Christ in Song:
Hymns of Immanuel
Selected from all Ages

compiled by

Philip Schaff

Solid Ground Christian Books
PO Box 660132 ~ Vestavia Hills AL 35266

SOLID GROUND CHRISTIAN BOOKS
Po Box 660132, Vestavia Hills AL 35266
205-443-0311
sgcb@charter.net
http://solid-ground-books.com

Christ in Song:
Hymns of Immanuel Selected from All Ages

Compiled by Philip Schaff (1819-1893)

Taken from the 1870 edition by Sampson Low, Son & Marston

Published by Solid Ground Christian Books

Classic Reprints Series

First printing of hardcover edition April 2003
First printing of paperback edition June 2004

ISBN: 1-932474-06-4 (hardcover)
ISBN: 1-932474-34-X (paperback)

Special thanks are extended to Dr. Mike DiMaio for his kindness in offering his copy of this volume for use in this project. May the peace of Christ rest upon your life.

Manufactured in the United States of America

PREFACE.

CHRIST is the centre of sacred art as well as of theology and religion. The noblest works of the master-painters are attempts to portray His "human face divine," now in the charm of childhood, now in the agony of the cross, now in the glory of the resurrection, now in His majesty as the judge of the world. From Him music has drawn its highest inspiration, and Handel transcended himself when he made "Messiah" his theme. The sweetest lyrics of Zion in all ages celebrate the events of His life and the boundless wealth of mercy and peace that is treasured up in His person and work for every believer.

The hymns of JESUS are the Holy of holies in the temple of sacred poetry. From this sanctuary every doubt is banished; here the passions of sense, pride, and unholy ambition give way to the tears of penitence, the joys of faith, the emotions of love, the aspirations of hope, the anticipations of heaven; here the dissensions of rival churches and theological schools are hushed into silence; here the hymnists of ancient, mediæval, and modern times, from every section of Christendom — profound divines, stately bishops, humble monks, faithful pastors, devout laymen, holy women—unite with one voice in the common adoration of a common Saviour. He is the theme of all ages, tongues, and creeds, the divine harmony of all human discords, the solution of all the dark problems of life.

What an argument this for the great mystery of " God manifest in the flesh," and for the communion of saints! Where is the human being, however great and good, that could open such a stream of grateful song, ever widening and deepening from generation to generation, in every land!

Blessed Saviour! Thou indeed, and Thou alone, with the Father and the Holy Ghost ever one God, art worthy to receive blessing and glory, praise and adoration from the innumerable army of the redeemed in the Church militant on earth, and the Church triumphant in heaven, for ever and for ever!

A complete and carefully selected LYRA CHRISTOLOGICA, embracing the choicest hymns on the Person and Work of our Lord from all ages, denominations, and tongues, must be welcome to every lover of sacred poetry.

Such a work is here attempted from the best hymnological sources. A large proportion of the poems are translations or transfusions from the Greek, Latin, and German; with a few from other languages. The English hymns, with a few necessary exceptions, are given as they came from the inspiration of the poet, without omission or alteration. Any other course would be contrary to good taste, and a violation of the sacredness of literary property. The *Lyra Sacra* of America is well represented. Although only about thirty years old, it takes already an honourable rank among its older and richer sisters.

About thirty pieces are especially prepared for this Collection, and will attract attention. The Editor begs leave here, publicly, to express his cordial thanks to his friends, the Rev. Drs. W. A. Muhlenberg, Ray Palmer, E. A. Washburn, A. R. Thompson, Prof. Thomas C. Porter, the Rev. James Inglis, the Hon. E. C. Benedict, Mr. A. D. F. Randolph, Mrs. G. W. Hinsdale, Mrs. Dr. H. B. Smith, and Mrs. G. L. Prentiss, for valuable original contributions, as well as to those English and American authors and publishers who kindly permitted him to use poems already known.[1]

Under each section the pieces are mostly arranged in chronological order, to enable the reader to trace the history of Christian life in song. It will be observed that the Church before the Reformation celebrated mainly the great objective facts in Christ's life (*Christus pro nobis*); while the hymnists after the Reformation, without neglecting the festival themes, brought out more fully the subjective appli-

---

[1] This privilege was freely granted to the Editor by the Rev. Dr. Horatius Bonar, Rev. John S. B. Monsell, Mrs. Alexander, Miss Borthwick, Dean Alford, Dean Stanley, Dr. Tregelles, Sir E. Denny, Mrs. H. Beecher Stowe, Dr. Muhlenberg, Dr. Palmer, Bishop Coxe, R. Massie, Miss Frances E. Cox, James Parker (publisher of Keble's "Christian Year"), J. T. Hayes (publisher of Neale's "Hymns of the Eastern Church"), and others.

From Messrs. Longmans, Green and Co., the Editor obtained, by purchase, the right to insert a number of the translations from Miss Winkworth's "Lyra Germanica," and from Messrs. Joseph Masters and Son the right to make similar use of Neale's "Mediæval Hymns."

Should the editor have inadvertently trespassed upon copyright

cation of Christ's merits, and our relation to Him (*Christus in nobis*). A few mediæval singers, especially St. Bernard in his "Jesu dulcis memoria," have anticipated the deep fervour of that true evangelical piety, which consists in a personal apprehension of Christ by faith, and immediate union and communion with Him, as the all-sufficient Fountain of grace and peace.

I need hardly add that the Collection is intended for private devotion, and hence includes many poems which would be out of place in a hymn-book for public worship.

May He, whose holy name shines on every page, own and bless this labour of love to His own glory and praise, and to the joy and comfort of His people; animating their songs in the house of their pilgrimage, until they adore Him face to face in the chorus of Redemption everlasting.

P. S.

London, *June* 1869.

---

in using a hymn which has not yet become the public property of the Christian Church, he trusts that the authors and publishers will exercise the same generosity which he experienced from others in applying for this privilege. The Editor begs leave to add a sentence from the reply of one of the best living hymn writers of the Church of England:

"I gladly give you the permission you ask . . . It is to me a great pleasure to feel that thus communion amongst God's people is deepened and widened by the circulation of those aspirations to Him, which He has put into many hearts, but which He has not given all lips equally the power to express. Are not our hymns drawing us all who love our Lord Jesus Christ in sincerity nearer to each other every day? It is remarkable how Christians occupying different sections in the great Family unite in choosing the same words in which to utter His praise."

LIST OF THE PRINCIPAL SOURCES USED AND AUTHORS QUOTED IN THIS COLLECTION.

I. *For Ancient and Mediæval (Greek and Latin) Hymnology.*

II. A. DANIEL: *Thesaurus Hymnologicus.* Lipsiae, 1841-1856. 5 vols. Contains Latin, Greek, and Syriac Hymns.

F. J. MONE: *Lateinische Hymnen des Mittelalters.* Freiburg, 1853-1855. 3 vols.

PHILIPP WACKERNAGEL: *Das Deutsche Kirchenlied von der ältesten Zeit bis zu Anfang des XVII. Jahrh.* Leipzig, 1864-1865. 2 vols. Part of Vol. I., pp. 9-362, is devoted to Latin hymnology, with much curious literary and bibliographical information.

RICHARD CHENEVIX TRENCH: *Sacred Latin Poetry, chiefly Lyrical.* Second edition, corrected and improved. London and Cambridge, 1864.

J. CHANDLER: *The Hymns of the Primitive Church, now first collected, translated, and arranged.* London, 1837.

J. M. NEALE: *Hymns of the Eastern Church.* London, 1862, third edition, 1866.

J. M. NEALE: *Mediæval Hymns and Sequences.* London, 1851, third edition, enlarged, 1867.

LYRA CATHOLICA, by EDWARD CASWALL. London, 1849. New York, 1851 (with additions from Faber and others).

ERASTUS C. BENEDICT: *The Hymn of Hildebert, and other Mediæval Hymns, with Translations.* New York, 1867. A new and enlarged edition, 1869.

ABRAHAM COLES: *Latin Hymns, with Original Translations (Dies Iræ ; Stabat Mater,* both *dolorosa* and *speciosa; Urbs cælestis,* &c.). New York, 5th ed., 1868.

II. *For German Hymnology.*

Ph. Wackernagel: *Das Deutsche Kirchenlied*, &c. 1864-1865. 2 vols.

Albert Knapp: *Evangelischer Liederschatz*. Stuttgart, third edition, 1865, which contains 3130 hymns.

Phil. Schaff: *Deutsches Gesangbuch*. Philadelphia, first published 1859, and often since. (Large edition, with notes, &c.)

Frances Elizabeth Cox: *Sacred Hymns from the German*. London, 1841; new edition, 1865.

Lyra Germanica, by Catherine Winkworth. First Series, London, 1855; Second Series, 1858. Sixth edition, 1866.

Horæ Germanicæ, by Henry Mills. New York and Auburn. Second edition, 1856.

Hymns from the Land of Luther. *Translated from the German* (by Miss Jane Borthwick, published first in four series, Edin. 1853, and in 1 vol. 1862).

Lyra Domestica: *Christian Songs for Domestic Edification. Translated from* Spitta *by* Richard Massie. London, 1860. Second Series, 1864.

III. *For English Hymnology.*

Good editions of the Poems of George Herbert, Watts, Wesley, Doddridge, Toplady, Cowper, Newton, Heber, Keble, Monsell, Faber, Bonar, Muhlenberg, Bethune, J. W. Alexander, Ray Palmer, Mrs. Stowe, and other hymn-writers, and a number of hymnological collections by Sir Roundell Palmer, Charles Rogers, and others.

TABLE OF CONTENTS.

[The date generally indicates the time of composition; or, where this could not be ascertained, the time of first publication, or the year of the author's death.]

INTRODUCTORY.

	Author	Time of composition	Page
SALVATOR MUNDI	Ray Palmer	1868	1

Part First.

CHRIST FOR US.

THE ADVENT.

O Thou Redeemer	Ambrose	397	9
Behold! the Bridegroom cometh	From the Greek		10
On Jordan's bank	From the Latin		12
Draw nigh, draw nigh	From the Latin		13
Once He came in blessing	M. Weiss	1531	14
Lift up your heads	G. Weissel	1630	15
Let the earth now praise	H. Held	1643	16
Lord, how shall I be meeting	P. Gerhardt	1653	17
Plunged in a gulf	Is. Watts	1709	19
Messiah, at Thy glad approach	Michael Bruce	1767	20
Lo, He comes!	Th. Kelly	1809	21
Watchman, tell us	Sir John Bowring	1825	22
When Jesus came to earth	Mrs. C. F. Alexander	1850	23
Zion, at thy shining gates	B. H. Kennedy	1862	24
He comes, no royal vesture	F. Rückert	1824	25
The Church has waited long	Horatius Bonar	1856	26
O'er the distant mountains	John S. B. Monsell	1863	27

THE INCARNATION.

A great and mighty wonder	Anatolius	450	31
From where the rising sun	Ambrose	397	32
Of the Father's love begotten	Prudentius	405	34

TABLE OF CONTENTS.

	Author	Time of composition	Page
From lands that see the sun	Cœlius Sedulius	450	35
To-day in Bethlehem hear I	John of Damascus	754	36
All hail thou night,	From the Latin		37
Come hither, ye faithful	From the Latin		37
A child is born in Bethlehem	From the Latin		38
Height of heaven	From the Latin		40
There comes a galley laden	John Tauler	1361	41
All praise to Thee	Notker and Luther		42
Good news from heaven	Luther	1535	43
We sing to Thee Immanuel	P. Gerhardt	1656	44
All my heart this night rejoices	P. Gerhardt	1656	45
While to Bethlehem	Violante do Ceo	1693	47
This is the month	John Milton	1674	48
Thou fairest Child Divine	G. Tersteegen	1731	49
Joy to the world	Isaac Watts	1709	50
Hark, how all the welkin rings	Chs. Wesley	1739	51
Hark, the glad sound	Ph. Doddridge	1751	52
Oh, how wondrous is the story	Hannah More	1833	53
When Jordan hushed his waters	Thomas Campbell	1844	55
Hark! what mean those holy	John Cawood	1852	56
Angels, from the realms of glory	J. Montgomery	1854	57
What sudden blaze of song	John Keble	1827	58
'Tis come, the time so oft	Thomas Grinfield	1836	60
The happy Christmas	From the Danish	1867	61
Carol, brothers, carol	Wm. A. Mühlenberg	1840	62
Come, ye lofty! come, ye lowly	Archer Gurney	1860	63
Joy and gladness	G. W. Bethune	1847	65
The time draws near	Alfred Tennyson	1850	66
It came upon the midnight clear	E. H. Sears	1860	67
Lo, God, our God, has come	H. Bonar	1868	68
In Bethlehem, the Lord of glory	Friedrich Rückert	1867	69

The Infant Saviour with the Virgin Mother.

The God whom earth and sea	From the Latin		75
When within His mother's arms	From the Latin		76
Sleep, Holy Babe	Edward Caswall		77
Thou stand'st between the earth	Mrs. G. W. Hinsdale	1867	78
Hail, infant martyrs	Prudentius	405	80
The Mater Dolorosa	Mrs. H. B. Stowe	1867	81

The Epiphany.

A star shines forth in heaven	Ephræm Syrus	379	85
Bethlehem! of noblest cities	Prudentius	405	86
What star is this	From the Latin		87
O Christ, our true and only	Johann Heermann	1630	88
They gave to Thee	Jeremy Taylor	1650	89
All ye Gentile lands awake	Johann Rist	1655	89
The wondering sages trace	Ernst Lange	1727	91
Sons of men, behold from far	Charles Wesley	1739	91
Brightest and best of the sons	Bishop Heber	1826	92
Christ, whose first appearance	Phil. Spitta	1859	93
O Thou, who by a star	J. M. Neale	1866	94

TABLE OF CONTENTS.   xiii

	Author	Time of composition	Page
As with gladness men of old	W. C. Dix	1860	95
The wise men to Thy cradle	C. F. Alexander	1867	96
We come not with a costly store	Anon.		96

CHRIST'S LIFE AND EXAMPLE.

	Author	Time of composition	Page
Most holy Jesus, Fount of light	From the German		101
Come, my Way	George Herbert	1632	102
Earth has nothing sweet or fair	Angelus Silesius	1677	103
My dear Redeemer	Is. Watts	1719	104
Jesus, still lead on	Ct. Zinzendorf	1721	105
Oh for a heart to praise my God	Chs. Wesley	1742	106
Behold, where, in a mortal form	William Enfield	1772	107
Oh, Jesus Christ, grow Thou	J. C. Lavater	1801	108
Ever would I fain be reading	Louise Hensel	1818	109
Jesus, I my cross have taken	H. F. Lite	1833	110
Thou art the way	G. W. Doane	1859	111
When o'er Judea's vales and hills	A. C. Coxe	1840	112
Thou Lord of all, on earth	S. P. Tregelles	1840	114
Thine handmaid, Saviour	W. A. Mühlenberg	1859	115
A Pilgrim through this lonely	E. Denny	1863	116
Immortal Love, for ever full	John G. Whittier	1867	117
Trustingly, trustingly	H. Bonar	1868	121

THE PASSION.

	Author	Time of composition	Page
Sing, my tongue	Fortunatus	600	125
The royal banners forward go	Fortunatus	600	128
Forth flames the standard	From the Latin		130
Hail, thou Head	St. Bernard	1153	130
Jesus' holy Cross and dying	Bonaventura	1274	132
Ponder thou the cross all holy	Bonaventura	1274	134
O'erwhelmed in depths of woe	From the Latin		135
At the cross her station keeping	Jacopone	1306	136
What laws, my blessed Saviour	Johann Heermann	1630	138
O world? behold upon the tree	Paul Gerhardt	1653	140
O sacred Head! now wounded	Paul Gerhardt	1656	142
O sacred Head, surrounded	Paul Gerhardt	1656	145
Christ, the Life of all the living	E. C. Homburg	1659	146
Thou Holiest Love	Anon	1704	147
When I survey	Is. Watts	1709	149
Not all the blood of beasts	Is. Watts	1748	149
O Love, too boundless	Bishop Ken	1721	150
Him on yonder cross I love	J. E. Greding	1723	151
Jesus, Thy Blood	Ct. Zinzendorf	1739	153
Sweet the moments	Walter Shirley	1774	154
Surely Christ thy griefs	A. M. Toplady	1778	155
There is a fountain	W. Cowper	1779	156
Hark! the voice of love	Jonathan Evans	1787	157
In the cross of Christ I glory	John Bowring	1825	158
We sing the praise of Him	Thomas Kelly	1855	159
Come to Calvary's holy mount	James Montgomery	1854	160
Fling out the Banner	Bishop Doane	1859	160
Wherefore weep we over Jesus	Phil. Spitta	1836	161

TABLE OF CONTENTS.

		Time of composition	Page
Ride on, ride on in majesty	H. H. Milman	1839	163
Bound upon the accursed tree	H. H. Milman	1839	163
Ask ye what great thing	B. H. Kennedy	1863	165
Oppressed with noon-day's	Horatius Bonar	1857	166
Cling to the Crucified	Horatius Bonar	1857	166
I lay my sins on Jesus	Horatius Bonar	1857	167
Wouldst thou learn the depth	J. S. B. Monsell	1860	168
My sins, my sins, my Saviour	J. S. B. Monsell	1863	169
Jesus! gentle Sufferer, say	J. S. B. Monsell	1863	170
Thou who didst hang	C. G. Rossetti	1866	171
O Jesus! sweet the tears I shed	Ray Palmer	1867	172
Wonder of wonders!	Ray Palmer	1867	173
O Head, so full of bruises!	Jos. Stammers	1867	173
When, wounded sore	Mrs. C. F. Alexander	1867	174
Are there no wounds for *me*?	Mrs. G. W. Hinsdale	1868	175

THE BURIAL OF CHRIST.

EASTER EVE.

			Page
The sepulchre is holding	From the Latin		179
Rest of the weary!	Salomon Frank	1716	180
Resting from His work to-day	Anon.	1860	181
Rest, weary Son of God	Horatius Bonar	1868	182

THE RESURRECTION.

			Page
Hail, Day of days!	Venant. Fortunatus	600	185
The Supper of the Lamb	Old Hymnus Paschalis		186
We keep the festival	From the R. Breviary		187
The Church of God	Greek Paschal Hymn		189
If the dark and awful tomb	John of Damascus	787	190
'Tis the Day of Resurrection	John of Damascus	787	190
Come, ye faithful	John of Damascus	787	191
This holy morn, so fair	R. Breviary	9th cent.	192
The morning purples all the sky	R. Breviary		193
Hallelujah! Hallelujah!	From the Latin	12th cent.	194
Behold the Day, the Lord	Adam of St. Victor	1172	195
Now thy gentle Lamb, O Sion	From the Latin		197
Jesus Christ is risen to-day	From the Latin	15th cent.	198
Let Zion's sons and daughters	From the Latin		199
Mary! put thy grief away	From the Latin		200
Still thy sorrow, Magdalena	From the Latin		201
Christ the Lord is risen again	Mich. Weiss	1531	203
In the bonds of death He lay	Martin Luther	1524	204
Ere yet the dawn	Johann Heermann	1630	206
Jesus, my Redeemer, lives	L. H. of Brandenburg	1649	207
O risen Lord	Justus H. Boehmer	1706	208
Blest morning	Is. Watts	1709	210
Welcome, Thou Victor	Benj. Schmolke	1712	210
Glorious Head, Thou livest	G. Tersteegen	1731	212
"Christ the Lord is risen"	Chs. Wesley	1739	212
Jesus lives, and so shall I	C. F. Gellert	1757	214
I say to all men, far and near	Novalis	1801	215

TABLE OF CONTENTS.

	Author	Time of composition	Page
The grave is empty now	Matt. Claudius	1812	216
Come, ye saints	Ths. Kelly	1804	217
Morning breaks upon the tomb.	W. B. Collyer	1812	218
Again the Lord of life and light	Anne L. Barbauld	1825	218
Sun, shine forth	Phil. Spitta	1833	220
Christ is arisen	Göthe and Coxe	1840	222
The foe behind, the deep before	J. M. Neale	1851	223
The Lord of life is risen	J. P. Lange	1851	224
We welcome thee, dear Easter	Meta Heusser	1859	225
The tomb is empty	H. Bonar	1862	227
Angels, roll the rock away	Episcopal Collection	1859	229
O Jesus! when I think	G. W. Bethune	1862	229
Awake, glad soul! awake	John S. B. Monsell	1863	230
In Thy glorious Resurrection	Chr. Wordsworth	1863	232
Sing aloud, children	A. R. Thompson	1865	233
Why should these eyes	Ray Palmer	1867	234

The Ascension.

	Author	Time of composition	Page
A hymn of glory let us sing	Beda Venerabilis	735	239
Exalt, exalt, the heavenly	Joseph of the Studium	830	240
Jesus, Lord of life eternal	Joseph of the Studium	830	241
On earth awhile	Peter Abelard	1142	241
To-day above the sky He soared	From the Latin		242
O Christ, who hast prepared	From the Latin		243
O Jesu, who art gone before	From the Latin		244
To-day our Lord went up	Johann Zwick	1540	244
Since Christ is gone to heaven	Jos. Wegelin	1637	245
Lo, God to heaven ascendeth	G. W. Sacer	1699	246
Hosanna to the Prince of light.	Is. Watts	1709	248
Heavenward still our pathway	Benj. Schmolke	1731	249
Conquering Prince and Lord	G. Tersteegen	1731	250
Hail the day that sees Him	Chs. Wesley	1739	251
Our Lord is risen from the dead	Chs. Wesley	1739	253
All hail the power	E. Perronet	1785	253
Soft cloud, that	John Keble	1827	255
Lamb, the once crucified	Meta Heusser	1831	256
See, the Conqueror mounts	Chr. Wordsworth	1863	259
He is gone; beyond the skies	A. P. Stanley	1869	261
Sing, O Heavens	J. S. B. Monsell	1863	262

Christ in Glory.

HIS INTERCESSION AND REIGN.

	Author	Time of composition	Page
Christ, Thou the champion	M. A. von Löwenstern	1644	267
My Jesus, if the seraphim	W. C. Dessler	1692	268
Jesus shall reign	Is. Watts	1719	270
Behold the glories of the Lamb	Is. Watts		271
Rejoice! the Lord is King	Charles Wesley	1745	272
Now let our cheerful eyes	Phil. Doddridge	1751	273
Where high the heavenly	Michael Bruce	1767	273
He who on earth as man	John Newton	1779	274
The Head that once	Thomas Kelly	1855	275
The atoning work is done	Thomas Kelly	1855	276

	Author	Time of composition	Page
Hosanna! raise the pealing	Anon.	1842	277
See, the ransomed millions	Josiah Conder	1855	277
Jesus is God! the solid earth	F. W. Faber	1862	278
King of kings, and wilt Thou	W. A. Mühlenberg	1859	280
O Christ, the Lord of heaven	Ray Palmer	1867	281

Christ Judging the World.

	Author	Time of composition	Page
God comes;—and who shall	Theod. of the Studium	826	285
The Day is near	Theod. of the Studium	826	286
That great Day of wrath	From the Latin	7th cent.	287
Day of wrath! that Day foretold	Thomas of Celano	1250	290
Day of wrath! O Day	Dies Iræ by Irons	1848	293
That Day of wrath	Sir Walter Scott	1805	295
Lo, the Day!—the Day of Life	From the Latin		296
Wake, the startling watch-cry	Phil. Nikolai	1597	297
Wake, awake	Phil. Nikolai	1597	298
Rejoice, all ye believers	Laurentius Laurenti	1700	299
Lo! He comes	Chs. Wesley	1758	301
Day of judgment!	John Newton	1807	303
The Lord will come	Bishop Heber	1826	304
Jesus, Thy Church	W. H. Bathurst	1830	305
The chariot! the chariot	H. H. Milman	1839	306
The Throne of His Glory	W. A. Mühlenberg	1839	306
Late, late, so late	Alfred Tennyson	1850	307
Come, Lord, and tarry not	H. Bonar	1857	308
Hope of our hearts	Sir Edward Denny	1863	309
Bride of the Lamb, awake	Sir Edward Denny	1863	310

Part Second.

CHRIST IN US.

The Love and Loveliness of Christ.

	Author	Time of composition	Page
Jesu, name all names above	Theoctistus	890	317
Jesu! the very thought of Thee	St. Bernard	1153	318
O Jesu! King most wonderful	St. Bernard		320
O Jesu! Thou the beauty art	St. Bernard		320
Jesus, how sweet Thy memory	St. Bernard		321
Heart of Christ, my King	St. Bernard		322
Fairest Lord Jesus	Old German Song	12th cent.	325
O Love, who formedst me	Angelus Silesius	1657	325
One thing's needful	J. H. Schröder	1697	327
Dearest of all the names	Is. Watts	1709	329
Love Divine, all loves	Chs. Wesley	1746	330
How wondrous are the works	Jos. Hart	1759	331
The Saviour! O, what charms	Anne Steele	1760	332
Hark, my soul! it is the Lord	William Cowper	1779	333
How sweet the name of Jesus	John Newton	1779	334
One there is above all others	John Newton	1779	335
I was a wandering sheep	Horatius Bonar	1857	336
Jesus, how much Thy name	Mary Peters	1856	337
Still on Thy loving heart	C. J. P. Spitta	1836	338
Our lot is fallen	C. J. P. Spitta	1836	339

TABLE OF CONTENTS.

	Author	Time of composition	Page
Beneath the shadow	S. Longfellow	1846	341
Jesus' name shall ever be	W. A. Mühlenberg	1842	341
In the silent midnight watches	A. C. Coxe	1838	342
There is no love like the love	W. E. Littlewood		343
Souls of men, why will ye	F. W. Faber	1862	344
I bore with thee long	C. G. Rossetti	1865	345
Listen to the wondrous story	Ellin Isab. Tupper	1867	346
There was no angel	Mrs. Hinsdale	1868	347

CHRIST OUR REFUGE AND STRENGTH.

Fierce was the wild billow	Anatolius	458	353
Art thou weary	Stephen the Sabaite	794	354
Lord Jesus Christ	Johann Schneesing	1522	355
Courage, my tempted heart	J. H. Böhmer	1704	356
Now I have found the ground	J. A. Rothe	1728	357
Jesu, lover of my soul	Chs. Wesley	1740	359
Rock of ages, cleft for me	A. M. Toplady	1776	360
Jesus, pro me perforatus	Toplady. Gladstone	1848	361
Awake, sweet harp of Judah	Henry Kirke White	1806	362
When through the torn sail	Bishop Heber	1826	363
From every stormy wind	Hugh Stowell	1831	364
Saviour! when, in dust	Sir Robert Grant	1838	365
When gathering clouds	Sir Robert Grant	1838	366
When our heads are bowed	H. H. Milman	1839	367
With tearful eyes	Hugh White	1841	368
Just as I am	Charlotte Elliott	1836	369
Just as thou art	Russell S. Cook	1864	370
Where is mercy and compassion	C. J. P. Spitta	1843	371
Long hast thou wept and sorrowed	Meta Heusser	1837	372
I heard the voice of Jesus say	Horatius Bonar	1856	374
A sinful man am I	Horatius Bonar	1868	374
Lo! the storms of life	Henry Alford	1864	375
There is an everlasting home	M. Bridges	1852	376
Tossed with rough winds	Mrs. Charles	1867	377
My Saviour, 'mid life's varied	Mrs. Godwin	1867	378
The way is long and dreary	Adelaide A. Procter	1864	379
In the hours of pain	Helen L. Parmelee	1865	380
Watcher, who watchest	Mrs. Sigourney	1865	381
Thus far the Lord has led us on	Jane Borthwick	1867	382
Amid the darkness	Ray Palmer	1867	383
I need Thee, precious Jesu	F. Whitfield	1867	384

CHRIST OUR PEACE.

Jesus, my chief pleasure	Johann Frank	1677	389
O Friend of souls! how blest	W. C. Dessler	1692	391
Thou hidden Source	Chs. Wesley	1740	392
The world can neither give	Lady Huntingdon	1780	393
Come, weary souls	Annie Steele	1778	394
Jesus, my Lord, Thy nearness	Christian Gregor	1778	394
O for a closer walk with God!	W. Cowper	1779	396
Why should I fear?	John Newton	1779	397
Jesus, my Lord! my life!	S. Medley	1799	398
If I only have Thee	Novalis	1801	399
Trembling before Thy throne	A. L. Hillhouse	1822	400

xviii   *TABLE OF CONTENTS.*

		Author	Time of composition	Page
Yes! our Shepherd leads		F. A. Krummacher	1830	401
Long did I toil		H. F. Lyte	1833	402
O blessed Sun, whose splendour		C. J. P. Spitta	1836	403
Now I have found a friend		Henry Hope	1852	405
Tell me not of earthly		Jane Borthwick	1762	406
Rest, weary soul!		Jane Borthwick	1859	409
Through the love of God		Mrs. Mary Peters	1847	407
Thou knowest, Lord		Jane Borthwick	1867	408
I've found a joy in sorrow		Mrs. Jane Crewdson	1863	410
Let not your heart be faint		John A. Latrobe	1863	411
Rest of the weary		John S. B. Monsell	1863	412
Jesus, my Lord, 'tis sweet		Anon.	1865	413
When across the heart		Canterbury Hymnal	1863	414
Sweet was the hour, O Lord		Sir E. Denny	1863	415
When winds are raging		Mrs. H. B. Stowe	1867	416
Alone with Thee!		Ray Palmer	1867	416
Jesus! the rays divine		Mrs. G. W. Hinsdale	1868	418
Abide with me!		H. F. Lyte	1847	419
The children of the world		Timm	1868	420

FAITH IN CHRIST.

When sins and fears' prevailing	Anne Steele	1778	423
See a poor sinner, dearest Lord	S. Medley	1799	424
Amid life's wild commotion	C. J. Asschenfeld	1819	425
I know in whom I put my trust	E. M. Arndt	1819	426
My faith looks up to Thee	Ray Palmer	1830	427
Hallelujah! I believe!	H. Möwes	1831	428
O holy Saviour, Friend unseen	Charlotte Elliott	1836	429
I once was a stranger	R. M. McCheyne	1843	430
While Faith is with me	Anne Bronte		431
We walk by faith	Henry Alford	1845	432
Strong Son of God	Alfred Tennyson	1849	433
We were not with the faithful	Canterbury Hymnal	1863	434
Life's mystery	Mrs. H. B. Stowe	1867	434
Yes!—my Redeemer lives	Meta Heusser	1859	435
When time seems short	G. W. Bethune	1862	437
Ever is my peril near	Kingo	1868	438

UNION WITH CHRIST.

How lovely shines	Phil. Nikolai	1597	441
Lord, Thou art mine	George Herbert	1632	443
I leave Thee not	W. C. Dessler	1722	444
My Saviour! I am Thine!	Phil. Doddridge	1755	446
Jesus immutably the same	A. M. Toplady	1776	446
Jesus, lead us with Thy power	W. Williams	1791	448
Sun of my soul	John Keble	1827	448
Ah! Jesus, let me hear	Andrew Reed	1841	450
When in the hour of lonely	Josiah Conder	1855	451
In Thy service will I ever	Phil. Spitta	1833	452
O happy house! where Thou	Phil. Spitta	1859	453
Chief of sinners though I be	Wm. McComb	1864	454
On Thee, O Jesus!	Horatius Bonar	1868	455
Lord! let my heart still turn	Lady Powerscourt	1865	456

TABLE OF CONTENTS. xix

	Author	Time of composition	Page
That mystic word of Thine	Mrs. H. B. Stowe	1867	457
Still, still with Thee	Mrs. H. B. Stowe	1867	458
Jesus! I live to Thee	H. Harbaugh	1867	459
O blessed Lord!	A. D. F. Randolph	1868	460

The Holy Communion.

	Author	Time of composition	Page
O Lamb of God, who, bleeding	Nik. Decius	1523	465
Sing, my tongue	Thomas Aquinas	1274	465
Sing, and the mystery declare	Thomas Aquinas	1274	468
O Bread of Life from heaven	From the Latin	14th cent.	469
Deck thyself, my soul	Johann Frank	1650	470
Suffering Saviour	Anon.		471
'Twas on that dark	Is. Watts	1748	472
In memory of the Saviour's	Anon.	1843	473
Body of Jesus, O sweet food!	A. C. Coxe	1858	474
O God, unseen, yet ever near	Anon.	1860	474
Jesu, to Thy table led	Robt. H. Baynes	1863	475
By Christ redeemed	Anon.	1863	476
Lo, the feast is spread to-day!	Henry Alford	1865	477

Love and Gratitude to Christ.

	Author	Time of composition	Page
Jesus, Thou Joy of loving hearts	St. Bernard	1153	481
I give my heart to Thee	From the Latin		482
Jesus, I love Thee	Francis Xavier	1540	483
Jesus, I love Thee evermore	From the Latin		484
O Lord! I love Thee	Martin Schalling	1571	485
Jesus, Thy boundless love	Paul Gerhardt	1653	486
I place an offering	Mme. Guyon	1717	487
The Lord of all things	Mme. Guyon	1717	488
Yes: I will always love	Mme. Guyon	1717	489
O Love divine	Chs. Wesley	1749	490
Jesus, I love Thy name	Ph. Doddridge	1751	491
Compared with Christ	A. M. Toplady	1772	492
When this passing world	R. M. McCheyne	1843	492
Oh how could I forget him	G. Chr. Kern	1820	494
O abide, abide in Jesus!	Ph. Spitta	1833	495
We are the Lord's	Phil. Spitta	1843	496
More than all	Albert Knapp	1823	497
Lovest thou Me?	J. Montgomery	1853	498
Jesu, my Lord, my God		1860	499
Jesus, these eyes have never	Ray Palmer	1858	500
That Holy One	A. D. F. Randolph	1867	500

For Ever with Christ.

	Author	Time of composition	Page
My home in heaven alone	Gregory Nazianzen	390	505
Cease, ye tearful mourners	Prudentius	405	506
No more, ah, no more	Prudentius	405	508
With terror Thou dost strike	Peter Damiani	1072	510
Brief life is here our portion	Bernard of Cluny	1145	512
For thee, O dear, dear Country	Bernard of Cluny	1145	513
Jerusalem the golden	Bernard of Cluny	1145	515
Region of life and light	Luis Ponce de Leon	1580	516

TABLE OF CONTENTS.

	Author	Time of composition	Page
The Life above	St. Teresa	1582	517
Lord, it belongs not to my care	Richard Baxter	1691	519
Thou shalt rise!	F. G. Klopstock	1803	520
Guide me, O Thou great Jehovah	W. Williams	1791	521
Asleep in Jesus!	Margaret Mackay	1832	521
Let me be with Thee	Charlotte Elliott	1836	522
We speak of the realms	Mrs. Wilson	1837	523
Forever with the Lord	Js. Montgomery	1853	523
I would not live alway	W. A. Muhlenberg	1824	525
Since o'er Thy footstool	W. A. Muhlenberg	1824	526
What shall we be?	Ph. Spitta	1833	527
Oh, Paradise must fairer be!	Friedrich Rückert	1866	529
O Paradise! O Paradise!	F. W. Faber	1862	530
No, no, it is not dying	Cæsar Malan	1841	531
It is not death to die	George W. Bethune	1847	532
O sweet home-echo	Mrs. M. Heusser	1845	533
Jesus, when my soul is parting	Thomas Mackellar	1860	535
Go and dig my grave	E. M. Arndt	1860	536
There is a blessed home	Sir H. W. Baker	1861	537
Star of morn and even	F. T. Palgrave	1862	538
O Heaven! Sweet Heaven!	Edwin H. Nevin	1862	539
Oh for the robes of whiteness!	Charitie Lees Smith		540
Oh for the peace which floweth	Jane Crewdson	1863	541
"Soon and for ever"	J. S. B. Monsell	1863	542
We shall see Him	Anon.	1868	543

PRAISE AND ADORATION OF CHRIST.

	Author	Time of composition	Page
Shepherd of tender youth	Clement of Alexandria	200	547
Thee we adore, eternal Lord	From the Te Deum	400	548
I greet Thee	John Calvin	1564	549
Come, let us join	Is. Watts	1700	551
O for a thousand tongues!	Chs. Wesley	1740	552
Ye servants of God	Chs. Wesley	1740	553
Awake, and sing the song	Wm. Hammond	1745	554
Hail, Thou once despised Jesus!	John Bakewell	1760	555
Now let us join	John Newton	1779	556
Awake, my soul, in joyful lays	S. Medley	1799	557
Hosanna to the living Lord!	Bishop Heber	1827	559
Thou whom we seek	L. Uhland	1833	560
To Him, who for our sins	A. T. Russell	1851	560
Thou that art the Father's	Henry Alford	1865	561
Praise to Jesus!	William Ball	1864	562
Thou King anointed	James Inglis	1868	564
As on a vast, eternal shore	Mrs. Prentiss	1869	565
Glory be to God the Father!	H. Bonar	1868	566

FINALE.

	Author	Time of composition	Page
Christ the theme of song	A. D. F. Randolph	1868	567

SALVATOR MUNDI.

By the Rev. RAY PALMER, D.D., New York. (Born at Little Compton, R.I., 1808; author of "My faith looks up to Thee.") Written for this Collection, as a Prelude, at the request of the Editor, February, 1868.

OH! long and darksome was the night
    That in dull watches wore away,
    With moon and stars alone to light
    A world bewildered and astray;
While oft thick shade and murky cloud
    Pale moon and stars did deep enshroud;
And nations looked, and hoped in vain
    That over earth, of guilt and sorrow,
Of sin and hate, the sad domain,
    Might dawn a bright and cheerful morrow.

'Twas not, Eternal Love, that Thou
    Hadst lost Thy care for mortal men:
No, Thou didst yearn of old, as now,
    To fold them to Thy heart again;
    Thou didst but wait till men might know
    That sin's ripe fruits were death and woe;
Till, worn and sick of fruitless grief,
    Of lust's foul cup to loathing taken,
With longing they might crave relief
    Ere yet of God and hope forsaken.

There were who heard with trusting heart,
    E'en then, Thy words of hope and cheer;
Who saw by faith the night depart,
    And morning break serene and clear.

On holy prophets shone afar
    The gleam of Jacob's promised Star;
The rising of the Lord of day,
    That, o'er the world his radiance throwing,
Should chase the spectral night away,
    And mount to noon resplendent glowing.

When Thou, O Christ! of flesh wast born,
    To greet Thee in Thy humble bed,
Though earth Thy lowliness should scorn,
    Celestial bands with rapture sped;
      At midnight on the silent air
      Thy birth their floating strains declare:
The shepherds catch the thrilling lay,
In harmonies their senses steeping;
Then to Thy manger take their way,
And gaze on Thee, an infant sleeping!

While Thou didst dwell with men below,
    'Twas morning twilight's early blush;
Thy light yet veiled, 'twas Thine to know
    Sweet childhood's dream, youth's joyous flush;
      Then manhood's burdens, cares, and fears,
      Its toils and weariness and tears;
Tears shed for human grief and woes
    Mark Thee, of all, the Man of Sorrows:
And through Thy life the grandeur grows
    That manhood from the Godhead borrows!

When, all forsaken of Thine own,
    Robed in mock purple Thou didst stand,
Thou wast a King—without a throne;
    A Sovereign Lord—without command;
      'Neath purple robe and thorns concealed,
      Divinity its light revealed;
Upon the Roman's heart it fell,
    And its keen flash, his conscience waking,
Wrought in him like some mighty spell,
    The pride of his strong spirit breaking.

When came at last Thy darkest hour,
    On which the sun refused to look,
Though hell seemed armed with conquering power,
    And earth, as seized with terror, shook;

SALVATOR MUNDI.

  Though from Thy lips the dying cry,
   By anguish wrung, went up on high;
 Still, 'mid the darkness and the fear,
   O Son of God! Thy life resigning,
 Thou didst to those that saw appear
   The Light of men,—eclipsed, yet shining!

 E'en the dark tomb of chiselled rock
   Thy glory could not all repress:
 A moment hid, with earthquake shock
   Abroad it streamed again to bless;
    Angels first caught the vision bright,
    Then broke its beams on mortal sight;
 The Conqueror of Death and Hell,
   Thou stood'st, Thine own each word attending.
 Till on their wistful eyes there fell
   Splendours divine from Thee ascending!

 For ever on the unveiled throne,
   O Lamb divine! enrobed in light,
 Thou life and love, and joy unknown,
   Dost shed while ages wing their flight;
    The cherubim before Thee bow;
    The fulness of the Godhead Thou!
 Thy uncreated beauty greets
   The longing eyes that, upward gazing,
 Feast on Thy smile, that ever meets
   Thy saints that wait before Thee praising.

 Head over all! 'tis Thine to reign;
   The groaning earth with joy shall see
 What ages sought, but sought in vain,
   The balm for all its woes in Thee;
    Eyes fixed on Thee shall dry their tears;
    Hearts stayed on Thee shall lose their fears;
 Fair innocence and love shall breathe
   Their fragrant breath o'er vale and mountain,
 And Faith pure altars shall enwreathe,
   And nations bathe in Calvary's fountain.

 Crowned Lord of lords, Thy power shall bring
   All Thine Thy glory to partake;
 Thyself enthroned Eternal King,
   Of them Thy love shall Princes make;

And Priests, that in the Holy Place
    Shall serve, adorned and full of grace;
The Church, Thy queenly Bride, shall stand
    In vesture like Thy brightness shining,
Content to clasp Thy royal hand,
    All other love for Thine resigning.

O Love beyond all mortal thought!
    Unquenchable by flood or sea!
Love that, through death, to man hath brought
    The life of Immortality!
        Thou dost enkindle Heaven's own fire
        In hearts all dead to high desire.
Let love for love our souls inflame,
    The perfect love that faileth never;
And sweet Hosannas to Thy Name
    Through Heaven's vast dome go up for ever!

PART FIRST.

CHRISTUS PRO NOBIS.

THE ADVENT.

"ARISE, shine; for thy light is come, and the glory of the Lord is risen upon thee."—*Isaiah* lx. 1.

"The night is far spent, the day is at hand: let us therefore cast off the works of darkness, and let us put on the armour of light."—*Rom.* xiii. 12.

ALMIGHTY GOD, Father of all mercies, we render Thee most hearty thanks, that after man, created in Thine own image, had fallen under the curse of sin and death, Thou didst not leave him to perish in helpless misery, but didst provide a Saviour, and proclaim to the fathers, by the mouth of Thy prophets and holy men of old, the Advent of Thy dear Son, the Hope of Israel, the Desire of all nations, the Redeemer of the world, that, by believing on Him, we might have the forgiveness of sins, and life everlasting: to whom, with Thee and the Holy Ghost, ever one God, be glory and thanksgiving, world without end. Amen.

> Tandem fluctus, tandem luctus,
> Sol erumpens temperat;
> Nunc aurora, rupta mora,
> Lucem lactam nunciat.
> *Old Hymn.*

Come, Jesus! come! return again;
  With brighter beam Thy servants bless,
Who long to feel Thy perfect reign,
  And share Thy kingdom's happiness!

Come, Jesus! come! and, as of yore
  The prophet went to clear Thy way,
A harbinger Thy feet before,
  A dawning to Thy brighter day:

So now may grace with heavenly shower
  Our stony hearts for truth prepare;
Sow in our souls the seed of power,
  Then come and reap Thy harvest there.

REGINALD HEBER.

THE ADVENT.

O THOU REDEEMER OF OUR RACE!

(Veni, Redemptor gentium.)

FROM the Latin of St. AMBROSE, Bishop of Milan, the father of Latin church poetry (died A.D. 397). Translated for this Collection by the Rev Dr. RAY PALMER, April, 1868. The best of the Ambrosian hymns (except the "Te Deum," which is older), full of faith, rugged vigour, austere simplicity, and bold contrasts, but of objectionable taste in st. 3, which is here smoothed down. It has been freely reproduced in German by LUTHER (" Nu komm der Heiden Heiland "), JOHN FRANK (" Komm, Heidenheiland, Lösegeld "), and others (see SCHAFF's " German Hymn Book," No. 72), and several times in English. Dr. J. M. NEALE's version,
"Come, Thou Redeemer of the Earth,"
retains the harsh features of the original.

St. Augustine, in his " Confessions," testifies to the effect of the hymns and music introduced into the church of Milan by Ambrose, his spiritual father. " How did I weep, O Lord! through Thy hymns and canticles, touched to the quick by the voices of Thy sweet-attuned church! The voices sank into mine ears, and the truths distilled into my heart, whence the affections of my devotions overflowed; tears ran down, and I rejoiced in them."

 THOU Redeemer of our race!
   Come, show the Virgin's Son to earth;
Let every age admire the grace;
   Worthy a God Thy human birth!

'Twas by no mortal will or aid,
   But by the Holy Spirit's might,
That flesh the Word of God was made,
   A babe yet waiting for the light.

Spotless remains the Virgin's name,
   Although the Holy Child she bears;
And virtue's banners round her flame,
   While God a temple so prepares.

As if from honour's royal hall,
  Comes forth at length the Mighty One,
Whom Son of God and Man they call,
  Eager His destined course to run.[1]

Forth from the Father's bosom sent,
  To Him returned, He claimed His own;
Down to the realms of death He went,
  Then rose to share the eternal throne.

An equal at the Father's side,
  Thou wear'st the trophy[2] of Thy flesh;
In Thee our nature shall abide
  In strength complete, in beauty fresh.

With light divine Thy manger streams,
  That kindles darkness into day;
Dimmed by no night henceforth, its beams
  Shine through all time with changeless ray.

BEHOLD, THE BRIDEGROOM COMETH.

MIDNIGHT Hymn of the Eastern Church. From the Greek, by G. MOULTRIE, "Hymns and Lyrics," &c., Lond. 1867.

EHOLD, the Bridegroom cometh in the middle
    of the night,
  And blest is he whose loins are girt, whose
    lamp is burning bright;

---

[1] In the original:
          "Geminæ gigas substantiæ,
          Alacris ut currat viam."

The *giant of two-fold substance* is an allusion to the "giants" of Gen. vi. 4, who, by some of the early Fathers, were supposed to have been of a double nature; being the offspring of the "sons of God," or angels (?), and the "daughters of men," and who furnished a forced resemblance to the two-fold nature of Christ, according to the mystical interpretation of Ps. xix. 5, "as a bridegroom cometh out of his chamber, . . . as a strong man to run a race," which was referred to the earthly course of the Redeemer. Comp. AMBROSIUS: "De incarnat. Domini," c. 5.

[2] Not "mantle." *Tropæo* or *trophæo* is undoubtedly the true reading (for *stropheo* or *strophio*). The Fathers frequently call the risen flesh of Christ *tropæum*, τρόπαιον κατὰ δαιμόνων, a trophy erected as a monument of His victory over death.—DANIEL: "Thesaurus Hymnol." I. p. 14; TRENCH: "Sacred Latin Poetry," 2nd ed. p. 69.

BEHOLD, THE BRIDEGROOM COMETH.

But woe to that dull servant whom the Master shall surprise
With lamp untrimmed, unburning, and with slumber in his eyes!

Do thou, my soul, beware, beware, lest thou in sleep sink down,
Lest thou be given o'er to death, and lose the golden crown;
But see that thou be sober, with watchful eyes, and thus
Cry, "Holy, holy, holy God, have mercy upon us!"

That day, the day of fear, shall come: my soul, slack not thy toil,
But light thy lamp, and feed it well, and make it bright with oil;
Who knowest not how soon may sound the cry at eventide,
"Behold, the Bridegroom comes! Arise! Go forth to meet the bride."[1]

Beware, my soul; beware, beware, lest thou in slumber lie,
And, like the five, remain without, and knock and vainly cry;
But watch, and bear thy lamp undimmed, and Christ shall gird thee on
His own bright wedding-robe of light,—the glory of the Son.

---

[1] For the received text, Matt. xxv. 1: "to meet the *bridegroom*." But there is another reading in Greek: "to meet the bridegroom *and the bride*" (the Church). It was a custom among the Jews and Greeks that the bridegroom, accompanied by his friends, went to the house of the bride, to lead her to his own home; and, on his returning with her, he was joined by the virgins, the friends of the bride.

ON JORDAN'S BANK.

(Jordanis oras prævia vox ecce Baptistæ quatit.)

FROM the Latin, by the Rev. J. CHANDLER. "The Hymns of the Primitive Church," Lond. 1837.

ON Jordan's bank, the Baptist's cry
Announces that the Lord is nigh:
Come, then, and hearken; for He brings
Glad tidings from the King of kings.

E'en now the air, the sea, the land,
Feel that their Maker is at hand;
The very elements rejoice,
And welcome Him with cheerful voice.

Then cleansed be every Christian breast,
And furnished for so great a Guest!
Yea, let us each our hearts prepare
For Christ to come and enter there.

For Thou art our salvation, Lord,—
Our refuge and our great reward;
Without Thy grace, our souls must fade,
And wither like a flower decayed.

Stretch forth Thy hand, to heal our sore,
And make us rise, to fall no more;
Once more upon Thy people shine,
And fill the world with love divine.

To Him, who left the throne of heaven
To save mankind, all praise be given!
Like praise be to the Father done,
And Holy Spirit,—Three in One!

DRAW NIGH, DRAW NIGH, EMMANUEL.

(*Veni, veni, Emmanuel.*)

From the Latin of the twelfth century, by Dr. J. M. Neale (died 1866): "Mediæval Hymns and Sequences," 3rd ed. Lond. 1867. "This Advent Hymn is little more than a versification of some of the Christmas antiphons commonly called the O's." It is found also in the "Hymnal Noted;" in "Hymns Ancient and Modern," and other collections. See the Latin in Daniel, "Thes." tom. ii. p. 336.

DRAW nigh, draw nigh, Emmanuel,
 And ransom captive Israel,
 That mourns in lonely exile here,
Until the Son of God appear.
Rejoice! rejoice! Emmanuel
Shall be born for thee, O Israel!

Draw nigh, O Jesse's Rod! draw nigh,
To free us from the enemy,
From hell's infernal pit to save,
And give us victory o'er the grave.
Rejoice! rejoice! Emmanuel
Shall be born for thee, O Israel!

Draw nigh, Thou Orient! Who shalt cheer
And comfort by Thine Advent here,
And banish far the brooding gloom
Of sinful night and endless doom.
Rejoice! rejoice! Emmanuel
Shall be born for thee, O Israel!

Draw nigh, draw nigh, O David's Key;
The heavenly gate will ope to Thee:
Make safe the way that leads on high,
And close the path to misery.
Rejoice! rejoice! Emmanuel
Shall be born for thee, O Israel!

Draw nigh, draw nigh, O Lord of Might,
Who to Thy tribes, from Sinai's height,
In ancient time didst give the law,
In cloud and majesty and awe.
Rejoice! rejoice! Emmanuel
Shall be born for thee, O Israel!

ONCE HE CAME IN BLESSING.

(Gottes Sohn ist kommen.)

FROM the German of MICHAEL WEISS, who reproduced the old hymns of the Bohemian (Moravian) Brethren in German, 1531. Translated by Miss CATHERINE WINKWORTH, 1862.

NCE He came in blessing,
All our ills redressing,—
Came in likeness lowly,
Son of God most holy;
Bore the Cross to save us,
Hope and freedom gave us.

Still He comes within us;
Still His voice would win us
From the sins that hurt us,
Would to Truth convert us
From our foolish errors,
Ere He comes in terrors.

Thus, if thou hast known Him,
Not ashamed to own Him,
Nor dost love Him coldly,
But will trust Him boldly,
He will now receive thee,
Heal Thee, and forgive thee.

But through many a trial,
Deepest self-denial,
Long and brave endurance,
Must thou win assurance
That His own He makes thee,
And no more forsakes thee.

He who thus endureth,
Bright reward secureth:
Come, then, O Lord Jesus!
From our sins release us;
Let us here confess Thee,
Till in heaven we bless Thee.

LIFT UP YOUR HEADS, YE MIGHTY GATES.

(Macht hoch die Thür', die Thor' macht weit.)

ABRIDGED from the German of GEORGE WEISSEL, 1630. Based upon Ps. xxiv., as applied to the coming of Christ in the flesh. The original has five stanzas, of eight unequal lines each. The "Canterbury Hymnal" has reduced the whole to three stanzas of six lines each.

LIFT up your heads, ye mighty gates!
Behold, the King of glory waits;
The King of kings is drawing near,
The Saviour of the world is here.

The Lord is just, a Helper tried;
Mercy is ever at His side:
His kingly crown is holiness;
His sceptre, pity in distress.

Oh, blest the land, the city blest,
Where Christ the Ruler is confessed!
Oh, happy hearts and happy homes
To whom this King of triumph comes!

Fling wide the portals of your heart;
Make it a temple, set apart
From earthly use for heaven's employ,
Adorned with prayer and love and joy.

Redeemer, come! I open wide
My heart to Thee: here, Lord, abide!
Let me Thy inner presence feel,
Thy grace and love in me reveal.

So come, my Sovereign! enter in,
Let new and nobler life begin;
Thy Holy Spirit guide us on,
Until the glorious crown be won!

LET THE EARTH NOW PRAISE THE LORD.

(Gott sei Dank durch alle Welt.)

A POPULAR German Advent hymn by HEINRICH HELD, a lawyer of Silesia, died 1643. Translated by Miss C. WINKWORTH, in the original metre, omitting ver. 7 ("Choral Book for England," 1862).

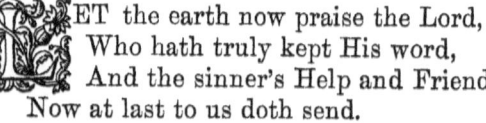ET the earth now praise the Lord,
Who hath truly kept His word,
And the sinner's Help and Friend
Now at last to us doth send.

What the fathers most desired,
What the prophets' hearts inspired,
What they longed for many a year,
Stands fulfilled in glory here.

Abram's promised great Reward,
Zion's Helper, Jacob's Lord,
Him of twofold race, behold,
Truly come, as long foretold.

Welcome, O my Saviour, now!
Hail! my Portion, Lord, art Thou!
Here, too, in my heart I pray,—
Oh prepare Thyself a way.

Enter, King of glory, in!
Purify the wastes of sin,
As Thou hast so often done:
This belongs to Thee alone.

As Thy coming was all peace,
Noiseless, full of gentleness,
Let the same mind dwell in me
That was ever found in Thee.

Bruise for me the serpent's head,
That, set free from doubt and dread,
I may cleave to Thee in faith,
Safely kept through life and death.

And when Thou dost come again,
As a glorious King to reign,
I with joy may see Thy face,
Freely ransomed by Thy grace.

LORD, HOW SHALL I BE MEETING?

(*Wie soll ich Dich empfangen?*)

By Paul Gerhardt, the prince of German hymnists, 1653. Translated in the spirit and metre of the original, by Dr. James W. Alexander, of N. York (died 1859), and first published in Schaff's "Deutsche Kirchenfreund," Mercersburg, Penns., for 1850 (p. 176). Another version by Miss Catherine Winkworth, 1855: "How shall I meet Thee? how, my heart?"

LORD, how shall I be meeting,
   And how shall I embrace
Thee, earth's Desire, when greeting
   My soul's adorning grace?
O Jesus, Jesus! holding
   Thyself the flame in sight,
Show how, Thy beam beholding,
   I may my Lord delight.

Fresh palms Thy Zion streweth,
   And branches ever green,
And psalms my voice reneweth,
   To raise my joy serene.
Such budding tribute paying,
   My heart shall hymn Thy praise,
Thy holy name obeying
   With chiefest of my lays.

What hast Thou left ungranted,
   To give me glad relief?
When soul and body panted
   In utmost depth of grief,
In hour of degradation,
   Thy peace and pity smiled,
Then Thou, my soul's salvation,
   Didst happy make Thy child.

THE ADVENT.

I lay in slavish mourning,
   Thou cam'st to set me free;
I sank in shame and scorning,
   Thou cam'st to comfort me.
Thou raisedst me to glory,
   Bestowing highest good,
Not frail and transitory,
   Like wealth on earth pursued.

Naught, naught did send Thee speeding
   From mansions of the skies,
But love all love exceeding,
   Love able to comprise
A world in pangs despairing,
   Weighed down with thousand woes
That tongue would fail declaring,
   But love doth fast inclose.

Grave on your heart this writing,
   O band of mourners poor!
With pains and sorrows fighting,
   That throng you more and more;
Dismiss the fear that sickens,
   For lo! beside you see
Him who your heart now quickens
   And comforts; here is He.

Why should you be detainèd
   In trouble day and night,
As though He must be gainèd
   By arm of human might?
He comes, He comes, all willing,
   All full of grace and love,
Those woes and troubles stilling,
   Well known to Him above.

Nor need ye tremble over
   The guilt that gives distress.
No! Jesus all will cover
   With grace and righteousness:
He comes, He comes, procuring
   The peace of sin forgiven,
To all God's sons securing
   Their part and lot in heaven.

Why heed ye, then, the crying
    Of crafty foemen nigh?
Your Lord shall send them flying
    In twinkling of an eye.
He comes, He comes, for ever
    A King; and earth's fell band
Shall prove in the endeavour
    Too feeble to withstand.

He comes to judge the nations,
    Wroth if they wrathful prove,
With sweet illuminations
    To those who seek and love.
Come, come, O Sun eternal!
    And all our souls convey
To endless bliss supernal,
    In yonder court of day.

PLUNGED IN A GULF OF DARK DESPAIR.

ISAAC WATTS, 1709. The fifth stanza is among the most familiar poetic descriptions of the Saviour's love. Sir Roundell Palmer, in his "Book of Praise," omits the fourth stanza. The hymn might as well be classed with the Passion hymns.

PLUNGED in a gulf of dark despair,
    We wretched sinners lay,
Without one cheerful beam of hope,
    Or spark of glimmering day.

With pitying eyes, the Prince of Grace
    Beheld our helpless grief;
He saw, and — oh, amazing love! —
    He ran to our relief.

Down from the shining seats above,
    With joyful haste He fled,
Entered the grave in mortal flesh,
    And dwelt among the dead.

He spoiled the powers of darkness thus,
    And brake our iron chains;

THE ADVENT.

Jesus has freed our captive souls
  From everlasting pains.

Oh! for this love let rocks and hills
  Their lasting silence break,
And all harmonious human tongues
  The Saviour's praises speak.

Angels, assist our mighty joys;
  Strike all your harps of gold!
But, when you raise your highest notes,
  His love can ne'er be told.

MESSIAH, AT THY GLAD APPROACH.

MICHAEL BRUCE, one of the most remarkable short-lived poets; born 1746; educated at the University of Edinburgh; died, of consumption, in 1767, in his twenty-first year. Some of his poems are erroneously ascribed to his friend, John Logan. See ROGERS'S " Lyr. Brit." 1867, p. 97.

MESSIAH, at Thy glad approach
  The howling winds are still;
Thy praises fill the lonely waste,
  And breathe from every hill.

The hidden fountains at Thy call
  Their sacred stores unlock;
Loud in the desert, sudden streams
  Burst living from the rock.

The incense of the spring ascends
  Upon the morning gale;
Red o'er the hill the roses bloom,
  The lilies in the vale.

Renewed, the earth a robe of light,
  A robe of beauty, wears;
And in new heavens a brighter sun
  Leads on the promised years.

The kingdom of Messiah come,
  Appointed times disclose;

And fairer in Emmanuel's land
　The new creation glows.

Let Israel to the Prince of Peace
　The loud hosanna sing!
With hallelujahs and with hymns
　O Zion, hail thy King!

LO, HE COMES! LET ALL ADORE HIM!

ISA. xl. 3-5. THOMAS KELLY, born in Dublin, 1769; educated for the law; ordained 1792; left the Established Church; laboured, for the London Missionary Society, with the brothers Haldane; died 1855. Author of 765 hymns, some of which are among the best in the English language.

LO, He comes! let all adore Him!
　　'Tis the God of grace and truth!
　　Go! prepare the way before Him,
　Make the rugged places smooth!
Lo, He comes, the mighty Lord!
Great His work, and His reward.

Let the valleys all be raisèd;
　Go, and make the crooked straight;
Let the mountains be abasèd;
　Let all nature change its state;
Through the desert mark a road,
Make a highway for our God.

Through the desert God is going,
　Through the desert waste and wild,
Where no goodly plant is growing,
　Where no verdure ever smiled;
But the desert shall be glad,
And with verdure soon be clad.

Where the thorn and brier flourished,
　Trees shall there be seen to grow,
Planted by the Lord and nourished,
　Stately, fair, and fruitful too;
They shall rise on every side,
They shall spread their branches wide.

THE ADVENT.

From the hills and lofty mountains
    Rivers shall be seen to flow;
There the Lord will open fountains,
    Thence supply the plains below;
As He passes, every land
Shall confess His powerful hand.

WATCHMAN! TELL US OF THE NIGHT.

SIR JOHN BOWRING, LL.D., born at Exeter, 1792; a distinguished diplomatist and colonial governor in China, now living in retirement; author of several important works of travel and on politics, and of a volume of excellent hymns published in 1825. This hymn is based on Isa. xxi. 11: "Watchman, what of the night?"

WATCHMAN! tell us of the night,
    What its signs of promise are.
Traveller! o'er yon mountain's height,
    See that glory-beaming star.

Watchman! does its beauteous ray
    Aught of hope or joy foretell?
Traveller! yes; it brings the day,
    Promised day of Israel.

Watchman! tell us of the night;
    Higher yet that star ascends.
Traveller! blessedness and light,
    Peace and truth, its course portends.

Watchman! will its beams alone
    Gild the spot that gave them birth?
Traveller! ages are its own;
    See, it bursts o'er all the earth!

Watchman! tell us of the night,
    For the morning seems to dawn.
Traveller! darkness takes its flight;
    Doubt and terror are withdrawn.

Watchman! let thy wanderings cease;
    Hie thee to thy quiet home:
Traveller! lo, the Prince of Peace,
    Lo, the Son of God is come!

WHEN JESUS CAME TO EARTH OF OLD.

MRS. CECIL FRANCES ALEXANDER, a highly accomplished authoress, daughter of Major Humphreys of Ireland; married, in 1850, to the Very Rev. William Alexander, Dean of Emly. Her "Hymns for Little Children" have an immense circulation in England (two hundred and fifty thousand copies were disposed of before 1867). She has published several volumes of poems, and contributed to the "Lyra Anglicana," and various magazines.

WHEN Jesus came to earth of old,
    He came in weakness and in woe;
He wore no form of angel mould,
    But took our nature, poor and low.

But, when He cometh back once more,
    There shall be set the great white throne,
And earth and heaven shall flee before
    The face of Him that sits thereon.

O Son of God, in glory crowned,
    The Judge ordained of quick and dead!
O Son of Man, so pitying found
    For all the tears Thy people shed!

Be with us in this darkened place,—
    This weary, restless, dangerous night;
And teach, oh teach us, by Thy grace,
    To struggle onward into light!

And since, in God's recording book,
    Our sins are written, every one,—
The crime, the wrath, the wandering look,
    The good we knew, and left undone.

Lord, ere the last dread trump be heard,
    And ere before Thy face we stand,
Look Thou on each accusing word,
    And blot it with Thy bleeding hand.

And by the love that brought Thee here,
    And by the cross, and by the grave,
Give perfect love for conscious fear,
    And in the day of judgment save.

And lead us on while here we stray,
   And make us love our heavenly home,
Till from our hearts we love to say,
   " Even so, Lord Jesus, quickly come."

ZION, AT THY SHINING GATES.

BENJAMIN HALL KENNEDY, D.D. born near Birmingham, 1804; educated at Cambridge; since 1865, Rector of West Felton, England.

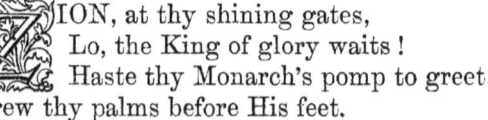

ZION, at thy shining gates,
   Lo, the King of glory waits!
   Haste thy Monarch's pomp to greet,
Strew thy palms before His feet.

Christ, for Thee their triple light
Faith and Hope and Love unite;
This the beacon we display,
To proclaim Thine Advent day.

Come, and give us peace within;
Loose us from the bands of sin;
Take away the galling weight
Laid on us by Satan's hate.

Give us grace Thy yoke to wear;
Give us strength Thy cross to bear;
Make us Thine in deed and word,
Thine in heart and life, O Lord!

Kill in us the carnal root,
That the Spirit may bear fruit;
Plant in us Thy lowly mind;
Keep us faithful, loving, kind.

So, when Thou shalt come again,
Judge of angels and of men,
We, with all Thy saints, shall sing
Hallelujahs to our King.

HE COMES, NO ROYAL VESTURE WEARING.

(Dein König kommt in niedern Hüllen.)

BY FRIEDRICH RÜCKERT, one of the greatest German poets of the 19th century; died 1867. A lyric of high order, first published 1824; admirably translated, for this Collection, by Professor THOMAS C. PORTER, of Lafayette College, Easton, Pa., April 5, 1868. (The original in SCHAFF's "G. Hymn Book," No. 81.) Based upon Matt. xxi. 1-11, which is the Gospel lesson for the first Sunday in Advent (and also a proper lesson for Palm Sunday.)

HE comes, no royal vesture wearing,
  An humble beast the Monarch bearing;
    Receive thy King, Jerusalem!
Go forth with palms, His triumph showing,
With branches green the pathway strewing,
    And shout hosannas to His name.

O Sovereign, by no host attended!
Strong Champion, by no spear defended!
    O Prince of Peace, and David's Son!—
Thy throne, from whose approach for ever
The kings of earth Thy step would sever,
    Is by Thee, without battle, won.

Unto the empire Thou hast founded,
Though not of earth, nor by earth bounded,
    All earthly realms shall subject be:
Forth into every land and nation,
Thy servants, armed with Thy salvation,
    March to prepare a way for Thee.

And at Thy coming, clothed with power,
The sullen storm forgets to lower,
    And waves grow calm beneath Thy tread;
The bonds, by man's rebellion blighted,
In a new covenant are united,
    And sin and death in fetters led.

O Lord of grace and truth unending,
And love all reach of thought transcending,
    Revisit us, so sorely tried!
Thine Advent once again is needed,
To form anew Thy peace, unheeded
    By worldly haughtiness and pride.

Oh, let Thy light, which ne'er shall vanish,
From earth the power of darkness banish;
  The lurid flames of discord quell;
That we, the thrones and people loyal,
As brethren 'neath Thy sceptre royal,
  In Thy great Father's house may dwell.

THE CHURCH HAS WAITED LONG.

By Horatius Bonar, D.D., of Kelso. Rev. xxii. 20. From his "Hymns of Faith and Hope," First Series, 1856, under the title "Advent."

THE Church has waited long,
  Her absent Lord to see;
  And still in loneliness she waits,
A friendless stranger she.
Age after age has gone,
Sun after sun has set,
And still, in weeds of widowhood,
  She weeps, a mourner yet.
  Come, then, Lord Jesus, come!

Saint after saint on earth
Has lived and loved and died;
And, as they left us one by one,
  We laid them side by side.
  We laid them down to sleep,
  But not in hope forlorn;
We laid them but to ripen there,
  Till the last glorious morn.
  Come, then, Lord Jesus, come!

The serpent's brood increase,
The powers of hell grow bold,
The conflict thickens, faith is low,
  And love is waxing cold.
  How long, O Lord our God!
  Holy and true and good,
Wilt Thou not judge thy suffering Church,
  Her sighs and tears and blood?
  Come, then, Lord Jesus, come!

We long to hear Thy voice,
  To see Thee face to face,
To share Thy crown and glory then,
  As now we share Thy grace.
  Should not the loving bride
    Her absent bridegroom mourn?
Should she not wear the signs of grief
    Until her Lord return?
    Come, then, Lord Jesus, come!

The whole creation groans,
  And waits to hear that voice,
That shall restore her comeliness,
  And make her wastes rejoice.
  Come, Lord, and wipe away
    The curse, the sin, the stain,
And make this blighted world of ours
    Thine own fair world again.
    Come, then, Lord Jesus, come!

O'ER THE DISTANT MOUNTAINS BREAKING.

BY JOHN S. B. MONSELL, LL.D. Vicar of Egham; author of "Parish Musings," "Spiritual Songs," &c. From his "Hymns of Love and Praise," London, 1863. "Surely I come quickly; Amen. Even so, come, Lord Jesus."—*Rev.* xxii. 20.

O'ER the distant mountains breaking
  Comes the redd'ning dawn of day,
  Rise, my soul, from sleep awaking,
Rise and sing, and watch and pray:
    'Tis thy Saviour
  On His bright returning way.

O Thou long-expected! weary
  Waits mine anxious soul for Thee,
Life is dark, and earth is dreary
  Where Thy light I do not see;
    O my Saviour!
  When wilt Thou return to me?

THE ADVENT.

Long, too long, in sin and sadness,
  Far away from Thee I pine,
When, O when, shall I the gladness
  Of Thy Spirit feel in mine?
    O my Saviour!
  When shall I be wholly Thine?

Nearer is my soul's salvation,
  Spent the night, the day at hand,
Keep me in my lowly station,
  Watching for Thee, till I stand,
    O my Saviour!
  In Thy bright and promised land.

With my lamp well trimm'd and burning,
  Swift to hear, and slow to roam,
Watching for Thy glad returning
  To restore me to my home,
    Come, my Saviour!
  O my Saviour, quickly come!

THE INCARNATION.

"UNTO us a Child is born, unto us a Son is given: and the government shall be upon his shoulder; and his name shall be called Wonderful, Counsellor, the Mighty God, the Everlasting Father, the Prince of Peace."—*Isa.* ix. 6.

"And the Word was made flesh, and dwelt among us (and we beheld his glory, the glory as of the only begotten of the Father), full of grace and truth."—*John* i. 14.

 THOU only-begotten Son of God, Light of Light, God of God, very God of very God, who, in the fulness of time, wast made flesh, and didst take upon Thyself all our sins and infirmities, that we might have salvation from sin, and eternal life, in Thee:—we bless Thee for Thy holy incarnation; and with the multitude of angels who proclaimed Thy birth, and with Thy people among all nations, we unite in singing, Glory to God in the highest, and on earth peace, good-will toward men! Amen.

> WELCOME to our wondering sight,
>   Eternity shut in a span!
> Summer in winter! day in night!
>   Heaven in earth! and God in man!
> Great Little One, whose glorious birth
> Lifts earth to heaven, stoops heaven to earth.
>   RICHARD CRASHAW, 1646.

THE angels never sang an air,
Which could in melody compare
　With that at Jesus' birth,
　When sent to tell the earth
That the co-gracious Three design'd
Great Filial God to save mankind.
　　　　　　　　　　BISHOP KEN.

Rise, happy morn! rise, holy morn!
　Draw forth the cheerful day from night:
O Father! touch the east, and light
The Light that shone when Hope was born.
　　　　　　　　　　ALFRED TENNYSON.

THE INCARNATION.

A GREAT AND MIGHTY WONDER.

(Μέγα καὶ παράδοξον θαῦμα.)

FROM the Greek of ANATOLIUS (Patriarch of Constantinople, and member of the Ecumenical Council of Chalcedon, A.D. 451), by Dr. J. MASON NEALE ("Hymns of the Eastern Church," Lond. 1862).

GREAT and mighty wonder
    The festal makes secure:
The Virgin bears the Infant
    With virgin-honour pure.

The Word is made incarnate,
    And yet remains on high;
And cherubim sing anthems
    To shepherds from the sky.

And we with them triumphant,
    Repeat the hymn again:
"To God on high be glory,
    And peace on earth to men!"

While thus they praise your Monarch,
    Those bright angelic bands,
Rejoice, ye vales and mountains!
    Ye oceans, clap your hands!

Since all He came to ransom,
    By all be He adored,
The Infant born in Bethlehem,
    The Saviour and the Lord!

And idol forms shall perish,
    And error shall decay;
And Christ shall wield His sceptre,
    Our Lord and God for aye.

FROM WHERE THE RISING SUN GOES FORTH.

(A solis ortûs cardine.)

ST. AMBROSE of Milan, A.D. 397. The original, as given by DANIEL ("Thes. Hymnol." I. p. 21), has fifty-six lines, but only a part of it (vers. 4, 5, 6) has passed into ecclesiastical use. The beginning is borrowed from Ps. cxii. 3: "A solis ortu usque ad occasum laudabile nomen."

FROM where the rising sun goes forth
To where he spans the utmost earth
Proclaim we Christ our King, this morn
Of Mary Virgin-mother born:

All climes unite in common voice;
Judea, Rome, and Greece rejoice;
Thrace, Egypt, Persia, Scythia, now
To one sole King's dominion bow.

All, all, confess your Lord and King;
Redeemed and lost, His praises sing;
Health, sickness, life, and death adore;
All live in Him, they die no more.

His beauteous portal, full of grace,
Is hallowed for the King to pass;
The King doth pass: the folded door
Abideth folded as before.[1]

Son of the Father's Might Divine,
Proceeding from His Virgin-shrine,
Maker, Redeemer, Bridegroom, He
The Giant of His Church shall be.[2]

---

[1] An allusion to the *porta clausa*, Ezek. xliv. 1-3, which was allegorically understood of the womb of the Virgin. This is one of the earliest testimonies of the belief in the perpetual virginity of Mary, which subsequently became a dogma of the Greek and Roman Catholic Churches, and is held also by many Protestant divines, although it cannot be proved from the New Testament, but seems to conflict with the obvious meaning of Matt. i. 25, and several passages where brothers of Jesus are mentioned.

[2] The expression, *Suæ gigas ecclesiæ*, refers to the double nature of Christ, in allusion to the mystical interpretation of the giants, Gen. vi. 4. Comp. *geminæ gigas substantiæ*, in Ambrose's "Veni Redemptor gentium," line 15 (see p. 10).

Of Mother-maid the light and joy,
Of all believers hope most high,
He the dark cup of death shall drain
Ere He unloose our guilty chain.

Fair Stone, cut out from mountain-height,
Filling the world with grace and light,
Whom, by no hand of mortal hewn,
The ancient sages had foreshown:[1]

'Tis done, what herald-angel said,
He, the True Word, true flesh is made,
A Virgin-birth of Virgin-womb,
Virgin of virgins, Christ is come.

The skies have shed the dew from heaven,
The outpouring clouds the Just One given,
Earth's open lap receives the birth,
And brings the Lord the Saviour forth.

Oh! 'twas a wondrous travail there
When Him, the Christ, the Virgin bare,
So bare the birth, the Offspring pure,
As Ever-virgin to endure.

Creator He of all the race,
For whom creation hath no place,
Hath found, chaste Mother, where to dwell,
Hath shrined Him in thy sacred cell:

Whom Sire most High, when time was not,
God Very God of God begot,
The bosom chaste of Mother mild
In time doth bear a new-born Child.

---

[1] Dan. ii. 34; Isa. xxviii. 16; Eph. ii. 20; 1 Cor. iii. 11; 1 Pet. ii. 4, 6, 7.

OF THE FATHER'S LOVE BEGOTTEN.

(Corde natus ex Parentis.)

FROM the Latin of CLEMENS AURELIUS PRUDENTIUS, of Spain, died 405 DANIEL, "Thesaurus," I. 122; WACKERNAGEL, I. 36; an English version in "The Hymnal Noted," No. 32; "Hymns Ancient and Modern," No. 46, and other collections.

OF the Father's love begotten,
    Ere the worlds began to be,
He is Alpha and Omega,
    He the source, the ending He,
Of the things that are, that have been,
    And that future years shall see,
        Evermore and evermore!

He is here, whom seers in old time
    Chanted of, while ages ran;
Whom the voices of the Prophets
    Promised since the world began:
Then foretold, now manifested,
    To receive the praise of man,
        Evermore and evermore!

Oh that ever-blessed birthday,
    When the Virgin, full of grace,
Of the Holy Ghost incarnate
    Bare the Saviour of our race;
And that Child, the world's Redeemer,
    First displayed His sacred Face,
        Evermore and evermore!

Praise Him, O ye heavens of heavens!
    Praise Him, angels in the height!
Every power and every virtue
    Sing the praise of God aright!
Let no tongue of man be silent,
    Let each heart and voice unite,
        Evermore and evermore!

Thee let age, and Thee let manhood,
    Thee let choirs of infants sing;

Thee the matrons and the virgins,
　And the children answering:
Let their modest song re-echo,
　And their heart its praises bring,
　　Evermore and evermore!

Laud and honour to the Father!
Laud and honour to the Son!
Laud and honour to the Spirit!
　Ever Three and ever One:
Consubstantial, co-eternal,
　While unending ages run,
　　Evermore and evermore.

FROM LANDS THAT SEE THE SUN.

(A solis ortûs cardine.)

FROM the Latin of CŒLIUS SEDULIUS, a native of Scotland or Ireland, and presbyter in the fifth century. This hymn is found in all the Breviaries. The first stanza is literally borrowed from a Nativity hymn of St. Ambrose (p. 32). See the Latin in DANIEL, "Thesaurus," I. p. 143

FROM lands that see the sun arise,
　To earth's remotest boundaries,
　The Virgin-born to-day we sing,
The Son of Mary, Christ the King.

Blest Author of this earthly frame,
To take a servant's form He came,
That, liberating flesh by flesh,
Whom He had made might live afresh.

In that chaste parent's holy womb
Celestial grace hath found its home:
And she, as earthly bride unknown,
Yet calls that Offspring blest her own.

The mansion of the modest breast
Becomes a shrine where God shall rest:
The pure and undefilèd one
Conceivèd in her womb the Son.

That Son, that Royal Son, she bore,
Whom Gabriel's voice had told afore:
Whom, in His Mother yet concealed,
The Infant Baptist had revealed.

The manger and the straw He bore,
The cradle did He not abhor:
By milk in infant portions fed,
Who gives e'en fowls their daily bread.

The heavenly chorus filled the sky,
The angels sang to God on high,
What time to shepherds, watching lone,
They made Creation's Shepherd known.

For that Thine Advent glory be,
O Jesu, Virgin-born, to Thee!
With Father, and with Holy Ghost,
From men and from the heavenly host.

TO-DAY IN BETHLEHEM HEAR I.

(Δόξα ἐν ὑψίστοις Θεῷ.)

FROM the Greek of JOHN OF DAMASCUS, died 754.

TO-DAY in Bethlehem hear I
    Sweet angel voices singing:
All glory be to God on high,
    Who peace to earth is bringing.
The Virgin Mary holdeth more
    Than highest heaven most holy:
Light shines on what was dark before,
    And lifteth up the lowly.

God wills that peace should be in earth,
    And holy exultation:
Sweet Babe, I greet Thy spotless birth
    And wondrous Incarnation.
To-day in Bethlehem hear I
    Even the lowly singing:
With angel-words they pierce the sky;
    All earth with joy is ringing.

ALL HAIL, THOU NIGHT, THAN DAY MORE BRIGHT!

(*O nox vel medio splendidior die.*)

FROM the Amiens Breviary, translated by W. J. BLEW, "Church Hymn and Tune Book," Lond. 1855.

ALL hail, thou night, than day more bright,
    Through whose mysterious shade,
    In wondrous birth, arose on earth,
  From bosom of pure Maid,
The Sun new-born, a Star of morn,
  Filling the world with light!

He who alone, from heaven's high throne,
  Rules all, and doth restore
To God's embrace man's fallen race,
  Lies on a cottage floor,
Like Him that we, save poverty,
  Have nought to call our own.

While o'er their sheep close watch they keep,
  Those shepherds first receive
The heavenly call, that doth to all
  Great joy and gladness give,—
The call from heaven, to watchmen given
  That wake and never sleep.

COME HITHER, YE FAITHFUL.

(*Adeste fideles.*)

FROM a Latin hymn of uncertain date. Another translation in the "Hymnal Noted:"

"Be present, ye faithful, joyful and triumphant."

COME hither, ye faithful;
    Triumphantly sing;
    Come, see in the manger
  Our Saviour and King!
To Bethlehem hasten,
  With joyful accord!
Oh, come ye, come hither,
  To worship the Lord!

True Son of the Father,
  He comes from the skies;
To be born of a Virgin
  He doth not despise.
To Bethlehem hasten,
  With joyful accord!
Oh, come ye, come hither,
  To worship the Lord!

Hark, hark to the angels!
  All singing in heaven:
"To God in the highest
  All glory be given!"
To Bethlehem hasten,
  With joyful accord!
Oh, come ye, come hither,
  To worship the Lord!

To Thee, then, O Jesus!
  This day of Thy birth,
Be glory and honour
  Through heaven and earth!
True Godhead Incarnate!
  Omnipotent Word!
Oh, come, let us hasten
  To worship the Lord!

A CHILD IS BORN IN BETHLEHEM.

(Puer natus in Bethlehem.)

A JOYOUS Christmas hymn of the fourteenth century, which continued in use, in the Lutheran churches of Germany, wellnigh to this day. Other English versions by R. F. LITTLEDALE, Mrs. CHARLES, and others. The Latin in DANIEL, I. 334; TRENCH, p. 97. WACKERNAGEL ("Das Deutsche Kirchenlied," vol. i. p. 198-200), gives ten forms of this hymn.

CHILD is born in Bethlehem;
  Rejoice and sing, Jerusalem.
  Within a manger He doth lie,
Whose throne is set above the sky.
  Hallelujah! hallelujah!

A CHILD IS BORN IN BETHLEHEM.

The wise men came, led by the star;
Gold, myrrh, and incense brought from far.
The ox and ass beheld that sight;
The creature knew the Lord of might.[1]
    Hallelujah! hallelujah!

His mother is the Virgin mild,
And He the Father's only child.
The serpent's wound He beareth not,
Yet takes our blood, and shares our lot.
    Hallelujah! hallelujah!

Our human flesh He enters in,
But free from every stain of sin.
To fallen man himself He bowed,
That He might lift us up to God.
    Hallelujah! hallelujah!

On this most blessed jubilee,
All glory be, O God! to Thee.
O Holy Three, we Thee adore,
This day, henceforth, for evermore.
    Hallelujah! hallelujah!

---

[1] "Cognovit bos et asinus
Quod puer erat Dominus."

The mediæval legend of the ox and ass recognizing and worshipping the Lord whom the Jews ignored and rejected, figures prominently in Catholic pictures of the holy family. It rests upon a fanciful interpretation of Isa. i. 3 ("Cognovit bos possessorem suum, et asinus præsepe domini sui") and Hab. iii. 2 ("In medio duorum animalium innotesceris"), which was understood as a prophetic allusion to the manger of Bethlehem.

HEIGHT OF HEAVEN, WHY ART THOU LYING.

(Altitudo, quid hic jaces.)

From the Latin by the Rev. E. A. Washburn, D.D., Rector of Calvary Church, New York, 1869. Contributed to this collection.

HEIGHT of heaven, why art thou lying
    Cradled in a stable base?
Maker of the starry torches,
    Hides a manger cold Thy face?
Oh, what marvels hast Thou lavished,
    Jesu, upon sinful men!
Exiles from the bliss of Eden,
    Yet Thy heart hath loved again.

Might divine becometh weakness;
    Infinite a babe could be;
In a mortal womb imprisoned,
    Born—behold Eternity!
Oh, what marvels hast Thou lavished,
    Jesu, upon sinful men!
Exiles from the bliss of Eden,
    Yet Thy heart hath loved again.

Thou with childish lips wast clinging
    To the stainless Virgin's breast;
Tear-drops from Thine eye were springing,—
    Thou, the Joy of heaven blest!
Oh, what marvels hast Thou lavished,
    Jesu, upon sinful men!
Exiles from the bliss of Eden,
    Yet Thy heart hath loved again.

THERE COMES A GALLEY LADEN.

(Es kommt ein Schiff geladen.)

FROM the German of JOHN TAULER, a celebrated mystic divine and revival preacher, died at Strassburg, 1361. See the original in WACKERNAGEL'S " Deutsches Kirchenlied von der ältesten Zeit," vol. ii. pp. 302, 303 (three forms). Another translation, by C. W. SHIELDS (" There comes a bark full laden"), in " Sacred Lyrics from the German," Phila. p. 109.

THERE comes a galley laden,
    A heavenly freight on board;
It bears God's Son, the Saviour,
    The great Undying Word.

And proudly floats that galley,
    From troubled coast to coast:
Its sail is love and mercy;
    Its mast, the Holy Ghost.

Now earth hath caught the anchor,
    The ship hath touched the strand;
God's Word, in fleshly garment,—
    The Son,—steps out on land.

Thou Bethlehem the lowly
    Receiv'st Him in thy stall;
Thou giv'st Him rest and shelter,
    Who comes to save us all.

Oh! haste, my brothers, quickly
    To kiss this little Child,
Who dies a glorious Martyr
    For souls with sin defiled.

And he who dies with Jesus,
    With Jesus he shall rise,
And love eternal waft him
    With Christ beyond the skies.

ALL PRAISE TO THEE, ETERNAL LORD!

(Grates nunc omnes reddamus.)

ON the basis of LUTHER's hymn, " Gelobet seist Du, Jesu Christ," 1523, which is itself freely reproduced and enlarged from the short sequence " De Nativitate Domini," by NOTKER of St. Gall in the ninth century. (Comp. WACKERNAGEL's " Kirchenlied," I. 69, who attributes the sequence to Gregory the Great, died 604; DANIEL's " Thes." II. 5; KOCH's " Geschichte des Kirchenlieds," IV. 134; SCHAFF's " Deutsches Gesangbuch," No. 83; and " Andover Sabbath H. B." No. 263.)

ALL praise to Thee, eternal Lord!
Clothed in a garb of flesh and blood;
Choosing a manger for Thy throne,
While worlds on worlds are Thine alone.

Once did the skies before Thee bow:
A Virgin's arms contain Thee now;
Angels, who did in Thee rejoice,
Now listen for Thine infant voice.

A little child, Thou art our guest,
That weary ones in Thee may rest;
Forlorn and lowly is Thy birth,
That we may rise to heaven from earth.

Thou comest in the darksome night
To make us children of the light,—
To make us, in the realms divine,
Like Thine own angels round Thee shine.

All this for us Thy love hath done;
By this to Thee our love is won:
For this we tune our cheerful lays,
And shout our thanks in ceaseless praise.

GOOD NEWS FROM HEAVEN THE ANGELS BRING.

(Von Himmel hoch da komm ich her.)

FROM LUTHER's childlike Christmas carol, written for his children, 1535, and abridged 1543 (" Vom Himmel kam der Engel Schaar"). There are several English translations, one by two little blind girls (commencing, " From highest heaven I just came," and published in the " Lutheran and Missionary," Philad.), one by ARTHUR TOZER RUSSELL (1851), and another by Miss C. WINKWORTH (" From heaven above to earth I come," " Lyra Germanica," First Series), etc.

GOOD news from heaven the angels bring,
Glad tidings to the earth they sing:
To us this day a child is given,
To crown us with the joy of heaven.

This is the Christ, our God and Lord,
Who in all need shall aid afford:
He will Himself our Saviour be,
From sin and sorrow set us free.

To us that blessedness He brings,
Which from the Father's bounty springs:
That in the heavenly realm we may
With Him enjoy eternal day.

All hail, Thou noble Guest, this morn,
Whose love did not the sinner scorn!
In my distress Thou cam'st to me:
What thanks shall I return to Thee?

Were earth a thousand times as fair,
Beset with gold and jewels rare,
She yet were far too poor to be
A narrow cradle, Lord, for Thee.

Ah, dearest Jesus, Holy Child!
Make Thee a bed, soft, undefiled,
Within my heart, that it may be
A quiet chamber kept for Thee.

Praise God upon His heavenly throne,
Who gave to us His only Son:
For this His hosts, on joyful wing,
A blest New Year of mercy sing.

WE SING TO THEE, IMMANUEL.

(Wir singen Dir, Immanuel.)

FROM the German of PAUL GERHARDT, 1656, by F. E. Cox. ("Hymns from the German," 2nd ed. Lond. 1865). Another version in "Lyra Germanica," I. p. 28:
"Thee, O Immanuel! we praise, the Prince of Life, and Fount of Grace." The hymn has twenty stanzas, but is much abridged in German hymn-books (SCHAFF's "G. H. B." No. 86).

WE sing to Thee, Immanuel,
   The Prince of life, salvation's Well,
   The Plant of Heaven, the Star of morn,
The Lord of Lords, the Virgin-born.

All glory, worship, thanks, and praise,
That Thou art come in these our days!
Thou Heavenly Guest expected long,
We hail Thee with a joyful song.

For Thee, since first the world was made,
Men's hearts have waited, watched, and prayed;
Prophets and patriarchs, year by year,
Have longed to see Thy light appear.

O God!—they prayed—from Sion rise,
And hear Thy captive people's cries;
At length, O Lord! salvation bring:
Then Jacob shall rejoice and sing.

Now Thou, by whom the world was made,
Art in Thy manger-cradle laid;
Maker of all things great, art small,
Naked Thyself, though clothing all.

Thou, who both heaven and earth dost sway,
In strangers' inn art fain to stay;
And though Thy power makes angels blest,
Dost seek Thy food from human breast.

Encouraged thus, our love grows bold
On Thee to lay our steadfast hold;
The Cross which Thou didst undergo
Has vanquished death and healed our woe.

WE SING TO THEE, IMMANUEL.   45

Thou art our Head: then, Lord, of Thee,
True, living members we will be;
And, in the strength Thy grace shall give,
Will live as Thou wouldst have us live.

As each short year goes quickly round,
Our Hallelujahs shall resound;
And, when we reckon years no more,
May we in heaven Thy Name adore!

ALL MY HEART THIS NIGHT REJOICES.

(Fröhlich soll mein Herze springen.)

PAUL GERHARDT, 1656. Translated by C. WINKWORTH. The original has fifteen stanzas, but is abridged in most German hymn books.

ALL my heart this night rejoices,
  As I hear,
  Far and near,
 Sweetest angel voices:
" Christ is born," their choirs are singing,
  Till the air
  Everywhere
 Now with joy is ringing.

Hark! a voice from yonder manger,
  Soft and sweet,
  Doth entreat:
" Flee from woe and danger;
Brethren, come: from all that grieves you
  You are freed;
  All you need
 I will surely give you."

Come, then, let us hasten yonder;
  Here let all,
  Great and small,
 Kneel in awe and wonder;
Love Him who with love is yearning;
  Hail the Star
  That from far
 Bright with hope is burning!

Ye who pine in weary sadness,
    Weep no more,
    For the door
Now is found of gladness.
Cling to Him, for He will guide you
    Where no cross,
    Pain or loss,
Can again betide you.

Hither come, ye heavy-hearted,
    Who for sin,
    Deep within,
Long and sore have smarted:
For the poisoned wounds you're feeling
    Help is near;
    One is here
Mighty for their healing.

Hither come, ye poor and wretched;
    Know His will
    Is to fill
Every hand outstretchèd;
Here are riches without measure,
    Here forget
    All regret,
Fill your hearts with treasure.

Blessed Saviour, let me find Thee!
    Keep Thou me
    Close to Thee,
Cast me not behind Thee!
Life of life, my heart Thou stillest,
    Calm I rest
    On Thy breast,
All this void Thou fillest.

Heedfully my Lord I'll cherish,
    Live to Thee,
    And with Thee
Dying shall not perish;
But shall dwell with Thee for ever,
    Far on high,
    In the joy
That can alter never.

WHILE TO BETHLEHEM.

VIOLANTE DO CEO, a celebrated Portuguese poetess, called "the Tenth Muse of Portugal;" b. at Lisbon, 1601; d. in a cloister, 1693. Translated by J. ADAMSON, "Lusitania Illustrata,' 1842.

WHILE to Bethlehem we are going,
   Tell me now, to cheer the road.
Tell me why this lovely Infant
   Quitted His divine abode.
" From that world to bring to this
Peace, which, of all earthly blisses,
   Is the brightest, purest bliss."

Wherefore from His throne exalted
   Came He on this earth to dwell;
All his pomp an humble manger,
   All His court a narrow cell?
" From that world to bring to this
Peace, which, of all earthly blisses,
   Is the brightest, purest bliss."

Why did He, the Lord Eternal,
   Mortal pilgrim deign to be;
He who fashioned for His glory,
   Boundless immortality?
" From that world to bring to this
Peace, which, of all earthly blisses,
   Is the brightest, purest bliss."

Well, then, let us haste to Bethlehem;
   Thither let us haste and rest;
For, of all Heaven's gifts, the sweetest.
   Sure, is peace,—the sweetest, best.

THIS IS THE MONTH, AND THIS THE HAPPY MORN.

"On the Morning of Christ's Nativity." By John Milton, born 1608, died 1674. The magnificent Nativity hymn of the immortal singer of " Paradise Lost," which follows this, is too long, and not sufficiently lyrical, for our Collection.

THIS is the month, and this the happy morn,
    Wherein the Son of heaven's eternal King,
  Of wedded Maid and Virgin Mother born,
  Our great redemption from above did bring;
  For so the holy sages once did sing,
  That He our deadly forfeit should release,
And with His Father work us a perpetual peace.

  That glorious form, that light unsufferable,
  And that far-beaming blaze of majesty,
  Wherewith He wont at heaven's high council-table
  To sit the midst of Trinal Unity,
  He laid aside; and, here with us to be,
  Forsook the courts of everlasting day,
And chose with us a darksome house of mortal clay.

  Say, heavenly Muse, shall not Thy sacred vein
  Afford a present to the Infant God?
  Hast thou no verse, no hymn, or solemn strain,
  To welcome Him to this His new abode,
  Now while the heaven by the sun's team untrod,
  Hath took no print of the approaching light,
And all the spangled host keep watch in squadrons bright?

  See how from far upon the eastern road
  The star-led wizards[1] haste with odours sweet:
  Oh run, prevent them with thy humble ode,
  And lay it lowly at His blessed feet;
  Have thou the honour first thy Lord to greet,
  And join thy voice unto the angel choir,
From out His secret altar touched with hallowed fire.

---

[1] Sages, Matt. ii.

THOU FAIREST CHILD DIVINE.

(Du schönstes Gottes-Kind.)

GERHARD TERSTEEGEN, 1731. Translated by C. WINKWORTH, " Lyra Germanica," Second Series.

THOU fairest Child Divine
    In yonder manger laid,
    In whom is God Himself well pleased,
  By whom were all things made,
  On me art Thou bestowed;
  How can such wonders be!
The dearest that the Father hath
    He gives me here in Thee!

    I was a foe to God,
    I fought in Satan's host,
I trifled all His grace away,
    Alas! my soul was lost.
    Yet God forgets my sin;
    His heart, with pity moved,
He gives me, Heavenly Child, in Thee:
    Lo! thus our God hath loved!

    Once blind with sin and self,
    Along the treacherous way,
That ends in ruin at the last,
    I hastened far astray;
    Then God sent down His Son;
    For with a love most deep,
Most undeserved, His heart still yearned
    O'er me, poor wandering sheep!

    God with His life of love
    To me was far and strange,
My heart clung only to the world
    Of sight and sense and change;
    In Thee, Immanuel,
    Are God and man made one;
In Thee my heart hath peace with God,
    And union in the Son.

Oh ponder this, my soul:
　Our God hath loved us thus,
That even His only dearest Son
　He freely giveth us.
　Thou precious gift of God,
　The pledge and bond of love,
With thankful heart I kneel to take
　This treasure from above.

　I kneel beside Thy couch,
　I press Thee to my heart,
For Thee I gladly all forsake
　And from the creature part:
　Oh deign to take my heart,
　And let Thy heart be mine,
That all my love flow out to Thee
　And lose itself in Thine.

JOY TO THE WORLD! THE LORD IS COME.

Isaac Watts, 1709. Ps. xcviii.

JOY to the world! the Lord is come:
　Let earth receive her King;
Let every heart prepare Him room,
　And heaven and nature sing.

Joy to the world! the Saviour reigns:
　Let men their songs employ;
While fields and floods, rocks, hills, and plains,
　Repeat the sounding joy.

No more let sin and sorrow grow,
　Nor thorns infest the ground:
He comes to make His blessings flow
　Far as the curse is found.

He rules the world with truth and grace,
　And makes the nations prove
The glories of His righteousness,
　And wonders of His love.

HARK, HOW ALL THE WELKIN RINGS!

CHARLES WESLEY. From his "Hymns and Sacred Poems," 1739.

HARK, how all the welkin rings!
Glory to the King of kings!
Peace on earth and mercy mild,
God and sinners reconciled!
Joyful, all ye nations, rise,
Join the triumph of the skies;
Universal nature say,
Christ the Lord is born to-day!

Christ, by highest Heaven adored;
Christ, the Everlasting Lord;
Late in time behold Him come,
Offspring of a Virgin's womb:
Veiled in flesh the Godhead see;
Hail the Incarnate Deity,
Pleased as man with men to appear,
Jesus, our Immanuel here!

Hail, the heavenly Prince of Peace!
Hail, the Son of Righteousness!
Light and life to all He brings,
Risen with healing in His wings.
Mild He lays His glory by,
Born that man no more may die,
Born to raise the sons of earth,
Born to give them second birth.

Come, Desire of nations, come,
Fix in us Thy humble home!
Rise, the Woman's conquering Seed,
Bruise in us the Serpent's head!
Now display Thy saving power,
Ruined nature now restore;
Now in mystic union join
Thine to ours, and ours to Thine!

Adam's likeness, Lord, efface;
Stamp Thine image in its place;

Second Adam from above,
Reinstate us in Thy love !
Let us Thee, though lost, regain,
Thee, the Life, the Heavenly Man :
Oh, to all Thyself impart,
Formed in each believing heart !

HARK, THE GLAD SOUND!

Philip Doddridge, D.D., died 1751.

HARK, the glad sound ! the Saviour comes,
    The Saviour promised long !
Let every heart prepare a throne,
    And every voice a song !

On Him the Spirit, largely poured,
    Exerts its sacred fire ;
Wisdom and might, and zeal and love,
    His holy breast inspire.

He comes, the prisoners to release,
    In Satan's bondage held ;
The gates of brass before Him burst,
    The iron fetters yield.

He comes, from thickest films of vice
    To clear the mental ray,
And on the eyeballs of the blind
    To pour celestial day.

He comes, the broken heart to bind,
    The bleeding soul to cure,
And with the treasure of His grace
    Enrich the humble poor.

His silver trumpets publish loud
    The jubilee of the Lord ;
Our debts are all remitted now,
    Our heritage restored.

Our glad hosannas, Prince of Peace,
   Thy welcome shall proclaim,
And heaven's eternal arches ring
   With Thy beloved name.

OH, HOW WONDROUS IS THE STORY!

Hannah More, born 1744, died 1833.

OH, how wondrous is the story
   Of our blest Redeemer's birth!
See, the mighty Lord of glory
   Leaves His heaven to visit earth.

Hear with transport, every creature,—
   Hear the gospel's joyful sound:
Christ appears in human nature,—
   In our sinful world is found.

Comes to pardon our transgression,
   Like a cloud our sins to blot;
Comes to His own favoured nation,
   But his own receive Him not.

If the angels who attended
   To declare the Saviour's birth,
Who from heaven with songs descended
   To proclaim good-will on earth,—

If, in pity to our blindness,
   They had brought the pardon needed,
Still Jehovah's wondrous kindness
   Had our warmest hopes exceeded.

If some prophet had been sent
   With salvation's joyful news,
Who that heard the blest event
   Could their warmest love refuse?

But 'twas He to whom in heaven
   Hallelujahs never cease;
He, the mighty God, was given
   Given to us,—a Prince of peace.

THE INCARNATION.

None but He who did create us
    Could redeem from sin and hell;
None but He could reinstate us
    In the rank from which we fell.

Had He come, the glorious Stranger,
    Decked with all the world calls great;
Had He lived in pomp and grandeur,
    Crowned with more than royal state,—

Still our tongues, with praise o'erflowing,
    On such boundless love would dwell;
Still our hearts with rapture glowing,
    Feel what words could never tell.

But what wonder should it raise,
    Thus our lowest state to borrow!
Oh, the high mysterious ways,
    God's own Son a child of Sorrow!

'Twas to bring us endless pleasure
    He our suffering nature bore;
'Twas to give us heavenly treasure
    He was willing to be poor.

Come, ye rich, survey the stable
    Where your infant Saviour lies;
From your full, o'erflowing table,
    Send the hungry good supplies.

Boast not your ennobled stations;
    Boast not that you're highly fed;
Jesus—hear it, all ye nations!
    Had not where to lay his head.

Learn of me, thus cries the Saviour,
    If my kingdom you'd inherit;
Sinner, quit your proud behaviour,
    Learn my meek and lowly spirit.

Come, ye servants, see your station
    Freed from all reproach and shame;
He who purchased your salvation
    Bore a servant's humble name.

Come, ye poor, some comfort gather;
　Faint not in the race you run:
Hard the lot your gracious Father
　Gave His dear, His only Son.

Think that, if your humbler stations
　Less of worldly good bestow,
You escape those strong temptations
　Which from wealth and grandeur flow.

See, your Saviour is ascended;
　See, He looks with pity down:
Trust Him, all will soon be mended;
　Bear His cross, you'll share His crown.

WHEN JORDAN HUSHED HIS WATERS STILL.

THOMAS CAMPBELL; born at Glasgow, 1777; died 1844, and interred in the Poets' Corner in Westminster Abbey.

WHEN Jordan hushed his waters still,
And silence slept on Zion's hill;
When Salem's shepherds through the night
Watched o'er their flocks by starry light,—

Hark! from the midnight hills around,
A voice, of more than mortal sound,
In distant hallelujahs stole,
Wild murmuring o'er the raptured soul.

Then swift to every startled eye,
New streams of glory gild the sky;
Heaven bursts her azure gates, to pour
Her spirits to the midnight hour.

On wheels of light, on wings of flame,
The glorious hosts to Zion came;
High heaven with songs of triumph rung,
While thus they smote their harps and sung:

O Zion! lift thy raptured eye:
The long-expected hour is nigh;

The joys of nature rise again;
The Prince of Salem comes to reign.

See Mercy, from her golden urn,
Pours a rich stream to them that mourn;
Behold, she binds, with tender care,
The bleeding bosom of Despair.

He comes to cheer the trembling heart,
Bid Satan and his host depart;
Again the day-star gilds the gloom,
Again the bowers of Eden bloom.

O Zion! lift thy raptured eye:
The long-expected hour is nigh;
The joys of nature rise again;
The Prince of Salem comes to reign.

HARK! WHAT MEAN THOSE HOLY VOICES?

Rev. JOHN CAWOOD (born at Matlock, in Derbyshire, 1775; died 1852). From the author's MS., furnished by his son for ROGERS's "Lyra Britannica," Lond. 1867. In the usual collections, the Hallelujah and the last stanza are omitted. Cawood wrote also, as a counterpart, a missionary hymn commencing,

    "Hark! what mean those lamentations,
    Rolling sadly through the sky?
    'Tis the cry of heathen nations,—
    'Come and help us, or we die!'"

HARK! what mean those holy voices
    Sweetly warbling in the skies?
Sure the angelic host rejoices,
    Loudest hallelujahs rise.
        Hallelujah!

Listen to the wondrous story,
    Which they chant in hymns of joy!
"Glory in the highest, glory,
    Glory be to God most high!
        Hallelujah!

"Peace on earth, good will from heaven,
  Reaching far as man is found;
Souls redeemed, and sins forgiven,
  Loud our golden harps shall sound.
    Hallelujah!

"Christ is born, the great Anointed!
  Heaven and earth His glory sing!
Glad receive whom God appointed
  For your Prophet, Priest, and King.
    Hallelujah!

"Hasten, mortals, to adore Him,
  Learn His name and taste His joy,
Till in heaven you sing before Him,
  Glory be to God most high!
    Hallelujah!"

Let us learn the wondrous story
  Of our great Redeemer's birth,
Spread the brightness of His glory,
  Till it cover all the earth.
    Hallelujah!

ANGELS, FROM THE REALMS OF GLORY.

JAMES MONTGOMERY, son of a Moravian Minister; born 1771; died at Sheffield, 1854. His first volume of poems was composed in prison, and published in 1797, under the title, "Prison Amusements."

ANGELS, from the realms of glory,
  Wing your flight o'er all the earth;
Ye who sang creation's story,
  Now proclaim Messiah's birth!
    Come and worship,—
  Worship Christ the new-born King.

Shepherds, in the field abiding,
  Watching o'er your flocks by night,
God with man is now residing,
  Yonder shines the infant-light.

Come and worship,—
Worship Christ the new-born King.

Sages, leave your contemplations:
  Brighter visions beam afar;
Seek the great Desire of nations:
  Ye have seen his natal star.
    Come and worship,—
  Worship Christ the new-born King.

Saints before the altar bending,
  Watching long in hope and fear,
Suddenly the Lord, descending,
  In His temple shall appear.
    Come and worship,—
  Worship Christ the new-born King.

Sinners, wrung with true repentance,
  Doomed for guilt to endless pains,
Justice now revokes the sentence;
  Mercy calls you, break your chains;
    Come and worship,—
  Worship Christ the new-born King.

WHAT SUDDEN BLAZE OF SONG.

D<small>R</small>. J<small>OHN</small> K<small>EBLE</small> (died 1866). From his "Christian Year," 1827.

WHAT sudden blaze of song
    Spreads o'er the expanse of heaven!
  In waves of light it thrills along,
    The angelic signal given:
"Glory to God!" from yonder central fire
Flows out the echoing lay beyond the starry choir.

    Like circles widening round
      Upon a clear blue river,
    Orb after orb, the wondrous sound
      Is echoed on for ever:
"Glory to God on high, on earth be peace,
And love towards men of love, salvation, and release!"

Yet stay, before thou dare
To join that festal throng;
Listen, and mark what gentle air
First stirred the tide of song:
'Tis not, " The Saviour born in David's home,
To whom for power and health obedient worlds should come."

'Tis not, " The Christ the Lord:"
With fixed adoring look
The choir of angels caught the word,
Nor yet their silence broke:
But when they heard the sign, where Christ should be,
In sudden light they shone, and heavenly harmony.

Wrapped in His swaddling bands,
And in His manger laid,
The Hope and Glory of all lands
Is come to the world's aid:
No peaceful home upon His cradle smiled;
Guests rudely went and came, where slept the royal Child.

But where Thou dwellest, Lord,
No other thought should be;
Once duly welcomed and adored,
How should I part with Thee?
Bethlehem must lose Thee soon; but Thou wilt grace
The single heart to be Thy sure abiding-place.

Thee, on the bosom laid
Of a pure virgin mind,
In quiet ever and in shade
Shepherd and sage may find;
They who have bowed untaught to Nature's sway,
And they who follow Truth along her star-paved way.

The pastoral spirits first
Approach Thee, Babe divine;
For they in lowly thoughts are nursed,
Meet for Thy lowly shrine:
Sooner than they should miss where Thou dost dwell,
Angels from heaven will stoop to guide them to Thy cell.

Still, as the day comes round
For Thee to be revealed,
By wakeful shepherds Thou art found,
Abiding in the field:
All through the wintry heaven and chill night air
In music and in light Thou dawnest on their prayer.

Oh faint not ye for fear!
What though your wandering sheep,
Reckless of what they see and hear,
Lie lost in wilful sleep?
High Heaven, in mercy to your sad annoy,
Still greets you with glad tidings of immortal joy.

Think on the eternal home
The Saviour left for you;
Think on the Lord most holy, come
To dwell with hearts untrue:
So shall ye tread untired His pastoral ways,
And in the darkness sing your carol of high praise.

'TIS COME, THE TIME SO OFT FORETOLD.

Thomas Grinfield, 1836.

'TIS come, the time so oft foretold,
    The time eternal love forecast;
Four thousand years of hope have rolled,
    And God hath sent His Son at last.
Let heaven, let earth, adore the plan:
Glory to God, and grace to man!

To swains that watched their nightly fold,
    Of lowly lot, of lowly mind,
To these the tidings first were told,
    That told of hope for lost mankind.
God gives His Son; no more He can:
Glory to God, and grace to man!

And well to shepherds first 'tis known,
    The Lord of angels comes from high,

In humblest aspect like their own,
   Good Shepherd, for His sheep to die.
O height and depth, which who shall span?
Glory to God, and grace to man!

Fain with those meek, those happy swains,
   Lord, I would hear that angel choir;
Till, ravished by celestial strains,
   My heart responds with holy fire,
(That holy fire Thy breath must fan,)
Glory to God, and grace to man!

THE HAPPY CHRISTMAS COMES ONCE MORE.

Translated from the Danish, by Dr. CHS. P. KRAUTH, Phila. 1867.

THE happy Christmas comes once more,
   The heavenly Guest is at the door:
   The blessed words the shepherds thrill,
The joyous tidings: Peace, good-will!

To David's city let us fly,
Where angels sing beneath the sky;
Through plain and village pressing near,
And news from God with shepherds hear.

Oh! let us go with quiet mind,
The gentle Babe with shepherds find,
To gaze on Him who gladdens them,
The loveliest Flower of Jesse's stem.

The lowly Saviour meekly lies,
Laid off the splendor of the skies;
No crown bedecks his forehead fair,
No pearl nor gem nor silk is there.

No human glory, might, and gold,
The lovely Infant's form enfold;
The manger and the swaddlings poor
Are His whom angels' songs adore.

O wake our hearts, in gladness sing!
And keep our Christmas with our King,

THE INCARNATION.

Till living song, from loving souls,
Like sound of mighty waters rolls.

O holy Child! Thy manger streams
Till earth and heaven glow with its beams,
Till midnight noon's broad light has won,
And Jacob's Star outshines the sun.

Thou Patriarchs' joy, Thou Prophets' song,
Thou heavenly Day-spring, looked for long.
Thou Son of Man, Incarnate Word,
Great David's Son, great David's Lord!

Come, Jesus, glorious, heavenly Guest,
Keep Thine own Christmas in our breast!
Then David's harp-strings, hushed so long,
Shall swell our Jubilee of song.

CAROL, BROTHERS, CAROL.

W. A. MUHLENBERG, D.D. A Christmas Carol, made for the boys of St. Paul's College, Long Island, N. Y., 1840.

CAROL, brothers, carol,
   Carol joyfully;
Carol the good tidings,
   Carol merrily;
And pray a gladsome Christmas
   For all good Christian men.
Carol, brothers, carol,
   Christmas times again.

Carol ye with gladness,
   Not in songs of earth;
On the Saviour's birthday,
   Hallowed be our mirth.
While a thousand blessings
   Fill our hearts with glee,
Christmas-day we'll keep, the
   Feast of Charity!

At the joyous table,
    Think of those who've none,—
The orphan and the widow,
    Hungry and alone.
Bountiful your offerings,
    To the altar bring;
Let the poor and needy
    Christmas carols sing.

Listening angel-music,
    Discord sure must cease;
Who dare hate his brother,
    On this day of peace?
While the heavens are telling
    To mankind good-will,
Only love and kindness
    Every bosom fill.

Let our hearts, responding
    To the seraph band,
Wish this morning's sunshine
    Bright in every land!
Word and deed and prayer
    Speed the grateful sound,
Bidding merry Christmas
    All the world around.

COME, YE LOFTY! COME, YE LOWLY!

By Archer Gurney. 1860.

COME, ye lofty! come, ye lowly!
    Let your songs of gladness ring!
    In a stable lies the Holy,
In a manger rests the King:
See, in Mary's arms reposing,
    Christ by highest heaven adored:
Come! your circle round Him closing,
    Pious hearts that love the Lord.

THE INCARNATION.

Come, ye poor! no pomp of station
    Robes the Child your hearts adore:
He, the Lord of all salvation,
    Shares your want, is weak and poor:
Oxen round about behold them,
    Rafters naked, cold, and bare:
See! the shepherds! God has told them
    That the Prince of Life lies there.

Come, ye children, blithe and merry!
    This one Child your model make;
Christmas holly, leaf, and berry,
    All be prized for His dear sake:
Come, ye gentle hearts and tender!
    Come, ye spirits keen and bold!
All in all your homage render,
    Weak and mighty, young and old.

High above a star is shining,
    And the Wise Men haste from far:
Come, glad hearts, and spirits pining!
    For you all has risen the Star.
Let us bring our poor oblations,
    Thanks and love and faith and praise:
Come, ye people! come, ye nations!
    All in all draw nigh to gaze.

Hark! the heaven of heavens is ringing:
    Christ the Lord to man is born:
Are not all our hearts, too, singing,
    Welcome, welcome, Christmas morn?
Still the Child, all power possessing,
    Smiles as through the ages past;
And the song of Christmas-blessing
    Sweetly sinks to rest at last.

JOY AND GLADNESS.

By George W. Bethune, D.D.; born at New York, 1805; died at Florence 1862. From " Lays of Love and Faith," Philad. 1847.

JOY and gladness! joy and gladness!
    O happy day!
Every thought of sin and sadness
    Chase, chase away.
Heard ye not the angels telling,
Christ the Lord of might excelling,
On the earth with man is dwelling,
    Clad in our clay?

With the shepherd throng around Him
    Haste we to bow:
By the angels' sign they found Him,
    We know Him now;
New-born Babe of houseless stranger,
Cradled low in Bethlehem's manger,
Saviour from our sin and danger,
    Jesus, 'tis Thou!

God of Life, in mortal weakness,
    Hail, Virgin-born!
Infinite in lowly meekness,
    Thou wilt not scorn;
Though all heaven is singing o'er Thee,
And gray wisdom bows before Thee,
When our youthful hearts adore Thee
    This holy morn.

Son of Mary, (blessed mother!)
    Thy love we claim;
Son of God, our elder brother,
    (O gentle name!)
To Thy Father's throne ascended,
With Thine own His glory blended.
Thou art, all Thy trials ended,
    Ever the same.

Thou wert born to tears and sorrows,
    Pilgrim divine;

Watchful nights and weary morrows,
    Brother, were Thine:
By Thy fight with strong temptation,
By Thy cup of tribulation,
O Thou God of our salvation,
    With mercy shine!

In Thy holy footsteps treading,
    Guide, lest we stray;
From Thy word of promise shedding
    Light on our way;
Never leave us nor forsake us,
Like Thyself in mercy make us,
And at last to glory take us,
    Jesus, we pray.

THE TIME DRAWS NEAR THE BIRTH OF CHRIST.

Alfred Tennyson, Poet Laureate of England; b. 1811. From "In Memoriam" (first pub. 1850), No. xxviii. I have added the last stanza from No. xxx.

THE time draws near the birth of Christ:
    The moon is hid; the night is still;
    The Christmas bells from hill to hill
Answer each other in the mist.

Four voices of four hamlets round,
    From far and near, on mead and moor,
    Swell out and fail, as if a door
Were shut between me and the sound.

Each voice four changes on the wind,
    That now dilate, and now decrease,
    Peace and good-will, good will and peace,
Peace and good-will, to all mankind.

This year I slept and woke with pain,
    I almost wished no more to wake,
    And that my hold on life would break
Before I heard those bells again.

But they my troubled spirit rule,
  For they controlled me when a boy;
  They bring me sorrow touched with joy,
The merry, merry bells of Yule.

Rise, happy morn! rise, holy morn!
  Draw forth the cheerful day from night:
  O Father! touch the east, and light
The light that shone when Hope was born.

IT CAME UPON THE MIDNIGHT CLEAR.

REV. EDMUND H. SEARS; b., in 1810, in Berkshire Co., Massachusetts, author of "Athanasia, or Foregleams of Immortality," and other works. 1860.

IT came upon the midnight clear,
  That glorious song of old,
From angels bending near the earth
  To touch their harps of gold:
"Peace to the earth, good-will to men
  From heaven's all-gracious King!"
The world in solemn stillness lay
  To hear the angels sing.

Still through the cloven skies they come,
  With peaceful wings unfurled;
And still their heavenly music floats
  O'er all the weary world:
Above its sad and lowly plains
  They bend on heavenly wing,
And ever o'er its Babel sounds
  The blessed angels sing.

Yet with the woes of sin and strife
  The world has suffered long;
Beneath the angel-strain have rolled
  Two thousand years of wrong;
And men, at war with men, hear not
  The love-song which they bring:
Oh! hush the noise, ye men of strife,
  And hear the angels sing.

And ye, beneath life's crushing load
  Whose forms are bending low ;
Who toil along the climbing way
  With painful steps and slow,—
Look now ! for glad and golden hours
  Come swiftly on the wing :
Oh ! rest beside the weary road,
  And hear the angels sing !

For lo ! the days are hastening on,
  By prophet bards foretold,
When with the ever-circling years
  Comes round the age of gold ;
When Peace shall over all the earth
  Its ancient splendours fling,
And the whole world send back the song
  Which now the angels sing.

LO, GOD, OUR GOD, HAS COME.

By Dr. Horatius Bonar. From " Hymns of Faith and Hope."
Third Series, 1868.

> Fœno jacere pertulit,
> Præsepe non abhorruit,
> Parvoque lacte pastus est,
> Per quem nec ales esurit.
>   *Old Hymn.*

LO, God, our God, has come !
  To us a Child is born,
  To us a Son is given ;
  Bless, bless the blessed morn,
O happy, lowly, lofty birth,
Now God, our God, has come to earth !

  Rejoice ! our God has come
    In love and lowliness !
  The Son of God has come,
    The sons of men to bless.
God with us now descends to dwell,
God in our flesh, Immanuel.

Praise ye the Word made flesh!
True God, true Man is He.
Praise ye the Christ of God!
To Him all glory be.
Praise ye the Lamb that once was slain,
Praise ye the King that comes to reign!

IN BETHLEHEM, THE LORD OF GLORY.

(Er ist in Bethlehem geboren.)

"BETHLEHEM AND GOLGOTHA." A lyric of rare beauty, by FRIEDRICH RÜCKERT, one of the greatest and purest of German poets (died 1867). Admirably translated by the Rev. THOMAS C. PORTER, Professor of Natural Sciences, Easton, Pennsylvania. Contributed.

IN Bethlehem, the Lord of glory,
   Who brought us life, first drew His breath;
On Golgotha,—oh, bloody story!—
   By suffering broke the power of death.
From Western shores, all danger scorning,
I travelled through the lands of morning;
   And greater spots I nowhere saw,
   Than Bethlehem and Golgotha.

Where are the seven works of wonder
   The ancient world beheld with pride?
They all have fallen, sinking under
   The splendour of the Crucified!
I saw them, as I wandered, spying,
Amid their ruins crumbled, lying;
   None stand in quiet gloria
   Like Bethlehem and Golgotha.

Away, ye pyramids, whose bases
   Lie shrouded in Egyptian gloom!
Eternal graves! no resting places,
   Where hope immortal gilds the tomb.
Ye sphinxes, vain was your endeavour
To solve life's riddle, dark for ever,
   Until the answer came with awe
   From Bethlehem and Golgotha.

THE INCARNATION.

Fair Paradise, where ever blowing
   The roses of Shiraz expand!
Ye stately palms of India, growing
   Along her scented ocean-strand!
I see, amid your loveliest bowers,
Death stalking in the sunniest hours.
    Look up! To you life comes from far,
    From Bethlehem and Golgotha.

Thou Caaba, half the world, benighted,
   Is stumbling o'er thee, as of old;
Now, by thy crescent faintly lighted,
   The coming day of doom behold:
The moon before the sun decreases,
A sign shall shiver thee to pieces;
    The Hero's sign! "Victoria!"
    Shout Bethlehem and Golgotha.

O Thou who, in a manger lying,
   Wert willing to be born a child,
And on the cross, in anguish dying,
   The world to God hast reconciled!
To pride, how mean Thy lowly manger!
How infamous Thy cross! yet stranger!
    Humility became the law
    At Bethlehem and Golgotha.

Proud kings, to worship One descended
   From humble shepherds, thither came;
And nations to the cross have wended,
   As pilgrims, to adore His name.
By war's fierce tempest rudely battered,
The world, but not the cross, was shattered,
    When East and West it struggling saw
    Round Bethlehem and Golgotha!

O let us not with mailèd legions,
   But with the spirit take the field,
To win again those holy regions,
   As Christ compelled the world to yield!
Let rays of light, on all sides streaming,
Dart onward, like apostles gleaming,
    Till all mankind their light shall draw
    From Bethlehem and Golgotha!

With staff and hat, the scallop wearing,
  The far-off East I journeyed through;
And homeward, now, a pilgrim bearing
  This message, I have come to you:
Go not with hat and staff to wander
Beside God's grave and cradle yonder;
  Look inward, and behold with awe
  His Bethlehem and Golgotha.

O heart! what profits all thy kneeling,
  Where once He laid His infant head,
To view with an enraptured feeling
  His grave, long empty of its dead?
To have Him born in thee with power
To die to earth and sin each hour,
  And live to Him,—this only, ah!
  Is Bethlehem and Golgotha.

THE INFANT SAVIOUR WITH THE VIRGIN MOTHER.

" HAIL, thou that art highly favoured, the Lord is with thee; blessed art thou among women."—*Luke* i. 28.
" Mary kept all these things, and pondered them in her heart."—*Luke* ii. 19.

"IF wedded Maid and Virgin Mother born."
                                JOHN MILTON.

" Say of me as the angel said,—' Thou art
The blessedest of women !'—blessedest,
Not holiest, not noblest,—no high name,
Whose height, misplaced, may pierce me like a shame,
When I sit meek in heaven !"
                                MRS. E. B. BROWNING.

      Stabat Mater speciosa
      Juxta fœnum gaudiosa,
        Dum jacebat parvulus—
      Cujus animam gaudentem,
      Lætabundam ac ferventem,
        Pertransivit jubilus.

      O quam læta et beata
      Fuit hæc immaculata
        Mater Unigeniti!
      Quæ gaudebat et ridebat,
      Exultabat, cum videbat
        Nati partum inclyti!
           JACOBUS DE BENEDICTIS. 1306.

THE INFANT SAVIOUR WITH THE VIRGIN MOTHER.

TO GOD WHOM EARTH AND SEA.

(Quem terra, pontus, sidera.)

OLD Latin hymn. DANIEL, Tome I. p. 172 (two forms); translated in " The Words of the Hymnal Noted," No. 88, and, with some changes, in " Hymns Ancient and Modern," No. 249. Abridged.

HE God whom earth and sea and sky
Adore and laud and magnify,
Whose might they own, whose praise they swell,
In Mary's womb vouchsafed to dwell.

The lord whom sun and moon obey,
Whom all things serve from day to day,
Was by the Holy Ghost conceived,
Of her who, through His grace, believed.

How blest that Mother, in whose shrine
The world's Creator, Lord divine,
Whose hand contains the earth and sky,
Once deigned, as in His ark, to lie!

Blest in the message Gabriel brought,
Blest by the work the Spirit wrought,
From whom the great Desire of earth
Took human flesh and human birth.

O Lord, the Virgin-born, to Thee
Eternal praise and glory be!
Whom, with the Father, we adore,
And Holy Ghost for evermore.

WHEN WITHIN HIS MOTHER'S ARMS.

(Parvum quando cerno Deum.)

By an anonymous author of the 14th-16th century. See DANIEL, II. p. 342. Translated by the Rev. Dr. E. A. WASHBURN, New York, May, 1868. Contributed.

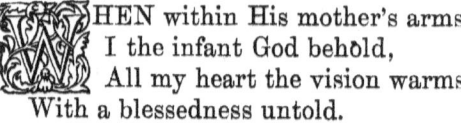HEN within His mother's arms
I the infant God behold,
All my heart the vision warms
With a blessedness untold.

Leaps He, mother! leaps the Boy,
Gazing at thy holy breast!
Kisses with a smile of joy,
Thousand kisses, fondly pressed!

As upon the stainless skies
Peaceful hangs the new-born sun,
So upon thy bosom lies,
Mother pure, thy Holy One.

Ah! how lovely that repose!
Mother with the Infant fair,
Twined as with the tender rose
Violet and lily are.

Many a silent clasp of bliss,
Many a look of smiling love,
As the flowers the meadows kiss,
As the starry eyes above.

Oh! if one such loving dart,
Falling on that mother mild,
May but fall upon my heart,
Infant Jesu, Holy Child![1]

---

[1] O! ut una ex sagittis,
Dulcis O puerule!
Quas in matris pectus mittis,
Cadat in me, Jesule!

SLEEP, HOLY BABE.

Edward E. Caswall.

"But see, the Virgin blest
Hath laid her babe to rest."
　　　　　　　　Milton.

SLEEP, Holy Babe,
　　Upon Thy mother's breast;
　　Great Lord of earth and sea and sky,
How sweet it is to see Thee lie
　　In such a place of rest!

　　Sleep, Holy Babe:
　　Thine angels watch around,
All bending low, with folded wings,
Before the Incarnate King of kings,
　　In reverent awe profound.

　　Sleep, Holy Babe,
　　While I with Mary gaze
In joy upon that face awhile,
Upon the loving Infant smile,
　　Which there divinely plays.

　　Sleep, Holy Babe;
　　Ah! take Thy brief repose:
Too quickly will Thy slumbers break,
And Thou to lengthened pains awake.
　　That death alone shall close.

　　Then must those hands
　　Which now so fair I see,
Those little pearly feet of Thine,
So soft, so delicately fine,
　　Be pierced and rent for me.

　　Then must that brow
　　Its thorny crown receive;
That cheek, more lovely than the rose,
Be drenched with blood, and marred with blows.
　　That I thereby may live.

THOU STAND'ST BETWEEN THE EARTH AND HEAVEN.

Mrs. Grace Webster Hinsdale, Brooklyn, N. Y. Written after viewing Raphael's Madonna di San Sisto, in the Royal Gallery of Dresden, August, 1867.

THOU stand'st between the earth and heaven,
    Sweet Mary, with thy boy;
And on thy young and lovely face
    Lingers surprise and joy.

The angel's words are sounding yet
    In thy attentive ear;
Thou hold'st thy child most tenderly,
    And yet with awe and fear.

Almost a frightened look thou hast,
    As if within thy thought
The glory of thy motherhood
    An anxious burden brought.

Thou dar'st not clasp the Holy Child
    With freedom to thy breast;
And yet, because He is Thine own,
    Thou look'st supremely blest.

God gave the Boy into thine arms,
    And thou His mother art;
And yet the words the angel spoke
    Are lingering in thy heart.

Thou canst not call Him quite thine own;
    And when, upon thy knee,
He sleeps as other infants sleep,
    Thou dost a glory see,

Which fills thee with a kind of awe,
    And makes thee tremble so,
That thou dost lay thy Baby down,
    And, bending very low,

Dost ask the Father why He sent
    A Babe divine to thee;
And, pouring out thy troubled heart,
    Dost seek His sympathy.

O Mary! loved of God and man,
    Let all thy fears depart:
For God will send His Spirit down,
    To guide thy anxious heart;

And thou shalt rear the Blessed Child,
    Cheered by His smile divine;
And, in thy sweet and humble home,
    Shall God's veiled glory shine.

But, oh! I dread for thee the hour
    When thou shalt stand alone
Beneath the cross where God's dear Son
    Shall for man's sin atone.

A sword shall enter then thine heart,
    And leave such bitter pain,
That thou wilt kneel in agony,
    Inquiring once again,

Why God should crush thee with a grief
    No other heart could share?
And why, in utter loneliness,
    Thou must the anguish bear?

And, oh! I see another day
    When thou shalt wondering stand,
Amidst a throng who welcome thee,
    In heaven, the blessed land!

And then the Lord, who lived on earth
    Clothed in humility,
Shall sit upon His Father's throne
    In radiant majesty.

The angels then shall lead thy feet
    Across the crystal sea;
And thou shalt reach the Blessed One
    Who lived and died for thee.

Thy grateful praise shall swell the song
    Which rises toward the throne;
For then the mysteries of earth
    Shall all be fully known.

Sweet Mary, when the gate of life
    Death's hand unlocks for me,
I shall discern thy lovely face
    By its humility.

HAIL, INFANT MARTYRS!

(Salvete, flores martyrum!)

THE Infant Martyrs of Bethlehem. From a famous hymn of PRUDENTIUS of Spain (d. 405), which is used in the Latin Church on Innocents' Day,—the second day after Christmas. Christ was born on earth, that we might be born in heaven. The ancient Church called the death of the martyrs their heavenly birthday. The translation is from CHANDLER's "Hymns of the Primitive Church," 1837. See the Latin in DANIEL, I. 124, and in TRENCH, p. 121. Other English translations by J. M. NEALE ("All hail, ye infant martyr-flowers!"), and by CASWALL ("Lovely flowers of martyrs, hail!") The VENERABLE BEDE (d. 735) wrote also a hymn for the Holy Innocents, commencing, "Hymnum canentes Martyrum" (repeating the first line in the last of every stanza), and JOHN KEBLE, in his "Christian Year" ("Say, ye celestial guards who wait!"), which is far superior in poetic merit to that of Bede.

HAIL, infant martyrs! new-born victims, hail!
    Hail, earliest flowerets of the Christian spring!
O'er whom, like rosebuds scattered by the gale,
    The cruel sword such havoc dared to fling.

The Lord's first votive offerings of blood,
    First tender lambs upon the altar laid,
Around in fearless innocence they stood,
    And sported gaily with the murderous blade.

Oh! what availed thee, Herod, this thy guilt,
    This load of crime that on thy conscience lies?
The Lord alone, whose blood thou wouldst have spilt,
    Now mocks thy malice, and thy power defies.

Yes! He alone survived, when all the ground
    Drank the red torrents of that carnage wild:
Though many a childless mother wailed around,
    The hand of murder spared the Virgin's Child!

O Jesu, Virgin-born! all praise to Thee,
  And to the Father and the Holy Ghost!
One God eternal, ever honoured be,
  By saints on earth, and by the heavenly host.

THE MATER DOLOROSA.

FROM Mrs. H. BEECHER STOWE'S "Mary at the Cross," "Religious Poems," Boston, 1867, pp. 22-27. I have selected the first and the last stanzas of this beautiful poem, which may be called a worthy Protestant pendant of the "Stabat Mater."

WONDROUS mother! since the dawn of time
Was ever love, was ever grief, like thine?
O highly favoured in thy joy's deep flow,
And favoured, even in this, thy bitterest woe!

* * * * *

By sufferings mighty as His mighty soul
  Hath the Redeemer risen for ever blest;
And through all ages must His heart-beloved
  Through the same baptism enter the same rest.

THE EPIPHANY.

"THE Gentiles shall come to Thy light, and kings to the brightness of Thy rising."—*Isa.* lx. 3.

"When they were come into the house, they saw the young Child, with Mary his mother, and fell down, and worshipped Him; and, when they had opened their treasures, they presented unto Him gifts, gold and frankincense and myrrh."—*Matt.* ii. 11.

ALMIGHTY GOD, who, by the light of a glorious star, didst make known Thine only-begotten Son to the wise men coming from afar to worship Him: mercifully grant, that all nations may come to the light of the gospel, and that we, who know Thee now by faith, may be conducted to the full vision of Thy glory in heaven; through Jesus Christ our Lord, who liveth and reigneth with Thee, and the Holy Ghost, ever one God, world without end. Amen.

> O JESU, mi dulcissime,
> Spes suspirantis animæ,
> Te quærunt piæ lacrymæ,
> Te clamor mentis intimæ.
>
> Tu cordis delectatio,
> Amoris consummatio,
> Tu mea gloriatio,
> Jesu mundi salvatio.
>   *From* ST. BERNARD.

LORD, make us with keen eye to heed
All lights by which Thou wouldst us lead;
Help us to toil o'er plain and hill,
In glad obedience to Thy will;
To see by faith, and humbly fall,
And give to Thee, who givest all.
CHRISTOPHER WORDSWORTH.

THE EPIPHANY.

A STAR SHINES FORTH IN HEAVEN SUDDENLY.

FROM the Syriac of EPHRÆM SYRUS, a monk and deacon in Mesopotamia, the father of Syrian psalmody (died 378). The original, with a German translation by ZINGERLE, in DANIEL's "Thes. Hymnol." III. pp. 149-151.

A STAR shines forth in heaven suddenly,
A wondrous orb, less than the sun, yet greater,—
Less in its outward light, but greater in
Its inward glory, pointing to a mystery.
That morning star sent forth its beams afar
Into the land of those who had no light;
Led them as blind men, by a way they knew not,
Until they came and saw the Light of men,
Offered their gifts, received eternal life,
Worshipped, and went their way.
Thus had the Son two heralds, one on high,
And one below. Above, the star rejoiced;
Below, the Baptist bore Him record:
Two heralds thus, one heavenly, one of earth;
That witnessing the nature of the Son,
The majesty of God, and this, His human nature.
O mighty wonder! thus were they the heralds,
Both of His Godhead and His manhood.
Who held Him only for a son of earth,
To such the star proclaimed His heavenly glory;
Who held Him only for a heavenly spirit,
To such the Baptist spoke of Him as man.
And in the holy temple Simeon held the Babe
Fast in his aged arms, and sang to Him—

> "To me, in Thy mercy,
>   An old man, Thou art come;
> Thou layest my body
>   In peace in the tomb.
> Thou soon wilt awake me,
>   And bid me arise;
> Wilt lead me transfigured
>   To paradise."

Then Anna took the Babe upon her arms,
And pressed her mouth upon His infant lips;
Then came the Holy Spirit on her lips,
As erst upon Isaiah's, when the coal
Had touched his silent lips, and opened them;
With glowing heart she sang—

> "O Son of the King!
>   Though Thy birthplace was mean,
> All-hearing, yet silent,
>   All-seeing, unseen,
> Unknown, yet all-knowing,
>   God, and yet Son of Man,
>   Praise to Thy name!"

BETHLEHEM! OF NOBLEST CITIES.

(O sola magnarum urbium.)

AURELIUS PRUDENTIUS CLEMENS, of Spain (died 405). From the Latin, by E. CASWALL (*Lyra Catholica*). The text of the Roman Breviary, in DANIEL, I. p. 127, and in the separate editions of the poems of Prudentius. This translation is altered, but not improved, in "Hymns Ancient and Modern," No. 59: "Earth has many a noble city."

BETHLEHEM! of noblest cities,
  None can once with thee compare;
  Thou alone the Lord from heaven
Didst for us incarnate bear.

Fairer than the sun at morning
  Was the star that told His birth;
To the lands their God announcing,
  Hid beneath a form of earth.

By its lambent beauty guided,
 See, the Eastern kings appear;
See them bend, their gifts to offer,—
 Gifts of incense, gold, and myrrh.

Offerings of mystic meaning!—
 Incense doth the God disclose;
Gold a royal child proclaimeth;
 Myrrh a future tomb foreshows.

Holy Jesu! in Thy brightness
 To the Gentile world displayed!
With the Father, and the Spirit,
 Endless praise to Thee be paid!

WHAT STAR IS THIS, WITH BEAMS SO BRIGHT?

(Quæ stella sole pulchrior?)

TRANSLATED from the Latin, by the Rev. J. CHANDLER, "Hymns of the Primitive Church," Lond. 1837. Altered in "Hymns Ancient and Modern."

WHAT star is this, with beams so bright,
Which shame the sun's less radiant light?
It shines to announce a new-born King,—
Glad tidings of our God to bring.

'Tis now fulfilled what God decreed,—
"From Jacob shall a Star proceed:"
And lo! the Eastern sages stand,
To read in heaven the Lord's command.

While outward signs the star displays,
An inward light the Lord conveys,
And urges them, with force benign,
To seek the Giver of the sign.

True love can brook no dull delay,
Nor toil nor dangers stop their way:
Home, kindred, fatherland, and all,
They leave at once, at God's high call.

O Jesu, while the star of grace
Invites us now to seek Thy face,
May we no more that grace repel,
Or quench that light which shines so well!

To God the Father, God the Son
And Holy Spirit, Three in One,
May every tongue and nation raise
An endless song of thankful praise!

O CHRIST, OUR TRUE AND ONLY LIGHT!

(O Jesu Christe, wahres Licht.)

From the German of Johann Heermann, 1653, by Miss C. Winkworth ("Lyra Germ." II. 43).

CHRIST, our true and only light!
Illumine those who sit in night;
Let those afar now hear Thy voice,
And in Thy fold with us rejoice.

Fill with the radiance of Thy grace
The souls now lost in error's maze,
And all in whom their secret minds
Some dark delusion hurts and blinds.

And all who else have strayed from Thee,
Oh, gently seek! Thy healing be
To every wounded conscience given,
And let them also share Thy heaven.

O make the deaf to hear Thy word,
And teach the dumb to speak, dear Lord,
Who dare not yet the faith avow,
Though secretly they hold it now.

Shine on the darkened and the cold,
Recall the wanderers from Thy fold,
Unite those now who walk apart,
Confirm the weak and doubting heart.

So they, with us, may evermore
Such grace with wondering thanks adore;
And endless praise to Thee be given,
By all Thy Church in earth and heaven.

THEY GAVE TO THEE.

By Bishop JEREMY TAYLOR (died 1667). 1650.

THEY gave to Thee
    Myrrh, frankincense, and gold;
    But, Lord, with what shall we
Present ourselves before Thy majesty,
  Whom Thou redeemedst when we were sold?
We've nothing but ourselves, and scarce that neither:
    Vile dirt and clay;
    Yet it is soft, and may
    Impression take.
Accept it, Lord, and say, this Thou hadst rather;
  Stamp it, and on this sordid metal make
  Thy holy image, and it shall outshine
  The beauty of the golden mine.

ALL YE GENTILE LANDS, AWAKE.

(*Werde Licht, du Volk der Heiden.*)

By JOHANN RIST, 1655. "Lyra Germ." I. 30. Abridged.

ALL ye Gentile lands, awake!
    Thou, O Salem, rise and shine!
    See the Dayspring o'er you break,
  Heralding a morn divine,
  Telling, God hath called to mind
  Those who long in darkness pined.

THE EPIPHANY.

Lo, the shadows flee away!
   For our Light is come at length,
Brighter than all earthly day,
   Source of being, life, and strength!
Whoso on this Light would gaze
Must forsake all evil ways.

Ah! how blindly did we stray,
   Ere shone forth this glorious Sun,
Seeking each his separate way,
   Leaving Heaven unsought, unwon!
All our looks were earthwards bent,
All our strength on earth was spent.

But the glory of the Lord
   Hath arisen on us to-day.
We have seen the light outpoured
   That must surely drive away
All things that to night belong,
All the sad earth's woe and wrong.

Thy arising, Lord, shall fill
   All my thoughts in sorrow's hour;
Thy arising, Lord, shall still
   All my dread of Death's dark power:
Through my smiles and through my tears
Still Thy light, O Lord! appears.

Let me, Lord, in peace depart
   From this evil world to Thee;
Where Thyself sole Brightness art,
   Thou hast kept a place for me:
In the radiant city there,
Crowns of light Thy saints shall wear.

THE WONDERING SAGES TRACE FROM FAR.

(Im Abend blinkt der Morgenstern.)

FROM the German of ERNST LANGE (1650-1727). By FRANCES ELIZABETH COX, "Sacred Hymns from the German," Lond. 1841.

THE wondering sages trace from far,
Bright in the west, the morning star;
A light illumes the western skies,
Seen never in the east to rise.

Eternity produced its blaze,
Time's fulness hails its nearer rays;
Its brightness chases night away,
And kindles darkness into day.

O Jesu! brightest Morning Star!
Shed forth Thy beams both near and far,
That all, in these our later days,
May know Thee, and proclaim Thy praise.

SONS OF MEN, BEHOLD FROM FAR!

CHARLES WESLEY, 1739.

SONS of men, behold from far!
Hail the long-expected Star!
Jacob's Star that gilds the night
Guides bewildered nature right.

Fear not hence that ill should flow,
Wars or pestilence below:
Wars it bids and tumults cease,
Ushering in the Prince of Peace.

Mild He shines on all beneath,
Piercing through the shades of death;
Scattering error's wide-spread night,
Kindling darkness into light.

Nations all, far off and near,
Haste to see your God appear !
Haste ! for Him your hearts prepare,
Meet Him manifested there.

Here behold the Dayspring rise,
Pouring eyesight on your eyes :
God in His own light survey,
Shining to the perfect day.

Sing, ye morning stars, again !
God descends on earth to reign ;
Deigns for man His life to employ :
Shout, ye sons of God, for joy !

BRIGHTEST AND BEST OF THE SONS OF THE MORNING.

Reginald Heber, D.D.; b. 1783, at Malpas, Cheshire; Bishop of Calcutta; d. 1827.

BRIGHTEST and best of the sons of the morning,
    Dawn on our darkness, and lend us Thine aid ;
  Star of the East, the horizon adorning,
    Guide where our infant Redeemer is laid.

Cold on His cradle the dew-drops are shining,
    Low lies His head with the beasts of the stall ;
Angels adore Him, in slumber reclining,
    Maker and Monarch and Saviour of all !

Say, shall we yield Him, in costly devotion,
    Odours of Edom, and offerings divine,
Gems of the mountain and pearls of the ocean,
    Myrrh from the forest or gold from the mine ?

Vainly we offer each ample oblation,
    Vainly with gifts would His favour secure ;
Richer by far is the heart's adoration,
    Dearer to God are the prayers of the poor.

Brightest and best of the sons of the morning,
   Dawn on our darkness, and lend us Thine aid;
Star of the East, the horizon adorning,
   Guide where our infant Redeemer is laid.

CHRIST, WHOSE FIRST APPEARANCE LIGHTED.

(*Der Du in der Nacht des Todes*)

" THE Appearance of Christ " (" Die Erscheinung Christi"), by C. J. PHILIPP SPITTA (1801-1859). From the First Series of his "Psaltery and Harp," which, since 1833, has passed through about thirty editions, and has given the author a place among the sweetest and most popular hymnists of Germany. Translated by RICHARD MASSIE (" Lyra Domestica," Lond. 1860).

CHRIST, whose first appearance lighted
      Gloomy Death's obscure domain,
   Long in Herod's courts benighted
      Sought I Thee, but sought in vain:
All was glitter, pomp and pleasure,
      Sensuality and pride;
But my heart found not its treasure,
      And remained unsatisfied.

Then to learned scribes and sages
      Seeking Christ I wandered on;
But upon their barren pages
      Jacob's Star had never shone:
True, indeed, like men in prison
      Groping for the light of day,
Spake they of the Light new-risen,
      But themselves saw not one ray.

To the temple I was guided
      By the altar-fire and lights;
But, though all else was provided,
      Christ was absent from the rites,
Then, more precious time I wasted
      In thy streets, Jerusalem;
But I sought in vain, and hasted
      On my way to Bethlehem.

In the streets I wandered slowly,
  Looking for some trusty guide;
All was dark and melancholy,
  None I met with, far and wide.
On a sudden I perceivèd
  O'er my head a star to shine;
Lo, because I had believèd,
  And had sought Him, Christ was mine!

Only seek and you will find Him:
  Never cease to seek the Lord;
And should He delay, remind Him
  Boldly of His plighted word.
Follow Him, and He will lead you;
  Trust Him in the darkest night;
Jacob's Star will still precede you,
  Jacob's Star will give you light.

O THOU! WHO BY A STAR DIDST GUIDE.

By Dr. John Mason Neale (died 1866).

O THOU! who by a star didst guide
  The wise men on their way,
Until it came and stood beside
  The place where Jesus lay;

Although by stars Thou dost not lead
  Thy servants now below,
Thy Holy Spirit, when they need,
  Will show them how to go.

As yet we know Thee but in part;
  But still we trust Thy word,
That blessed are the pure in heart,
  For they shall see the Lord.

O Saviour! give us, then, Thy grace,
  To make us pure in heart;
That we may see Thee face to face,
  Hereafter, as Thou art.

AS WITH GLADNESS MEN OF OLD.

WILLIAM CHATTERTON DIX (born at Bristol, 1837; educated to mercantile pursuits; residing at Glasgow). Contributed to "Hymns Ancient and Modern," 1860, No. 64.

AS with gladness men of old
Did the guiding star behold;
As with joy they hailed its light,
Leading onward, beaming bright:
So, most gracious Lord, may we
Evermore be led to Thee.

As with joyful steps they sped
To that lowly manger-bed;
There to bend the knee before
Him whom heaven and earth adore:
So may we, with willing feet,
Ever seek Thy mercy-seat.

As they offered gifts most rare
At that manger rude and bare;
So may we with holy joy,
Pure, and free from sin's alloy,
All our costliest treasures bring,
Christ, to Thee, our Heavenly King!

Holy Jesus! every day
Keep us in the narrow way;
And, when earthly things are past,
Bring our ransomed souls at last
Where they need no star to guide,
Where no clouds Thy glory hide.

In the heavenly country bright
Need they no created light;
Thou its Light, its Joy, its Crown,—
Thou its Sun, which goes not down:
There for ever may we sing
Hallelujahs to our King.

THE WISE MEN TO THY CRADLE-THRONE.

MRS. CECIL FRANCES ALEXANDER. Contributed to BAYNES's
"Lyra Anglicana," 1863.

THE wise men to Thy cradle-throne,
 O Infant Saviour! brought, of old,
The incense meet for God alone,
 Sharp myrrh, and shining gold.

Shine on us too, sweet Eastern Star,
 Thine own baptizèd Gentile band,
Till we have found our Lord from far,
 An offering in our hand!

Till we have brought the fine gold rare,
 Of zeal that giveth all for love;
Till we have prayed the glowing prayer,
 Like incense borne above;

Till bitter tears our eyes have wet,
 Because our wilful hearts would err;
Worship and love and sorrow met,
 Gold, frankincense, and myrrh.

All meet for Thee, our own adored,
 Our suffering Saviour, God, and King;
Accept the gold and incense, Lord:
 Accept the myrrh, we bring.

WE COME NOT WITH A COSTLY STORE.

WE come not with a costly store,
 O Lord! like them of old,
The masters of the starry lore,
 From Ophir's shore of gold;
No weepings of the incense-tree;
 Are with the gifts we bring;
No odorous myrrh of Araby
 Blends with our offering.

WE COME NOT WITH A COSTLY STORE.

But faith and love may bring their best,
    A spirit keenly tried
By fierce affliction's fiery test,
    And seven times purified:
The fragrant graces of the mind,
    The virtues that delight
To give their perfume out, will find
    Acceptance in Thy sight.

CHRIST'S LIFE AND EXAMPLE.

"He hath done all things well."—*Mark* vii. 37.
"I am the Way, the Truth, and the Life."—*John* xiv. 6.
"Follow Me."—*Matt.* iv. 19.

BLESSED JESUS! who wast tempted, as we are tempted, yet without sin, and who, by Thy perfect obedience to the will of Thy Heavenly Father, didst fulfil all righteousness, and leave us an example: assist us, we beseech Thee, in our infirmity; and enable us, by Thy Spirit, so to follow Thy steps, that we may daily grow in grace, and be transformed more and more into Thy glorious image, to the praise of Thy holy name. Amen.

> "Thou seemest human and divine,
> The highest, holiest manhood Thou:
> Our wills are ours, we know not how;
> Our wills are ours, to make them Thine."
> Alfred Tennyson.
>
> "Jesu, divinest when Thou most art man!"

ETERNAL Word, who, clothed in human dust,
Didst teach lapsed man the wisdom of the just;
Illustrate by example Thy discourse,
Confirm it by a wonder-working force;
Open my ears, my eyes, my tongue unloose,
Into my heart Thy heavenly truth infuse;
That I Thy praise incessantly may sing,
That love may give my heart a heavenward spring!
That I may never more towards earth propend,
In vigorous, sweet efforts to Thee ascend;
Thy bright idea in my heart enchase,
To copy out each imitable grace.
                              BISHOP KEN.

CHRIST'S LIFE AND EXAMPLE.

MOST HOLY JESUS, FOUNT OF LIGHT!

(*Heiligster Jesu, Heil'gungsquelle.*)

THE first two stanzas are freely reproduced, in the metre of the original, from a German hymn of BARTHOLOMÆUS CRASSELIUS (about 1700); the third is added by the Ed. The German poem has nine stanzas (SCHAFF's "G. H. B.," No. 103), and is a translation from the Dutch of JODOCUS VON LODENSTEIN, 1655. A close, but not very smooth, version, by Dr. HENRY MILLS, in "Horæ Germanicæ" ("Most Holy Jesus, Fount unfailing, Of joy all other joys excelling"), who erroneously attributes the original to Gottfried Arnold.

MOST holy Jesus, Fount of light!
  As crystal clear, for ever bright,
    Thou Stream o'erflowing, pure and free :
  The brightness of the cherubim,
The glow of burning seraphim,
  Are darkness when compared with Thee.
    Be Thou my pattern bright,
    My study and delight,
      My all in all.
Oh, teach Thou me, that I may be
All pure and holy, like to Thee :

Most humble Jesus ! self-denying,
And with Thy Father's will complying,
  Yea, even unto death resigned ;
Let me, Thy humble path pursuing,
And pride and haughtiness subduing,
  Be guided by Thy gentle mind.
    May I be ever mild
    And humble as a child,
      And docile too !
Oh, teach Thou me, that I may be
Meek and obedient, like Thee :

Most loving Jesus! dearest treasure,
Whose love to man no more can measure,
  Conform me to Thine image bright;
Thy Spirit and Thy strength bestowing,
That I, in every virtue growing,
  May reach in Thee perfection's height.
    Lord, give me from above
    A heart all filled with love
      To God and man;
Oh, teach Thou me to die for Thee,
That I may live and reign with Thee!

COME, MY WAY, MY TRUTH, MY LIFE.

"THE CALL." Comp. John xiv. 6. By GEORGE HERBERT: b. at Montgomery Castle, Wales, 1593; d. 1632. Rector of Bemerton, near Salisbury; remarkable for the beautiful harmony of purity and poetry, goodness and happiness, in his secluded pastoral life; generally known as "holy George Herbert." As a poet, he is quaint, but pregnant with pious thought, and belongs to the same school as Quarles, Donne, Herrick, and Crashaw, of the age of Charles I.

COME, my Way, my Truth, my Life:
  Such a Way as gives us breath;
  Such a Truth as ends all strife;
Such a Life as killeth death.

Come, my Light, my Feast, my Strength:
  Such a Light as shows a feast;
  Such a Feast as mends in length;
Such a Strength as makes his guest.

Come, my Joy, my Love, my Heart:
  Such a Joy as none can move;
  Such a Love as none can part;
Such a Heart as joys in love.

EARTH HAS NOTHING SWEET OR FAIR.

(Keine Schönheit hat die Welt.)

FROM the German of ANGELUS SILESIUS (JOHANN ANGELUS SCHEFFLER), b. at Breslau, Silesia, 1624; d. 1677; author of 205 hymns and poetic proverbs, most of which were composed before he joined the Roman Catholic Church. Several of his hymns are among the deepest and most tender in the German language, and breathe a glowing love to the Saviour. Of the following poem, we have two excellent English translations,—one by CATHERINE WINKWORTH ("Nothing fair on earth I see, But I straightway think of Thee"), and one by FRANCES ELIZABETH COX (Lond. 1841). The latter is more literal, and is here given.

EARTH has nothing sweet or fair,
Lovely forms or beauties rare,
But before my eyes they bring
Christ of beauty Source and Spring.

When the morning paints the skies,
When the golden sunbeams rise,
Then my Saviour's form I find
Brightly imaged on my mind.

When the day-beams pierce the night,
Oft I think on Jesu's light,
Think how bright that light will be,
Shining through eternity.

When, as moonlight softly steals,
Heaven its thousand eyes reveals,
Then I think: Who made their light
Is a thousand times more bright.

When I see, in spring-tide gay,
Fields their varied tints display,
Wakes the thrilling thought in me,
What must their Creator be!

If I trace the fountain's source,
Or the brooklet's devious course,
Straight my thoughts to Jesus mount,
As the best and purest fount.

Sweetly sings the nightingale,
Sweet the flute's soft, plaintive tale;

Sweeter than the richest tone
Is the name of Mary's Son.[1]

Sweetness fills the air around,
At the echo's answering sound;
But more sweet than echo's fall,
Is to me the Bridegroom's call.

Lord of all that's fair to see!
Come, reveal Thyself to me;
Let me, 'mid Thy radiant light,
See Thine unveiled glories bright.

Let Thy Deity profound
Me in heart and soul surround;
From my mind its idols chase,
Weaned from joys of time and place.

Come, Lord Jesus! and dispel
This dark cloud in which I dwell;
Thus to me the power impart,
To behold Thee as Thou art.

MY DEAR REDEEMER, AND MY LORD.

By Isaac Watts, 1674-1748. From his "Hymns and Spiritual Songs," 1719

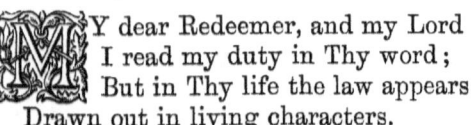

Y dear Redeemer, and my Lord!
I read my duty in Thy word;
But in Thy life the law appears,
Drawn out in living characters.

Such was Thy truth, and such Thy zeal,
Such deference to Thy Father's will,

---

[1] This stanza I have borrowed from Miss Winkworth's translation. Miss Cox renders it, less happily,—

"Sweet the song the night-bird sings,
Sweet the lute, with quivering strings;
Far more sweet than every tone
Are the words 'Maria's Son.'"

Such love and meekness so divine,
I would transcribe and make them mine.

Cold mountains and the midnight air
Witnessed the fervour of Thy prayer;
The desert Thy temptations knew,
Thy conflict, and Thy victory too.

Be Thou my pattern; make me bear
More of Thy gracious image here:
Then God, the Judge, shall own my name
Among the followers of the Lamb.

JESUS, STILL LEAD ON.

(Jesu, geh voran.)

COUNT NIKOLAUS LUDWIG VON ZINZENDORF, 1721. (SCHAFF'S " G. H. B.," No. 106.) Translation by JANE BORTHWICK, in the " Hymns from the Land of Luther," Edinb. 1853.

JESUS, still lead on,
  Till our rest be won:
  And, although the way be cheerless,
We will follow, calm and fearless:
    Guide us by Thy hand
    To our Fatherland!

  If the way be drear,
  If the foe be near,
Let not faithless fears o'ertake us,
Let not faith and hope forsake us;
    For, through many a foe,
    To our home we go!

  When we seek relief
  From a long-felt grief,
When temptations come alluring,
Make us patient and enduring:
    Show us that bright shore
    Where we weep no more!

Jesus, still lead on,
  Till our rest be won!
Heavenly Leader, still direct us,
Still support, console, protect us,
  Till we safely stand
  In our Fatherland:

OH FOR A HEART TO PRAISE MY GOD!

Charles Wesley, 1742.

OH for a heart to praise my God!
  A heart from sin set free!
  A heart that always feels Thy blood,
So freely spilt for me:

A heart resigned, submissive, meek,
  My great Redeemer's throne:
Where only Christ is heard to speak,
  Where Jesus reigns alone:

A humble, lowly, contrite heart,
  Believing, true, and clean;
Which neither life nor death can part
  From Him that dwells within:

A heart in every thought renewed,
  And full of love divine;
Perfect and right, and pure and good,
  A copy, Lord, of Thine.

My heart, Thou knowest, can never rest
  Till Thou create my peace;
Till, of my Eden repossest,
  From every sin I cease.

Fruit of Thy gracious lips, on me
  Bestow that peace unknown;
The hidden manna, and the tree
  Of life, and the white stone.

Thy nature, gracious Lord, impart;
  Come quickly from above;
Write Thy new name upon my heart,
  Thy new, best name of Love.

BEHOLD, WHERE, IN A MORTAL FORM.

WILLIAM ENFIELD [?], 1772. I have been unable to trace this hymn to its source. It is not found in the Warrington Collection, edited by Enfield, 1772, to whom it is attributed in most hymn books. He disowns, in the preface, the authorship of any of the original compositions, for which he acknowledges himself " wholly indebted to his friends." Enfield was a Presbyterian minister with semi-Arian sentiments.

BEHOLD, where, in a mortal form,
    Appears each grace divine;
    The virtues, all in Jesus met,
With mildest radiance shine.

To spread the rays of heavenly light,
    To give the mourner joy,
To preach glad tidings to the poor,
    Was His divine employ.

'Mid keen reproach and cruel scorn,
    Patient and meek He stood:
His foes, ungrateful, sought His life;
    He laboured for their good.

In the last hour of deep distress,
    Before His Father's throne,
With soul resigned, He bowed, and said,
    " Thy will, not mine, be done ! "

Be Christ our pattern and our guide;
    His image may we bear;
Oh, may we tread His holy steps,
    His joy and glory share !

OH, JESUS CHRIST, GROW THOU IN ME.

(O Jesus Christus, wachs in mir.)

"HE must increase, but I must decrease." The best hymn of JOHANN CASPAR LAVATER, of Zurich, died 1801. Translated from the German by Mrs. Dr. H. B. SMITH, of New York, 1869, and here published for the first time.

OH, Jesus Christ, grow Thou in me,
   And all things else recede;
My heart be daily nearer Thee,
   From sin be daily freed!

Each day, let Thy supporting might
   My weakness still embrace;
My darkness vanish in Thy light,
   Thy life my death efface.

In Thy bright beams, which on me fall,
   Fade every evil thought;
That I am nothing, Thou art all,
   I would be daily taught.

Come near, I cast myself away,
   Before Thee silent weep;
Come, with Thy pure, divinest sway,
   My spirit rule and keep.

More of Thy glory let me see,
   Thou Holy, Wise and True!
I would Thy living image be
   In joy and sorrow too.

Fill me with gladness from above,
   Hold me by strength divine;
Lord, let the glow of Thy great love
   Through my whole being shine!

Weak is the power of sloth and pride,
   And vain desires are still,
When, to Thy realm and Thee allied,
   I haste to do Thy will.

Make this poor self grow less and less,
   Be Thou my life and aim.
Oh, make me daily, through Thy grace,
   More worthy of Thy name;

Daily more filled with Thee my heart,
  Daily from self more free;
Thou, to whom prayer did strength impart,
  Of my prayer hearer be!

Let faith in Thee and in Thy might
  My every motive move,
Be Thou alone my soul's delight,
  My passion and my love!

EVER WOULD I FAIN BE READING.

(Immer muss ich wieder lesen.)

FROM the German of LOUISE HENSEL; b. 1798; daughter of a Lutheran clergyman in the Mark Brandenburg; joined the Roman Catholic Church 1818; authoress of several sweet and childlike hymns, which led to the conversion of Clemens Brentano. Translated by Miss C. WINKWORTH.

EVER would I fain be reading,
  In the ancient holy Book,
Of my Saviour's gentle pleading,
  Truth in every word and look.

How when children came He blessed them,
  Suffered no man to reprove,
Took them in His arms, and pressed them
  To His heart with words of love.

How to all the sick and tearful
  Help was ever gladly shown;
How He sought the poor and fearful,
  Called them brothers and His own.

How no contrite soul e'er sought Him,
  And was bidden to depart,
How with gentle words He taught him,
  Took the death from out his heart.

Still I read the ancient story,
  And my joy is ever new,
How for us He left His glory,
  How He still is kind and true.

How the flock He gently leadeth
   Whom His Father gave Him here;
How His arms He widely spreadeth
   To His heart to draw us near.

Let me kneel, my Lord, before Thee,
   Let my heart in tears o'erflow,
Melted by Thy love adore Thee,
   Blest in Thee 'mid joy or woe.

JESUS, I MY CROSS HAVE TAKEN.

Rev. Henry Francis Lyte. Born at Kelso, 1793; died at Nice, 1847.

JESUS, I my cross have taken,
   All to leave and follow Thee;
Destitute, despised, forsaken,
   Thou from hence my all shalt be.
Perish every fond ambition,
   All I've sought or hoped or known;
Yet how rich is my condition!
   God and heaven are still my own.

Let the world despise and leave me;
   They have left my Saviour too;
Human hearts and looks deceive me:
   Thou art not like them, untrue.
And while Thou shalt smile upon me,
   God of wisdom, love, and might!
Foes may hate, and friends may shun me:
   Show Thy face and all is bright.

Go, then, earthly fame and treasure;
   Come, disaster, scorn and pain:
In Thy service pain is pleasure;
   With Thy favour, loss is gain.
I have called Thee Abba, Father,
   I have stayed my heart on Thee:
Storms may howl, and clouds may gather,
   All must work for good to me.

Man may trouble and distress me,
   'Twill but drive me to Thy breast;
Life with trials hard may press me,
   Heaven will bring me sweeter rest.
Oh, 'tis not in grief to harm me,
   While Thy love is left to me!
Oh, 'twere not in joy to charm me,
   Were that joy unmixed with Thee!

Take, my soul, thy full salvation!
   Rise o'er sin and fear and care;
Joy to find, in every station,
   Something still to do or bear.
Think what Spirit dwells within thee,
   What a Father's smile is thine,
What a Saviour died to win thee;
   Child of heaven, should'st thou repine?

Haste, then, on from grace to glory,
   Armed by faith, and winged by prayer;
Heaven's eternal day's before thee,
   God's own hand shall guide thee there.
Soon shall close thy earthly mission,
   Swift shall pass thy pilgrim days;
Hope soon change to full fruition,
   Faith to sight, and prayer to praise.

THOU ART THE WAY; TO THEE ALONE.

GEORGE WASHINGTON DOANE, Bishop of the Protestant Episcopal Diocese of New Jersey; died at Burlington, N.J., 1859. "I am the Way, the Truth, and the Life."—*John* xiv. 6.

THOU art the Way; to Thee alone
   From sin and death we flee;
And he who would the Father seek,
   Must seek Him, Lord, by Thee.

Thou art the Truth; Thy word alone
   True wisdom can impart;
Thou only canst inform the mind,
   And purify the heart.

Thou art the Life ! the rending tomb
  Proclaims Thy conquering arm;
And those who put their trust in Thee
  Nor death nor hell shall harm.

Thou art the Way, the Truth, the Life;
  Grant us that Way to know;
That Truth to keep, that Life to win,
  Whose joys eternal flow.

WHEN O'ER JUDEA'S VALES AND HILLS.

"HYMN to the Redeemer," by Dr. A. C. COXE, born at Mendham, New Jersey, 1818; since 1865 bishop of Western New York; author of "Christian Ballads," &c. This poem was written 1840, and passed in mutilated form into several American hymn books, where it commences with the fifth line of the first stanza: "How beauteous were," etc. We give it in its original form as printed in "Halloween, with Lays, Meditative and Devotional," Philad., 1869, with final corrections kindly furnished by the author (1869).

WHEN o'er Judea's vales and hills,
  Or by her olive-shaded rills,
  Thy weary footsteps went of old,
Or walked the lulling waters bold,
How beauteous were the marks divine,
That in Thy meekness used to shine,
That lit Thy lonely pathway, trod
In wondrous love, O Lamb of God!

Oh! who like Thee, so mild, so bright,
Thou Son of Man, Thou Light of Light,
Oh! who like Thee, did ever go
So patient, through a world of woe,
Oh! who like Thee, so humbly bore
The scorn, the scoffs of men before,
So meek, so lowly—yet so high,
So glorious in humility !

The morning saw Thee, like the day,
Forth on Thy light bestowing way;
And evening in her holy hues,
Shed down her sweet baptismal dews,

Where bending angels stoop'd to see
The lisping infant clasp Thy knee,
And smile, as in a father's eye,
Upon Thy mild divinity.

The hours when princes sought their rest
Beheld Thee, still, no chamber's guest;
But when the chilly night hung round,
And man from Thee sweet slumber found,
Thy wearied footsteps sought, alone,
The mountain to Thy sorrows known,
And darkness heard thy patient prayer,
Or hid Thee in the prowler's lair.

And all Thy life's unchanging years,
A man of sorrows and of tears,
The cross, where all our sins were laid
Upon Thy bending shoulders weigh'd;
And death, that sets the prisoner free,
Was pang, and scoff, and scorn to thee;
Yet love through all thy torture glow'd,
And mercy with Thy life blood flow'd.

O wondrous Lord! my soul would be
Still more and more conformed to Thee,
Would lose the pride, the taint of sin,
That burns these fevered veins within,
And learn of Thee, the lowly One,
And like Thee, all my journey run,
Above the world, and all its mirth,
Yet weeping still with weeping earth.

THOU LORD OF ALL, ON EARTH HAST DWELT.

By Samuel Prideaux Tregelles, LL.D., a learned and devout biblical scholar, editor of a Greek Testament from the oldest manuscripts; born at Wodehouse Place, near Falmouth, 1813; formerly a member of the Plymouth Community. This poem was composed in 1840, as the author kindly informed me when I saw him in London, May, 1869.

THOU Lord of all, on earth hast dwelt,
    Rejected and unknown;
What bitter grief Thy heart hath felt,
    Endured by Thee alone!

But oh! how full of truth and grace
    Through all Thou dost appear!
And thus with wonder we retrace
    Thy path of sorrow here.

Thou on the cross didst suffer, too,
    More than man's eye could see;
For then the wrath that was our due,
    Was poured, O Lord, on Thee!

But Thou art risen; and now we know
    That Thou, in heaven above,
For all God's children here below,
    Dost feel a brother's love.

Oh, may we ever look to Thee
    For needed grace and strength,
Till we Thy face in glory see,
    And reign with Thee at length!

Till then may we, who bear Thy name,
    Thy blest example take,
And count the world's reproach and shame
    As glory, for Thy sake.

Since Thou the cup of wrath didst drain,
    None now for us is there;
The drops of sorrow that remain,
    Shall we refuse to share?

THINE HANDMAID, SAVIOUR! CAN IT BE?

WILLIAM A. MUHLENBERG, D.D., founder of St. Luke's Hospital, New York. Written on the words "Come, follow me," for the reception of a "Sister" at St. Luke's Hospital, 1859.

THINE Handmaid, Saviour! can it be?
Such honour dost Thou put on me?
To wait on Thee, do Thy commands,
The works once hallowed by Thy hands?

Daily Thy mercy paths to go,
Bearing Thy balm for every woe;
Thy sick and weary ones to cheer,
Bid them Thy words of pity hear;

Parting with earth Thy cross to bear,
Content Thy poverty to share,
Rich in Thy Love,—Thou blessed Lord,
This life to me dost Thou accord?

Oh, marvellous grace,—yea, even so!
The call I heard,—'twas Thine I know,—
"Come, follow me;" the heavenly voice,
How could it but constrain my choice!

My heart's free choice, yet bound by Thee:
Thrice welcome, sweet captivity,
My soul and all its powers to fill
With love of Thee and Thy dear will!

Lord, give but light to show the way,
Strength from Thyself to be my stay,
Grace, always,—grace to feel Thee nigh,—
Thine Handmaid then, I live and die.

A PILGRIM THROUGH THIS LONELY WORLD.

By Sir Edward Denny, Bart. [1863].

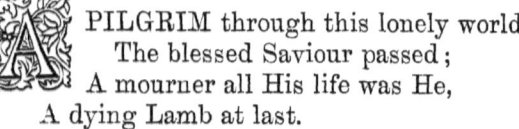A PILGRIM through this lonely world
    The blessed Saviour passed;
A mourner all His life was He,
    A dying Lamb at last.

That tender heart that felt for all,
    For all its life-blood gave;
It found on earth no resting-place,
    Save only in the grave.

Such was our Lord; and shall we fear
    The Cross with all its scorn,
Or love a faithless, evil world,
    That wreathed His brow with thorn?

No; facing all its frowns and smiles,
    Like Him obedient still,
We homeward press, through storm or cloud,
    To yon Celestial Hill.

In tents we dwell amid the waste,
    Nor turn aside to roam
In folly's paths, nor seek our rest,
    Where Jesus had no home.

Dead to the world with Him who died
    To win our hearts, our love;
We, risen with our risen Head,
    In spirit dwell above.

By faith His boundless glories there
    Our wondering eyes behold,
Those glories which eternal years
    Shall never all unfold.

This fills our hearts with deep desire
    To lose ourselves in love,
Bears all our hopes from earth away,
    And fixes them above.

IMMORTAL LOVE, FOR EVER FULL.

"OUR MASTER," by JOHN GREENLEAF WHITTIER, one of the first American poets, born 1807, in Haverhill, Massachusetts. From his "Tent on the Beach, and Other Poems," Boston, 1867. An exquisite tribute of the Quaker poet to our common Lord and Master.

    IMMORTAL love, for ever full,
        For ever flowing free;
    For ever shared, for ever whole,
        A never-ebbing sea!

Our outward lips confess the name
    All other names above;
Love only knoweth whence it came,
    And comprehendeth love.

Blow, winds of God, awake and blow
    The mists of earth away!
Shine out, O Light Divine, and show
    How wide and far we stray!

Hush every lip, close every book,
    The strife of tongues forbear;
Why forward reach, or backward look,
    For love that clasps like air?

We may not climb the heavenly steeps
    To bring the Lord Christ down:
In vain we search the lowest deeps,
    For Him no depths can drown.

Nor holy bread, nor blood of grape,
    The lineaments restore,
Of Him we know in outward shape,
    And in the flesh, no more.

He cometh not a king to reign;
    The world's long hope is dim;
The weary centuries watch in vain,
    The clouds of heaven for Him.

Death comes, life goes, the asking eye
    And ear are answerless;
The grave is dumb, the hollow sky
    Is sad with silentness.

The letter fails, and systems fall,
   And every symbol wanes;
The Spirit over-brooding all
   Eternal Love remains.

And not for signs in heaven above
   Or earth below they look,
Who know with John His smile of love,
   With Peter His rebuke.

In joy of inward peace, or sense
   Of sorrow over sin,
He is His own best evidence,
   His witness is within.

No fable old, nor mythic lore,
   Nor dream of bards and seers,
No dead fact stranded on the shore
   Of the oblivious years,—

But warm, sweet, tender, even yet
   A present help is He;
And faith has still its Olivet,
   And love its Galilee.

The healing of His seamless dress
   Is by our beds of pain;
We touch Him in life's throng and press,
   And we are whole again.

Through Him the first fond prayers are said
   Our lips of childhood frame,
The last low whispers of our dead
   Are burdened with His name.

O Lord and Master of us all!
   Whate'er our name or sign,
We own Thy sway, we hear Thy call,
   We test our lives by Thine.

Thou judgest us; Thy purity
   Doth all our lusts condemn;
The love that draws us nearer Thee
   Is hot with wrath to them.

IMMORTAL LOVE, FOR EVER FULL.

Our thoughts lie open to Thy sight;
  And naked to Thy glance,
Our secret sins are in the light
  Of Thy pure countenance.

Thy healing pains, a keen distress
  Thy tender light shines in;
Thy sweetness is the bitterness,
  Thy grace the pang of sin.

Yet weak and blinded though we be,
  Thou dost our service own;
We bring our varying gifts to Thee,
  And Thou rejectest none.

To Thee our full humanity,
  Its joys and pains belong;
The wrong of man to man on Thee
  Inflicts a deeper wrong.

Who hates, hates Thee; who loves, becomes
  Therein to Thee allied;
All sweet accords of hearts and homes
  In Thee are multiplied.

Deep strike thy roots, O heavenly vine,
  Within our earthly sod!
Most human and yet most divine,
  The flower of man and God!

O Love! O Life! our faith and sight
  Thy presence maketh one;
As through transfigured clouds of white
  We trace the noon-day sun.

So to our mortal eyes subdued,
  Flesh-veiled, but not concealed,
We know in Thee the fatherhood
  And heart of God revealed.

We faintly hear, we dimly see,
  In differing phrase we pray;
But dim or clear, we own in Thee
  The Light, the Truth, the Way!

The homage that we render Thee
    Is still our Father's own;
Nor jealous claim or rivalry
    Divides the Cross and Throne.

To do Thy will is more than praise,
    As words are less than deeds,
And simple trust can find Thy ways
    We miss with chart of creeds.

No pride of self Thy service hath,
    No place for me and mine;
Our human strength is weakness, death
    Our life, apart from Thine.

Apart from Thee all gain is loss,
    All labour vainly done;
The solemn shadow of Thy Cross
    Is better than the sun.

Alone, O Love ineffable!
    Thy saving name is given;
To turn aside from Thee is hell,
    To walk with Thee is heaven.

How vain, secure in all Thou art,
    Our noisy championship!
The sighing of the contrite heart
    Is more than flattering lip.

Not Thine the bigot's partial plea,
    Nor Thine the zealot's ban;
Thou well canst spare a love of Thee
    Which ends in hate of man.

Our Friend, our Brother, and our Lord,
    What may Thy service be?
Nor name, nor form, nor ritual word,
    But simply following Thee.

We bring no ghastly holocaust,
    We pile no graven stone;
He serves Thee best who loveth most
    His brothers and Thy own.

Thy litanies, sweet offices
  Of love and gratitude;
Thy sacramental liturgies,
  The joy of doing good.

In vain shall waves of incense drift
  The vaulted nave around,
In vain the minster turret lift
  Its brazen weights of sound.

The heart must ring Thy Christmas bells,
  Thy inward altars raise;
Its faith and hope Thy canticles,
  And its obedience praise!

TRUSTINGLY, TRUSTINGLY.

HORATIUS BONAR, D.D. From "Hymns of Faith and Hope," Third Series, 1868: "My Pilgrimage."

TRUSTINGLY, trustingly,
  Jesus, to Thee
Come I: Lord, lovingly
  Come Thou to me!
Then shall I lovingly,
Then shall I joyfully,
  Walk here with Thee.

Peacefully, peacefully,
  Walk I with thee;
Jesus, my Lord, Thou art
  All, all to me.
Peace Thou hast left us,
Thy peace hast given us;
  So let it be.

Whom but Thyself, O Lord!
  Have I above?
What have I left on earth?
  Only Thy love!

Come then, O Saviour! come:
Come then, O Spirit! come
  Heavenly Dove.

Happily, happily,
  Pass I along,
Eager to work for Thee,
  Earnest and strong.
Life is for service true,
Life is for battle too;
  Life is for song.

Hopefully, hopefully,
  Onward I go,
Cheerfully, cheerfully,
  Meet I the foe.
Crowns are awaiting us,
Glory prepared for us;
  Joys overflow.

THE PASSION.

"SURELY He hath borne our griefs, and carried our sorrows; yet we did esteem Him stricken, smitten of God, and afflicted. But He was wounded for our transgressions, He was bruised for our iniquities; the chastisement of our peace was upon Him, and with His stripes we are healed."—*Isa.* liii. 4, 5.

"Christ also hath once suffered for sins, the just for the unjust, that He might bring us to God."—1 *Pet.* iii. 18.

"Unto Him that loved us, and washed us from our sins in His own blood, and has made us kings and priests unto God and his Father,—to Him be glory and dominion for ever and ever. Amen."—*Rev.* i. 5, 6.

LORD JESUS CHRIST! who, by Thy bitter passion and crucifixion, hast redeemed me from the curse of sin, the power of death, and the woe of damnation: most heartily do I thank Thee for Thine unspeakable love, for every burden Thou didst bear, for every tear Thou didst weep, for every pain Thou didst suffer, for every conflict Thou didst endure, for every drop of blood Thou didst shed, for me, Thine enemy; and I humbly beseech Thee to give me grace, that, being dead unto sin, I may live unto righteousness all the days of my life, and attain, at last, to the glory of the blessed resurrection. Amen.

O LORD, the only-begotten Son, Jesus Christ!
O Lord God, Lamb of God, Son of the Father,
That takest away the sin of the world,
Have mercy upon us.
Thou that takest away the sin of the world,
Have mercy upon us.
Thou that takest away the sin of the world,
Receive our prayer.
Thou that sittest at the right hand of God the Father,
Have mercy upon us,
And grant us Thy peace. Amen.
From the " Gloria in Excelsis."

THE PASSION.

SING, MY TONGUE, THE SAVIOUR'S BATTLE.

(Pange, lingua, gloriosi prœlium certaminis.)

THE masterpiece of VENANTIUS FORTUNATUS, Bishop of Poitiers, in France, about 600, and one of the finest hymns in the Latin language ("in pulcherrimorum numero recensendum," says Daniel). FORTUNATUS (530-609) was the favourite poet of his age, a friend of St. Gregory of Tours and Queen Rhadegunda, and marks the transition from the ancient to the mediæval hymnology. This passion-hymn, like the one that follows, found a place in the Roman Breviary, with some alterations. DANIEL, I. p. 163-165, gives the original and the altered text; WACKERNAGEL, I. pp. 61, 62, gives two forms, one of 10, and the other of 11, stanzas, from old MSS. (TRENCH strangely omits the two best productions of this gifted poet.) The Latin is without rhyme, and in the measure of the trochaic tetrametre, which was first grouped into stanzas by Fortunatus, and which, subsequently, with various modifications, became the favourite measure of the mediæval hymn. The translation here given is chiefly from E. CASWALL ("Lyra Catholica"), with some changes and additions by the Editor. Another version by Dr. J. M. NEALE ("Mediæval Hymns and Sequences," p. 1), and one by Mrs. CHARLES, "Spread, my tongue, the wondrous story Of the glorious battle far" ("Christian Life in Song," p. 133).

SING, my tongue, the Saviour's battle;[1]
  Tell His triumphs far and wide;
Tell aloud the wondrous story
  Of His body crucified,
How upon the cross a victim,
  Vanquishing in death, He died.

---

[1] Caswall has "the Saviour's glory," following the reading of the Roman Breviary, which substitutes "*lauream* certaminis," for the original "*prælium certaminis.*" Thomas Aquinas borrowed from Fortunatus a part of the first line of his famous eucharistic hymn :—
      "Pange, lingua, gloriosi *corporis mysterium.*"

Eating of the Tree forbidden,
  Man had sunk in Satan's snare,
When our pitying Creator
  Did this second Tree prepare,
Destined, many ages later,
  That first evil to repair.

Such the order God appointed,
  When for sin He would atone,
To the serpent thus opposing
  Schemes yet deeper than his own;
Thence the remedy procuring,
  Whence the fatal wound had come.

So, when now at length the fulness
  Of the time foretold drew nigh,
Then the Son, the world's Creator,
  Left His Father's throne on high,
From a virgin's womb appearing,
  Clothed in our mortality.

All within a lowly manger,
  Lo, a tender babe He lies!
See His gentle Virgin-mother
  Lull to sleep His infant cries!
While the limbs of God Incarnate
  Round with swathing bands she ties.

Thus did Christ to perfect manhood
  In our mortal flesh attain;
Then of His free choice He goeth
  To a death of bitter pain;
He, the Lamb upon the altar
  Of the cross, for us was slain.

Lo, with gall His thirst He quenches!
  See the thorns upon His brow;
Nails His hands and feet are rending;
  See, His side is open now!
Whence, to cleanse the whole creation,
  Streams of blood and water flow.

Faithful Cross! above all other,
  One and only noble Tree!

None in foliage, none in blossom,
    None in fruit thy peers may be;
Sweetest wood and sweetest iron,
    Sweetest weight is hung on thee![1]

Bend thy boughs, O Tree of Glory!
    Thy relaxing sinews bend;
For a while the ancient rigour,
    That thy birth bestowed, suspend;
And the King of heavenly beauty
    On thy bosom gently tend.

Thou alone wast counted worthy
    This world's ransom to uphold;
For a shipwrecked race preparing
    Harbour, like the ark of old:
With the sacred blood anointed,
    From the smitten Lamb that rolled.

When, O Judge of this world! coming
    In Thy glory all divine,
Thou shalt bid Thy Cross's trophy
    Bright above the stars to shine;
Be the Light and the Salvation
    Of the people that are Thine![2]

Blessing, honour everlasting,
    To the immortal Deity;

---

[1] This and the two following stanzas are strangely omitted by Caswall (in the "Lyra Catholica," and in another copy before me), and have been supplemented from Neale's version. The eighth stanza is the finest in the poem. In the second recension given by Wackernagel (No. 79), from Munich and other MSS. it opens the hymn. The Latin is a gem of rare beauty, although not free from a taint of superstition:—

    "Crux fidelis, inter omnes arbor una nobilis!
    Nulla talem silva profert fronde, flore, germine:
    Dulce lignum, dulces clavos, dulce pondus sustinens."

In the Roman breviary,

    "Dulce ferrum, dulce lignum, dulce pondus sustinent."

Daniel reads, "dulci clavo;" Wackernagel twice, "dulces clavos." Mrs. Charles translates thus:—

    "Faithful cross! of all earth's produce only rich and noble tree;
    No such flower or leaf or fruitage we in all the world can see:
    Sweet to us thy wood and nails, for sweetest weight is hung on thee."

[2] This verse is no part of the original, but is added in some copies, and translated by Neale.

To the Father, Son, and Spirit,
Equal praises ever be;
Glory through the earth and heaven
To the blessed Trinity!

THE ROYAL BANNERS FORWARD GO.

(Vexilla Regis prodeunt.)

FROM the Latin of VENANTIUS FORTUNATUS (died 609), by J. M. NEALE ("Mediæval Hymns," p. 6), with slight alterations. The original (in DANIEL, I. p. 160, who gives also the variations of the Roman Breviary, and WACKERNAGEL, I. p. 63) is sung, in the Roman Church, on Good Friday, during the procession in which the consecrated host is carried to the altar. Neale calls it "one of the grandest in the treasury of the Latin Church;" but it does not reach the depth of Bernard's or Gerhardt's passion-hymns. The second stanza is omitted by Neale, as it is also in the Roman Breviary. Another English translation by EDWARD CASWALL: "Forth comes the standard of the King" (in the "Lyra Catholica"); and one by Mrs. CHARLES: "The banner of the King goes forth" ("Christian Life in Song," p. 131).

THE Royal Banners forward go,
The Cross shines forth in mystic glow;
Where He in flesh, our flesh Who made,
Our sentence bore, our ransom paid.

There, whilst He hung, His sacred side
By soldier's spear was opened wide,
To cleanse us in the precious flood
Of water mingled with His blood.

Fulfilled is all that David told
In true prophetic song of old,
How God the nation's King should be,
For God is reigning from the Tree.[1]

---

[1] Ps. xcvi. 10, which reads, in the old Latin version, "Tell it out among the heathen, that the Lord reigneth *from the Tree.*" Justin Martyr accuses the Jews, that they have erased the words "a ligno," ἀπὸ ξύλου, which are wanting in the original and in the Septuagint. See the note in Daniel, I. p. 162. Mrs. Charles renders the verse thus:—

"The truth that David learned to sing,
Its deep fulfilment here attains:
'Tell all the earth, the Lord is King!'
Lo, from the cross, a King He reigns!"

THE ROYAL BANNERS FORWARD GO.

O Tree of Glory, Tree most fair!
Ordained those Holy Limbs to bear;
How bright in purple robe it stood,
The purple of a Saviour's blood!

Upon its arms, so widely flung,
The weight of this world's ransom hung:
The ransom He alone could pay,
Despoiling Satan of his prey.

With fragrance dropping from each bough
Sweeter than sweetest nectar Thou;
Decked with the fruit of peace and praise,
And glorious with triumphal lays.

Hail, Altar! hail, O Victim! Thee
Decks now Thy Passion's victory;
Where life for sinners death endured,
And life, by death, for man procured.[1]

To Thee, Eternal Three in One,
Let homage meet by all be done:
As by the Cross Thou dost restore,
So rule and guide us evermore.

---

[1] In the Roman Breviary, the last two verses of Fortunatus, which seem to reflect upon the cross itself the glory of the victory won upon it, are replaced by the following one, which shows the gradual change of the original contemplation of the cross, as the mere instrument of the humiliation and torture of our Lord, into the superstitious worship of the same:—

"O Cross! our only hope, all hail!
This holy Passion-tide, avail
To give fresh merit to the saint,
And pardon to the penitent."

FORTH FLAMES THE STANDARD OF OUR KING.

The "Vexilla Regis," in an abridged translation, by Bishop WILLIAMS, of Connecticut (from RIDER's "Lyra Americana," 1865).

FORTH flames the standard of our King,
    Bright gleams the mystic sign,
When life bore death of suffering,
    And death wrought life divine.

The stabs of the accursed spear
    Brought forth the healing flood,
To cleanse sin's stains so dark and drear,
    With water and with blood.

Fulfilled is each prophetic word,
    Each faith-inspiring strain,
Telling the nations of that Lord,
    Who by the Cross should reign.

Hail, Cross of Christ! man's only hope;
    While now we gaze and pray,
Dear Lord, th' exhaustless fountains ope.
    And wash our sins away.

HAIL, THOU HEAD! SO BRUISED AND WOUNDED.

(*Salve, Caput cruentatum.*)

ST. BERNARD, of Clairvaux, the best and greatest man of his age, d. 1153. See WACKERNAGEL, I. p. 124; DANIEL, I. p. 232. Translated by Mrs. CHARLES ("Christian Life in Song," p. 159). The original, in fifty lines, in five stanzas, addressed to the face of Christ ("Ad faciem Christi in cruce pendentis"), is the best of Bernard's seven passion-hymns, and has been happily reproduced and much improved by Gerhardt in German, by Alexander and others in English.

HAIL, thou Head! so bruised and wounded,
    With the crown of thorns surrounded;
    Smitten with the mocking reed,
Wounds which may not cease to bleed.

Trickling faint and slow.
Hail! from whose most blessed brow
None can wipe the blood-drops now;
All the flower of life has fled,
Mortal paleness there instead;
Thou, before whose presence dread
   Angels trembling bow.

All Thy vigour and Thy life
Fading in this bitter strife;
Death his stamp on Thee has set,
Hollow and emaciate,
   Faint and drooping there.
Thou this agony and scorn
Hast for me, a sinner, borne,
Me, unworthy, all for me!
With those signs of love on Thee,
   Glorious Face, appear!

Yet, in this Thine agony,
Faithful Shepherd, think of me;
From whose lips of love divine
Sweetest draughts of life are mine,
   Purest honey flows.
All unworthy of Thy thought,
Guilty, yet reject me not;
Unto me Thy head incline,
Let that dying head of Thine
   In mine arms repose!

Let me true communion know
With Thee in Thy sacred woe,
Counting all beside but dross,
Dying with Thee on Thy Cross:
   'Neath it will I die!
Thanks to Thee with every breath,
Jesus, for Thy bitter death;
Grant Thy guilty one this prayer,
When my dying hour is near,
   Gracious God, be nigh!

When my dying hour must be,
Be not absent then from me;
In that dreadful hour, I pray,

THE PASSION.

Jesus, come without delay :
See and set me free !
When Thou biddest me depart,
Whom I cleave to with my heart,
Lover of my soul, be near ;
With Thy saving Cross appear,
Show Thyself to me.

JESUS' HOLY CROSS AND DYING.

(Recordare sanctæ crucis.)

FROM the Latin of JOHN BONAVENTURA, a celebrated scholastic and mystic divine of the Franciscan order, professor of theology in Paris, called the "Seraphic Doctor ;" died at Lyons, 1274. This " Laudismus de S. Cruce" is his best poem. DANIEL, II. pp. 101, 102. (TRENCH omits it, but gives two other passion-hymns of Bonav., pp. 143-147.) The original has fifteen stanzas, the last bearing a strong resemblance to the second last of the " Stabat Mater Dolorosa." Translated by Dr. JAMES W. ALEXANDER, of New York (d. 1859). Another English version by Dr. H. HARBAUGH, in the " Mercersburg Review," 1858, p. 481 (" Make the cross your meditation ") ; a German version by Rambach in SCHAFF'S " G. H. B." No. 119. See next hymn.

JESUS' holy Cross and dying
O remember ! ever eyeing
Endless pleasure's pathway here ;
At the Cross Thy mindful station
Keep, and still in meditation
All unsated persevere.

When thou toilest, when thou sleepest,
When thou smilest, when thou weepest,
Or in mirth, or woe, hast part ;
When thou comest, when thou goest,
Grief or consolation showest,—
Hold the Cross within thy heart.

'Tis the Cross, when comforts languish,
In the heaviest hour of anguish,
Makes the broken spirit whole.
When the pains are most tormenting,
Sweetly here the heart relenting
Finds the refuge of the soul.

Christ's Cross is the gate of heaven,
Trust to all disciples given,
  Who have conquered all their foes;
Christ's Cross is the people's healing,
Heavenly goodness o'er it stealing
  In a stream of wonders flows.

'Tis the cure of soul-diseases,
Truth that guides, and light that pleases,
  Sweetness in the heart's distress;
Life of souls in heavenly pleasure,
And of raptured saints the treasure,
  Ornament and blissfulness.

Jesus' Cross is virtue's mirror,
Guide to safety out of error,
  True believers' single rest;
Crown of Pilgrims unto heaven,
Solace to the weary given,
  Longed for by the humble breast.

Jesus' Cross, the Tree once scorned,
All with crimson drops adorned,
  Laden hangs with rich supplies;
These the souls from death are leading,
Who, with heavenly spirits feeding,
  Taste the manna of the skies.

Crucified! Thy strength supplying,
Let me, till my day of dying,
  Gaze upon Thy dying face!
Yea, Thy deepest wounds desiring,
Thee, though on the Cross expiring,
  Ever pant I to embrace

PONDER THOU THE CROSS ALL HOLY.

(Recordare sanctæ crucis.)

ANOTHER version of BONAVENTURA's passion-hymn, by the Rev. E. A. WASHBURN, D.D., of New York. Contributed.

PONDER thou the cross all-holy,
Who wilt tread the pathway lowly
  To the perfect joy above:
Thou the Holy Cross, aye, ponder,
And, with an uncloying wonder,
  Drink its mysteries of love.

When thou toilest, when thou sleepest,
When thou smilest, when thou weepest,
  Sad or gladsome if thou art,—
In thy coming, in thy going,
Whether pain or solace knowing,
  Keep the Cross within thy heart.

In the Cross, mid burdens aching,
Heaviest waves above thee breaking,
  Thine unending comfort find;
Though midst cruel foes thou languish,
Sweet the cross in every anguish,
  Refuge of the pious mind.

Cross, of Paradise the portal,
Where have clung the souls immortal,
  Victors in this earthly strife;
Holy Cross, the whole world's healing;
By it is God's love revealing
  Marvels of eternal life.

Cross of Christ, the soul's well being,
Light unshadowed for our seeing,
  For the heart its sweetest good;
Cross, the life all saints indwelling,
Storehouse of all gifts excelling,
  Beauty and beatitude.

Cross, the glass of brave endeavour;
Leader of our triumph ever;
  Hope the faithful to inspire;

Badge of the elect of heaven;
Succour in our trial given;
   Fulness of the soul's desire.

Cross, the tree in beauty growing,
Hallowed by Christ's life-blood flowing,
   Hanging with full-ripened load;
Bounty for all spirits bearing,
An immortal banquet sharing
   With the blessed sons of God.

Crucified, O, make me stronger,
While my life is spared me longer,
   Still to know Thy suffering;
With Thee wounded, with Thee dying,
To that Form before me lying
   On the holy Cross I cling.

O'ERWHELMED IN DEPTHS OF WOE.

(Sævo dolorum turbine.)

From the Latin, by Edward Caswall ("Lyra Catholica," 1848.)

O'ERWHELMED in depths of woe,
   Upon the tree of scorn,
Hangs the Redeemer of mankind,
   With wracking anguish torn.

See! how the nails those hands
   And feet so tender rend!
See! down His face, and neck, and breast,
   His sacred blood descend.

Hark! with what awful cry
   His spirit takes its flight;
That cry,—it pierced His Mother's heart,
   And whelmed her soul in night.

Earth hears, and to its base
   Rocks wildly to and fro;
Tombs burst; seas, rivers, mountains quake;
   The veil is rent in two.

The sun withdraws his light;
The midday heavens grow pale;
The moon, the stars, the universe,
  Their Maker's death bewail.

Shall man alone be mute?
Come, youth and hoary hairs!
Come, rich and poor! come, all mankind!
  And bathe those feet in tears.

Come! fall before His Cross,
Who shed for us His blood;
Who died the victim of pure love,
  To make us sons of God.

Jesu, all praise to Thee,
Our joy and endless rest!
Be Thou our guide while pilgrims here,
  Our crown amid the blest.

AT THE CROSS HER STATION KEEPING.

(Stabat Mater Dolorosa.)

FROM the Latin of JACOPÔNE or JACOBUS DE BENEDICTIS, a Franciscan monk (d. 1306). The "Stabat Mater," as it is familiarly called, or, better, the "Mater Dolorosa," Mary by the Cross of Calvary (to distinguish it from its recently discovered companion-hymn, the "Mater Speciosa," or Mary by the cradle of Bethlehem). It is the most pathetic, as the "Dies Iræ" is the most sublime, hymn of the middle ages, and occupies the second rank in Latin hymnology. Suggested by the incident related by St. John xix. 25 ("Stabat juxta crucem mater ejus"), and the prophecy of Simeon, Luke ii. 35, it describes, with overpowering effect, the piercing agony of Mary at the cross, and the burning desire to be identified with her, by sympathy, in the intensity of her grief. It furnished the text for some of the noblest musical compositions of Palestrina, Pergolesi, Haydn, Rossini, and others. Unfortunately, like the "Mater Speciosa," it is disfigured by Mariolatry. The objectionable stanzas, which contain a prayer to Mary, have been here omitted. For the original, in ten stanzas, see WACKERNAGEL, I. 136, 162; MONE, II. 147-154; DANIEL, II. 133. Many German, and several English translations (by Lord Lindsay, Caswall, Coles, Benedict, &c.). The soft, sad melody of its verse is untranslatable. Comp. LISCO, "Stabat Mater," Berlin, 1843 (with fifty-three German, and several Dutch, translations); OZANAM, "Les Poëtes Franciscains en Italie au troisième siècle," Paris,

1852; and my article on the two "Stabat Maters" in the "Hours at Home" for May, 1867, pp. 50-58. The best *Protestant* companion-hymn of the "Stabat Mater" is Mrs. H. BEECHER STOWE's "O wondrous mother!" but too long for this collection.

AT the cross her station keeping,
Stood the mournful Mother weeping,
 Where He hung, her Son and Lord;
For her soul, of joy bereavèd,
Bowed with anguish, deeply grievèd,
 Felt the sharp and piercing sword.

Oh, how sad and sore distressèd
Now was she, that Mother blessèd
 Of the sole-begotten One;
Deep the woe of her affliction
When she saw the Crucifixion [1]
 Of her ever-glorious Son.

Who, on Christ's dear Mother gazing,
Pierced by anguish so amazing,
 Born of woman, would not weep?
Who, on Christ's dear Mother thinking,
Such a cup of sorrow drinking,
 Would not share her sorrows deep?

For His people's sins chastisèd
She beheld her Son despisèd,
 Scourged, and crowned with thorns entwined;
Saw Him then from judgment taken,
And in death by all forsaken,
 Till His Spirit He resigned.

. . . .

Jesu, may such deep devotion
Stir in me the same emotion,
 Fount of love, Redeemer kind!

---

[1] It is difficult to render the musical quadruplication of the double rhymes in the Latin :—

  Quæ mœrebat et dolebat,
  Et tremebat, cum videbat.
  "Who stood grieving, sighs upheaving,
  Spirit-reaving, bosom-cleaving;"

or (as Dr. COLES has it) :—

  "Trembling, grieving, bosom-heaving;
  While perceiving, scarce believing," &c.

That my heart, fresh ardour gaining,
And a purer love attaining,
   May with Thee acceptance find.

WHAT LAWS, MY BLESSED SAVIOUR?

(Herzliebster Jesu, was hast Du verbrochen?)

JOHANN HEERMANN, 1630 (SCHAFF'S "G. H. B." No. 108). Translated by F. E. COX, 1841. Based upon the seventh Meditation of St. AUGUSTINE (d. 430). Comp. Mark xv. 14, "What evil hath He done?" and Isa. liii. 5, "He was wounded for our transgressions, He was bruised for our iniquities." Another excellent translation, by C. WINKWORTH, "Alas! dear Lord, what evil hast Thou done?" ("Lyra Germ." I. p. 77).

WHAT laws, my blessed Saviour, hast Thou broken,
That so severe a sentence should be spoken?
How hast Thou 'gainst Thy Father's will contended,
   In what offended?

With scourges, blows, and spitting, they reviled Thee:
They crowned Thy brow with thorns, while King they styled Thee;
When, faint with pains, Thy tortured body suffered,
   Then gall they offered.

Say! wherefore thus by woes wast Thou surrounded?
Ah! Lord, for my transgressions Thou wast wounded:
God took the guilt from me, who should have paid it;
   On Thee He laid it.

How strange and marvellous was this correction!
Falls the good Shepherd in His sheep's protection;
The servants' debt behold the Master paying,
   For them obeying.

The righteous dies, who walked with God true-hearted:
The sinner lives, who has from God departed;
By man came death, yet man its fetters breaketh;
   God it o'ertaketh.

Shame and iniquity had whelmed me over:
From head to foot no good couldst Thou discover;
For this in hell should I, with deep lamenting,
    Be aye repenting.

But oh! the depth of love beyond comparing,
That brought Thee down from heaven, our burden bearing!
I taste all peace and joy that life can offer,
    Whilst Thou must suffer!

Eternal King! in power and love excelling,
Fain would my heart and mouth Thy praise be telling;
But how can man's weak powers at all come nigh Thee,
    How magnify Thee?

Such wondrous love would baffle my endeavour
To find its equal, should I strive for ever:
How should my works, could I in all obey Thee,
    Ever repay Thee!

Yet this shall please Thee, if devoutly trying
To keep Thy Laws, mine own wrong will denying,
I watch my heart, lest sin again ensnare it
    And from Thee tear it.

But since I have not strength to flee temptation,
To crucify each sinful inclination,
Oh! let Thy Spirit, grace, and strength provide me,
    And gently guide me.

Then shall I see Thy grace, and duly prize it,
For Thee renounce the world, for Thee despise it;
Then of my life Thy laws shall be the measure,
    Thy will my pleasure.

For Thee, my God, I'll bear all griefs and losses:
No persecution, no disgrace or crosses,
No pains of death or tortures e'er shall move me,
    Howe'er they prove me.

This, though at little value Thou dost set it,
Yet Thou, O gracious Lord! wilt not forget it;
E'en this Thou wilt accept with grace and favour,
    My blessed Saviour.

And when, O Christ! before Thy throne so glorious,
Upon my head is placed the crown victorious,
Thy praise I will, while heaven's full choir is ringing,
    Be ever singing.

O WORLD! BEHOLD UPON THE TREE.

(O Welt, sieh hier dein Leben.)

From the German of Paul Gerhardt (1653), by C. Winkworth ("Lyra Germ." II. p. 52; Schaff, No. 113).

WORLD! behold upon the tree
  Thy Life is hanging now for thee,
    Thy Saviour yields His dying breath;
The mighty Prince of glory now
For thee doth unresisting bow
    To cruel stripes, to scorn and death.

Draw near, O world! and mark Him well;
Behold the drops of blood that tell
    How sore His conflict with the foe:
And hark! how from that noble heart
Sigh after sigh doth slowly start,
    From depths of yet unfathomed woe.

Alas! my Saviour, who could dare
Bid Thee such bitter anguish bear,
    What evil heart entreat Thee thus?
For Thou art good, hast wrongèd none,
As we and ours too oft have done:
    Thou hast not sinned, dear Lord, like us.

I and my sins, that number more
Than yonder sands upon the shore,
    Have brought to pass this agony.
'Tis I have caused the floods of woe
That now Thy dying soul o'erflow,
    And those sad hearts that watch by Thee.

'Tis I to whom these pains belong,
'Tis I should suffer for my wrong,
    Bound hand and foot in heavy chains;

O WORLD, BEHOLD UPON THE TREE.

Thy scourge, Thy fetters, whatsoe'er
Thou bearest, 'tis my soul should bear,
   For she hath well deserved such pains.

Yet Thou dost even for my sake
On Thee, in love, the burdens take,
   That weighed my spirit to the ground.
Yes: Thou art made a curse for me,
That I might yet be blest through Thee:
   My healing in Thy wounds is found.

To save me from the monster's power,
The Death that all things would devour,
   Thyself into his jaws dost leap:
My death Thou takest thus away,
And buriest in Thy grave for aye;
   O love most strangely true and deep!

From henceforth there is nought of mine
But I would seek to make it Thine,
   Since all myself to Thee I owe.
Whate'er my utmost powers can do,
To Thee to render service true,
   Here at Thy feet I lay it low.

Ah! little have I, Lord, to give,
So poor, so base the life I live;
   But yet, till soul and body part,
This one thing I will do for Thee,—
The woe, the death endured for me,
   I'll cherish in my inmost heart,

Thy cross shall be before my sight,
My hope, my joy by day and night,
   Whate'er I do, where'er I rove;
And, gazing, I will gather thence
The form of spotless innocence,
   The seal of faultless truth and love.

And from Thy sorrows will I learn
How fiercely doth God's anger burn,
   How terribly His thunders roll;
How sorely this our loving God
Can smite with His avenging rod,
   How deep His floods o'erwhelm the soul.

And I will study to adorn
My heart with meekness under scorn,
    With gentle patience in distress ;
With faithful love that yearning cleaves
To those o'er whom to death it grieves,
    Whose sins its very soul oppress,

When evil tongues with stinging blame
Would cast dishonour on my name,
    I'll curb the passions that upstart ;
And take injustice patiently,
And pardon, as Thou pardon'st me,
    With an ungrudging generous heart.

And I will nail me to Thy cross,
And learn to count all things but dross
    Wherein the flesh doth pleasure take :
Whate'er is hateful in Thine eyes,
With all the strength that in me lies,
    Will I cast from me and forsake.

Thy heavy groans, Thy bitter sighs,
The tears that from Thy dying eyes
    Were shed when Thou wast sore oppressed,
Shall be with me, when at the last
Myself on Thee I wholly cast,
    And enter with Thee into rest.

O SACRED HEAD! NOW WOUNDED.

(O Haupt voll Blut und Wunden.)

By Paul Gerhardt, 1656 (Schaff, No. 109), on the basis of St. Bernard's "Salve, caput cruentatum," 1153 (Daniel, I. 232; Wackernagel, I. 124, in five stanzas, of ten lines each ; comp. the version on p. 162). Both the Latin of the Catholic monk and the German of the Lutheran pastor are conceived in the spirit of deep repentance, and glowing gratitude to Christ, who "was wounded for our transgressions, and bruised for our iniquities." Faithfully reproduced by Dr. James W. Alexander, a Presbyterian clergyman of New York (d. 1859), for Schaff's "Kirchenfreund," 1849, and since introduced, with abridgments and changes, into several American hymnbooks.—This classical hymn has shown an imperishable vitality in passing from the Latin into the German, and from the German into the English, and proclaiming in three tongues, and in the name of three confessions,—the

O SACRED HEAD, NOW WOUNDED.

Catholic, the Lutheran, and the Reformed,—with equal effect, the dying love of our Saviour, and our boundless indebtedness to him. Other English versions in Moravian and Methodist H. Bs. ("O head so full of bruises!"), by C. WINKWORTH, ("O wounded Head! must Thou endure?") and by MASSIE ("Hymns Ancient and Modern," No. 97).

SACRED head! now wounded,
 With grief and shame weighed down,
Now scornfully surrounded
 With thorns, Thy only crown;
O sacred Head! what glory,
 What bliss, till now was Thine!
Yet, though despised and gory,
 I joy to call Thee mine.

O noblest brow, and dearest!
 In other days the world
All feared when Thou appearedst:
 What shame on Thee is hurled!
How art Thou pale with anguish,
 With sore abuse and scorn;
How does that visage languish,
 Which once was bright as morn!

The blushes late residing
 Upon that holy cheek,
The roses once abiding
 Upon those lips so meek,
Alas! they have departed;
 Wan Death has rifled all!
For weak and broken-hearted,
 I see Thy body fall.

What Thou, my Lord, hast suffered,
 Was all for sinners' gain:
Mine, mine, was the transgression,
 But Thine the deadly pain.
Lo! here I fall, my Saviour:
 'Tis I deserve Thy place;
Look on me with Thy favour,
 Vouchsafe to me Thy grace,

Receive me, my Redeemer:
 My Shepherd, make me Thine;
Of every good the fountain,
 Thou art the spring of mine.

THE PASSION.

Thy lips with love distilling,
    And milk of truth sincere,
With heaven's bliss are filling
    The soul that trembles here.

Beside Thee, Lord, I've taken
    My place—forbid me not!
Hence will I ne'er be shaken,
    Though Thou to death be brought.
If pain's last paleness hold Thee,
    In agony opprest,
Then, then, will I enfold Thee
    Within this arm and breast!

The joy can ne'er be spoken,
    Above all joys beside,
When in Thy body broken
    I thus with safety hide.
My Lord of Life, desiring
    Thy glory now to see,
Beside the cross expiring,
    I'd breathe my soul to Thee.

What language shall I borrow
    To thank Thee, dearest Friend,
For this, Thy dying sorrow,
    Thy pity without end!
O make me Thine for ever;
    And should I fainting be,
Lord, let me never, never
    Outlive my love to Thee.

And when I am departing,
    O part not Thou from me!
When mortal pangs are darting,
    Come, Lord, and set me free!
And when my heart must languish
    Amidst the final throe,
Release me from mine anguish
    By Thine own pain and woe![1]

---

[1] This verse, which is admirably rendered from the German,—

Be near me when I'm dying,
   Oh! show Thy cross to me;
And for my succour flying,
   Come, Lord, and set me free!
These eyes new faith receiving
   From Jesus shall not move;
For he, who dies believing,
   Dies safely through Thy love.

O SACRED HEAD, SURROUNDED.

(O Haupt voll Blut und Wunden)

ANOTHER version of GERHARDT's hymn, abridged. From "Hymns Ancient and Modern," No. 97.

SACRED Head, surrounded
   By crown of piercing thorn!
O bleeding Head, so wounded,
   Reviled, and put to scorn!
Death's pallid hue comes o'er Thee,
   The glow of life decays,
Yet angel-hosts adore thee,
   And tremble as they gaze.

I see Thy strength and vigour
   All fading in the strife,
And death with cruel rigour
   Bereaving Thee of life;
O agony and dying!
   O love to sinners free!
Jesu, all grace supplying,
   O turn Thy face on me!

" Wann ich einmal soll scheiden
So scheide nicht von mir," &c.,—

is a gem, and well worthy to be the last *suspirium* of a dying Christian. In several American collections it is arbitrarily changed or omitted altogether. The sainted Dr. Alexander, in transmitting to me his translation from Princeton, in 1849, gave me a touching account of a poor German labourer who, on his death-bed in a foreign land, found his last strength and comfort in this verse, which he had committed to memory, in early youth, in his fatherland.

In this Thy bitter passion,
  Good Shepherd, think of me,
With Thy most sweet compassion,
  Unworthy though I be:
Beneath Thy Cross abiding,
  For ever would I rest;
In Thy dear love confiding,
  And with Thy presence blest.

CHRIST, THE LIFE OF ALL THE LIVING.

(Jesu, meines Lebens Leben.)

FROM the German of ERNST CHRISTOPH HOMBURG, 1659: "Jesu, meines Lebens Leben, Jesu, meines Todes Tod" (SCHAFF, No. 122; "Choral Book for England," 1862.)

CHRIST, the Life of all the living,
  Christ, the Death of death, our foe,
Who Thyself for me once giving
  To the darkest depths of woe,
Patiently didst yield Thy breath
But to save my soul from death;
Thousand, thousand thanks shall be,
Blessed Jesus, unto Thee.

Thou, ah, Thou, hast taken on Thee
  Bitter strokes, a cruel rod;
Pain and scorn were heaped upon Thee,
  O Thou sinless Son of God!
Only thus for me to win
Rescue from the bonds of sin;
Thousand, thousand thanks shall be,
Blessed Jesus, unto Thee.

Thou didst bear the smiting only
  That it might not fall on me;
Stoodest falsely charged and lonely,
  That I might be safe and free;
Comfortless, that I might know
Comfort from Thy boundless woe;
Thousand, thousand thanks shall be
Blessed Jesus, unto Thee.

Then for all that wrought our pardon,
  For Thy sorrows deep and sore,
For Thine anguish in the garden,
  I will thank Thee evermore;
  Thank Thee with my latest breath
  For Thy sad and cruel death;
  For that last and bitter cry,
  Praise Thee evermore on high.

THOU HOLIEST LOVE, WHOM MOST I LOVE.

(O Du Liebe meiner Liebe.)

FROM the German by an anonymous author, first published in FREYLING-
HAUSEN'S "Gesangbuch," Halle, 1704 (SCHAFF, No. 124). Translated by
CATHERINE WINKWORTH (who, with many others, erroneously attributes this
hymn to Angelus Silesius).

THOU Holiest Love, whom most I love,
  Who art my longed-for only bliss,
Whom tenderest pity erst did move
  To fathom woe and death's abyss;
Thou who didst suffer for my good,
  And die my guilty debts to pay,
Thou Lamb of God, whose precious blood
  Can take a world's misdeeds away!

Thou who didst bear the agony
  That made e'en Thy strong spirit quail,
Yet ever yearnest still for me
  With longing love that ne'er shall fail,—
'Twas Thou wast willing, Thou alone,
  To bear the righteous wrath of God;
Thy death hath stilled it, else had none
  Found shelter from its awful load.

O Love! who with unflinching heart
  Didst bear all worst disgrace and shame;
O Love! who 'mid the keenest smart
  Of dying pangs wert still the same;

Who didst Thy changeless virtue prove
   E'en with Thy latest parting breath,
And spakest words of gentlest love
   When soul and body sank in death!

O Love! through sorrows manifold
   Hast Thou betrothed me as a bride,
By ceaseless gifts, by love untold,
   Hast bound me ever to Thy side.
Oh, let the weary ache, the smart,
   Of life's long tale of pain and loss,
Be gently stilled within my heart
   At thought of Thee and of Thy cross!

O Love! who gav'st Thy life for me,
   And won an everlasting good
Through Thy sore anguish on the tree,
   I ever think upon Thy blood;
I ever thank Thy sacred wounds,
   Thou wounded Love, Thou Holiest!
But most when life is near its bounds,
   And in Thy bosom safe I rest.

O Love! who unto death hast grieved
   For this cold heart, unworthy Thine,
Whom the cold grave and death received,
   I thank Thee for that grief divine.
I give Thee thanks that Thou didst die
   To win eternal life for me,
To bring salvation from on high:
   Oh, draw me up through love to Thee!

WHEN I SURVEY THE WONDROUS CROSS.

Dr. Isaac Watts, 1709. Glorying in the cross. Gal. vi. 14. One of the noblest hymns in the English or any other language, and truly classical in expression. The fourth stanza is omitted in most hymn-books.

WHEN I survey the wondrous cross
   On which the Prince of glory died,
   My richest gain I count but loss,
And pour contempt on all my pride.

Forbid it, Lord, that I should boast,
   Save in the death of Christ, my God!
All the vain things that charm me most,
   I sacrifice them to His blood.

See, from His head, His hands, His feet,
   Sorrow and love flow mingled down!
Did e'er such love and sorrow meet?
   Or thorns compose so rich a crown?

His dying crimson, like a robe,
   Spreads o'er His body on the tree;
Then am I dead to all the globe,
   And all the globe is dead to me.

Were the whole realm of nature mine,
   That were a present far too small;
Love so amazing, so divine,
   Demands my soul, my life, my all.

NOT ALL THE BLOOD OF BEASTS.

Dr. Isaac Watts (d. 1748). "Faith in Christ our sacrifice."

NOT all the blood of beasts
   On Jewish altars slain,
Could give the guilty conscience peace,
   Or wash away the stain.

But Christ, the heavenly Lamb,
   Takes all our sins away,
A sacrifice of nobler name,
   And richer blood, than they.

My faith would lay her hand
   On that dear head of Thine,
While like a penitent I stand,
   And there confess my sin.

My soul looks back to see
   The burdens Thou didst bear
When hanging on the cursèd tree,
   And hopes her guilt was there.

Believing, we rejoice
   To see the curse remove;
We bless the Lamb with cheerful voice,
   And sing His bleeding love.

O LOVE, TOO BOUNDLESS TO BE SHOWN.

SELECTED from a long poem of Bishop KEN on 1 Cor. xv. 3, for Eleventh Sunday after Trinity, commencing:

    "When Adam sinned, and all his line
    Lost the similitude divine."

Bishop KEN, the author of the celebrated L. M. doxology: "Praise God, from whom all blessings flow" (the true English Te Deum), which closes his three Morning, Evening, and Midnight Hymns, composed also during his declining years poems for every Sunday and festival of the Christian Year, and anticipated Keble's great work. They were first published posthumously in 1721, but were almost forgotten till they were revived in a new edition, London, 1867.

LOVE, too boundless to be shown
By any but great God alone!
O Love offended, which sustains
The bold offender's curse and pains!
O Love which could no motive have,
But mere benignity to save.

O sacrifice from blemish free,
Worthy the God of Purity!

O LOVE, TOO BOUNDLESS TO BE SHOWN.   151

O sacrifice, like God, immense,
Atoning by equivalence!
O sacrifice too dear to fail
With God Paternal to prevail!

O Love, which at the Throne remains,
Which all inflammatives contains,
Which gives to all a free access,
Compassion shows to all distress!
O Love, in which all joys conspire,
Which fill and terminate desire!

O sin, God's hatred for which, none
But filial God could God atone!
Past sins which grieve me, Lord, forgive,
Thy priest and sacrifice I'll live,
Till I, like Thee, in Heaven above
Re-offer and complete my love.

HIM ON YONDER CROSS I LOVE.

FROM the German of J. E. GREDING, 1723, by CATHERINE WINKWORTH, II. 57. The German begins with the beautiful lines :—

"Der am Kreuz ist meine Liebe,
Und sonst nichts auf dieser Welt!
O dass Er's doch ewig bliebe,
Der mir jetzt so wohl gefällt!"

It is not to be confounded with a similar hymn of JOHN MENTZER (1670) :—

"Der am Kreuz ist meine Liebe,
Meine Lieb' ist Jesus Christ!
Weg, ihr argen Seelendiebe,
Satan, Welt und Fleischeslist!"

Both in SCHAFF's "G. H. B.," Nos. 125 and 126.

HIM on yonder cross I love;
    Nought on earth I else count dear!
    May He mine for ever prove,
  Who is now so inly near!
Here I stand: whate'er may come,
Days of sunshine or of gloom,
From this word I will not move:
Him upon the cross I love!

THE PASSION.

'Tis not hidden from my heart,
    What true love must often bring;
Want and grief have sorest smart,
    Care and scorn can sharply sting;
Nay, but if Thy will were such,
Bitterest death were not too much!
Dark though here my course may prove,
Him upon the cross I love!

Rather sorrows such as these,
    Rather love's acutest pain,
Than without Him days of ease,
    Riches false and honours vain.
Count me strange, when I am true,
What He hates I will not do;
Sneers no more my heart can move:
Him upon the cross I love!

Know ye whence my strength is drawn,
    Fearless thus the fight to wage?
Why my heart can laugh to scorn
    Fleshly weakness, Satan's rage?
'Tis, I know, the love of Christ:
Mighty is that love unpriced!
What can grieve me, what can move?
Him upon the cross I love!

Once the eyes that now are dim,
    Shall discern the changeless love
That hath led us home to Him,
    That hath crowned us far above:
Would to God that all below
What that love is now might know!
And their hearts this word approve:
Him upon the cross I love!

JESUS, THY BLOOD AND RIGHTEOUSNESS.

(Christi Blut und Gerechtigkeit.)

COUNT NIC. LUDWIG VON ZINZENDORF, 1739. Originally thirty stanzas (complete in A. KNAPP's edition of Zinzendorf's " Spiritual Songs," Stuttgart, 1845, p. 135; abridged in SCHAFF's " G. H. B.," No. 291). Freely reproduced by JOHN WESLEY, 1740, who drew his poetic inspiration mostly from Moravian hymns and from Tersteegen.

JESUS, Thy Blood and Righteousness
My beauty are, my glorious dress;
'Midst flaming worlds, in these arrayed,
With joy shall I lift up my head.[1]

Bold shall I stand in Thy great day,
For who aught to my charge shall lay?
Fully absolved through these I am,
From sin and fear, from guilt and shame.

The holy, meek, unspotted Lamb,
Who from the Father's bosom came,
Who died for me, e'en me to atone,
Now for my Lord and God I own.

Lord, I believe Thy precious blood,
Which at the mercy-seat of God
For ever doth for sinners plead,
For me—e'en for my soul—was shed.

Lord, I believe were sinners more
Than sands upon the ocean shore,
Thou hast for all a ransom paid,
For all a full atonement made.

When from the dust of death I rise
To claim my mansion in the skies,
E'en then, this shall be all my plea:
Jesus hath lived, hath died for me.

---

[1] The first stanza—which is literally borrowed from an older German hymn of P. Eber (1569)—is very popular among German Christians, and often quoted at death-beds:—

" Christi Blut und Gerechtigkeit:
Das ist mein Schmuck und Ehrenkleid;
Damit werd ich vor Gott bestehn,
Wann ich zum Himmel werd eingehn."

THE PASSION.

Thus Abraham, the Friend of God,
Thus all heaven's armies bought with blood,
Saviour of sinners, Thee proclaim;
Sinners of whom the chief I am.

Jesus, be endless praise to Thee,
Whose boundless mercy hath for me,
For me, and all Thy hands have made,
An everlasting ransom paid.

Ah! give to all Thy servants, Lord,
With power to speak Thy gracious word;
That all who to Thy wounds will flee,
May find eternal life in Thee.

Thou, God of power, Thou, God of love,
Let the whole world Thy mercy prove!
Now let Thy word o'er all prevail;
Now take the spoils of death and hell.

SWEET THE MOMENTS, RICH IN BLESSING.

REV. WALTER SHIRLEY, 1725-1786. This hymn first appeared, 1774, in Lady Huntingdon's Hymn-Book, which he revised. It is an older hymn of Rev. JAMES ALLEN, popularized. It found its way, with two or three other Protestant hymns, into the "Lyra Catholica" (under the heading "Sub Cruce Christi"). Much altered in the Andover and other hymn-books.

SWEET the moments, rich in blessing,
 Which before the cross I spend;
Life and health and peace possessing,
 From the sinner's dying Friend.
Here I'll sit, for ever viewing
 Mercy's streams in streams of blood
Precious drops, my soul bedewing,
 Plead and claim my peace with God.

Truly blessed is this station,
 Low before His cross to lie;
While I see Divine compassion
 Floating in His languid eye.

Here it is I find my heaven,
   While upon the Lamb I gaze ;
Love I much ? I'm much forgiven,—
   I'm a miracle of grace.

Love and grief my heart dividing,
   With my tears His feet I'll bathe ;
Constant still, in faith abiding,
   Life deriving from His death.
May I still enjoy this feeling,
   In all need to Jesus go ;
Prove His wounds each day more healing,
   And Himself most deeply know !

SURELY CHRIST THY GRIEFS HAS BORNE.

Rev. Aug. M. Toplady (d. 1776). Isa. liii. 4, 5, 12.

SURELY Christ thy griefs has borne ;
   Weeping soul, no longer mourn :
   View Him bleeding on the tree,
Pouring out His life for thee ;
There thy every sin He bore ;
Weeping soul, lament no more.

All thy crimes on Him were laid :
See, upon His blameless head
Wrath its utmost vengeance pours,
Due to my offence and yours ;
Wounded in our stead He is,
Bruised for our iniquities.

Weary sinner, keep thine eyes
   On th' atoning sacrifice ;
There th' incarnate Deity,
Numbered with transgressors, see ;
There, his Father's absence mourns,
Nailed and bruised, and crowned with thorns.

See thy God His head bow down,
Hear the Man of Sorrows groan !

For thy ransom there condemned,
Stripped, derided, and blasphemed;
Bleed the guiltless for th' unclean,
Made an offering for thy sin.

Cast thy guilty soul on Him,
Find him mighty to redeem;
At His feet thy burden lay,
Look thy doubts and cares away;
Now by faith the Son embrace,
Plead His promise, trust His grace.

Lord, Thine arm must be revealed,
Ere I can by faith be healed;
Since I scarce can look to Thee,
Cast a gracious eye on me:
At thy feet myself I lay;
Shine, O shine, my fears away!

THERE IS A FOUNTAIN FILLED WITH BLOOD.

WILLIAM COWPER (1731-1800). "Olney Hymns," 1779, Book I. No. 79: "Praise, for the Fountain opened." Zech. xiii. 1. This hymn, drawn from the fountain of atoning blood, "opened to the house of David and to the inhabitants of Jerusalem, for sin and for uncleanness," is itself a fountain of comfort and peace. The last two stanzas are omitted in most hymn-books.

THERE is a fountain filled with blood
    Drawn from Immanuel's veins,
And sinners plunged beneath that flood
    Lose all their guilty stains.

The dying thief rejoiced to see
    That fountain in his day;
And there have I, as vile as he,
    Washed all my sins away.

Dear dying Lamb, Thy precious blood
    Shall never lose its power,
Till all the ransomed church of God
    Be saved, to sin no more.

E'er since, by faith, I saw the stream
  Thy flowing wounds supply,
Redeeming love has been my theme,
  And shall be till I die.

Then, in a nobler, sweeter song,
  I'll sing thy power to save,
When this poor lisping, stammering tongue
  Lies silent in the grave.

Lord, I believe Thou hast prepared
  (Unworthy though I be)
For me a blood-bought, free reward,
  A golden harp for me!

'Tis strung and tuned for endless years,
  And formed by power divine,
To sound in God the Father's ears
  No other name but Thine.

HARK! THE VOICE OF LOVE AND MERCY.

"FINISHED Redemption." By the Rev. JONATHAN EVANS (1749-1799). First published in Ripon's Selection, 1787. The authorship of this hymn is not quite certain. See the note in ROGERS's "Lyra Brit." p. 677.

HARK! the voice of love and mercy
  Sounds aloud from Calvary;
See! it rends the rocks asunder,
  Shakes the earth, and veils the sky:
    "It is finished!"
  Hear the dying Saviour cry.

"It is finished!" O what pleasure
  Do these charming words afford
Heavenly blessings, without measure,
  Flow to us from Christ, the Lord:
    "It is finished!"
  Saints, the dying words record.

Finished all the types and shadows
    Of the ceremonial law;
Finished all that God had promised,
    Death and hell no more shall awe:
        " It is finished ! "
Saints, from hence your comfort draw.

Happy souls, approach the table,
    Taste the soul-reviving food;
Nothing half so sweet and pleasant
    As the Saviour's flesh and blood:
        " It is finished ! "
Christ has borne the heavy load.

Tune your harps anew, ye seraphs;
    Join to sing the pleasing theme;
All on earth, and all in heaven,
    Join to praise Immanuel's name !
        Hallelujah !
Glory to the bleeding Lamb !

IN THE CROSS OF CHRIST I GLORY.

"THE Cross of Christ." By Sir JOHN BOWRING, LL.D., a distinguished diplomatist and colonial governor (b. 1792), author of several important works of travel and on politics; and of a volume of excellent hymns, published in 1825.

IN the Cross of Christ I glory,
    Towering o'er the wrecks of time;
All the light of sacred story
    Gathers round its head sublime.

When the woes of life o'ertake me,
    Hopes deceive, and fears annoy,
Never shall the cross forsake me;
    Lo ! it glows with peace and joy.

When the sun of bliss is beaming
    Light and love upon my way,
From the cross the radiance streaming,
    Adds more lustre to the day.

Bane and blessing, pain and pleasure,
   By the cross are sanctified:
Peace is there that knows no measure;
   Joys that through all time abide.

In the cross of Christ I glory,
   Towering o'er the wrecks of time;
All the light of sacred story
   Gathers round its head sublime.

WE SING THE PRAISE OF HIM WHO DIED.

Rev. Thomas Kelly, 1769-1855.

WE sing the praise of Him who died,
   Of Him who died upon the cross:
The sinner's hope let men deride;
   For this we count the world but loss.

Inscribed upon the cross we see
   The shining letters "God is love:"
He bears our sins upon the tree,
   He brings us mercy from above.

The cross, it takes our guilt away,
   It holds the fainting spirit up;
It cheers with hope the gloomy day,
   And sweetens every bitter cup.

It makes the coward spirit brave,
   And nerves the feeble arm for fight;
It takes its terror from the grave,
   And gilds the bed of death with light.

The balm of life, the cure of woe,
   The measure and the pledge of love,
The sinner's refuge here below,
   The angels' theme in heaven above.

COME TO CALVARY'S HOLY MOUNTAIN.

JAMES MONTGOMERY (born 1771; died at Sheffield, 1854). Zech. xiii. 1; "In that day, there shall be a Fountain opened." 1819.

COME to Calvary's holy mountain,
   Sinners ruined by the fall;
Here a pure and healing fountain
   Flows to you, to me, to all,
In a full, perpetual tide,
Opened when our Saviour died.

Come in poverty and meanness,
   Come defiled, without, within;
From infection and uncleanness,
   From the leprosy of sin,
Wash your robes, and make them white:
Ye shall walk with God in light.

Come, in sorrow and contrition,
   Wounded, impotent, and blind;
Here the guilty, free remission,
   Here the troubled, peace may find;
Health this fountain will restore,
He that drinks shall thirst no more.

He that drinks shall live for ever;
   'Tis a soul-renewing flood:
God is faithful,—God will never
   Break His covenant in blood;
Signed when our Redeemer died,
Sealed when He was glorified.

FLING OUT THE BANNER! LET IT FLOAT.

BISHOP G. W. DOANE, of New Jersey, U.S. Died at Burlington, New Jersey, 1859.

FLING out the Banner! let it float
   Skyward and seaward, high and wide;
The sun, that lights its shining folds,
   The Cross, on which the Saviour died.

Fling out the Banner! Angels bend,
  In anxious silence o'er the sign;
And vainly seek to comprehend
  The wonder of the love divine.

Fling out the Banner! Heathen lands
  Shall see, from far, the glorious sight;
And nations, crowding to be born,
  Baptize their spirits in its light.

Fling out the Banner! Sin-sick souls,
  That sink and perish in the strife,
Shall touch in faith its radiant hem,
  And spring immortal into life.

Fling out the Banner! Let it float
  Skyward and seaward, high and wide;
Our glory, only in the Cross,
  Our only hope, the Crucified.

Fling out the Banner! Wide and high,
  Seaward and skyward, let it shine :
Nor skill, nor might, nor merit, ours;
  We conquer only in that sign.

WHEREFORE WEEP WE OVER JESUS?

(*Weint nicht über Jesu Schmerzen.*)

BY the Rev. PHILIP SPITTA, died 1859. Translated by RICHARD MASSIE, 1860. "Weep not for me, but weep for yourselves."—*Luke* xxiii. 28.

WHEREFORE weep we over Jesus,
  O'er His death and bitter smart?
Weep we rather that He sees us
  Unconvinced and hard of heart;
For His soul was never tainted
  With the smallest spot or stain :
'Twas for us He was acquainted
  With such depths of grief and pain.

THE PASSION.

Oh! what profits it with groaning
    Underneath His cross to stand;
Oh! what profits our bemoaning
    His pale brow and bleeding hand?
Wherefore gaze on Him expiring,
    Railed at, pierced, and crucified,
Whilst we think not of inquiring,
    Wherefore, and for whom He died?

If no sin could be discovered
    In the pure and spotless Lord.
If the cruel death He suffered
    Is sin's just and meet reward:
Then it must have been for others
    That the Lord on Calvary bled,
And the guilt have been a brother's,
    Which was laid upon His head.

And for whom hath He contended
    In a strife so strange and new?
And for whom to hell descended?
    Brothers! 'twas for me and you!
Now you see that He was reaping
    Punishment for us alone;
And we have great cause for weeping,
    Not for His guilt, but our own.

If we then make full confession
    Joined with penitence and prayer,
If we see our own transgression
    In the punishment He bare,
If we mourn with true repentance,
    We shall hear the Saviour say,
" Fear not: I have borne your sentence;
    Wipe your bitter tears away."

RIDE ON, RIDE ON IN MAJESTY.

CHRIST's final entrance into Jerusalem. John xii. 12-15. By the Very Rev. HENRY HART MILMAN, D.D.; b. London, 1791; since 1849, Dean of St. Paul's; author of " History of Latin Christianity," &c. His poetical works were published, 1839, in 3 vols. 12mo. He died Sept. 1868.

RIDE on, ride on in majesty!
In lowly pomp ride on to die:
O Christ! Thy triumphs now begin
O'er captive death and conquered sin.

Ride on, ride on in majesty!
The wingèd squadrons of the sky
Look down, with sad and wondering eyes,
To see th' approaching sacrifice.

Ride on, ride on in majesty!
Thy last and fiercest strife is nigh:
The Father, on His sapphire throne,
Expects his own anointed Son.

Ride on, ride on in majesty!
In lowly pomp ride on to die:
Bow Thy meek head to mortal pain;
Then take, O God, Thy power, and reign!

BOUND UPON THE ACCURSÈD TREE.

DR. HENRY HART MILMAN, Dean of St. Paul's, London; d. 1868.

BOUND upon th' accursèd tree,
Faint and bleeding, who is He?
By the eyes so pale and dim,
Streaming blood, and writhing limb;
By the flesh, with scourges torn;
By the crown of twisted thorn;
By the side so deeply pierced;
By the baffled, burning thirst;
By the drooping death-dewed brow:
Son of Man, 'tis Thou! 'tis Thou!

Bound upon th' accursèd tree,
Dread and awful, who is He?
By the sun at noon-day pale,
Shivering rocks, and rending veil;
By earth, that trembles at his doom;
By yonder saints who burst their tomb;
By Eden promised, ere He died,
To the felon at his side;
Lord, our suppliant knees we bow:
Son of God, 'tis Thou! 'tis Thou!

Bound upon th' accursèd tree,
Sad and dying, who is He?
By the last and bitter cry;
The ghost given up in agony;
By the lifeless body laid
In the chamber of the dead;
By the mourners come to weep
Where the bones of Jesus sleep;
Crucified! we know Thee now:
Son of Man, 'tis Thou! 'tis Thou!

Bound upon th' accursèd tree,
Dread and awful, who is He?
By the prayer for them that slew,—
"Lord, they know not what they do!"
By the spoiled and empty grave;
By the souls He died to save;
By the conquest He hath won;
By the saints before His throne;
By the rainbow round His brow:
Son of God, 'tis Thou! 'tis Thou!

ASK YE WHAT GREAT THING I KNOW.

REV. DR. BENJAMIN HALL KENNEDY, b. 1804; Rector of West Felton, England. Editor of "Hymnologia Christiana," London, 1863. *"Jesus Christ and Him crucified."*—1 *Cor.* ii.

ASK ye what great thing I know
That delights and stirs me so?
What the high reward I win?
Whose the name I glory in?
    Jesus Christ, the Crucified.

What is faith's foundation strong?
What awakes my lips to song?
He who bore my sinful load
Purchased for me peace with God,
    Jesus Christ, the Crucified.

Who is He that makes me wise
To discern where duty lies?
Who is He that makes me true,
Duty, when discerned, to do?
    Jesus Christ, the Crucified,

Who defeats my fiercest foes?
Who consoles my saddest woes?
Who revives my fainting heart,
Healing all its hidden smart?
    Jesus Christ, the Crucified.

Who is life in life to me?
Who the death of death will be?
Who will place me on His right,
With the countless hosts of light?
    Jesus Christ, the Crucified.

This is that great thing I know;
This delights and stirs me so:
Faith in Him who died to save,
Him who triumphed o'er the grave,—
    Jesus Christ, the Crucified.

OPPRESS'D WITH NOON-DAY'S SCORCHING HEAT.

"The Shadow of the Cross." By Horatius Bonar, D.D., "Hymns of Faith and Hope," First Series.

OPPRESSED with noon-day's scorching heat,
   To yonder cross I flee;
   Beneath its shelter take my seat;
No shade like this for me!

Beneath that cross clear waters burst,
   A fountain sparkling free;
And there I quench my desert thirst;
   No spring like this for me!

A stranger here, I pitch my tent
   Beneath this spreading tree;
Here shall my pilgrim life be spent;
   No home like this for me!

For burdened ones a resting-place,
   Beside that cross I see;
Here I cast off my weariness;
   No rest like this for me!

CLING TO THE CRUCIFIED.

"Abide in Him." Horatius Bonar, D.D.; b. Edinburgh, 1808.

   " Tecum volo vulnerari
   Te libenter amplexari
   In cruce desidero."
             Old Hymn.

CLING to the Crucified!
   His death is life to thee,—
   Life for eternity.
His pains thy pardon seal;
His stripes thy bruises heal;
His cross proclaims thy peace,

Bids every sorrow cease.
His blood is all to thee:
It purges thee from sin;
It sets thy spirit free;
It keeps thy conscience clean.
Cling to the Crucified!

Cling to the Crucified!
His is a heart of love,
Full as the hearts above;
Its depths of sympathy
Are all awake for thee:
His countenance is light,
Even to the darkest night.
That love shall never change;
That light shall ne'er grow dim:
Charge thou thy faithless heart
To find its all in Him.
Cling to the Crucified!

I LAY MY SINS ON JESUS.

HORATIUS BONAR, D.D. "The Substitute." From the First Series of his "Hymns of Faith and Hope."

> "Jesu, plena caritate
> Manus tuæ perforatæ
> Laxent mea crimina;
> Latus tuum lanceatum,
> Caput spinis coronatum,
> Hæc sint medicamina."
> *Old Hymn.*

I LAY my sins on Jesus,
  The spotless Lamb of God;
He bears them all, and frees us
  From the accursèd load.
I bring my guilt to Jesus,
  To wash my crimson stains
White in His blood most precious,
  Till not a stain remains.

I lay my wants on Jesus;
    All fulness dwells in Him:
He heals all my diseases,
    He doth my soul redeem.
I lay my griefs on Jesus,
    My burdens and my cares:
He from them all releases,
    He all my sorrows shares.

I rest my soul on Jesus,
    This weary soul of mine:
His right hand me embraces,
    I on his breast recline.
I love the name of Jesus,
    Immanuel, Christ, the Lord:
Like fragrance on the breezes,
    His name abroad is poured.

I long to be like Jesus,
    Meek, loving, lowly, mild:
I long to be like Jesus,
    The Father's holy Child.
I long to be with Jesus
    Amid the heavenly throng,
To sing with saints His praises,
    To learn the angels' song.

WOULDST THOU LEARN THE DEPTH OF SIN?

GETHSEMANE. By the Rev. JOHN S. B. MONSELL, LL.D., b. 1811, one of the Rural Deans in the see of Winchester, author of several volumes of sacred lyrics, which breathe the genuine fire of poetry and devout piety.

WOULDST thou learn the depth of sin,
    All its bitterness and pain?
What it cost thy God to win
    Sinners to Himself again?
Come, poor sinner, come with me;
Visit sad Gethsemane.

Wouldst thou know God's wondrous love?
Seek it not beside the throne;
List not angels' praise above,
But come and hear the heavy groan
By the Godhead heaved for thee,
Sinner, in Gethsemane.

When His tears and bloody sweat,
When His passion and His prayer,
When His pangs on Olivet,
Wake within thee thoughts of care,—
Remember, sinner, 'twas for thee
He suffered in Gethsemane!

Hate the sin that cost so dear;
Love the God that loved thee so;
Weep if thou wilt, but likewise fear
To bid that fountain freshly flow,
That gushed so freely once for thee
In sorrowful Gethsemane.

MY SINS, MY SINS, MY SAVIOUR!

JOHN S. B. MONSELL, LL.D, Vicar of Egham, Surrey. From his "Hymns of Love and Praise for the Church's Year," Lond. 1863. For Ash Wednesday. On Ps. xi. 15: "My sins have taken such hold upon me, that I am not able to look up; yea, they are more in number than the hairs of my head, and my heart hath failed me."

MY sins, my sins, my Saviour!
  They take such hold on me,
  I am not able to look up,
    Save only, Christ, to Thee:
  In Thee is all forgiveness,
    In Thee abundant grace,
  My shadow and my sunshine
    The brightness of Thy face.

My sins, my sins, my Saviour!
  How sad on Thee they fall!
Seen through Thy gentle patience,
  I tenfold feel them all.

I know they are forgiven;
  But still, their pain to me
Is all the grief and anguish
  They laid, my Lord, on Thee.

My sins, my sins, my Saviour!
  Their guilt I never knew,
Till, with Thee, in the desert
  I near Thy passion drew,—
Till, with Thee, in the garden
  I heard Thy pleading prayer,
And saw the sweat-drops bloody
  That told Thy sorrow there.

Therefore my songs, my Saviour!
  E'en in this time of woe,
Shall tell of all Thy goodness
  To suffering man below,—
Thy goodness and Thy favour,
  Whose presence from above,
Rejoice those hearts, my Saviour,
  That live in Thee, and love.

JESUS! GENTLE SUFFERER, SAY.

For Good Friday. By John S. B. Monsell, LL.D., Vicar of Egham, born 1811. From his "Hymns of Love and Praise," Lond. 1863, p. 82. The "Canterbury Hymnal" gives this hymn with abridgments and unnecessary changes ("Jesu, *mighty* Sufferer, say," &c.)

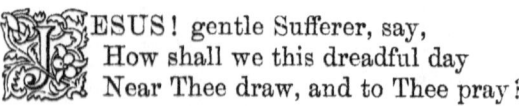

JESUS! gentle Sufferer, say,
  How shall we this dreadful day
  Near Thee draw, and to Thee pray?

We, whose proneness to forget
Thy dear love, on Olivet
Bathed Thy brow with bloody sweat;

We, whose sins, with awful power,
Like a cloud did o'er Thee lower,
In that God-excluding hour;

We, who still, in thought and deed,
Often hold the bitter reed
To Thee, in Thy time of need,—

Canst Thou pardon us, and pray,
As for those who on this day
Took Thy precious life away?

Yes! Thy blood is all my plea;
It was shed, and shed for me,
Therefore to Thy cross I flee.

At Thy feet, in dust and shame,
I dare breathe Thy holy name,
And a great salvation claim.

Save me, Jesus: stoop and take
Pity on my soul, and make
This day bright, for Thy dear sake.

THOU WHO DIDST HANG UPON A BARREN TREE.

"Long Barren." By Christina G. Rossetti, 1866 ("Poems," Boston ed., p. 245).

THOU who didst hang upon a barren tree,
    My God, for me;
Though I till now be barren, now at length,
    Lord, give me strength
To bring forth fruit to Thee.

Thou who didst bear for me the crown of thorn,
    Spitting and scorn;
Though I till now have put forth thorns, yet now
    Strengthen me Thou,
That better fruit be borne.

Thou Rose of Sharon, Cedar of broad roots,
    Vine of sweet fruits,
Thou Lily of the vale, with fadeless leaf,
    Of thousands Chief,
Feed Thou my feeble shoots.

O JESUS! SWEET THE TEARS I SHED.

"At the Cross." "I am crucified with Christ."—*Gal.* ii. 20. Rev. Dr. RAY PALMER; b. 1808, in the State of Rhode Island. From his "Hymns of my Holy Hours," New York, 1867. One of his best hymns.

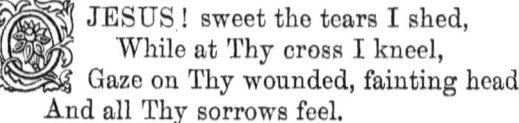 JESUS! sweet the tears I shed,
   While at Thy cross I kneel,
Gaze on Thy wounded, fainting head,
   And all Thy sorrows feel.

My heart dissolves to see Thee bleed,
   This heart so hard before;
I hear Thee for the guilty plead,
   And grief o'erflows the more.

'Twas for the sinful Thou didst die,
   And I a sinner stand:
What love speaks from Thy dying eye,
   And from each piercèd hand!

I know this cleansing blood of Thine
   Was shed, dear Lord, for me,—
For me, for all—O grace divine!—
   Who look by faith on Thee.

O Christ of God! O spotless Lamb!
   By love my soul is drawn;
Henceforth, for ever, Thine I am;
   Here life and peace are born.

In patient hope the cross I'll bear,
   Thine arm shall be my stay;
And Thou, enthroned, my soul shalt spare,
   On Thy great judgment-day.

WONDER OF WONDERS! ON THE CROSS.

"THE SACRIFICE." A sonnet, by Dr. RAY PALMER. From his "Hymns and Sacred Pieces," New York, 1865.

WONDER of wonders! On the cross He dies!
  Man of the ages, David's mighty Son,
  The Eternal Word, who spake and it was done,
What time, of old, He formed the earth and skies.

Abashed be all the wisdom of the wise!
  Let the wide earth through all her kingdoms know
  The promised Lamb of God, whose blood should flow,—
For human guilt the grand, sole sacrifice.

No more need altar smoke, nor victim bleed:
  'Tis finished!—the great mystery of love.
Ye sin-condemned, by this blood, 'tis decreed.
  Ye stand absolved: behold the curse remove!
O Christ! Thy deadly wounds, Thy mortal strife
Crush death and hell, and give immortal life!

O HEAD, SO FULL OF BRUISES!

"THE CRUCIFIXION." JOSEPH STAMMERS, born 1801, barrister in London. Contributed to ROGERS's "Lyr. Brit." 1867, p. 517.

O HEAD, so full of bruises!
  Brow, that its life-blood loses!
    Oh! great humility!
  Across His face are flying
  The shadows of the dying:
    'Twas suffered all for me!

O Back, by scourges ploughèd!
O Soul, by sorrow bowèd
    Upon the accursèd tree!
  He hears the bitter scorning;
  'Tis night, without a dawning:
    'Twas suffered all for me!

Eye, that in darkness sinketh!
Lip, that the red cup drinketh!
  Hands, bound to misery!
See, from His feet forth streameth
The fountain that redeemeth!
  'Twas suffered all for me!

And now He speaks: oh, hearken,
While clouds all nature darken!
  " Lama sabachthani?"
His head is bent, and droopeth!
To such a death He stoopeth!
  'Twas suffered all for me!

WHEN, WOUNDED SORE, THE STRICKEN SOUL.

"Touched with a feeling of our infirmities."—*Heb.* iv. 15. By Mrs. Cecil Frances Alexander. 1858. One of the best hymns of this gifted poetess.

WHEN, wounded sore, the stricken soul
  Lies bleeding and unbound,
One only hand, a piercèd hand,
  Can salve the sinner's wound.

When sorrow swells the laden breast,
  And tears of anguish flow,
One only heart, a broken heart,
  Can feel the sinner's woe.

When penitence has wept in vain
  Over some foul, dark spot,
One only stream, a stream of blood,
  Can wash away the blot.

'Tis Jesu's blood that washes white,
  His hand that brings relief;
His heart that's touched with all our joys,
  And feeleth for our grief.

Lift up Thy bleeding hand, O Lord!
  Unseal that cleansing tide:
We have no shelter from our sin
  But in Thy wounded side.

ARE THERE NO WOUNDS FOR *ME* ?

"Who loved me, and gave Himself for me."—*Gal.* ii. 20. By Mrs. Grace Webster Hinsdale, of Brooklyn, N. Y., April, 1868. Contributed to this Collection.

ARE there no wounds for *me* ?
  Hast Thou received them all ?
How can I, Lord, the anguish see,
  Beneath which Thou didst fall!

Shedding such tears for me!
  Sweating such drops of blood!
That by Thy stripes my soul might be
  Saved from the wrath of God!

'Tis over now, I know,—
  That suffering life of Thine;
Thy precious blood has ceased to flow,
  Thou wear'st Thy crown divine;

But yet, I weeping see
  The thorns which pierced Thy head;
Thou faint'st beneath Thy cross for me,
  For me to death Thou'rt led!

Stretched on the cruel tree,
  And fastened by my sin,—
Lord, at Thy cross, with shame, I see
  How guilty I have been.

Meekly, with love divine,
  Thy holy head is bent,
And streams of blood, for sins of mine,
  Flow where Thy side is rent.

Such grief did well atone
    For all our sinful race;
But yet, O Christ! for me alone
    The Father hid His face!

Oh, how this crimson tide
    O'erwhelms my soul with shame!
Within Thy bleeding wounds I hide:
    Wilt Thou, Lord, own my name?

Beneath this sacred flood
    I bow my sinful soul:
Dear Saviour, let Thy precious blood
    O'er my defilement roll.

THE BURIAL OF CHRIST.

EASTER EVE.

"AND when Joseph had taken the body, he wrapped it in a clean linen cloth, and laid it in his own new tomb, which he had hewn out in the rock: and he rolled a great stone to the door of the sepulchre, and departed. And there was Mary Magdalene and the other Mary, sitting over against the sepulchre."—*Matt.* xxvii. 59-61.

 LORD JESUS, who by Thy rest in the grave, and Thy descent into the world of departed spirits, hast sanctified the tomb, and opened the gate of paradise to all believers: grant unto us, we beseech Thee, that, being crucified with Thee to sin, we may rest in peace, and attain, with the whole army of the Redeemed, unto the glorious resurrection to life everlasting. Amen.

> COME and deck the grave with flowers,
>   That is now a blessed bed,
> Where the truest Friend of ours
>   Stooped to rest His Holy head;
> For the Saviour, in it lying,
>   Did its grief and gloom destroy,
> Took from death the dread of dying,
>   Gave to life its crown and joy.
>   JOHN S. B. MONSELL.

Pourrais-je craindre encore
　Le sommeil du tombeau ?
Le trépas est l'aurore
　D'un jour pur et nouveau.
Jésus rend l'existence
　Au mortel ranimé ;
Ravissante espérance
　Pour ceux qui l'ont aimé !

*Recueil de Psaumes et Cantiques, à l'usage
des églises réformées. Paris*, 1862.

THE BURIAL OF CHRIST.

EASTER EVE.

THE SEPULCHRE IS HOLDING.

TRANSLATED from the Latin. "The People's Hymnal," Lond. 1867. No. III.

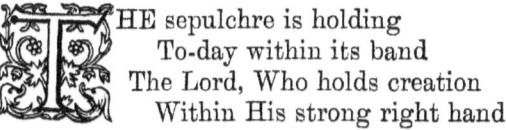HE sepulchre is holding
    To-day within its band
The Lord, Who holds creation
    Within His strong right hand.

To-day a stone is hiding
    From gaze of mortal eye
The Lord, whose glory hideth
    The brightness of the sky.

The Life of all is sleeping,
    But Hell is quaking sore;
And Adam bursts the fetters
    Which prisoned him before.

All praise to Thee, Lord Jesu,
    Whose Providence of love
Hath won for us, Thy people,
    The Sabbath rest above.

To Christ, the King of glory,
    Who in the tomb was laid,
To Father and to Spirit
    Eternal laud be paid.

REST OF THE WEARY!

(So ruhest Du, O meine Ruh'.)

SALOMON FRANK, 1716. Trsl. by Miss C. WINKWORTH,
"Lyra Germ.," I.

REST of the weary! Thou
    Thyself art resting now,
Where lowly in Thy sepulchre Thou liest.
    From out her deathly sleep,
    My soul doth start, to weep,
So sad a wonder, that Thou Saviour diest!

    Thy bitter anguish o'er,
    To this dark tomb they bore
Thee, Life of life,—Thee, Lord of all creation!
    The hollow rocky cave
    Must serve Thee for a grave,
Who wast Thyself the Rock of our Salvation!

    O Prince of Life! I know
    That when I, too, lie low,
Thou wilt at last my soul from death awaken;
    Wherefore I will not shrink
    From the grave's awful brink:
The heart that trusts in Thee shall ne'er be shaken.

    To me the darksome tomb
    Is but a narrow room,
Where I may rest in peace, from sorrow free.
    Thy death shall give me power
    To cry in that dark hour,
O Death, O Grave, where is your victory?

    The grave can nought destroy,
    Only the flesh can die;
And e'en the body triumphs o'er decay:
    Clothed by Thy wondrous might
    In robes of dazzling light,
This flesh shall burst the grave at that last Day.

My Jesus, day by day,
Help me to watch and pray,
Beside the tomb where in my heart Thou'rt laid:
Thy bitter death shall be
My constant memory,
My guide at last into Death's awful shade.

RESTING FROM HIS WORK TO-DAY.

FROM " Hymns Ancient and Modern," Lond. 1860, No. 105.

RESTING from His work to-day,
In the tomb the Saviour lay;
Still He slept, from head to feet
Shrouded in the winding-sheet,
Lying in the rock alone,
Hidden by the sealèd stone.

Late at even there was seen,
Watching long, the Magdalene;
Early, ere the break of day,
Sorrowful she took her way
To the holy garden glade,
Where her buried Lord was laid.

So with Thee, till life shall end,
I would solemn vigil spend;
Let me hew Thee, Lord, a shrine
In this rocky heart of mine,
Where, in pure embalmèd cell,
None but Thou may ever dwell.

Myrrh and spices will I bring,
True affection's offering;
Close the door from sight and sound
Of the busy world around;
And in patient watch remain
Till my Lord appear again.

REST, WEARY SON OF GOD.

Horatius Bonar. "Hymns of Faith and Hope," Third Series, 1868.

Rest, weary Son of God; and I, with Thee,
    Rest in that rest of Thine.
My weariness was Thine; Thou barest it,
    And now Thy rest is mine.

Rest, weary Son of God; we joy to think
    That all Thy toil is done.
No ache, no pang, no sigh for Thee again;
    Thy joy is now begun.

Thy life on earth was one sad weariness;
    Nowhere to lay Thy head.
Thy days were toil and heat; Thy lonely nights
    Sought some cold mountain bed.

How calmly in that tomb Thou liest now,
    Thy rest how still and deep!
O'er Thee in love the Father rests: He gives
    To His beloved sleep.

On Bethel-pillow now Thy head is laid,
    In Joseph's rock-hewn cell;
Thy watchers are the angels of Thy God:
    They guard Thy slumbers well.

With Thee Thy God and Father still abides,
    And Thou art not alone.
He in that still dark chamber is with Thee,
    The well-beloved Son.

Oh, silent, silent is Thy earthly tomb!
    The raging of Thy foes
Is ended all! nor Jew nor Roman now
    Can ruffle Thy repose.

Rest, weary Son of God: Thy work is done,
    And all Thy burdens borne;
Rest on that stone, till the third sun has brought
    Thine everlasting morn.

Then to a higher, brighter, truer rest,
    Upon the throne above,
Rise, weary Son of Man, to carry out
    Thy glorious work of love.

THE RESURRECTION.

"CHRIST is risen from the dead, and become the first-fruits of them that slept. For since by man came death, by man came also the resurrection of the dead. For as in Adam all die, even so in Christ shall all be made alive."
—1 *Cor.* xv. 20-22.

" If ye, then, be risen with Christ, seek those things which are above, where Christ sitteth on the right hand of God."—*Col.* iii. 1.

THOU Prince of Life and First-Begotten of the dead! who, by Thy glorious resurrection, hast overcome death, and opened unto us the gate of everlasting life: enable us, by Thy heavenly grace, to walk in newness of life, and to abound in the fruits of righteousness; so that we may at last triumph over death and the grave, and rise in Thy likeness, having our vile bodies changed into the fashion of Thine own glorious body, who art God over all, blessed for ever. Amen.

> STUPENDA lex mysterii,
> Novum genus prœlii:
> Ligatus nexos liberat,
> Mortuus vivificat,
> Dumque Vita perimitur,
> Mortis mors efficitur.
> PETER DAMIANI (DANIEL, I. 223).

YES,—the Easter-bells are ringing!
　Yes,—it is the Easter-day!
Hark,—their merry chimes are singing,
　In their sweet old-fashioned way!
　Listen,—for they seem to say,
In their ivied turret swinging,
　Hear, oh Earth, 'tis Easter-day!
A. C. COXE.

HEIL! Jesus Christus ist erstanden!
Aus den zerspreugten Todesbanden
　　Tritt siegverkläret Gottes Sohn.
Hoch durch des Himmels Tempelhallen
Hört man das Hallelujah schallen,
　　Und Friede glänzt um Gottes Thron.
Heil dem, der ewig liebt,
Der Allen Leben giebt,
　　Jesu Christo,
　　Und unserm Gott!
　　Des Todes Noth
Ist aufgelöst in Morgenroth!
ALBERT KNAPP.

THE RESURRECTION.

HAIL, DAY OF DAYS! IN PEALS OF PRAISE.

(*Salve, festa dies, toto venerabilis ævo.*)

FREE, from the Latin of VENANTIUS FORTUNATUS, Bishop of Poictiers, 600. In this sweet poem, the whole nature, born anew in the spring, and arrayed in the bridal garment of hope and promise, welcomes the risen Saviour, the Prince of spiritual and eternal life. The original (DANIEL, I. 170) has fourteen stanzas, of three lines each. TRENCH (p. 152) gives only ten lines. DANIEL remarks, "Ex hoc suavissimo poëmate ecclesia decem versus sibi vindicavit, qui efficerent canticum triumphale Paschatis." It passed also into several German forms, *e.g.*, "Sei gegrüsst, du heiliger Tag." The version here given is a very free transfusion, in a different measure. Another English version, more closely following the original, by Mrs. CHARLES :

"Hail, festal Day! ever exalted high;"

and one by Dr. NEALE :

"Hail, festal Day! for evermore adored."

HAIL, Day of days! in peals of praise
   Throughout all ages owned,
When Christ, our God, hell's empire trod,
   And high o'er heaven was throned.[1]

This glorious morn the world new-born
   In rising beauty shows;
How, with her Lord to life restored,
   Her gifts and graces rose!

---

[1] "Salve, festa dies, toto venerabilis ævo,
   Qua Deus infernum vicit et astra tenet.
Salve, festa dies, toto venerabilis ævo."

THE RESURRECTION.

The spring serene in sparkling sheen
    The flower-clad earth arrays,
Heaven's portal bright its radiant light
    In fuller flood displays.

The fiery sun in loftier noon,
    O'er heaven's high orbit shines,
As o'er the tide of waters wide
    He rises and declines.

From hell's deep gloom, from earth's dark tomb,
    The Lord in triumph soars;
The forests raise their leafy praise;
    The flowery field adores.

As star by star He mounts afar,
    And hell imprisoned lies,
Let stars and light, and depth and height
    In Hallelujahs rise.

Lo! He Who died, the Crucified,
    God over all He reigns;
On Him we call, His creatures all,
    Who heaven and earth sustains.

THE SUPPER OF THE LAMB TO SHARE.

(Ad cœnam Agni providi.)

AN old *hymnus paschalis*, which may have been sung, in the early Church, by the newly baptized catechumens, when, in their white robes, they first approached the Lord's table. DANIEL, I. 88, gives the original, and the altered form of the Roman Breviary ("Ad regias Agni dapes"). Trsl. in "Voice of Christian Life in Song," p. 103. Another version by NEALE:

    "The Lamb's high banquet we await."

THE Supper of the Lamb to share,
    We come in vesture white and fair;
The Red Sea crossed, our hymn we sing
To Christ, our Captain and our King.

His holy body on the cross,
Parched, on that altar hung for us;
And, drinking of His crimson blood,
We live upon the living God.

Protected in the Paschal night
From the destroying angel's might,
And by a powerful hand set free
From Pharaoh's bitter slavery.

For Christ our Passover is slain,
The Lamb is offered not in vain;
With truth's sincere unleavened bread,
His flesh He gave, His blood He shed.

O Victim, worthy Thou for ever,
Who didst the bands of hell dissever!
Redeem Thy captives from the foe,
The gift of life afresh bestow.

When Christ from out the tomb arose,
Victor o'er hell and all His foes,
The tyrant forth in chains He drew,
And planted Paradise anew.

Author of all, to Thee we pray,
In this our Easter joy to-day;
From every weapon death can wield
Thy trusting people ever shield.

WE KEEP THE FESTIVAL.

(Ad regias Agni dapes.)

FROM the Roman Breviary (Sabbato in Albis infra Octavam Paschæ). DANIEL, I. 88. Compare the preceding hymn and note. Reproduced (with a doxology added) by the Rev. Dr. A. R. THOMPSON, of the Dutch Reformed Church, New York, Easter, 1868. Contributed to this Collection.

WE keep the festival
   Of the slain Lamb our King.
     The Red Sea passed,
  And safe at last,
Our Leader's praise we sing.

His love ineffable
He pledged in precious blood;
  And Priest most high,
  The altar by,
Himself devoting, stood.

THE RESURRECTION.

The sacred crimson sign
The avenging angel knew;
   And the sea fled
   Back at Christ's tread,
And gave a pathway through.

Christ is our Passover!
And we will keep the feast
   With the new leaven,
   The bread of heaven:
All welcome, even the least!

O Heavenly Champion!
Death thought to vanquish Thee!
   But Death is slain;
   And thou again
Art risen, and we are free.

Hail, mighty Conqueror!
Under Thy glorious feet
   The tyrant lies,
   And gasps, and dies:
What praise for Thee is meet?

Forth from the gloomy prison,
Jesus, we follow Thee,
   With broken chain,
   With ended pain,
To life and liberty!

All glory be to Thee!
All worship to Thy name!
   Thee we adore,
   And evermore
Will celebrate Thy fame

THE CHURCH OF GOD LIFTS UP HER VOICE.

GREEK Paschal Hymn. From the offices of the Greek Church, by W. C. DIX.

THE Church of God lifts up her voice:
To-day both heaven and earth rejoice;
The gladsome Passover is here,
The Passover of Christ most dear.

The Passover that frees from woe,
That binds in chains the ancient foe,
That opens wide the heavenly gate,
The Lord's own day we celebrate.

From "very early" until night,
One strain we lift, one shout of might:
With Eucharist the morn arose,
With Hallelujahs day shall close.

O Christ, eternal Pascha, Thou,
And crown for every willing brow!
Thou spotless Lamb, and Victor bright,
Arrayed in more than morning light!

On this Thy Resurrection-day
Be strife and hate put far away,
That those who in Thy likeness live
May each his brother's wrongs forgive.

The earth in festal raiment stands,
The floods for gladness clap their hands;
Then higher still, and higher raise,
The true, the living Pascha's praise.

IF THE DARK AND AWFUL TOMB.

(Εἰ καὶ ἐν τάφῳ.)

GREEK ode of JOHN DAMASCENE, 787, the greatest poet, and one of the first divines, of the Oriental Church, though very little is known of his life. Translated by W. C. DIX.

IF the dark and awful tomb
 Thou, immortal One, hast known,
 Rising, in Thy deathless bloom,
Hades Thou hast overthrown.

Yes: as Victor Thou hast burst
 All the bands of hell, and said,
Hail! to those who sought Thee first,
 Bearing ointment for the dead.

Peace, Thy earliest, sweetest gift,
 Unto Thine Apostles given;
All the fallen Thou didst lift
 From the gates of hell to heaven.

'TIS THE DAY OF RESURRECTION.

(Ἀναστάσεως ἡμέρα.)

FROM the Greek of ST. JOHN OF DAMASCUS (d. before 787). His "Canon for Easter," which we give here in part, is called "the Golden Canon," or "the Queen of Canons," and is sung in the Greek Churches after midnight before Easter Day. Translated by Dr. J. M. NEALE ("Hymns of the Eastern Church," 1862).

TIS the day of Resurrection,
 Earth, tell it out abroad!
 The Passover of gladness,
 The Passover of God!
From death to life eternal,
 From earth unto the sky,
Our Christ hath brought us over,
 With hymns of victory.

Our hearts be pure from evil,
  That we may see aright
The Lord in rays eternal
  Of resurrection light:
And, listening to His accents,
  May hear, so calm and plain,
His own " All hail !"—and hearing,
  May raise the victor strain.

Now let the heavens be joyful!
  Let earth her song begin!
Let the round world keep triumph,
  And all that is therein:
In grateful exultation
  Their notes let all things blend,
For Christ the Lord hath risen,
  Our joy that hath no end.

COME, YE FAITHFUL, RAISE THE STRAIN.

("Ἄσωμεν πάντες λάοι)

FROM the Greek of ST. JOHN OF DAMASCUS, 787, by Dr. J. M. NEALE. This ode is the first of his canon for St. Thomas' Sunday, called also Renewal Sunday, or Low Sunday.

COME, ye faithful, raise the strain
  Of triumphant gladness!
God hath brought His Israel
  Into joy from sadness;
Loosed from Pharaoh's bitter yoke
  Jacob's sons and daughters;
Led them with unmoistened foot
  Through the Red Sea waters.

'Tis the spring of souls to-day:
  Christ hath burst His prison;
And from three days' sleep in death,
  As a sun, hath risen.
All the winter of our sins,
  Long and dark, is flying
From His light, to whom we give
  Laud and praise undying.

Now the queen of seasons, bright
　With the day of splendour,
With the royal Feast of feasts,
　Comes its joy to render:
Comes to glad Jerusalem,
　Who with true affection
Welcomes, in unwearied strains,
　Jesu's Resurrection.

Neither might the gates of death,
　Nor the tomb's dark portal,
Nor the watchers, nor the seal,
　Hold Thee as a mortal:
But to-day amidst the twelve
　Thou didst stand, bestowing
That Thy peace, which evermore
　Passeth human knowing.

THIS HOLY MORN, SO FAIR AND BRIGHT.

(Aurora cœlum purpurat.)

FREE, from the Latin of the Roman Breviary (Dominica in Albis), by the Rev. J. CHANDLER, 1837. Two different texts of this ancient *hymnus paschalis* in DANIEL, I. p. 83; MONE, I. p. 190 ("Aurora lucis rutilat"). Mone found a copy at Reichenau from the beginning of the ninth century. The Latin text is often divided into two hymns. Another version by CASWALL:

　　　"The Dawn was purpling over the sky;"
and in the "Hymnal Noted:"
　　　"Light's glittering morn bedecks the sky."
Compare also the next hymn.

THIS holy morn, so fair and bright,
　Shall hear our praises swell:
For oh, what joy prevails on earth,
　What wild despair in hell!

This morn our mighty King arose
　From death's infernal cave,
And many a saint, to welcome Him,
　Hath left his ancient grave.

In vain they sealed His sepulchre,
  And watched around His tomb:
The Lord hath gained the victory,
  And death is overcome.

Then calm your grief, dismiss your fears,
  Let no more tears be shed:
The mighty Vanquisher of death
  Is risen from the dead.

O, Jesu! may we ever live
  From sin and sorrow free;
Then let us ever die to sin,
  And ever live to Thee.

THE MORNING PURPLES ALL THE SKY.

(Aurora cœlum purpurat.)

ON the basis of the same hymn of the Roman Breviary for the Dominica in Albis. DANIEL, I. 83. By Dr. A. R. THOMPSON, New York, 1867. Contributed.

THE morning purples all the sky,
  The air with praises rings;
Defeated hell stands sullen by,
  The world exulting sings:
Glory to God! our glad lips cry;
  All praise and worship be
On earth, in heaven, to God Most High,
  For Christ's great victory!

While He, the King all strong to save,
  Rends the dark doors away,
And through the breaches of the grave
  Strides forth into the day.
Glory to God! our glad lips cry;
  All praise and worship be
On earth, in heaven, to God Most High,
  For Christ's great victory!

THE RESURRECTION.

Death's captive, in his gloomy prison
    Fast fettered He has lain;
But He has mastered death, is risen,
    And death wears now the chain.
Glory to God! our glad lips cry;
    All praise and worship be
On earth, in heaven, to God Most High,
    For Christ's great victory!

The shining angels cry, " Away
    With grief; no spices bring;
Not tears, but songs, this joyful day,
    Should greet the rising King!"
Glory to God! our glad lips cry;
    All praise and worship be
On earth, in heaven, to God Most High,
    For Christ's great victory!

That Thou our Paschal Lamb mayst be,
    And endless joy begin,
Jesus, Deliverer, set us free
    From the dread death of sin.
Glory to God! our glad lips cry;
    All praise and worship be
On earth, in heaven, to God Most High,
    For Christ's great victory!

HALLELUJAH! HALLELUJAH!

(Alleluia, Alleluia! finita jam sunt prœlia!)

FROM the Latin of the 12th century (see DANIEL, II. 363), translated by Dr. J. M. NEALE ("Mediæval Hymns and Sequences," 3d ed. 1867, p. 168).

HALLELUJAH! Hallelujah!
    Finished is the battle now:
    The crown is on the Victor's brow!
    Hence with sadness!
    Sing with gladness,
        Hallelujah!

Hallelujah! Hallelujah!
After sharp death that him befell,
Jesus Christ hath conquered hell.
    Earth is singing,
    Heaven is ringing,
        Hallelujah!

Hallelujah! Hallelujah!
On the third morning He arose,
Bright with victory o'er his foes.
    Sing we lauding,
    And applauding,
        Hallelujah!

Hallelujah! Hallelujah!
He hath closed hell's brazen door,
And heaven is open evermore!
    Hence with sadness!
    Sing with gladness,
        Hallelujah!

Hallelujah! Hallelujah!
Lord, by Thy wounds we call on Thee,
So from ill death to set us free,
    That our living
    Be thanksgiving!
        Hallelujah!

BEHOLD THE DAY THE LORD HATH MADE!

(Salve, Dies dierum gloria.)

FROM the Latin of ADAM OF ST. VICTOR, the most fertile, and, in the estimation of Trench and Neale, the greatest of the Latin hymnologists of the middle ages, d. at Paris after 1172. SHIPLEY'S "Lyra Messianica," p. 340. He wrote several Easter hymns,—" Mundi Renovatio;" " Zyma vetus expurgetur;" " Ecce dies celebris," &c. See TRENCH, p. 161, *seq.*

EHOLD the Day the Lord hath made!
That peerless day which cannot fade;
That day of light, that day of joy,
Of glory which shall never cloy.

THE RESURRECTION.

The day on which the world was framed
Has signal honour ever claimed;
But Christ, arising from the dead,
Unrivalled brightness o'er it shed.

In hope of their celestial choice,
Now let the sons of light rejoice:
Christ's members in their lives declare
What likeness to their Head they bear.

For solemn is our feast to-day,
And solemn are the vows we pay:
This day's surpassing greatness claims
Surpassing joy, surpassing aims.

The Paschal victory displays
The glory of our festal days;
Which type and shadow dimly bore,
In promise to the saints of yore.

The veil is rent; and, lo! unfold
The things the ancient Law foretold:
The figure from the substance flies,
And light the shadow's place supplies.

The type the spotless Lamb conveyed,
The goat, where Israel's sins were laid;
Messiah, purging our offence,
Disclosed in all their hidden sense.

By freely yielding up His breath,
He freed us from the bonds of death.
Who on that Prey forbidden flew,
And lost the prey that was his due.

The ills on sinful flesh that lay
His sinless flesh hath done away,
Which blooming fresh on that third morn
Assurance gave to souls forlorn.

O wondrous Death of Christ! may we
Be made to live to Christ by thee!
O deathless Death, destroy our sin,
Give us the prize of life to win!

NOW THY GENTLE LAMB, O SION.

(Mitis Agnus, Leo fortis.)

TRANSLATED from the Latin by H. TREND. The original in DU MERIL, II. 53; and DANIEL, IV. 160.

NOW thy gentle Lamb, O Sion,
  Shows the strength of Judah's Lion;
    Hell's stern fetters hold Him not:
Dawns the third day o'er His prison,
And our Mighty Saviour risen,
    Makes us share His glorious lot.

Holy women, with devotion
Such as springs from love's emotion,
    Bring sweet unguents to His tomb;
There, O wonderful transition!
Worthy of the heavenly vision,
    Glory meets them in the gloom.

One in faith that scorns defection,
Equal in their warm affection
    For His name whose grave they seek,
Back they see the stone is taken,
And the opened tomb forsaken,
    Whence they hear an Angel speak:

Fear not, loving souls; but going
Quickly back, the vision showing,
    Say to Peter and the rest:
Jesus lives, o'er death victorious,
Now to reign for ever glorious,
    In the regions of the blest.[1]

---

[1] " Festinantes ite retro;
  Nuntiantes visa Petro
    Cæterisque propere!
  Resurrexit vere Jesus;
  Immortalis et illæsus
    Vivit jam in æthere."

JESUS CHRIST IS RISEN TO-DAY.

(Surrexit Christus hodie.)

REPRODUCED from a Latin hymn of the 15th century, which exists in different forms. See WACKERNAGEL, I. pp. 175-177; DANIEL, I. 341. Roundell Palmer (No. LX.) adds a Hallelujah to each line, and erroneously ascribes the hymn to the year 1762, the last stanza (which differs from ours) to Charles Wesley.

JESUS Christ is risen to-day,
Our triumphant holy day;
Who did once upon the cross
Suffer to redeem our loss.
    Hallelujah!

Hymns of praise then let us sing
Unto Christ, our heavenly King;
Who endured the cross and grave,
Sinners to redeem and save.
    Hallelujah!

But the pains which He endured
Our salvation have procured;
Now above the sky He's King,
Where the angels ever sing.
    Hallelujah!

Now be God the Father praised,
With the Son, from death upraised,
And the Spirit, ever blest;
One true God, by all confest.
    Hallelujah!

LET ZION'S SONS AND DAUGHTERS SAY.

(O Filii et Filiæ.)

TRANSLATED from the Latin, by Prof. THOMAS C. PORTER, Easton, Pa., March, 1859; revised, April, 1868. Contributed. Another translation, by Dr. NEALE ("Alleluia! ye sons and daughters of the King"), and one in E. J. HOPKINS' "Temple-Church Choral Service," Lond. 1867 ("Ye sons and daughters of the Lord"). 13th century.

LET Zion's sons and daughters say:
"Heaven's glorious King, our King for aye,
Hath broke the bonds of death to-day!"
    Hallelujah!

Their Sabbath, o'er, with sweet perfume,
Amid the morning's early gloom,
His followers hasten to the tomb.
    Hallelujah!

With Mary Magdalene view
Salome,—James' mother too;
They come the sacred corse t' imbue.
    Hallelujah!

White-robed and seated on the stone,
God's angel speaks in thrilling tone:
"Your Lord to Galilee hath gone."
    Hallelujah!

His best-beloved, with eager pace,
Outstripping Peter in the race,
First cometh to th' appointed place.
    Hallelujah!

Where gathered His disciples true,
There in the midst Christ stood to view,
Proclaiming: "Peace be unto you!"
    Hallelujah!

When Didymus now heard it said,
That Jesus rising left the dead,
Strong doubt possessed his heart and head.
    Hallelujah!

"See, Thomas, see My wounded side,
These hands and feet!" the Saviour cried,
"Doubt not: believe; in Me confide."
    Hallelujah!

When Thomas searched with earnest heed
Feet, hands, and side, from doubting freed,
He said: "Thou art my God indeed!"
    Hallelujah!

Who have not seen with mortal eyes,
And yet believe, shall win the prize,
Eternal life beyond the skies.
    Hallelujah!

Upon this hallowed festal day,
Triumphant swell the joyful lay;
O let us bless the Lord alway!
    Hallelujah!

For grace like this, so rich and free,
Most humble thanks we pay to Thee,
Great Three in One and One in Three!
    Hallelujah!

MARY! PUT THY GRIEF AWAY.

(Pone luctum, Magdalena!)

FROM the Latin. DANIEL, II. p. 365. By W. J. C. ("Lyra Mess.," p. 328). Mary Magdalena is here, as in the "Dies Iræ" and other Latin hymns, identified with the sinful woman, Luke vii. 37. See the note in TRENCH, p. 159.

MARY! put thy grief away,
    And thy drooping eyelid clear:
'Tis not Simon's feast to-day,
  'Tis no time to shed a tear;
There are thousand springs of joy,
Thousand springs of transport high.

Mary! learn to smile again,
  Let thy beaming forehead brighten;

Far is banished every pain,
　Now the Sun of suns doth lighten:
Christ the world from death hath freed;
Yea, the Lord is risen indeed.

Mary! leap for joy and gladness,
　Christ hath triumphed o'er the tomb;
He hath closed the scene of sadness,
　He of death hath sealed the doom;
Whom thou late in death wast mourning,
Welcome now to life returning.

Mary! lift thy trembling glance,
　View Him risen with deep amaze;
See! how fair that countenance!
　On those wounds resplendent gaze;
How like purest pearls they shine,
Sparkling all with life Divine!

Mary! live, yea, live again,
　Now thy Light again hath shone;
Transport swell through every vein,
　Now the sting of death has gone:
Far away be gloom and sadness,
All once more be joy and gladness.

STILL THY SORROW, MAGDALENA!

(Pone luctum, Magdalena!)

ANOTHER and better version of this sweet and cheering Easter hymn, by the Rev. Dr. E. A. WASHBURN, New York, June, 1868. Contributed.

STILL thy sorrow, Magdalena!
　Wipe the tear-drops from thine eyes;
　Not at Simon's board thou kneelest,
Pouring thy repentant sighs:
All with thy glad heart rejoices;
All things sing with happy voices,
　　　Hallelujah!

THE RESURRECTION.

Laugh with rapture, Magdalena!
  Be thy drooping forehead bright;
Banished now is every anguish,
  Breaks anew thy morning light:
Christ from death the world hath freed;
He is risen, is risen indeed:
    Hallelujah!

Joy! exult, O Magdalena!
  He hath burst the rocky prison;
Ended are the days of darkness;
  Conqueror hath He arisen.
Mourn no more the Christ departed;
Run to welcome Him, glad-hearted:
    Hallelujah!

Lift thine eyes, O Magdalena!
  See! thy living Master stands;
See His face, as ever, smiling;
  See those wounds upon His hands,
On His feet, His sacred side,—
Gems that deck the Glorified:
    Hallelujah!

Live, now live, O Magdalena!
  Shining is thy new-born day;
Let thy bosom pant with pleasure,
  Death's poor terror flee away;
Far from thee the tears of sadness,
Welcome love, and welcome gladness!
    Hallelujah!

CHRIST THE LORD IS RISEN AGAIN!

(Christus ist erstanden.)

An Easter hymn of the BOHEMIAN BRETHREN, translated into German by MICHAEL WEISS, 1531, and, after him, into English by Miss C. WINKWORTH, 1858 ("L. G.'" II. 62). The German begins, like similar mediæval hymns: "Christus ist erstanden von des Todes Banden" (in KNAPP's "Liederschatz," 3d ed., No. 626). Compare the note on the next hymn.

CHRIST the Lord is risen again!
Christ hath broken every chain!
Hark! the angels shout for joy,
Singing evermore on high:
    Hallelujah!

He who gave for us His life,
Who for us endured the strife,
Is our Paschal Lamb to-day!
We, too, sing for joy, and say:
    Hallelujah!

He who bore all pain and loss
Comfortless upon the cross,
Lives in glory now on high,
Pleads for us and hears our cry:
    Hallelujah!

He whose path no records tell,
Who descended into hell,
Who the strong man armed hath bound,
Now in the highest heaven is crowned:
    Hallelujah!

He who slumbered in the grave,
Is exalted now to save;
Now through Christendom it rings
That the Lamb is King of kings:
    Hallelujah!

Now He bids us tell abroad,
How the lost may be restored,
How the penitent forgiven,
How we, too, may enter heaven:
    Hallelujah!

Thou our Paschal Lamb indeed,
Christ, to-day Thy people feed;
Take our sins and guilt away;
Let us sing by night and day:
    Hallelujah!

IN THE BONDS OF DEATH HE LAY.

(Christ lag in Todesbanden.)

FROM the German of Dr. MARTIN LUTHER, 1524 (SCHAFF's " G. H. B.," No. 132; " Lyra Germ.," I. p. 87). Based upon a Latin hymn of the 15th century : " Surrexit Christus hodie " (DANIEL, I. 341; and WACKERNAGEL, I. 175-177, who gives five forms), also upon an old German Easter hymn : " Christ ist erstanden " (several forms in WACKERNAGEL, II. 43 and 726-737). Luther's hymn is a great improvement upon its predecessors.

IN the bonds of Death He lay,
    Who for our offence was slain;
But the Lord is risen to-day,
Christ hath brought us life again.
Wherefore let us all rejoice,
Singing loud, with cheerful voice:
        Hallelujah!

Of the sons of men was none
    Who could break the bonds of Death:
Sin this mischief dire had done,
    Innocent was none on earth;
Wherefore Death grew strong and bold,
Would all men in his prison hold:
        Hallelujah!

Jesus Christ, God's only Son,
    Came at last our foe to smite;
All our sins away hath done,
    Done away Death's power and right;
Only the form of Death is left,
Of his sting he is bereft:
        Hallelujah!

IN THE BONDS OF DEATH HE LAY.

That was a wondrous war, I trow,
    When Life and Death together fought;
But Life hath triumphed o'er his foe,
    Death is mocked and set at nought;
'Tis even as the Scripture saith,
Christ through death has conquered Death:
        Hallelujah![1]

The rightful Paschal Lamb is He,
    On whom alone we all must live,
Who to death upon the tree,
    Himself in wondrous love did give.
Faith strikes His blood upon the door,
Death sees, and dares not harm us more:
        Hallelujah!

Let us keep high festival,
    On this most blessed Day of days,
When God His mercy showed to all!
    Our Sun is risen with brightest rays;
And our dark hearts rejoice to see
Sin and night before Him flee:
        Hallelujah!

To the Supper of the Lord,
    Gladly will we come to-day:
The word of peace is now restored,
    The old leaven is put away.
Christ will be our food alone,
Faith no life but His doth own:
        Hallelujah!

---

[1] In the original, this description of the marvellous duel between Life and Death is peculiarly forcible:

    "Es war ein wunderlicher Krieg,
        Da Tod und Leben rungen;
    Das Leben das behielt den Sieg,
        Es hat den Tod verschlungen.
    Die Schrift hat verkündet das,
    Wie da ein Tod den andern frass:
        Ein Spott aus dem Tod ist worden. Hallelujah."

This verse bears a striking resemblance to the Latin of Peter Damiani (see p. 183).

ERE YET THE DAWN HAS FILLED THE SKIES.

(Früh morgens da die Sonn' aufgeht.)

FROM the German of JOHANN HEERMANN, 1630. The original has nineteen stanzas, but is abridged in all the German hymn-books. "Lyra Germ.," II. 64.

ERE yet the dawn has filled the skies,
Behold my Saviour Christ arise,
He chaseth from us sin and night,
And brings us joy and life and light:
    Hallelujah! Hallelujah!

O stronger Thou than Death and Hell!
Where is the foe Thou canst not quell?
What heavy stone Thou canst not roll
From off the prisoned anguished soul?
    Hallelujah! Hallelujah!

If Jesus lives, can I be sad?
I know He loves me, and am glad;
Though all the world were dead to me,
Enough, O Christ, if I have Thee!
    Hallelujah! Hallelujah!

He feeds me, comforts and defends,
And when I die His angel sends
To bear me whither He is gone,
For of His own He loseth none:
    Hallelujah! Hallelujah!

No more to fear or grief I bow,
God and the angels love me now;
The joys prepared for me to-day
Drive fear and mourning far away:
    Hallelujah! Hallelujah!

Strong Champion! For this comfort see
The whole world brings her thanks to Thee;
And once we, too, shall raise above
More sweet and loud the song of love:
    Hallelujah! Hallelujah!

JESUS, MY REDEEMER, LIVES.

(Jesus, meine Zuversicht.)

FROM the German of LOUISA HENRIETTA, Electress of Brandenburg, 1649, after the death of her first son (SCHAFF, No. 488). A favourite German hymn. Based on Job xix. 25-27, and 1 Cor. xv. Translated by Miss C. WINKWORTH, 1855. Other translations in the English Moravian hymn-book, and in "Sacred Lyrics from the German," 1859 ("Jesus, my eternal trust, And my Saviour, ever liveth ").

JESUS, my Redeemer, lives,
   Christ, my trust, is dead no more !
In the strength this knowledge gives,
   Shall not all my fears be o'er;
Calm, though death's long night be fraught
Still with many an anxious thought?

Jesus, my Redeemer, lives,
   And His life I soon shall see;
Bright the hope this promise gives;
   Where He is, I too shall be.
Shall I fear then? Can the Head
Rise and leave the members dead?

Close to Him my soul is bound,
   In the bonds of hope enclasped;
Faith's strong hand this hold hath found,
   And the Rock hath firmly grasped.
Death shall ne'er my soul remove
From her refuge in Thy love.

I shall see Him with these eyes,
   Him whom I shall surely know;
Not another shall I rise;
   With His love my heart shall glow;
Only there shall disappear
Weakness in and round me here.

Ye who suffer, sigh and moan,
   Fresh and glorious there shall reign;
Earthly here the seed is sown,
   Heavenly it shall rise again;
Natural here the death we die,
Spiritual our life on high.

Body, be thou of good cheer,
   In thy Saviour's care rejoice;
Give not place to gloom and fear,
   Dead, thou yet shalt know His voice,
When the final trump is heard,
And the deaf, cold grave is stirred.

Laugh to scorn, then, death and hell,
   Fear no more the gloomy grave;
Caught into the air to dwell
   With the Lord who comes to save,
We shall trample on our foes,
Mortal weakness, fear, and woes.

Only see ye that your heart
   Rise betimes from earthly lust;
Would ye there with Him have part,
   Here obey your Lord and trust.
Fix your hearts beyond the skies,
Whither ye yourselves would rise!

O RISEN LORD! O CONQUERING KING!

(auferstand'ner Siegesfürst.)

From the German of Dr. Justus H. Boehmer (a celebrated jurist; born at Hanover, 1674; died at Halle, 1749), 1706. Translated by C. Winkworth.

O RISEN Lord! O conquering King!
   O Life of all that live!
   To-day that peace of Easter bring
Which only Thou canst give!
   Once Death, our foe,
   Had laid Thee low:
Now hast Thou rent his bonds in twain,
Now art Thou risen who once wast slain!

The power of Thy great majesty
   Bursts rocks and tombs away,
Thy victory raises us with Thee
   Into the glorious day;

  Now Satan's might
  And Death's dark night
Have lost their power this blessed morn,
And we to higher life are born.

Oh that our hearts might inly know
  Thy victory over death,
And gazing on Thy conflict glow
  With eager, dauntless faith!
   Thy quenchless light,
   Thy glorious might
Still comfortless and lonely leave
The soul that cannot yet believe.

Then break through our hard hearts Thy way,
  O Jesus, conquering King!
Kindle the lamp of faith to-day;
  Teach our faint hearts to sing
   For joy at length,
   That in Thy strength
We, too, may rise whom sin had slain,
And Thine eternal rest attain.

And, when our tears for sin o'erflow,
  Do Thou in love draw near,
The precious gift of peace bestow,
  Shine on us bright and clear;
   That so may we,
   O Christ! from Thee
Drink in the life that cannot die,
And keep true Easter feasts on high.

Yes, let us truly know within
  Thy rising from the dead;
And quit the grave of death and sin,
  And keep that gift, our Head,
   That Thou didst leave
   For all who cleave
To Thee through all this earthly strife:
So shall we enter into life.

THE RESURRECTION.

BLEST MORNING, WHOSE YOUNG RAYS.

Dr. Isaac Watts, 1674-1748.

BLEST morning, whose young dawning rays
    Beheld our rising God;
That saw Him triumph o'er the dust,
    And leave His dark abode.

In the cold prison of a tomb
    The dead Redeemer lay,
Till the revolving skies had brought
    The third, th' appointed day.

Hell and the grave unite their force
    To hold our God, in vain;
The sleeping Conqueror arose,
    And burst their feeble chain.

To Thy great name, Almighty Lord,
    These sacred hours we pay;
And loud hosannas shall proclaim
    The triumph of the day.

Salvation and immortal praise
    To our victorious King!
Let heaven and earth, and rocks and seas,
    With glad hosannas ring!

WELCOME, THOU VICTOR IN THE STRIFE!

(*Willkommen, Held im Streite.*)

Benjamin Schmolke, 1712 (Schaff, No. 135). Translated by C. Winkworth.

WELCOME, Thou Victor in the strife,
    Welcome from out the cave!
To-day we triumph in Thy life
    Around Thine empty grave.

WELCOME, THOU VICTOR IN THE STRIFE.

Our enemy is put to shame,
  His short-lived triumph o'er;
Our God is with us, we exclaim,
  We fear our foe no more.

The dwellings of the just resound
  With songs of victory;
For in their midst, Thou, Lord, art found,
  And bringest peace with Thee.

O share with us the spoils, we pray,
  Thou diedst to achieve!
We meet within Thy house to-day
  Our portion to receive.

And let Thy conquering banner wave
  O'er hearts Thou makest free,
And point the path that from the grave
  Leads heavenwards up to Thee.

We bury all our sin and crime
  Deep in our Saviour's tomb;
And seek the treasure there, that time
  Nor change can e'er consume.

We die with Thee; oh, let us live
  Henceforth to Thee aright!
The blessings Thou hast died to give
  Be daily in our sight.

Fearless we lay us in the tomb,
  And sleep the night away,
If Thou art there to break the gloom,
  And call us back to day.

Death hurts us not; his power is gone,
  And pointless are his darts;
God's favour now on us hath shone,
  Joy filleth all our hearts.

GLORIOUS HEAD, THOU LIVEST NOW!

PART of a German hymn of G. TERSTEEGEN (1731), which commences " Willkomm, verklärter Gottessohn." The stanzas here translated are verses 7-10 (" Verklärtes Haupt! nun lebest Du," &c.).

GLORIOUS Head, Thou livest now!
 Let us, Thy members, share Thy life;
Canst Thou behold their need, nor bow
 To raise Thy children from the strife
With self and sin, with death and dark distress,
That they may live to Thee in holiness?

Earth knows Thee not, but evermore
 Thou liv'st in Paradise, in peace;
Thither my soul would also soar,
 Let me from all the creatures cease:
Dead to the world, but to Thy Spirit known,
I live to Thee, O Prince of Life! alone.

Break through my bonds whate'er it cost;
 What is not Thine within me slay;
Give me the lot I covet most,
 To rise as Thou hast risen to-day.
Nought can I do, a slave to death I pine:
Work Thou in me, O Power and Life Divine!

Work Thou in me, and heavenward guide
 My thoughts and wishes, that my heart
Waver no more nor turn aside,
 But fix for ever where Thou art.
Thou art not far from us: who love Thee well
While yet on earth, in heaven with Thee may dwell.

"CHRIST THE LORD IS RISEN TO-DAY."

CHARLES WESLEY. From his " Hymns and Sacred Poems," 1739.

CHRIST the Lord is risen to-day,"
 Sons of men and angels say:
Raise your joys and triumphs high;
 Sing, ye heavens, and earth reply.

CHRIST THE LORD IS RISEN TO-DAY.

Love's redeeming work is done,
Fought the fight, the battle won;
Lo! our Sun's eclipse is o'er;
Lo! He sets in blood no more.

Vain the stone, the watch, the seal;
Christ hath burst the gates of hell!
Death in vain forbids His rise;
Christ has opened Paradise.

Lives again our glorious King;
Where, O Death! is now thy sting?
Once He died our souls to save;
Where thy victory, O Grave?

Soar we now where Christ has led,
Following our exalted Head;
Made like Him, like Him we rise;
Ours the cross, the grave, the skies.

What though once we perished all,
Partners in our parents' fall?
Second life we all receive,
In our Heavenly Adam live[1].

Risen with him, we upward move;
Still we seek the things above;
Still pursue and kiss the Son,
Seated on His Father's throne.

Scarce on earth a thought bestow,
Dead to all we leave below;
Heaven our aim and loved abode,
Hid our life with Christ in God:

Hid, till Christ our life appear
Glorious in His members here;
Joined to Him, we then shall shine,
All immortal, all divine.

Smoother :—
"Second life we now receive,
And in Christ for ever live."

Hail the Lord of earth and heaven!
Praise to Thee by both be given!
Thee we greet triumphant now!
Hail, the Resurrection Thou!

King of glory, Soul of bliss!
Everlasting life is this,
Thee to know, Thy power to prove,
Thus to sing, and thus to love!

JESUS LIVES, AND SO SHALL I.

(Jesus lebt, mit Ihm auch ich.)

From the German of Chr. Fürchtegott Gellert, 1757. Another English translation, by Frances Elizabeth Cox, commencing,
"Jesus lives! no longer now
Can thy terrors, Death, appal me."

JESUS lives, and so shall I:
   Death, thy sting is gone for ever:
He who deigned for me to die,
   Lives, the bands of death to sever.
He shall raise me with the just:
Jesus is my Hope and Trust.

Jesus lives, and reigns supreme;
   And, His kingdom still remaining,
I shall also be with Him,
   Ever living, ever reigning.
God has promised; be it must:
Jesus is my Hope and Trust.

Jesus lives, and God extends
   Grace to each returning sinner;
Rebels He receives as friends,
   And exalts to highest honour.
God is true as He is just:
Jesus is my Hope and Trust.

Jesus lives, and by His grace,
   Victory o'er my passions giving,
I will cleanse my heart and ways,
   Ever to His glory living.
Th' weak He raises from the dust:
Jesus is my Hope and Trust.

Jesus lives, and I am sure
   Naught shall e'er from Jesus sever:
Satan's wiles and Satan's power,
   Pain or pleasure, ye shall never!
Christian armour cannot rust:
Jesus is my Hope and Trust.

Jesus lives, and death is now
   But my entrance into glory.
Courage! then, my soul, for thou
   Hast a crown of life before thee;
Thou shalt find thy hopes were just:
Jesus is the Christian's Trust.

I SAY TO ALL MEN, FAR AND NEAR.

(Ich sag es jedem, dass Er lebt.)

FROM the German of FRIED. VON HARDENBERG, better known under the name of NOVALIS, d. 1801. Translated by C. WINKWORTH.

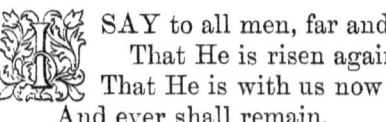SAY to all men, far and near,
   That He is risen again;
That He is with us now and here,
   And ever shall remain.

And what I say, let each this morn
   Go tell it to his friend,
That soon in every place shall dawn
   His kingdom without end.

Now first to souls who thus awake
   Seems earth a fatherland:
A new and endless life they take
   With rapture from His hand.

The fears of death and of the grave
    Are whelmed beneath the sea,
And every heart now light and brave
    May face the things to be.

The way of darkness that He trod
    To heaven at last shall come,
And he who hearkens to His word
    Shall reach His Father's home.

Now let the mourner grieve no more,
    Though his beloved sleep;
A happier meeting shall restore
    Their light to eyes that weep.

Now every heart each noble deed
    With new resolve may dare:
A glorious harvest shall the seed
    In happier regions bear.

He lives: His presence hath not ceased,
    Though foes and fears be rife;
And thus we hail in Easter's feast
    A world renewed to life!

THE GRAVE IS EMPTY NOW.

(Das Grab ist leer, das Grab ist leer.)

MATTHIAS CLAUDIUS, popularly called, from the title of his periodical, the "Wandsbecker Bote." 1812. Trsl. by Dr. HENRY MILLS, of Auburn, New York, and sent to the editor in MS., 1859. The original in SCHAFF's "G. H. B.," No. 139.

THE grave is empty now,—its prey
    Has forth victorious gone!
Life over death has gain'd the day,
    Redemption's work is done!

The learned scribes, with shrewd intent
    To stop this strange affair,
Their guard, to watch the grave, had sent,
    Its stone had seal'd with care:

But all their wisdom's utmost skill
    To shame is quickly turn'd:
God has a wisdom higher still
    Than any they had learn'd:

They could not understand the path
    He in His grace pursues,
When now, by suff'rings and by death,
    Our living He renews.

Thank God! The grave has lost its prey,
    Redemption's work is done!
Life over death has won the day
    Thro' God's victorious Son!

COME, YE SAINTS, LOOK HERE AND WONDER.

THOMAS KELLY; b. 1769, in Dublin; d. 1855. The first edition of his hymn-book (96 hymns) appeared in Dublin, 1804; the seventh (with 765 hymns), in 1853.

COME, ye saints, look here and wonder:
    See the place where Jesus lay;
    He has burst His bands asunder;
He has borne our sins away;
    Joyful tidings!
Yes, the Lord has risen to-day.

Jesus triumphs! Sing ye praises;
    By His death He overcame:
Thus the Lord His glory raises,
    Thus He fills His foes with shame.
        Sing ye praises!
Praises to the Victor's name.

Jesus triumphs! Countless legions
    Come from heaven to meet their King;
Soon, in yonder blessed regions,
    They shall join His praise to sing.
        Songs eternal
Shall through heaven's high arches ring.

MORNING BREAKS UPON THE TOMB.

WILLIAM BENGO COLLYER, D.D., LL.D.; b. 1782; minister at Peckham, Surrey; d. 1854. He published a Collection of Hymns, 1812.

MORNING breaks upon the tomb,
Jesus dissipates its gloom !
Day of triumph through the skies;
See the glorious Saviour rise.

Christians, dry your flowing tears,
Chase those unbelieving fears;
Look on His deserted grave;
Doubt no more His power to save.

Ye who are of death afraid,
Triumph in the scattered shade:
Drive your anxious cares away;
See the place where Jesus lay.

So the rising sun appears,
Shedding radiance o'er the spheres;
So returning beams of light
Chase the terrors of the night.

AGAIN THE LORD OF LIFE AND LIGHT.

ANNE LETITIA BARBAULD, 1743-1825. From her collected works, published 1825, by her niece, Miss Lucy Aikin.

AGAIN the Lord of life and light
Awakes the kindling ray,
Unseals the eyelids of the morn,
And pours increasing day.

O what a night was that which wrapt
The heathen world in gloom !
O what a sun which broke this day
Triumphant from the tomb !

AGAIN THE LORD OF LIFE AND LIGHT.

This day be grateful homage paid,
    And loud hosannas sung;
Let gladness dwell in every heart,
    And praise on every tongue.

Ten thousand differing lips shall join
    To hail this welcome morn,
Which scatters blessings from its wings
    To nations yet unborn.

Jesus, the friend of human kind,
    With strong compassion moved,
Descended, like a pitying God,
    To save the souls He loved.

The powers of darkness leagued in vain
    To bind His soul in death;
He shook their kingdom when He fell,
    With His expiring breath.

Not long the toils of hell could keep
    The Hope of Judah's line;
Corruption never could take hold
    On aught so much Divine.

And now His conquering chariot wheels
    Ascend the lofty skies;
While, broke beneath his powerful cross,
    Death's iron sceptre lies.

Exalted high at God's right hand,
    And Lord of all below,
Through Him is pardoning love dispensed,
    And boundless blessings flow.

And still for erring, guilty man,
    A brother's pity flows;
And still His bleeding heart is touched
    With memory of our woes.

To Thee, my Saviour and my King,
    Glad homage let me give;
And stand prepared, like Thee, to die,
    With Thee that I may live.

SUN, SHINE FORTH IN ALL THY SPLENDOUR.

(Wandle leuchtender und schöner, Ostersonne, deinen Lauf.)

From the German of C. J. P. Spitta (d. 1859), 1833. Translated by R. Massie, 1860.

SUN, shine forth in all thy splendour,
　　Joyfully pursue thy way;
　For thy Lord and my Defender
Rose triumphant on this day.
When He bowed His head, sore troubled
　Thou didst hide thyself in night;
Shine forth now with rays redoubled,
　He is risen who is thy light.

Earth, be joyous and glad-hearted,
　Spread out all thy vernal bloom;
For thy Lord is not departed,
　He has broken through the tomb.
When the Lord expired, wide-yawning
　Thy strong rocks were rent with fright;
Greet thy risen Lord this morning,
　Bathed in floods of rosy light.

Say, my soul, what preparation
　Makest thou for this high day,
When the God of thy salvation
　Opened through the tomb a way?
Dwellest thou with pure affection
　On this proof of power and love?
Doth thy Saviour's resurrection
　Raise thy thoughts to things above?

Hast thou, borne on Faith's strong pinion,
　Risen with the risen Lord?
And, released from sin's dominion,
　Into purer regions soared?
Or art thou, in spite of warning,
　Dead in trespasses and sin?
Hath to thee the purple morning
　No true Easter ushered in?

O, then, let not death o'ertake thee
    By the shades of night o'erspread!
See! thy Lord is come to wake thee,
    He is risen from the dead.
While the time as yet allows thee,
    Hear; the gracious Saviour cries,
" Sleeper, from thy sloth arouse thee,
    To new life at once arise."

See, with looks of tender pity
    He extends His wounded hands,
Bidding thee, with fond entreaty,
    Shake off sin's enthralling bands:
" Wait not for some future meetness,
    Dread no punishment from me,
Rouse thyself, and taste the sweetness
    Of the new life offered thee."

Let no precious time be wasted,
    To new life arise at length:
He who death for thee hath tasted,
    For new life will give new strength.
Try to rise, at once bestir thee,
    Still press on and persevere;
Let no weariness deter thee,
    He who woke thee still is near.

Waste not so much time in weighing
    When and where thou shalt begin;
Too much thinking is delaying,
    Rivets but the chain of sin.
He will help thee and provide thee
    With a courage not thine own,
Bear thee in His arms and guide thee,
    Till thou learn'st to walk alone.

See! thy Lord himself is risen,
    That thou mightest also rise,
And emerge from sin's dark prison
    To new life and open skies.
Come to Him who can unbind thee,
    And reverse thy awful doom;
Come to Him, and leave behind thee
    Thy old life,—an empty tomb!

CHRIST IS ARISEN.

FROM Bishop A. C. COXE's "Halloween," first printed 1840. This ode is suggested by, and partly translated from, the famous Easter-chorus in GOETHE's "Faust:"

> "Christ ist erstanden!
> Freude dem Sterblichen,
> Den die verderblichen,
> Schleichenden, erblichen
> Mängel umwanden," &c.

CHRIST is arisen,
   Joy to thee, mortal!
Out of His prison,
   Forth from its portal!
Christ is not sleeping,
   Seek Him no longer;
Strong was His keeping—
   Jesus was stronger!

Christ is arisen,
   Seek Him not here;
Lonely His prison,
   Empty His bier;
Vain His entombing,
   Spices, and lawn,
Vain the perfuming,
   Jesus is gone!

Christ is arisen,
   Joy to thee, mortal!
Empty His prison,
   Broken its portal:
Rising, he giveth
   His shroud to the sod;
Risen, He liveth,
   And liveth to God!

THE FOE BEHIND, THE DEEP BEFORE.

By Dr. JOHN MASON NEALE (d. 1866), 1851.

THE foe behind, the deep before,
    Our hosts have dared and passed the sea;
And Pharaoh's warriors strew the shore,
    And Israel's ransomed tribes are free.
  Lift up, lift up your voices now!
  The whole wide world rejoices now!
  The Lord hath triumphed gloriously!
  The Lord shall reign victoriously!
      Happy morrow,
      Turning sorrow
    Into peace and mirth!
      Bondage ending,
      Love descending
    O'er the earth!
      Seals assuring,
      Guards securing,
    Watch His earthly prison:
      Seals are shattered,
      Guards are scattered,
        Christ hath risen!

No longer must the mourners weep,
  Nor call departed Christians dead;
For death is hallowed into sleep
  And every grave becomes a bed.
    Now once more
    Eden's door
Open stands to mortal eyes;
For Christ hath risen, and men shall rise.
    Now at last,
    Old things past,
Hope and joy and peace begin:
For Christ has won, and man shall win.

It is not exile, rest on high;
  It is not sadness, peace from strife:
To fall asleep is not to die;
  To dwell with Christ is better life.

Where our banner leads us,
  We may safely go;
Where our Chief precedes us,
  We may face the foe.
His right arm is o'er us,
  He will guide us through:
Christ hath gone before us;
  Christians, follow you!

THE LORD OF LIFE IS RISEN!

(Der Herr ist auferstanden.)

FROM the German of Dr. J. P. LANGE, Professor in Bonn (editor of the well-known "Biblework"), 1832. Translated, at the request of the editor, by Dr. HENRY HARBAUGH, Mercersburg, Pa., who died, Dec. 28, 1867, before he saw this in print.

THE Lord of life is risen!
  Sing, Easter heralds! sing:
  He burst His rocky prison,
  Wide let the triumph ring.
Tell how the graves are quaking,
The saints their fetters breaking;
  Sing, heralds: Jesus lives!

In death no longer lying,
  He rose, the Prince, to-day:
Life of the dead and dying,
  He triumphed o'er decay.
The Lord of Life is risen,
In ruins lies Death's prison,
  Its keeper bound in chains.

We hear, in Thy blest greeting,
  Salvation's work is done!
We worship Thee, repeating,
  Life for the dead is won!
O Head of all believing!
O Joy of all the grieving!
  Unite us, Lord, to Thee.

Here at Thy tomb, O Jesus!
  How sweet the morning's breath!
We hear in all the breezes,
  Where is thy sting, O Death!
Dark hell flies in commotion;
While, far o'er earth and ocean,
  Loud Hallelujahs ring!

O publish this salvation,
  Ye heralds, through the earth!
To every buried nation
  Proclaim the day of birth!
Till, rising from their slumbers,
The countless heathen numbers
  Shall hail the risen light.

Hail, hail, our Jesus risen!
  Sing, ransomed brethren! sing;
Through Death's dark, gloomy prison,
  Let Easter chorals ring.
Haste, haste, ye captive legions!
Come forth from sin's dark regions,
  In Jesus' Kingdom live.

WE WELCOME THEE, DEAR EASTER-DAY.

(Willkommen, lieber Ostertag.)

AN Easter hymn for children, by Mrs. META HEUSSER-SCHWEIZER; born 1797, in the Canton Zürich, Switzerland. Translated (not reproduced) by the late Rev. Dr. HENRY MILLS, of Auburn, New York (from SCHAFF'S "G. H. B.," No. 142), 1859.

WE welcome thee, dear Easter-day!
  In grave made sure our Saviour,—
  He leaves the dead:—with glad surprise,
The angels see the Conq'ror rise.

Fill'd up with sorrows was his life;
His death, an agonizing strife;
Then, briefly resting from its woes,
To fit a place for us—he goes.

THE RESURRECTION.

Bright day that out of darkness breaks!
He now, the Lord of all, awakes;
But, made supreme o'er all beside,
He will our brother yet abide.

Blest vernal fields!—Ye well afford
Your emblems of our risen Lord;
And ev'ry flow'r, to life that springs,
Reminds us of the King of kings.

Oh, could these eyes the Saviour see
Who left the grave to set us free,—
Like Salem's children, in their day,
With palms would I bestrew His way.

Tho' we cannot, faith that is true
Can bring our absent Lord to view,
And leaving childhood's sportive band,
Before Him I, a suppliant, stand,

Accept, O Lord, my offering.
Instead of palms, my heart I bring:
'Tis vile,—but form it all anew!
A work myself could never do.

For Easter-present—give to me
A heart that's full of love to Thee;
And lead me on,—as seems Thee best,
Thro' earthly cares with Thee to rest.

An Easter-day, far brighter still,
Shall all the heart with rapture fill,
When we, thro' death, reach our reward,
To be for ever with the Lord.

Now, looking to Thy throne above,
I fain would grow in faith and love;
Nor can I here more happy be
Than when Thou sayest, "Peace be with thee!"

THE TOMB IS EMPTY.

HORATIUS BONAR, D.D. "Hymns of Faith and Hope," Second Series, 1862.

THE tomb is empty; wouldst thou have it full?
   Still sadly clasping the unbreathing clay:
O weak in faith, O slow of heart and dull,
   To dote on darkness, and shut out the day!

The tomb is empty; He who, three short days,
   After a sorrowing life's long weariness,
Found refuge in this rocky resting-place,
   Has now ascended to the throne of bliss.

Here lay the Holy One, the Christ of God,
   He who for death gave death, and life for life;
Our heavenly Kinsman, our true flesh and blood;
   Victor for us on hell's dark field of strife.

This was the Bethel, where, on stony bed,
   While angels went and came from morn till even,
Our truer Jacob laid his wearied head;
   This was to Him the very gate of heaven.

The Conqueror, not the conquered, He to whom
   The keys of death and of the grave belong,
Crossed the cold threshold of the stranger's tomb,
   To spoil the spoiler and to bind the strong.

Here Death had reign'd; into no tomb like this
   Had man's fell foe aforetime found his way;
So grand a trophy ne'er before was his,
   So vast a treasure, so divine a prey.

But now his triumph ends; the rock-barred door
   Is opened wide, and the Great Pris'ner gone:
Look round and see, upon the vacant floor,
   The napkin and the grave-clothes lie alone.

Yes: Death's last hope, his strongest fort and prison,
   Is shattered, never to be built again;
And He, the mighty Captive, He is risen,
   Leaving behind the gate, the bar, the chain.

THE RESURRECTION.

Yes, He is risen who is the First and Last;
   Who was and is; who liveth and was dead:
Beyond the reach of death He now has passed,
   Of the one glorious Church the glorious Head.

The tomb is empty; so, ere long, shall be
   The tombs of all who in this Christ repose;
They died with Him who died upon the tree,
   They live and rise with Him who lived and rose.

Death has not slain them; they are freed, not slain.
   It is the gate of life, and not of death,
That they have entered; and the grave in vain
   Has tried to stifle the immortal breath.

All that was death in them is now dissolved;
   For death can only what is death's destroy;
And, when this earth's short ages have revolved,
   The disimprisoned life comes forth with joy.

Their life-long battle with disease and pain
   And mortal weariness is over now:
Youth, health, and comeliness return again;
   The tear has left the cheek, the sweat the brow.

They are not tasting death, but taking rest,
   On the same holy couch where Jesus lay,
Soon to awake all glorified and blest,
   When day has broke and shadows fled away.

ANGELS, ROLL THE ROCK AWAY.

FROM the Protestant Episcopal Collection, prepared by Drs. BURGESS, COXE, MÜHLENBERG, and other eminent American Episcopalians, as an Appendix to the Common-Prayer Book, and publ. Philad. 1861. It is there ascribed to Gibbons, but is based upon an older and longer hymn of THOMAS SCOTT (a Presbyterian minister with Arian sentiments, at Lowestoft in Suffolk, who published "104 Lyric Poems and Hymns," mostly of inferior merit, 1773). It commences: "Trembling earth gave awful signs," and was transferred to the "Warrington Collection" (p. 77), in seven verses, with a "Hallelujah" after each verse. It was altered by the Rev. THOMAS GIBBONS (a Congregational minister in England, 1720-1785), and has passed since through various transformations. The following reads like another hymn.

ANGELS, roll the rock away!
Death, yield up the mighty prey!
See, the Saviour quits the tomb,
Glowing with immortal bloom.
   Hallelujah! Hallelujah!
Christ the Lord is risen to-day.

Shout, ye seraphs; angels, raise
Your eternal song of praise;
Let the earth's remotest bound
Echo to the blissful sound:
   Hallelujah! Hallelujah!
Christ the Lord is risen to-day.

Holy Father, Holy Son,
Holy Spirit, Three in One,
Glory as of old to Thee
Now and evermore shall be!
   Hallelujah! Hallelujah!
Christ the Lord is risen to-day.

O JESUS! WHEN I THINK OF THEE.

By GEORGE W. BETHUNE, D.D.; died in the Easter season, 1862, in Florence, on a Lord's Day, on which he preached his last sermon. First published in his "Memoir" by Dr. A. R. van Nest, New York, 1867, p. 423.

O JESUS! when I think of Thee,
   Thy manger, cross, and throne,
My spirit trusts exultingly
   In Thee, and Thee alone.

I see Thee in Thy weakness first;
   Then, glorious from Thy shame,
I see Thee death's strong fetters burst,
   And reach heaven's mightiest name.

In each a brother's love I trace
   By power divine exprest,
One in Thy Father God's embrace,
   As on Thy mother's breast.

For me Thou didst become a man,
   For me didst weep and die;
For me achieve Thy wondrous plan,
   For me ascend on high.

O let me share Thy holy birth,
   Thy faith, Thy death to sin!
And, strong amidst the toils of earth,
   My heavenly life begin.

Then shall I know what means the strain
   Triumphant of Saint Paul:
"To live is Christ, to die is gain;"
   Christ is my all in all.

AWAKE, GLAD SOUL! AWAKE! AWAKE!

By JOHN S. B. MONSELL, LL.D., Vicar of Egham, Surrey, b. 1811. From his "Hymns of Love and Praise," Lond. 1863. "Arise, shine; for thy light is come, and the glory of the Lord is risen upon thee."—*Isa.* lx. 1.

AWAKE, glad soul! awake! awake!
   Thy Lord hath risen long,
Go to His grave, and with thee take
   Both tuneful heart and song;
Where life is waking all around,
   Where love's sweet voices sing,
The first bright Blossom may be found
   Of an Eternal Spring.

O Love! which lightens all distress,
  Love, death cannot destroy:
O Grave! whose very emptiness
  To Faith is full of joy;
Let but that Love our hearts supply
  From Heaven's exhaustless Spring,
Then, Grave, where is thy victory?
  And, Death, where is thy sting?

The shade and gloom of life are fled
  This Resurrection-day;
Henceforth in Christ are no more dead,
  The grave hath no more prey:
In Christ we live, in Christ we sleep,
  In Christ we wake and rise;
And the sad tears death makes us weep,
  He wipes from all our eyes.

And every bird and every tree
  And every opening flower
Proclaim His glorious victory,
  His resurrection-power:
The folds are glad, the fields rejoice,
  With vernal verdure spread;
The little hills lift up their voice,
  And shout that Death is dead.

Then wake, glad heart! awake! awake!
  And seek thy risen Lord,
Joy in His resurrection take,
  And comfort in His word;
And let thy life, through all its ways,
  One long thanksgiving be,
Its theme of joy, its song of praise,
  "Christ died, and rose for me."

IN THY GLORIOUS RESURRECTION.

By Dr. Chr. Wordsworth, formerly Archdeacon of Westminster, now Bishop of Lincoln. From his "Holy Year; or, Hymns for Sundays and Holydays," &c., 3rd ed., Lond. 1863, p. 105.

IN Thy glorious Resurrection,
 Lord, we see a world's erection:
  Man in Thee is glorified;
Bliss for which the Patriarchs panted,
Joys by ancient sages chanted,
  Now in Thee are verified.

Oracles of former ages,
Veiled in dim prophetic pages,
  Now lie open to the sight;
Now the Types, which glimmered darkling
In the twilight gloom, are sparkling
  In the blaze of noonday light.

Isaac from the wood is risen;
Joseph issues from the prison;
  See the Paschal Lamb which saves.
Israel through the sea is landed;
Pharaoh and his hosts are stranded,
  And o'erwhelmèd in the waves.

See the cloudy Pillar leading,
Rock refreshing, Manna feeding;
  Joshua fights, and Moses prays:
See the lifted Wave-sheaf, cheering
Pledge of Harvest-fruits appearing,
  Joyful dawn of happy days.

Samson see at night uptearing
Gaza's brazen gates, and bearing
  To the top of Hebron's hill;
Jonah comes from stormy surges,
From his three days' grave emerges,
  Bids beware of coming ill.

Thus Thy Resurrection's glory
Sheds a light on ancient story;
  And it casts a forward ray,—

Beacon-light of solemn warning,
To the dawn of that great morning
   Ushering in the Judgment-Day.

Ever since Thy death and rising
Thou the nations art baptizing
   In Thy death's similitude;
Dead to sin, and ever dying,
And our members mortifying,
   May we walk with life renewed!

Forth, from Thy first Easter going,
Sundays are for ever flowing
   Onward to a boundless sea;
Lord, may they for Thee prepare us,
On a holy river bear us
   To a calm eternity!

Glory be to God the Father,
And to Him who all does gather
   In Himself, the Eternal Son,
And the dead to life upraises;
And to Holy Ghost be praises:
   Glory to the Three in One.

SING ALOUD, CHILDREN!

An Easter hymn for children, by the Rev. Dr. A. R. THOMPSON, New York, 1865. Contributed.

SING aloud, children! sing
   To the glorious King
Of Redemption, who sits on the throne;
   For the seraphim high
   Veil their faces, and cry,
And the angels are praising the Son.

   With His raiment blood-dyed,
   And with wounds in His side,
He returns like a chief from the war,

>   Where His champion blow
>   Hath laid death and hell low,
> And hath driven destruction afar.
>
>   Not a helper stood by
>   When the foemen drew nigh,
> And arrayed their leagued hosts for the fight;
>   But He met them alone,
>   And the victory won
> By His own irresistible might.
>
>   Yes! the triumph He won!
>   Give the Crucified Son
> Hallelujahs of praise ever new;
>   Hail Him, children, and say,
>   Hallelujah! to-day;
> For the Saviour is risen for you.

WHY SHOULD THESE EYES BE TEARFUL?

"THE Victory of Faith." 1 Cor. xv. 57. By Dr. RAY PALMER. From his "Hymns of my Holy Hours," New York, 1867. Written 1867.

> WHY should these eyes be tearful
>   For years too swiftly fled?
> And why these feet be fearful
>   The onward path to tread?
> Why should a chill come o'er me
>   At thoughts of death as near?
> Or when I see before me
>   The silent gates appear?
>
> Behold my Saviour dying!
>   I hear His parting breath;
> Entombed I see Him lying,
>   A captive held of death;
> Yet peacefully He sleepeth,
>   No foe disturbs Him now,
> And love divine still keepeth
>   Its impress on His brow.

But lo! the seal is broken!
　　Rolled back the mighty stone,
In vain was set the token
　　That friend and foe should own.
The weeping Mary bending
　　Sees not her Saviour there;
But sons of light attending
　　A joyful message bear.

The Lord is risen: He liveth,
　　The First-born from the dead;
To Him the Father giveth
　　To be creation's Head.
O'er all for ever reigning,
　　Of death He holds the keys;
And hell—His might constraining—
　　Obeys His high decrees.

Flies now the gloom that shaded
　　The vale of death to me;
The terrors that invaded
　　Are lost, O Christ, in Thee!
The grave, no more appalling,
　　Invites me to repose;
Asleep in Jesus falling,
　　To rise as Jesus rose.

Oh! when to life awaking,
　　The night for ever gone,
My soul, this dust forsaking,
　　Puts incorruption on,
Lord, in Thy lustre shining,
　　In Thine own beauty drest,
My sun no more declining,
　　Thy service be my rest!

THE ASCENSION.

"And when He had spoken these things, while they beheld, He was taken up, and a cloud received Him out of their sight."—*Acts* i. 9.

"Set your affection on things above, not on things on the earth."—*Col.* iii. 2.

O LORD JESUS, who sittest at the right hand of God the Father, as King of saints and eternal High Priest, far above all principality and power, and every name that is named: give us grace, we beseech Thee, that, being delivered from the curse and power of sin, we may ever seek the things that are above; and, when Thou who art our life shalt appear, we also may appear with Thee in glory everlasting, to praise and to enjoy Thee, with the Father and the Holy Ghost, one God, world without end. Amen.

> Qui penetravit inferas
>   Domos Redemptor pacifer,
> Se fert in sedes superas
>   Mundi supremus arbiter.
>
> Ab ascendente ducitur
>   Regnatura captivitas:
> Palma victis asseritur,
>   Mortuis immortalitas.
>   Daniel, II. 367.

GOD Filial pleased to condescend
To be our all-sufficient Friend,
And though exalted to His Throne
That dear relation still to own,
And send the boundless Source of grace,
The Spirit, to supply His place.
From Bishop Ken's Christian Year.

THE ASCENSION.

A HYMN OF GLORY LET US SING.

(Hymnum canamus gloriæ.)

BY BEDA VENERABILIS, an Anglo-Saxon monk and Presbyter at Yarrow, the most learned man of his age, d. 735. DANIEL, I. p. 206; SCHAFF (German translation), No. 143. Translated by Mrs. CHARLES ("Christian Life in Song," p. 141).

A HYMN of glory let us sing;
New songs throughout the world shall ring;
By a new way none ever trod,
Christ mounteth to the throne of God.

The apostles on the mountain stand,—
The mystic mount, in Holy Land;
They, with the Virgin-mother, see
Jesus ascend in majesty.

The angels say to the eleven:
"Why stand ye gazing into heaven?
This is the Saviour,—this is He!
Jesus hath triumphed gloriously!"

They said the Lord should come again,
As these beheld Him rising then,
Calm soaring through the radiant sky,
Mounting its dazzling summits high.

May our affections thither tend,
And thither constantly ascend,
Where, seated on the Father's throne,
Thee reigning in the heavens we own!

Be Thou our present joy, O Lord!
Who wilt be ever our reward;
And, as the countless ages flee,
May all our glory be in Thee!

EXALT, EXALT THE HEAVENLY GATES.

(Ἐπάρατε πυλάς.)

FROM the Greek of ST. JOSEPH OF THE STUDIUM, 830. This most prolific of Greek hymn-writers was a Sicilian by birth; became a monk at Thessalonica and Constantinople; for some years, a slave in Crete; a friend of Photius, the Patriarch of Constantinople, whom he followed into exile. His hymns are tedious, full of verbiage and bombast, and unsuited to our taste. But his canon for Ascension is highly praised by Dr. J. M. NEALE, as being equal to the hymns of John of Damascus. The following is the third ode of this canon, from NEALE'S "Hymns of the Eastern Church," p. 143.

EXALT, exalt, the heavenly gates,
    Ye chiefs of mighty name!
The Lord and King of all things waits,
    Enrobed in earthly frame:"
So to the higher seats they cry,
The humbler legions of the sky.

For Adam, by the serpent's guile,
    Distressed, deceived, o'erthrown,
Thou left'st Thy native home awhile,
    Thou left'st the Father's throne:
Now he is decked afresh with grace,
Thou seek'st once more the heavenly place.

Glad festal keeps the earth to-day,
    Glad festal heaven is keeping:
The ascension-pomp, in bright array,
    Goes proudly skyward sweeping;
The Lord the mighty deed hath done,
And joined the severed into one.

JESUS, LORD OF LIFE ETERNAL.

(Ἰησοῦς ὁ Ζωοδότης.)

From the Greek of Joseph of the Studium, 830, by Dr. Neale.

JESUS, Lord of life eternal,
    Taking those He loved the best,
    Stood upon the mount of Olives,
    And His Own the last time blest:
Then, though He had never left it,
    Sought again His Father's breast.

Know, O world! this highest festal:
    Floods and oceans, clap your hands!
Angels, raise the song of triumph;
    Make response, ye distant lands;
For our flesh is knit to Godhead,
    Knit in everlasting bands.

Loosing death with all its terrors,
    Thou ascendedst up on high;
And to mortals, now Immortal,
    Gavest immortality,
As Thine own disciples saw Thee
    Mounting Victor to the sky.

ON EARTH AWHILE, 'MID SUFFERINGS.

(*In terris adhuc positam.*)

By Peter Abelard (1079-1142), the celebrated schoolman, and unfortunate friend of Heloise. Translated by the Rev. Dr. E. A. Washburn, New York. June, 1868. Contributed.

ON earth awhile, 'mid sufferings tried,
    Still hears the Church, the holy Bride,
    Her Lord from heaven, calling with daily cry,
Bidding her heart ascend to Him on high.

"Draw me," she answers, "after Thee;
Stretch Thy right hand to succour me:
On wingèd winds Thou soarest to the skies;
Without Thy wings, how can I thither rise?"

Ask for the pinions of the dove,
To hasten to that nest of love;
Ask thou the eagle's plumes of tireless might,
That thou may'st climb to the eternal height.

Both wings and eyes will He bestow,
That thou the sun's unclouded glow
With thine undazzled glances may'st behold,
And drink the blessedness to man untold.

Only to wingèd beings given
Is that fair home of upper heaven;
And there the holy soul finds kindred place,
To whom our God shall grant the wings of grace.

TO-DAY ABOVE THE SKY HE SOARED.

(Cœlos ascendit hodie.)

TRANSLATED from the Latin of the 12th century, by Dr. NEALE ("Mediæval Hymns," p. 173). Another translation, by J. W. HEWETT, in SHIPLEY's "Lyra Messianica," p. 419 ("The King of glory, Christ most high, Ascends this day above the sky," &c.).

TO-DAY above the sky He soared:
    Hallelujah!
The King of glory, Christ the Lord!
    Hallelujah!

He sitteth on the Father's hand:
    Hallelujah!
And ruleth sky and sea and land:
    Hallelujah!

Now all things have their end foretold:
    Hallelujah!
In holy David's song of old:
    Hallelujah!

My Lord is seated with the Lord:
　　Hallelujah!
Upon the throne of God adored:
　　Hallelujah!

In this great triumph of our King,
　　Hallelujah!
To God on high all praise we bring:
　　Hallelujah!

To Him all thanks and laud give we:
　　Hallelujah!
The ever-blessed Trinity!
　　Hallelujah!

O CHRIST, WHO HAST PREPARED.

(Nobis Olympo redditus.)

FROM the Latin, by the Rev. J. CHANDLER ("Hymns of the Primitive Church," pp. 86 and 204).

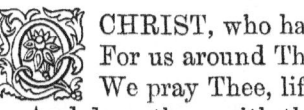CHRIST, who hast prepared a place
For us around Thy throne of grace,
We pray Thee, lift our hearts above,
And draw them with the cords of love!

Source of all good, Thou, gracious Lord,
Art our exceeding great reward;
How transient is our present pain,
How boundless our eternal gain!

With open face and joyful heart,
We then shall see Thee as Thou art:
Our love shall never cease to glow,
Our praise shall never cease to flow.

Thy never-failing grace to prove,
A surety of Thine endless love,
Send down Thy Holy Ghost, to be
The raiser of our souls to Thee.

O future Judge, Eternal Lord,
Thy name be hallowed and adored!
To God the Father, King of heaven,
And Holy Ghost, like praise be given.

THE ASCENSION.

O JESU, WHO ART GONE BEFORE.

(O Christe, qui noster poli.)

From the Latin, by J. Chandler (l. c. p. 87).

O JESU, who art gone before
    To Thy blest realms of light,
Oh, thither may our spirits soar,
    And wing their upward flight!

Make us to those delights aspire,
    Which spring from love to Thee,
Which pass the carnal heart's desire,
    Which faith alone can see:

When to His saints, as their reward,
    Himself Jehovah gives,
And thus its all-sufficient Lord
    The faithful soul receives.

To guide us to Thy glories, Lord,
    To lift us to the sky,
Oh, may Thy Holy Ghost be poured
    Upon us from on high!

Praise to the Father and the Son,
    Who dwells aloft in heaven:
And to the Spirit, Three in One,
    Let equal praise be given.

TO-DAY OUR LORD WENT UP.

(Auf diesen Tag bedenken wir.)

From the German of Johann Zwick (the editor of the first German Reformed Hymn-Book, Zürich, 1540). The best hymn of this author. Translated by Miss C. Winkworth ("Lyra Germ." II. 73). The original has six stanzas.

TO-DAY our Lord went up on high,
    And so our songs we raise:
To Him with strong desire we cry
    To keep us in His grace;

For we poor sinners here beneath
Are dwelling still 'mid woe and death.
  All hope in Him we place :
    Hallelujah ! Hallelujah !

Thank God that now the way is made !
  The cherub-guarded door,
Through Him on whom our help was laid,
  Stands open evermore ;
Who knoweth this is glad at heart,
And swift prepares him to depart
  Where Christ is gone before :
    Hallelujah ! Hallelujah !

Our heavenward course begins when we
  Have found our Father, God,
And join us to His sons, and flee
  The paths that once we trod ;
For He looks down, and they look up :
They feel His love, they live in hope,
  Until they meet their Lord :
    Hallelujah ! Hallelujah !

Then all the depths of joy that lie
  In this day we shall know,
When we are made like Him on high,
  Whom we confess below ;
When, bathed in life's eternal flood,
We dwell with Him, the highest Good :
  God grant us this to know !
    Hallelujah ! Hallelujah !

SINCE CHRIST IS GONE TO HEAVEN.

(Allein auf Christi Himmelfahrt.)

JOSUA WEGELIN, 1637. Translated from the German, by C. WINKWORTH
("Lyra Germ." II. 75).

SINCE Christ is gone to heaven, His home
  I, too, must one day share ;
And in this hope I overcome
All anguish, all despair ;

For where the Head is, well we know
The members He hath left below
  In time He gathers there.

Since Christ hath reached His glorious throne
  And mighty gifts are His,
My heart can rest in heaven alone;
  On earth my Lord I miss:
I long to be with Him on high,
And heart and thoughts would hourly fly
  Where now my treasure is.

From Thy ascension let such grace,
  My Lord, be found in me,
That steadfast faith may guide my ways
  Unfaltering up to Thee,
And at Thy voice I may depart
With joy to dwell where Thou, Lord, art;
  Oh, grant this prayer to me!

LO, GOD TO HEAVEN ASCENDETH!

(Gott führet auf gen Himmel.)

FROM the German of GOTTFRIED WILHELM SACER (1635-1699). "God is gone up with a shout, the Lord with the sound of a trumpet."—*Ps.* xlvii. 5. Translated by Miss FRANCES ELIZABETH COX ("Sacred Hymns from the German," Lond. 1841, p. 39).

LO, God to heaven ascendeth!
    Throughout its regions vast,
  With shouts triumphant blendeth
    The trumpet's thrilling blast:
  Sing praise to Christ the Lord,
    Sing praise with exultation,
    King of each heathen nation
  The God of Hosts adored!

With joy is heaven resounding,
    Christ's glad return to see;
  Behold the saints surrounding
    The Lord who set them free:

LO, GOD TO HEAVEN ASCENDETH.

Bright myriads thronging come;
 The cherub band rejoices,
 And loud seraphic voices
Welcome Messiah home.

No more the way is hidden,
 Since Christ our Head arose:
No more to man forbidden
 The road to heaven that goes.
Our Lord is gone before,
 But here He will not leave us;
 In heaven He'll soon receive us:
He opens wide the door.

Christ is our place preparing,
 To heaven we, too, shall rise,
And, joys angelic sharing,
 Be where our treasure lies:
There may each heart be found!
 Where Jesus Christ has entered,
 There let our hopes be centred,
Our course still heavenward bound!

May we, His servants, thither
 In heart and mind ascend;
And let us sing together,
 "We seek Thee, Christ our Friend,
Thee, God's Anointed Son!
 Our Life, and Way to heaven,
 To whom all power is given,
Our Joy and Hope and Crown!"

When, on our vision dawning,
 Will break the wished-for hour
Of that all-glorious morning,
 When Christ shall come with power?
O come, thou welcome Day!
 When we, our Saviour meeting,
 His second advent greeting,
Shall hail the heaven-sent ray.

HOSANNA TO THE PRINCE OF LIGHT!

Isaac Watts, 1709.

HOSANNA to the Prince of light,
    Who clothed Himself in clay;
Entered the iron gates of death,
    And tore the bars away.

Death is no more the king of dread,
    Since our Immanuel rose;
He took the tyrant's sting away,
    And conquered all our foes.

See, how the Conqueror mounts aloft,
    And to His Father flies!
With scars of honour in His flesh,
    And triumph in His eyes.

There our exalted Saviour reigns,
    And scatters blessings down
From the right hand of Majesty,
    On the celestial throne.

Raise your devotion, mortal tongues,
    To reach this blest abode;
Sweet be the accents of your songs
    To our incarnate God.

Bright angels, strike your loudest strings,
    Your sweetest voices raise!
Let heaven, and all created things,
    Sound our Immanuel's praise!

HEAVENWARD STILL OUR PATHWAY TENDS.

(Himmelan geht unsre Bahn.)

By Benjamin Schmolke, 1731. Translated by Miss Frances Elizabeth Cox. Another translation by Miss C. Winkworth: "Heavenward doth our journey tend."

HEAVENWARD still our pathway tends,
    Here on earth we are but strangers;
    Till our road in Canaan ends,
    Safely passed this wild of dangers,
Pilgrims we, a scattered band,
Seek above our Fatherland.

Heavenward still my soul ascend!
    Thou art one of heaven's creations;
Earth can ne'er give aim or end
    Fit to fill thy aspirations:
Turns a heaven-illumined mind
Evermore its source to find.

Heavenward still! God's volume blest,
    Thus, throughout its sacred pages,
Calls me on, and speaks of rest,
    Rest with Him through endless ages;
While my heart that call attends,
Still to heaven my path ascends.

Heavenward still my thoughts arise,
    When His festal board invites me;
Then my spirit upward flies,
    Foretaste then of heaven delights me:
When on earth this food has ceased
Comes the Lamb's own Marriage-feast.

Heavenward still my spirit wends,
    That fair land by faith exploring;
Heavenward still my heart ascends,
    Sun and moon and stars out-soaring;
Their faint rays in vain would try
Once with light of heaven to vie.

Heavenward still, when life shall close,
   Death to my true home shall guide me;
There, triumphant o'er my woes,
   Lasting bliss shall God provide me;
Christ Himself the way has led,
Joyful in His steps I tread.

Still then heavenward! heavenward still!
   That shall be my watchword ever!
Joys of heaven my heart shall fill,
   Chasing joys that filled it never:
Heavenward still my thoughts shall run,
Till the gate of heaven is won.

CONQUERING PRINCE AND LORD OF GLORY.

(Siegesfürst und Ehrenkönig.)

FROM the German of GERHARD TERSTEEGEN, a deeply spiritual hymnist, 1731. Translated by Miss C. WINKWORTH "Lyra Germ." II. 76; changed, 1862).

CONQUERING Prince and Lord of glory,
   Majesty enthroned in light!
All the heavens are bowed before Thee,
   Far beyond them spreads Thy might.
Shall I fall not at Thy feet,
And my heart with rapture beat,
Now Thy glory is displayed,
Thine ere yet the worlds were made?

As I watch Thee far ascending
   To the right hand of the throne,
See the host before Thee bending,
   Praising Thee in sweetest tone,
Shall I not, too, at Thy feet
Hear the angels' strain repeat,
And rejoice that heaven doth sing
With the triumph of my King?

Power and Spirit are overflowing;
   On me also be they poured:
Every hinderance overthrowing,
   Make Thy foes Thy footstool, Lord.
Yea, let earth's remotest end
To Thy righteous sceptre bend;
Make Thy way before Thee plain,
O'er all hearts and spirits reign.

Lo, Thy presence now is filling
   All Thy Church in every place!
Fill my heart, too: make me willing
   In this season of Thy grace.
Come, Thou King of glory! come:
Deign to make my heart Thy home:
There abide and rule alone,
As upon Thy heavenly throne.

Thou art leaving me, yet bringing
   God and heaven most inly near:
From this earthly life upspringing,
   As though still I saw Thee here,
Let my heart, transplanted hence,
Strange to earth and time and sense,
Dwell with Thee in heaven e'en now,
Where our only joy art Thou!

HAIL THE DAY THAT SEES HIM RISE!

Rev. Charles Wesley. From his "Hymns and Sacred Poems," 1739. In "Hymns Ancient and Modern," this hymn is radically changed so as to be hardly recognizable.

HAIL the day that sees Him rise,
   Ravished from our wishful eyes!
Christ, awhile to mortals given,[1]
Re-ascends His native heaven.

---

[1] Or:—
      Christ, the Lamb for sinners given.

THE ASCENSION.

There the pompous triumph waits:
"Lift your heads, eternal gates,
Wide unfold the radiant scene;
Take the King of glory in!"

Circled round with angel powers,
Their triumphant Lord and ours,
Conqueror over death and sin;
Take the King of glory in!

Him though highest heaven receives,
Still He loves the earth He leaves;
Though returning to His throne,
Still He calls mankind His own.

See, He lifts His hands above!
See, He shows the prints of love!
Hark! His gracious lips bestow
Blessings on His Church below!

Still for us His death He pleads;
Prevalent He intercedes;
Near Himself prepares our place,
Harbinger of human race.

Master (will we ever say),
Taken from our head to-day,
See Thy faithful servants, see,
Ever gazing up to Thee.

Grant, though parted from our sight,
High above yon azure height,
Grant our hearts may thither rise,
Following Thee beyond the skies.

Ever upward let us move,
Wafted on the wings of love;
Looking when our Lord shall come,
Longing, gasping after home.

There we shall with Thee remain,
Partners of Thy endless reign;
There Thy face unclouded see,
Find our heaven of heavens in Thee.

OUR LORD IS RISEN FROM THE DEAD.

Rev. CHARLES WESLEY, 1739.

OUR Lord is risen from the dead:
   Our Jesus is gone up on high;
The powers of hell are captive led,
   Dragged to the portals of the sky.
There His triumphant chariot waits,
   And angels chant the solemn lay:
Lift up your heads, ye heavenly gates;
   Ye everlasting doors, give way!

Loose all your bars of massy light,
   And wide unfold the ethereal scene:
He claims these mansions as His right;
   Receive the King of glory in!
Who is the King of glory? who?
   The Lord who all our foes o'ercame;
The world, sin, death, and hell o'erthrew;
   And Jesus is the Conqueror's name.

Lo! His triumphant chariot waits,
   And angels chant the solemn lay:
Lift up your heads, ye heavenly gates;
   Ye everlasting doors, give way!
Who is the King of glory? who?
   The Lord, of glorious power possessed;
The king of saints and angels too;
   God over all, for ever blest!

ALL HAIL THE POWER OF JESUS' NAME.

By the Rev. EDWARD PERRONET (son of Rev. Vincent Perronet), an associate of the Wesleys; afterwards employed by Lady Huntingdon; then pastor of a dissenting congregation; d. at Canterbury, in 1792. From his "Occasional Verses, Moral and Social, published for the instruction and amusement of the candidly Serious and Religious," London, 1785 (216 pages). A copy of this rare volume, published by a friend of Perronet, without his name, with some written remarks of the former owner, John Gaddsby, on the back of the title page, is preserved in the Library of the British Museum, from which I have copied the text, May 28, 1869. The hymn there is on p. 22, and bears the title "On the Resurrection." It is full of joyous inspiration, and very popular in America. It is far superior to the other poems of the same author. It is often falsely ascribed to DUNCAN, or others, and arbitrarily changed, or abridged. Charles Rogers (" Lyr. Brit." p. 150) gives the correct text, from the original in the British Museum.

ALL hail the power of Jesu's name!
    Let angels prostrate fall;
    Bring forth the royal diadem,
To crown Him Lord of all.

Let high-born seraphs tune the lyre,
    And, as they tune it, fall
Before His face, who tunes their choir,
    And crown Him Lord of all.

Crown Him, ye morning-stars of light,
    Who fixed this floating ball;
Now hail the strength of Israel's might,
    And crown Him Lord of all.

Crown Him, ye martyrs of our God,
    Who from His altar call;
Extol the Stem of Jesse's rod,
    And crown Him Lord of all.

Ye seed of Israel's chosen race,
    Ye ransom'd of the fall,
Hail Him who saves you by His grace,
    And crown Him Lord of all.

Hail Him, ye heirs of David's line,
    Whom David Lord did call;
The God incarnate, Man Divine;
    And crown Him Lord of all.

Sinners! whose love can ne'er forget
    The wormwood and the gall,
Go—spread your trophies at His feet,
    And crown Him Lord of all.

Let every tribe, and every tongue,
    That bound creation's call,[1]
Now shout in universal song,
    The crownèd Lord of all![2]

---

[1] Others: "On this terrestrial ball;" or "That hear the Saviour's call."
[2] Hymn-books generally read here again: "And crown Him Lord of all."

SOFT CLOUD, THAT, WHILE THE BREEZE OF MAY.

BY the Rev. JOHN KEBLE, D.D. (d. 1866). From his "Christian Year" (31st ed., 1857). "Why stand ye gazing up into heaven? This same Jesus, which is taken up from you into heaven, shall so come in like manner as ye have seen Him go into heaven."—*Acts* i. 11.

SOFT cloud, that, while the breeze of May
   Chants her glad matins in the leafy arch,
Draw'st thy bright veil across the heavenly way,
   Meet pavement for an angel's glorious march:

My soul is envious of mine eye,
   That it should soar and glide with thee so fast,
The while my grovelling thoughts half-buried lie,
   Or lawless roam around this earthly waste.

Chains of my heart, avaunt, I say:
   I will arise, and in the strength of love
Pursue the bright track ere it fade away,
   My Saviour's pathway to His home above.

Sure, when I reach the point where earth
   Melts into nothing from th' uncumbered sight,
Heaven will o'ercome th' attraction of my birth,
   And I shall sink in yonder sea of light:

Till resting by th' incarnate Lord,
   Once bleeding, now triumphant for my sake,
I mark Him,—how, by seraph hosts adored,
   He to earth's lowest cares is still awake.

The sun and every vassal star,
   All space, beyond the soar of angel wings,
Wait on His word; and yet He stays His car
   For every sigh a contrite suppliant brings.

He listens to the silent tear,
   For all the anthems of the boundless sky;
And shall our dreams of music bar our ear
   To His soul-piercing voice for ever nigh?

THE ASCENSION.

Nay, gracious Saviour; but as now
  Our thoughts have traced Thee to Thy glory throne,
So help us ever more with Thee to bow
  Where human sorrow breathes her lowly moan.

We must not stand to gaze too long,
  Though on unfolding Heaven our gaze we bend,
Where, lost behind the bright angelic throng,
  We see Christ's entering triumph slow ascend.

No fear but we shall soon behold,
  Faster than now it fades, that gleam revive,
When, issuing from His cloud of fiery gold,
  Our wasted frames feel the true Sun, and live.

Then shall we see Thee as Thou art,
  For ever fixed in no unfruitful gaze,
But such as lifts the new-created heart,
  Age after age, in worthier love and praise.

LAMB, THE ONCE CRUCIFIED!

(Lamm, das gelitten, und Löwe, der siegreich gerungen.)

FROM the German of Mrs. Dr. META HEUSSER-SCHWEIZER, the most gifted and sweetest of female poets in the German tongue; born, 1797, at Hirzel, near Zürich, Switzerland, where she resides, in modest retirement, to this day. This truly sublime hymn is the second part of a larger hymn composed in spring, 1831, and has passed into several German hymn-books (SCHAFF, Nos. 149 and 388). Translated, April, 1868, at the request of the editor, by the Rev. Professor THOMAS C. PORTER, of Lafayette College, Easton, Pa., who has successfully overcome the unusual difficulties of the German dactylic metre (adapted to the favorite choral, "Lobe den Herren, den mächtigen König der Ehren"). Albert Knapp has edited a collection of poems of Mrs. H., under the title, "Lieder einer Verborgenen," Leipz. 1858; 2nd ed. 1863. A second collection, under her proper name, appeared 1867. They are apples of gold in baskets of silver, and exhibit a rare union of lofty genius with humble piety.

LAMB, the once crucified! Lion, by triumph
    surrounded!
Victim all bloody, and Hero, Who hell hast
    confounded!

LAMB, THE ONCE CRUCIFIED.

   Pain-riven Heart,
  That from earth's deadliest smart
O'er all the heavens hast bounded![1]

Thou in the depths wert to mortals the highest revealing,
God in humanity veiled, Thy full glory concealing!
   "Worthy art Thou!"
  Shouteth eternity now,
Praise to Thee endlessly pealing.

Heavenly Love, in the language of earth past expression!
Lord of all worlds, unto whom every tongue owes confession!
   Didst Thou not go,
  And, under sentence of woe,
Rescue the doomed by transgression?

O'er the abyss of the grave, and its horrors infernal,
Victory's palm Thou art waving in triumph supernal:
   Who to Thee cling,
  Circled by hope, shall now bring
Out of its gulf life eternal.

Son of Man, Saviour, in whom, with deep tenderness
  blending,
Infinite Pity to wretches her balm is extending,
   On Thy dear breast,
  Weary and numb, they may rest,
Quickened to joy never ending.

Strange condescension! immaculate Purity, deigning
Union with souls where the vilest pollution is reigning,
   Beareth their sin,
  Seeketh the fallen to win,
Even the lowest regaining.

---

[1] The first stanza is truly classical in thought and expression, but almost untranslatable:—

  "Lamm, das gelitten, und Löwe, der siegreich gerungen!
  Blutendes Opfer, und Held, der die Hölle bezwungen!
   Brechendes Herz,
    Das sich aus irdischem Schmerz
  Ueber die Himmel geschwungen!"

The whole range of German poetry furnishes no finer specimen of dactylic versification. What sublime contrasts, and what noble language!

Sweetly persuasive, to me, too, Thy call has resounded;
Melting my heart so obdurate, Thy love has abounded;
      Back to the fold,
      Led by Thy hand, I behold
Grace all my path has surrounded.

Bless thou the Lord, O my soul! who, thy pardon assuring,
Heals thy diseases, and grants thee new life ever during,
      Joy amid woe,
      Peace amid strife here below,
Unto thee ever securing.

Upward, on pinions celestial, to regions of pleasure,
Into the land whose bright glories no mortal can measure,
      Strong hope and love
      Bear Thee, the fulness to prove
Of Thy salvation's rich treasure.

There, as He is, we shall view Him, with rapture abiding,
Cheered even here by His glance, when the darkness dividing
      Lets down a ray,
      Over the perilous way
Thousands of wanderers guiding.

Join, O my voice! the vast chorus, with trembling emotion:
Chorus of saints, who, though sundered by land and by ocean,
      With sweet accord
      Praise the same glorious Lord,
One in their ceaseless devotion.

Break forth, O nature! in song, when the spring tide is nighest;
World that hast seen His salvation, no longer thou sighest!
      Shout, starry train,
      From your empyreal plain,
"Glory to God in the highest!"

SEE, THE CONQUEROR.

By Chr. Wordsworth, D.D., Bishop of Lincoln. From his "Hymns for the Holy Year," Lond., 1863, p. 129. Verse 10 (a doxology) is omitted.

SEE, the Conqueror mounts in triumph,
    See the King in royal state,
Riding on the clouds His chariot,
    To His heavenly palace-gate;
Hark, the choirs of angel-voices
    Joyful Hallelujahs sing!
And the portals high are lifted,
    To receive their heavenly King.

Who is this that comes in glory,
    With the trump of Jubilee?
Lord of battles, God of armies,
    He has gained the victory;
He who on the cross did suffer,
    He who from the grave arose,
He has vanquished sin and Satan,
    He by death has spoiled His foes.

Now our heavenly Aaron enters,
    With His blood within the veil;
Joshua now is come to Canaan,
    And the kings before Him quail;
Now He plants the tribes of Israel
    In their promised resting-place;
Now our great Elijah offers
    Double portion of His grace.

Thou hast raised our human nature
    On the clouds to God's right hand;
There we sit in heavenly places,
    There with Thee in glory stand;
Jesus reigns, adored by angels;
    Man with God is on the throne;
Mighty Lord, in Thine Ascension
    We by faith behold our own.

THE ASCENSION.

Holy Ghost, Illuminator,
   Shed Thy beams upon our eyes,
Help us to look up with Stephen,
   And to see beyond the skies,
Where the Son of Man in glory
   Standing is at God's right hand,
Beckoning on His Martyr army,
   Succouring His faithful band.

See Him, who is gone before us,
   Heavenly mansions to prepare,
See Him, who is ever pleading
   For us with prevailing prayer;
See Him, who with sound of trumpet
   And with His angelic train
Summoning the world to judgment
   On the clouds shall come again.

Lift us up from earth to heaven,
   Give us wings of faith and love,
Gales of holy aspiration
   Wafting us to realms above;
That, with hearts and minds uplifted,
   We with Christ our Lord may dwell,
Where He sits enthroned in glory
   In the heavenly citadel.

So at last, when He appeareth,
   We from out our graves may spring,
With our youth renewed like eagles',
   Flocking round our heavenly King,
Caught up on the clouds of heaven,
   And may meet Him in the air,
Rise to realms where He is reigning,
   And may reign for ever there.

HE IS GONE; BEYOND THE SKIES.

A. P. STANLEY, D.D., Dean of Westminster, author of "History of Israel," and other works, 1859. Of this hymn Dean ALFORD has transferred three stanzas to his "Year of Praise," for Ascension Day, Hymn 133. It is here given complete from a MS. copy kindly furnished by the author to the editor on Ascension Day, May 6, 1869. The Dean informs me that this hymn "was written about ten years ago (1859), at the request of a friend, whose children had complained to him that there was no suitable hymn for Ascension Day, and who were eagerly asking what had been the feelings of the disciples after that event."

HE is gone—beyond the skies,
A cloud receives Him from our eyes:
Gone beyond the highest height
Of mortal gaze or angel's flight:
Through the veils of time and space,
Passed into the holiest place:
All the toil, the sorrow done,
All the battle fought and won.

He is gone—and we return,
And our hearts within us burn;
Olivet no more shall greet
With welcome shout His coming feet:
Never shall we track Him more
On Gennesareth's glistening shore:
Never in that look or voice
Shall Zion's walls again rejoice.

He is gone—and we remain
In this world of sin and pain:
In the void which He has left,
On this earth, of Him bereft,
We have still His work to do,
We can still His path pursue:
Seek Him both in friend or foe,
In ourselves His image show.

He is gone—we heard Him say,
" Good that I should go away;"
Gone is that dear form and face,
But not gone His present grace;

THE ASCENSION.

Tho' Himself no more we see,
Comfortless we cannot be—
No! His Spirit still is ours,
Quickening, freshening all our powers.

He is gone—towards their goal,
World and church must onward roll;
Far behind we leave the past;
Forward are our glances cast:
Still His words before us range
Through the ages, as they change:
Wheresoe'er the truth shall lead,
He will give whate'er we need.

He is gone—but we once more
Shall behold Him as before,
In the heaven of heavens the same
As on earth He went and came.
In the many mansions there,
Place for us He will prepare:
In that world, unseen, unknown,
He and we may yet be one.

He is gone—but, not in vain,
Wait, until He comes again:
He is risen, He is not here;
Far above this earthly sphere:
Evermore in heart and mind,
Where our peace in Him we find,
To our own Eternal Friend,
Thitherward let us ascend.

SING, O HEAVENS! O EARTH, REJOICE!

By JOHN S. B. MONSELL, LL.D., Vicar of Egham, England, author of several poetic volumes, b. 1811. From his "Hymns of Love and Praise," 1863.

SING, O Heavens! O Earth, rejoice!
Angel harp and human voice,
Round Him, as He rises, raise
Your ascending Saviour's praise:
Hallelujah!

Bruisèd is the serpent's head,
Hell is vanquished, Death is dead;
And to Christ, gone up on high,
Captive is captivity:
    Hallelujah!

All His work and warfare done,
He into His heaven is gone,
And, beside His Father's throne,
Now is pleading for His own:
    Hallelujah!

Asking gifts for sinful men,
That He may come down again,
And, the fallen to restore,
In them dwell for evermore:
    Hallelujah!

Sing, O Heavens! O Earth, rejoice!
Angel harp and human voice,
Round Him, in His glory, raise
Your ascended Saviour's praise:
    Hallelujah!

CHRIST IN GLORY.

HIS INTERCESSION AND REIGN.

"AND [God] hath put all things under His feet, and gave Him to be the head over all things to the church, which is His body, the fulness of Him that filleth all in all."—*Eph.* i. 22, 23.

"Who is he that condemneth? It is Christ that died; yea, rather, that is risen again, who is even at the right hand of God, who also maketh intercession for us."—*Rom.* viii. 34.

"We have such an High Priest, who is set on the right hand of the throne of the Majesty in the heavens."—*Heb.* viii. 1.

THOU art the King of glory, O Christ!
   Thou art the everlasting Son of the Father.
   When Thou tookest upon Thee to deliver man,
Thou didst not abhor the Virgin's womb.
When Thou hadst overcome the sharpness of death,
Thou didst open the kingdom of heaven to all believers.
Thou sittest at the right hand of God,
In the glory of the Father.
We believe that Thou shalt come to be our Judge,
We therefore pray Thee, help Thy servants,
Whom Thou hast redeemed with Thy precious blood.
Make them to be numbered with Thy saints,
In glory everlasting. Amen.
                     From the " Te Deum."

BRIGHT with all his crowns of glory,
  See the royal Victor's brow;
Once for sinners marred and gory,
  See the Lamb exalted now
    While before Him
  All his ransomed brethren bow.

LET worlds above, and worlds below,
  In songs united sing;
And, while eternal ages flow,
  Loud shout, the Lord is King.
      —EDWARD PERRONET (*from a copy of his
      "Occasional Verses," 1785, p. 25, in the
      British Museum*).

CHRIST IN GLORY.

HIS INTERCESSION AND REIGN.

CHRIST, THOU THE CHAMPION.

(Christe, Du Beistand Deiner Kreuzgemeine.)

FROM the German of MATTHÆUS APELLES VON LÖWENSTERN, a statesman; b. 1594, d. 1648; author of thirty hymns. This hymn was written, 1644, during the Thirty Years' War. "Be of good cheer: I have overcome the world."—*John* xvi. 33. Translated by C. WINKWORTH ("Lyra Germ." I. 105). It was a favourite hymn of Niebuhr and Bunsen.

CHRIST, Thou the champion of the band who own
    Thy cross, oh, make Thy succour quickly known!
The schemes of those who long our blood have sought
    Bring Thou to nought.

Do Thou Thyself for us Thy children fight,
Withstand the devil, quell his rage and might,
Whate'er assails Thy members left below,
    Do Thou o'erthrow.

And give us peace: peace in the church and school,
Peace to the powers who o'er our country rule,
Peace to the conscience, peace within the heart,
    Do Thou impart.

So shall Thy goodness here be still adored,
Thou guardian of Thy little flock, dear Lord;
And heaven and earth through all eternity
    Shall worship Thee.

MY JESUS, IF THE SERAPHIM.

(Mein Jesu, dem die Seraphinen.)

THE eternal Priesthood of Christ. By WOLFGANG CHRISTOPH DESSLER, 1692 (SCHAFF, No. 150). Translated by C. WINKWORTH, under the title, "The Throne of Grace" ("Lyra Germ." II. 78).

MY Jesus, if the seraphim,
    The burning host that near Thee stand,
  Before Thy Majesty are dim,
    And veil their face at Thy command;
How shall these mortal eyes of mine,
    Now dark with evil's hateful night,
    Endure to gaze upon the light
That aye surrounds that throne of Thine?

Yet grant the eye of faith, O Lord!
    To pierce within the Holy Place;
For I am saved and Thou adored,
    If I am quickened by Thy grace.
Behold, O King! before Thy throne
    My soul in lowly love doth bend,
    O show Thyself her gracious Friend!
And say, "I choose thee for Mine own."

Have mercy, Lord of Love! for long
    My spirit for Thy mercy sighs:
My inmost soul hath found a tongue,
    "Be merciful, O God!" she cries:
I know Thou wilt not bid me go,
    Thou canst not be ungracious, Lord,
    To one for whom Thy blood was poured,
Whose guilt was cancelled by Thy woe.

Here in Thy gracious hands I fall,
    To Thee I cling with faith's embrace:
O righteous Sovereign, hear my call!
    And turn, O turn, to me in grace!
For through Thy sorrows I am just,
    And guilt no more in me is found:
    Thus reconciled, my soul is bound
To Thee in endless love and trust.

And let Thy wisdom be my guide,
  Nor take Thy light from me away;
Thy grace be ever at my side,
  That from the path I may not stray
That Thou dost love, but evermore
  In steadfast faith my course fulfil,
  And keep Thy word, and do Thy will,
Thy love within, Thy heaven before!

Reach down, and arm me with Thy hand,
  And strengthen me with inner might,
That I, through faith, may strive and stand,
  Though craft and force against me fight:
So shall the kingdom of Thy love
  Be through me and within me spread,
  That honours Thee, our glorious Head,
And crowneth us in realms above.

Yes, yes, to Thee my soul would cleave:
  O choose it, Saviour, for Thy throne!
Couldst Thou in love to me once leave
  The glory that was all Thine own?
So honour Thou my life and heart
  That Thou mayst find a heaven in me;
  And, when this house decayed shall be,
Then grant the heaven where now Thou art.

To Thee I rise in faith on high:
  Oh, bend Thou down in love to me!
Let nothing rob me of this joy,
  That all my soul is filled with Thee:
As long as I have life and breath,
  Thee will I honour, fear, and love;
  And when this heart hath ceased to move
Yet Love shall live and conquer death.

JESUS SHALL REIGN.

Isaac Watts, D.D., 1719. *Ps.* lxxii.

JESUS shall reign where'er the sun
  Does his successive journeys run;
  His kingdom stretch from shore to shore,
Till moons shall wax and wane no more.

Behold the islands with their kings,
And Europe her best tribute brings;
From north to south the princes meet
To pay their homage at His feet.

There Persia, glorious to behold,
There India shines in eastern gold;
And barb'rous nations, at His word,
Submit and bow, and own their Lord.

For Him shall endless prayer be made,
And praises throng to crown His head;
His name, like sweet perfume, shall rise
With every morning sacrifice.

People and realms of every tongue
Dwell on His love with sweetest song;
And infant voices shall proclaim
Their early blessings on His name.

Blessings abound where'er He reigns;
The prisoner leaps to lose his chains;
The weary find eternal rest,
And all the sons of want are blest.

Where He displays His healing power,
Death and the curse are known no more;
In Him the tribes of Adam boast
More blessings than their father lost.

Let every creature rise, and bring
Peculiar honours to our King;
Angels descend with songs again,
And earth repeat the long Amen!

BEHOLD THE GLORIES OF THE LAMB!

Isaac Watts, DD., 1674-1748.   "A new song to the Lamb that was slain."—
Rev. v. 6, 8-12.

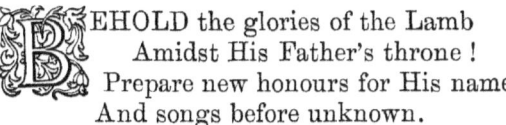EHOLD the glories of the Lamb
　　Amidst His Father's throne !
Prepare new honours for His name,
　　And songs before unknown.

Let elders worship at His feet,
　　The Church adore around,
With vials full of odours sweet,
　　And harps of sweeter sound.

Those are the prayers of the saints,
　　And these the hymns they raise;
Jesus is kind to our complaints,
　　He loves to hear our praise.

Eternal Father, who shall look
　　Into Thy secret will?
Who but the Son should take that book,
　　And open every seal?

He shall fulfil Thy great decrees :
　　The Son deserves it well;
Lo, in His hand the sov'reign keys
　　Of heaven and death and hell!

Now to the Lamb, that once was slain,
　　Be endless blessings paid;
Salvation, glory, joy, remain
　　For ever on Thy head.

Thou hast redeemed our souls with blood,
　　Hast set the prisoners free,
Hast made us kings and priests to God,
　　And we shall reign with Thee.

The worlds of nature and of grace
　　Are put beneath Thy power;
Then shorten these delaying days,
　　And bring the promised hour.

REJOICE! THE LORD IS KING.

Rev. Charles Wesley, 1745.

REJOICE! the Lord is King:
    Your Lord and King adore;
  Mortals, give thanks and sing,
    And triumph evermore:
Lift up your heart, lift up your voice,
Rejoice, again I say, rejoice.

  Jesus the Saviour reigns,
    The God of truth and love;
  When He had purged our stains,
    He took His seat above:
Lift up your heart, lift up your voice;
Rejoice, again I say, rejoice.

  His kingdom cannot fail;
    He rules o'er earth and heaven;
  The keys of death and hell
    Are to our Jesus given:
Lift up your heart, lift up your voice;
Rejoice, again I say, rejoice.

  He sits at God's right hand,
    Till all His foes submit,
  And bow to His command,
    And fall beneath His feet:
Lift up your heart, lift up your voice;
Rejoice, again I say, rejoice.

  He all His foes shall quell,
    Shall all our sins destroy,
  And every bosom swell
    With pure seraphic joy:
Lift up your heart, lift up your voice;
Rejoice, again I say, rejoice.

  Rejoice in glorious hope;
    Jesus the Judge shall come,
  And take His servants up
    To their eternal home:
We soon shall hear the archangel's voice;
The trump of God shall sound, Rejoice!

NOW LET OUR CHEERFUL EYES SURVEY.

Philip Doddridge, D.D.; born in London, 1702; died at Lisbon, 1751.

NOW let our cheerful eyes survey
    Our great High Priest above,
And celebrate His constant care,
    His sympathy and love.

Though raised to a superior throne,
    Where angels bow around,
And high o'er all the heavenly host,
    With matchless honour crowned,—

The names of all His saints He bears,
    Deep graven on His heart;
Nor shall the meanest Christian say,
    That he hath lost his part.

Those characters shall fair abide
    Our everlasting trust,
When gems and monuments and crowns
    Are mouldered down to dust.

So, gracious Saviour, on my breast
    May Thy dear name be worn,
A sacred ornament and guard,
    To endless ages borne.

WHERE HIGH THE HEAVENLY TEMPLE STANDS.

Michael Bruce, 1746-1767.

WHERE high the heavenly temple stands,
The house of God not made with hands,
A great High Priest our nature wears,
The Patron of mankind appears.

He who for men in mercy stood,
And poured on earth His precious blood,
Pursues in heaven His plan of grace,
The Guardian God of human race.

Though now ascended up on high,
He bends on earth a brother's eye;
Partaker of the human name,
He knows the frailty of our frame.

Our Fellow-sufferer yet retains
A fellow-feeling of our pains;
And still remembers in the skies
His tears and agonies and cries.

In every pang that rends the heart,
The Man of sorrows had a part;
He sympathizes with our grief,
And to the sufferer sends relief.

With boldness, therefore, at the throne
Let us make all our sorrows known;
And ask the aids of heavenly power
To help us in the evil hour.

HE WHO ON EARTH AS MAN WAS KNOWN.

JOHN NEWTON, 1779. From the "Olney Hymns," Book I. No. 59.
On *Isa.* xxxii. 2.

HE who on earth as man was known,
   And bore our sins and pains,
Now, seated on the eternal throne,
   The God of glory reigns.

His hands the wheels of nature guide
   With an unerring skill;
And countless worlds, extended wide,
   Obey His sovereign will.

While harps unnumbered sound His praise
   In yonder world above,
His saints on earth admire His ways,
   And glory in His love.

His righteousness, to faith revealed,
   Wrought out for guilty worms,
Affords a hiding-place and shield
   From enemies and storms.

This land, through which His pilgrims go,
  Is desolate and dry;
But streams of grace from Him o'erflow,
  Their thirst to satisfy.

When troubles, like a burning sun,
  Beat heavy on their head,
To this Almighty Rock they run,
  And find a pleasing shade.

How glorious He! how happy they
  In such a glorious Friend!
Whose love secures them all the way,
  And crowns them at the end.

THE HEAD THAT ONCE WAS CROWNED.

Rev. THOMAS KELLY, 1769-1855.

THE Head that once was crowned with thorns
  Is crowned with glory now;
A royal diadem adorns
  The mighty Victor's brow.

The highest place that heaven affords
  Is His, is His by right,—
"The King of kings, and Lord of lords,"
  And heaven's eternal Light!

The joy of all who dwell above,
  The joy of all below,
To whom He manifests His love,
  And grants His name to know.

To them, the cross, with all its shame,
  With all its grace, is given;
Their name an everlasting name,
  Their joy the joy of heaven.

They suffer with their Lord below,
  They reign with Him above;
Their profit and their joy to know
  The mystery of His love.

The cross He bore is life and health,
  Though shame and death to Him;
His people's hope, His people's health,
  Their everlasting theme.

THE ATONING WORK IS DONE.

Rev. Thomas Kelly; died, at Dublin, 1855.

THE atoning work is done,
  The Victim's blood is shed;
And Jesus now is gone
  His people's cause to plead;
He stands in heaven their great High Priest,
And bears their names upon His breast.

  He sprinkles with His blood
    The mercy-seat above;
  For justice hath withstood
    The purposes of love;
But justice now objects no more,
And mercy yields her boundless store.

  No temple made with hands
    His place of service is;
  In heaven itself He stands,
    An heavenly priesthood His;
In Him the shadows of the law
Are all fulfilled, and now withdraw.

  And though awhile He be
    Hid from the eyes of men,
  His people look to see
    Their great High Priest again;
In brightest glory He will come,
And take His waiting people home.

HOSANNA! RAISE THE PEALING HYMN.

Anonymous [1842]. From Sir R. PALMER's "Book of Praise," No. LXXIX.

HOSANNA! raise the pealing hymn
  To David's Son and Lord;
With Cherubim and Seraphim
Exalt the Incarnate Word.

Hosanna! Lord, our feeble tongue
  No lofty strains can raise;
But Thou wilt not despise the young,
  Who meekly chant Thy praise.

Hosanna! Sovereign, Prophet, Priest,
  How vast Thy gifts, how free!
Thy Blood, our life; Thy Word, our feast;
  Thy Name, our only plea.

Hosanna! Master, lo, we bring
  Our offerings to Thy throne;
Not gold, nor myrrh, nor mortal thing,
  But hearts to be Thine own.

Hosanna! once Thy gracious ear
  Approved a lisping throng;
Be gracious still, and deign to hear
  Our poor but grateful song.

O Saviour! if, redeemed by Thee,
  Thy temple we behold,
Hosannas through eternity
  We'll sing to harps of gold.

SEE, THE RANSOMED MILLIONS STAND!

JOSIAH CONDER, a publisher and editor; born in London, 1789; died 1855.

SEE, the ransomed millions stand,
  Palms of conquest in their hand!
This before the throne their strain:
  "Hell is vanquished; death is slain;

Blessing, honour, glory, might,
Are the Conqueror's native right;
Thrones and powers before Him fall;
Lamb of God, and Lord of all!"

Hasten, Lord! the promised hour;
Come in glory and in power;
Still Thy foes are unsubdued;
Nature sighs to be renewed:
Time has nearly reached its sum,
All things with Thy Bride say, Come;
Jesus whom all worlds adore,
Come and reign for evermore!

JESUS IS GOD! THE SOLID EARTH.

"JESUS is God." By FREDERICK WILLIAM FABER, D.D. Born 1815; graduated in Oxford, 1836; rector of Elton in Northamptonshire; entered the Roman-Catholic Church, 1845; priest of the Oratory of St. Philip Neri; died 1863. One of the most fervent devotional writers of the Roman-Catholic Church. One (polemical) stanza is omitted. From the last edition of FABER'S "Hymns," Lond. 1862, p. 33.

JESUS is God! the solid earth,
    The ocean broad and bright,
The countless stars, like golden dust,
    That strew the skies at night,
The wheeling storm, the dreadful fire,
    The pleasant, wholesome air,
The summer's sun, the winter's frost,
    His own creations were.

Jesus is God! the glorious bands
    Of golden angels sing
Songs of adoring praise to Him,
    Their Maker and their King.
He was true God in Bethlehem's crib;
    On Calvary's cross, true God:
He who in heaven eternal reigned,
    In time on earth abode.

JESUS IS GOD, THE SOLID EARTH.

Jesus is God! there never was
    A time when He was not;
Boundless, eternal, merciful,
    The Word the Sire begot.
Backward our thoughts through ages stretch,
    Onward through endless bliss;
For there are two eternities,
    And both alike are His!

Jesus is God! let sorrow come,
    And pain and every ill;
All are worth while, for all are means
    His glory to fulfil;
Worth while a thousand years of life
    To speak one little word,
If by our Credo we might own
    The Godhead of our Lord.

Jesus is God! oh, could I now
    But compass land and sea,
To teach and tell this single truth,
    How happy should I be!
Oh, had I but an angel's voice,
    I would proclaim so loud,—
Jesus, the good, the beautiful,
    Is everlasting God!

Jesus is God! if on the earth
    This blessed faith decays,
More tender must our love become,
    More plentiful our praise.
We are not angels, but we may
    Down in earth's corners kneel,
And multiply sweet acts of love,
    And murmur what we feel.

KING OF KINGS, AND WILT THOU DEIGN?

W. A. MUHLENBERG, D.D., author of "I would not live alway." 1859.

KING of kings, and wilt Thou deign
O'er this wayward heart to reign?
Henceforth take it for Thy throne,[1]
Rule here, Lord, and rule alone.

Then, like heaven's angelic bands,
Waiting for Thine high commands,
All my powers shall wait on Thee,
Captive, yet divinely free.

At Thy Word my will shall bow,
Judgment, reason, bending low;
Hope, desire, and every thought,
Into glad obedience brought.

Zeal shall haste on eager wing,
Hourly some new gift to bring;
Wisdom, humbly casting down
At Thy feet her golden crown.

Tuned by Thee in sweet accord,
All shall sing their gracious Lord;
Love, the leader of the choir,
Breathing round her seraph fire.

Be it so: my heart's Thy throne,
All my powers Thy sceptre own,
And, with them on Thine own hill,
Live rejoicing in Thy will.

---

[1] So reads the written copy, kindly furnished me by the author. In the printed volume of his poems, this line is changed thus:—

"Other Sovereign, none I'll own."

O CHRIST, THE LORD OF HEAVEN!

Ray Palmer, D.D., May 9, 1867. Praise to Christ. Rev xix. 16.

CHRIST, the Lord of heaven, to Thee,
    Clothed with all majesty divine,
    Eternal power and glory be,
Eternal praise of right is Thine!

Reign, Prince of Life! that once Thy brow
    Didst yield to wear the wounding thorn;
Reign throned beside the Father now,
    Adored the Son of God first-born!

From angel hosts that round Thee stand,
    With forms more pure than spotless snow,
From the bright, burning seraph band,
    Let praise in loftiest numbers flow!

To Thee, the Lamb, our mortal songs,
    Born of deep, fervent love shall rise;
All honour to Thy name belongs,
    Our lips would sound it to the skies.

Jesus! all earth shall speak the word;
    Jesus! all heaven resound it still;
Immanuel, Saviour, Conqueror, Lord,
    Thy praise the universe shall fill!

CHRIST JUDGING THE WORLD.

"When the Son of Man shall come in His glory, and all the holy angels with Him, then shall He sit upon the throne of His glory. And before Him shall be gathered all nations: and He shall separate them one from another, as a shepherd divideth his sheep from the goats."—*Matt.* xxv. 31, 32.

"We must all appear before the judgment-seat of Christ; that every one may receive the things done in his body."—2 *Cor.* v. 10.

JUDEX mundi quum sedebit,
 Quidquid latet apparebit,
Nil inultum remanebit.

Quid sum, miser, tunc dicturus,
Quem patronum rogaturus,
Quum vix justus sit securus?

Rex tremendæ majestatis,
Qui salvandos salvas gratis,
Salva me, Fons pietatis!

Recordare, Jesu pie,
Quod sum causa tuæ viæ;
Ne me perdas illa die!

Quærens me sedisti lassus,
Redemisti crucem passus;
Tantus labor non sit cassus!

Justæ Judex ultionis,
Donum fac remissionis
Ante diem rationis!

Oro supplex et acclinis,
Cor contritum, quasi cinis;
Gere curam mei finis. Amen.
From the "Dies Iræ," 1250.

Bring near Thy great salvation,
Thou Lamb for sinners slain,
Fill up the roll of Thine elect,
Then take Thy power, and reign:
Appear, Desire of nations,—
Thine exiles long for home:
Shew in the heaven Thy promised sign,—
Thou Prince and Saviour, come!
Dean Alford *of Canterbury*, 1869. (*Contributed.*)

What shall we be, when we shall hear Him say:
  "Come, O ye blessed," when we see Him stand,
Robed in the light of everlasting day,
  Before the throne of God at His right hand;
When we behold the eyes from which once flowed
  Tears o'er the sin and misery of man,
And the deep wounds from which the precious blood,
  That made atonement for the world, once ran!

What shall we be, when hand in hand we go
  With blessed spirits risen from the tomb,
Where streams of living water softly flow,
  And trees still flourish in primeval bloom;
Where in perpetual youth no cheek looks old
  By the sharp tooth of cruel time imprest,
Where no bright eye is dimmed, no heart grows cold,
  No grief, no pain, no death invades the blest!
From the German of SPITTA.

How long, O Lord? our hearts are sad and weary,
  Our voices join the whole creation's groan;—
With eager gaze we watch for Thine appearing,—
  When wilt Thou come again, and claim Thine own!

Return! return! come in Thy power and glory,
  With all Thy risen saints and angel throng;
Bring to a close time's strange, mysterious story,—
  How long dost Thou delay,—O Lord, how long?
MISS JANE BORTHWICK.

CHRIST JUDGING THE WORLD.

GOD COMES;—AND WHO SHALL STAND?

(Ὁ Κύριος ἔρχεται.)

ODE of ST. THEODORE OF THE STUDIUM (an abbey at Constantinople), distinguished for his sufferings and influence in the Iconoclastic controversy; died in exile, 826. Translated from the Greek, by Dr. J. M. NEALE, 1862.

GOD comes;—and who shall stand before His
    fear?
Who bide His Presence, when He draweth
    near?
    My soul, my soul, prepare
    To kneel before Him there!

Haste,—weep,—be reconciled to Him before
The fearful judgment knocketh at the door:
    Where, in the Judge's eyes,
    All bare and naked lies.

Have mercy, Lord! have mercy, Lord! I cry,
When with Thine angels Thou appear'st on high:
    And man a doom inherits,
    According to his merits.

How can I bear Thy fearful anger, Lord?
I, that so often have transgressed Thy word?
    But put my sins away,
    And spare me in that day!

O miserable soul! return, lament,
Ere earthly converse end, and life be spent:
    Ere, time for sorrow o'er,
    The Bridegroom close the door!

Yea, I have sinned, as no man sinned beside:
With more than human guilt my soul is dyed;
    But spare, and save me here,
    Before that Day appear!

Three Persons in One Essence uncreate,
On Whom, both Three and One, our praises wait,
    Give everlasting light
    To them that sing Thy might!

THE DAY IS NEAR.

(Ἐφέστηκεν ἡ ἡμέρα.)

From the Greek of St. Theodore of the Studium, 826. Translated by Dr. J. M. Neale, 1862.

THE Day is near, the judgment is at hand:
    Awake, my soul! awake, and ready stand!
    Where chiefs shall go with them that filled the throne,
Where rich and poor the same tribunal own;
    And every thought and deed
    Shall find its righteous meed.

There with the sheep the Shepherd of the fold
Shall stand together; there the young and old,
Master and slave, one doom shall undergo;
Widow and maiden one tribunal know:
    Oh, woe, oh, woe, to them
    Whom lawless lives condemn!

That Judgment-seat, impartial in decree,
Accepts no bribe, admits no subtilty:
No orator persuasion may exert,
No perjured witness wrong to right convert;
    But all things, hid in night,
    Shall then be dragged to light.

Let me not enter in the land of woe;
Let me not realms of outer darkness know!

Nor from the wedding-feast reject Thou me,
For my soiled vest of immortality;
    Bound hand and foot, and cast
    In anguish that shall last!

When Thou, the nations ranged on either side,
The righteous from the sinners shalt divide,
Then give me to be found amongst Thy sheep,
Then from the goats Thy trembling servant keep,
    That I may hear the voice
    That bids Thy saints rejoice!

When righteous inquisition shall be made,
And the books opened, and the thrones arrayed,
My soul, what plea to shield thee canst thou know,
Who hast no fruit of righteousness to show,
    No holy deeds to bring
    To Christ the Lord and King?

I hear the rich man's wail and bitter cry,
Out of the torments of eternity:
I know, beholding that devouring flame,
My guilt and condemnation are the same;
    And spare me, Lord, I say,
    In the great Judgment-Day!

The Word and Spirit, with the Father One,
One Light and emanation of One Sun,
The Word by generation, we adore,
The Spirit by procession, evermore;
    And with creation raise
    The thankful hymn of praise.

THAT GREAT DAY OF WRATH AND TERROR.

(Apparebit repentina magna Dies Domini.)

AN anonymous Latin poem, based on Matt. xxv. 31-46, first quoted by the Venerable Bede (d. 735), in his work "De Metris," and then lost sight of till Cassander published it in his "Hymni Ecclesiastici." See DANIEL, I. pp. 194 *seq.;* TRENCH, pp. 290-292. Translated by Dr. JOHN M. NEALE, who introduces it with the remark, "This rugged but grand judgment-hymn is at least as early as the 7th century, because quoted by the Venerable Bede. It manifestly contains the germ of the "Dies Iræ," to which however inferior in lyric fervour and effect, it scarcely yields in devotion and simple realization of its subject." Daniel and Trench likewise put it on a par with the "Dies Iræ," as to simplicity and faith, but below it in majesty and terror Both breathe the mediæval spirit of legalistic, rather than of joyous evangelic, piety. This poem is more narrative than lyrical. The Latin is alphabetic and acrostical, every other line in its first letter following the alphabet,—an artificial arrangement for the eye rather than the ear, borrowed from Ps. cxix. and the Lamentations of Jeremiah. Other versions by Mrs. Charles, and E. C. Benedict.

THAT great Day of wrath and terror,
That last Day of woe and doom,
Like a thief at darkest midnight,
On the sons of men shall come;
When the pride and pomp of ages
All shall utterly have passed,
And they stand in anguish, owning
That the end is here at last.
Then the trumpet's pealing clangour,
Through the earth's four quarters spread,
Waxing loud and ever louder,
Shall convoke the quick and dead;
And the King of heavenly glory
Shall assume His throne on high,
And the cohorts of His angels
Shall be near Him in the sky.
Then the sun shall turn to darkness,[1]
And the moon be red as blood;
And the stars shall fall from heaven,
Whelmed beneath destruction's flood.
Flame and fire and desolation
At the Judge's feet shall go:
Earth and sea and all abysses
Shall His mighty sentence know.

Then th' elect upon the right hand
Of the Lord shall stand around;
But, like goats, the evil-doers
Shall upon the left be found.
"Come, ye Blessed, take the kingdom,"
Shall be there the King's award,

---

[1] Neale translates "shall turn to *sackcloth*," which is an improper figure, and not implied in the original :—

"Erubescit orbis lunæ, sol vel *obscurabitur*."

" Which for you, before the world was,
Of My Father was prepared:
I was naked, and ye clothed Me,
Poor, and ye relieved Me; hence,
Take the riches of My glory
For your endless recompense."
Then the righteous shall make question:
" When have we beheld Thee poor,
Lord of glory?   When relieved Thee
Lying needy at our door?"
Whom the Blessed King shall answer:
" When ye showed your charity,
Giving bread and home and raiment,
What ye did was done to Me."
In like manner, to the left hand
That most righteous Judge shall say,
" Go, ye cursed, to Gehenna,
And the fire that is for aye:
For in prison ye came not nigh Me;
Poor, ye pitied not My lot;
Naked, ye have never clothed Me;
Sick, ye visited Me not."
They shall say : " O Christ! when saw we
That Thou calledst for our aid,
And in prison, or sick or hungry,
To relieve have we delayed?"
Whom again the Judge shall answer:
" Since ye never cast your eyes
On the sick and poor and needy,
It was Me ye did despise."

Backward, backward, at the sentence,
To Gehenna they shall fly,
Where the flame is never-ending,
Where the worm can never die;
Where are Satan and his angels
In profoundest dungeon bound;
Where are chains and lamentation,
Where are quenchless flames around.

But the righteous, upward soaring,
To the heavenly land shall go,
Midst the cohorts of the angels,

Where is joy for evermo :
To Jerusalem, exulting,
They with shouts shall enter in ;
That true " sight of peace " and glory
That sets free from grief and sin.
Christ shall they behold for ever,
Seated at the Father's hand,
As in Beatific Vision
His elect before Him stand.

Wherefore man, while yet thou mayest,
From the dragon's malice fly :[1]
Give thy bread to feed the hungry,
If thou seek'st to win the sky ;
Let thy loins be straitly girded,
Life be pure, and heart be right ;
At the coming of the Bridegroom,
That thy lamp may glitter bright.

DAY OF WRATH! THAT DAY FORETOLD.

(Dies iræ, dies illa.)

THE DIES IRÆ (DANIEL, II. p. 103; TRENCH, p. 293, and in many other collections). An act of humiliation, and prayer for mercy, in view of the impending Day of judgment, based upon Zeph. i. 15, 16; Matt. xxv.; 2 Pet. iii. 10-12, &c. Written, for private devotion, in a lonely monastic cell, about 1250, by THOMAS OF CELANO, the friend and biographer of St. Francis of Assisi. This marvellous hymn is the acknowledged masterpiece of Latin poetry, and the most sublime of all uninspired hymns, often translated, reproduced, and imitated, but never equalled. It is one of those rare productions which can never die, but which increase in value as the ages advance. It has commanded the admiration of secular poets, and men of letters, like Goethe, Walter Scott, and Macaulay, and has inspired some of the greatest musicians, from Palestrina down to Mozart. The secret of the irresistible power of the " Dies Iræ " lies in the awful grandeur of the theme, the intense earnestness and pathos of the poet, the simple majesty and solemn music of its language, the stately metre, the triple rhyme, and the vowel assonances chosen in striking adaptation to the sense,—all combining to produce an overwhelming effect, as if we heard the final crash of the universe, the commotion of the opening graves, the trumpet of the arch-angel that summons the quick and the dead, and as if we saw the " King of tremendous majesty " seated on the throne of justice and mercy, and ready to dispense everlasting

---

[1] " Ydri [= Hydri, from ὑδρός] fraudes ergo cave," refers to " the old serpent" (ὁ ὄφις ὁ ἀρχαῖος), as Satan is called, Rev. xii. 9, 14; xx. 2, with reference to the history of temptation, Gen. iii. 1, 4.

life or everlasting woe. Goethe thus describes its effect upon the guilty conscience, in the cathedral-scene of " Faust :"—

> " Horror seizes thee !
> The trump sounds !
> The grave trembles !
> And thy heart
> From the repose of its ashes,
> For fiery torment
> Brought to life again,
> Trembles up ! "

The opening line is literally borrowed from the Vulgate version of Zeph. i. 15 (as the " Stabat Mater " likewise opens with a Scripture sentence,—John xix. 25) ; it strikes with a startling sound the key-note to the whole, and brings up at once the judgment-scene as an awful, impending reality. The feeling of terror occasioned by the contemplation of that event, culminates in the cry of repentance, ver. 7 ; " Quid sum, miser, tunc dicturus ;" but from this the poet rises at once to the prayer of faith, and takes refuge from the wrath to come in the infinite mercy of Him who suffered nameless pain for a guilty world, who pardoned the sinful Mary Magdalene, and saved the dying robber.

For further information, see LISCO's "Dies Iræ," Berlin, 1840; and my articles in the " Hours at Home," New York, May and July, 1868, with specimens of about a hundred translations. This new version, suggested in part by older ones, although quite faithful, is offered by the Editor with a lively sense of the untranslatableness of the DIES IRÆ.

AY of wrath ! that Day foretold,
By the saints and seers of old,
Shall the world in flames infold.[1]

What a trembling, what a fear,
When the dread Judge shall appear,
Strictly searching far and near !

Hark ! the trumpet's wondrous tone,
Through the tombs of every zone,
Summons all before the throne.

Death shall shiver, nature quake,
When the creatures shall awake,
Answer to their Judge to make.

---

[1] A more literal version would be :—

> " Day of wrath, that woful Day,
> Shall the world in ashes lay :
> David and the Sibyl say."

But the mythical Sibyl, which, as the representative of the unconscious prophecies of heathendom, is placed by the poet alongside the singer and prophet of Israel, has long since lost the importance which it once occupied in the apologetic theology of the fathers and schoolmen. Yet there is a truth underlying this use made of the Sibylline oracles, and the fourth Eclogue of Virgil, inasmuch as heathenism, in its nobler spirits, was groping in the dark

Lo, the book of ages spread,[1]
From which all the deeds are read
Of the living and the dead.

Now, before the Judge severe,
Hidden things must all appear:
Nought shall pass unpunished here.

Wretched man, what shall I plead,
Who for me will intercede,
When the righteous mercy need?

King of dreadful majesty,
Author of salvation free,
Fount of pity, save Thou me!

Recollect, good Lord, I pray,
I have caused Thy bitter way:
Don't forget me on that Day!

Weary sat'st Thou seeking me,[2]
Died'st, redeeming, on the tree,
Let such toil not fruitless be![3]

Judge of righteousness severe,
Grant me full remission here,
Ere the reckoning-Day appear.

Sighs and tears my sorrow speak,
Shame and grief are on my cheek:
Mercy, mercy, Lord! I seek.

Thou didst Mary's guilt forgive,
And absolve the dying thief:
Even I may hope relief.[4]

---

after "the unknown God," and bore negative and indirect testimony to Christ, while the Old Testament positively and directly predicted and foreshadowed His coming.

[1] The *liber scriptus* is not the written Bible (as a translator in the London "Spectator," for March 7, 1868, strangely mistook it), but the record of all human actions, Dan. vii. 10; Rev. xx. 12.

[2] A touching allusion to Christ's fatigue on his journey to Samaria John iv. 6. (Vulgate: "Jesus *fatigatus* ex itinere, *sedebat* sic supra fontem.")

[3] It is related of the celebrated Dr. Samuel Johnson, that, rough and coarse as he was, he could never repeat this stanza in Latin without bursting into a flood of tears.

[4] Copernicus composed the following epitaph for himself:—

"Not the grace bestowed upon Paul do I pray for;
Not the mercy by which Thou pardonedst Peter:
That alone which Thou grantedst the crucified robber,—
That alone do I pray for."

Worthless are my prayers, I know;
Yet, O Christ! Thy mercy show:
Save me from eternal woe!

Make me with Thy sheep to stand,
Far from the convicted band,
Placing me at Thy right hand.

When the cursed are put to shame,
Cast into devouring flame,
With the blest then call my name!

Suppliant at Thy feet I lie,
Contrite in the dust I cry:
Care Thou for me when I die![1]

DAY OF WRATH! O DAY OF MOURNING!

THE "Dies Iræ," translated by Dr. W. J. IRONS, 1848. In England, this is considered the best of those versions which preserve the double rhyme of the Latin. It is introduced into the "Hymnal Noted," "The People's Hymnal" (1867); and other Collections. Several American translations (by Dr. Coles, Dr. Williams, and others) likewise retain the double rhyme, while Trench, Alford, Caswell, and others have chosen the single rhyme which is more congenial to the monosyllabic character of the English language.

AY of wrath! O Day of mourning!
See! once more the Cross returning,[2]
Heaven and earth in ashes burning!

O what fear man's bosom rendeth,
When from heaven the Judge descendeth,
On Whose sentence all dependeth!

---

[1] The Earl of Roscommon, in the moment of his death, repeated, with the most fervent devotion, these last lines, in his own version:—

"My God, my Father, and my Friend,
Do not forsake me in my end!"

The remaining seven lines of the received text of the original are here omitted for the reason stated in the note on p. 293.

[2] Dr. Irons, like Dean Alford in his translation, adopts—in the place of the usual, and no doubt original: "Teste David cum Sibylla"—the reading of the Paris missal:—

"Dies iræ, dies illa,
Crucis expandens vexilla [Matt. xxiv. 30],
Solvet sæclum in favilla."

It would be better to substitute for the second line:—

"See fulfilled the prophet's warning."

Wondrous sound the Trumpet flingeth,
Through earth's sepulchres it ringeth,
All before the throne it bringeth!

Death is struck, and nature quaking;
All creation is awaking,
To its Judge an answer making!

Lo, the book exactly worded,
Wherein all hath been recorded;
Thence shall judgment be awarded.

When the Judge His seat attaineth,
And each hidden deed arraigneth,
Nothing unavenged remaineth.

What shall I, frail man, be pleading,
Who for me be interceding,
When the just are mercy needing!

King of majesty tremendous,
Who dost free salvation send us,
Fount of pity, then befriend us!

Think, kind Jesu!—my salvation
Caused Thy wondrous Incarnation;
Leave me not to reprobation!

Faint and weary Thou hast sought me,
On the cross of suffering bought me:
Shall such grace be vainly brought me?

Righteous Judge of retribution,
Grant Thy gift of absolution,
Ere that reckoning-Day's conclusion!

Guilty, now I pour my moaning,
All my shame with anguish owning:
Spare, O God, Thy suppliant groaning!

Thou the sinful woman savedst;
Thou the dying thief forgavest;
And to me a hope vouchsafest.

Worthless are my prayers and sighing,
Yet, good Lord, in grace complying,
Rescue me from fires undying!

With Thy favoured sheep, O place me!
Nor among the goats abase me;
But to Thy right hand upraise me!

While the wicked are confounded,
Doomed to flames of woe unbounded,
Call me, with Thy saints surrounded.

Low I kneel, with heart-submission:
See, like ashes, my contrition;
Help me, in my last condition!

[Ah! that day of tears and mourning!
From the dust of earth returning,
Man for judgment must prepare him.

Spare, O God! in mercy spare him!
Lord, who didst our souls redeem,
Grant a blessed Requiem!][1]

THAT DAY OF WRATH!

AN abridged version or imitation of the "Dies Iræ," by Sir WALTER SCOTT (d. 1832), which has passed into many hymn-books. Following the example of Goethe's "Faust," Sir W. Scott introduced these stanzas in the sixth canto of his "Lay of the Last Minstrel." On his death-bed, he distinctly repeated portions of the Latin original. "To my Gothic ear," he once wrote to Crabbe, "the 'Stabat Mater,' the 'Dies Iræ,' and some of the other hymns of the Catholic Church, are more solemn and affecting than the fine classical poetry of Buchanan."

THAT Day of wrath! that dreadful Day,
When heaven and earth shall pass away!
What power shall be the sinner's stay?
How shall he meet that dreadful Day?

When, shrivelling like a parched scroll,
The flaming heavens together roll;
And louder yet, and yet more dread,
Swells the high trump that wakes the dead,—

---

[1] The last six lines (seven in the Latin) are in different metre, and no part of the original hymn, but were added, in the "Breviary," from older funeral services already in use.

Oh! on that Day, that wrathful Day,
When man to judgment wakes from clay,
Be Thou, O Christ! the sinner's stay,
Though heaven and earth shall pass away!

LO, THE DAY!—THE DAY OF LIFE.

(Dies illa, dies vitæ.)

THIS poem is a counterpart of the "Dies Iræ," although perhaps of earlier date, and presents the cheerful aspect of the Day of judgment, as the day of the complete redemption of the faithful. Translated by Mrs. CHARLES ("The Voice of Christian Life in Song," p. 190).

LO, the Day!—the Day of Life,
    Day of unimagined light,
Day when Death itself shall die,
    And there shall be no more night!

Steadily that Day approacheth,
    When the just shall find their rest,
When the wicked cease from troubling,
    And the patient reign most blest.

See the King desired for ages,
    By the just expected long,
Long implored, at length He hasteth,
    Cometh with salvation strong.

Oh, how past all utterance happy,
    Sweet, and joyful it will be
When they who, unseen, have loved Him,
    Jesus face to face shall see!

In that Day, how good and pleasant
    This poor world to have despised!
And how mournful, and how bitter,
    Dear that lost world to have prized!

Blessed, then, earth's patient mourners,
    Who for Christ have toiled and died,
Driven by the world's rough pressure
    In those mansions to abide!

There shall be no sighs or weeping,
  Not a shade of doubt or fear;
No old age, no want or sorrow,
  Nothing sick or lacking there.

There the peace will be unbroken,
  Deep and solemn joy be shed,
Youth in fadeless flower and freshness,
  And salvation perfected.

What will be the bliss and rapture
  None can dream and none can tell,
There to reign among the angels,
  In that heavenly home to dwell.

To those realms, just Judge, oh, call me!
  Deign to open that blest gate,
Thou whom, seeking, looking, longing,
  I, with eager hope, await!

WAKE, THE STARTLING WATCH-CRY PEALETH.

(Wachet auf! ruft uns die Stimme.)

FROM the German of PHILIPP NIKOLAI, of Unna, Westphalia, d. 1608. "Behold, the Bridegroom cometh; go out to meet Him."—Matt. xxv. 1-13. The midnight call of a Christian watchman, full of majesty and solemnity, composed during the raging of a pestilence, 1599, with an appropriate tune, which is called the "king of German chorals" (SCHAFF'S "German Hymn-Book," No. 157). Translated, in the metre of the original, by Miss FRANCES ELIZABETH COX.

WAKE! the startling watch-cry pealeth,
  While slumber deep each eyelid sealeth;
    Awake! Jerusalem, awake!
Midnight's solemn hour is tolling,
And cherub notes are onward rolling;
  They call on us our part to take.
    Come forth, ye virgins wise!
    The Bridegroom comes, arise!
      Alleluia!
      Each lamp be bright,
      With ready light,
To grace the Marriage-Feast to-night!

Zion hears the Watchman singing;
With sudden joy her heart is springing;
  At once she wakes, she stands arrayed:
See her Light, her Star ascending,
Lo! girt with truth, with mercy blending,
  Her Bridegroom there, so long delayed!
    All hail, our Joy and Crown!
    God's Son, from heaven come down!
      Alleluia!
      The joyful call
      We answer all,
And follow to the Nuptial Hall.

Praise to Him Who went before us!
Let men and angels join in chorus,
  Let harp and cymbal add their sound!
Twelve the gates, a pearl each portal,
We haste to join the choir immortal,
  Within the Holy City's bound.
    Ear ne'er heard aught like this,
    Nor heart conceived such bliss,
      Alleluia!
      We raise the song,
      We swell the throng,
To praise Thee ages all along.

WAKE, AWAKE, FOR NIGHT IS FLYING.

(Wachet auf! ruft uns die Stimme.)

THE same hymn of NICOLAI, translated, with a slight deviation from the metre of the original, by Miss C. WINKWORTH.

WAKE, awake, for night is flying,
  The watchmen on the heights are crying:
    Awake, Jerusalem, at last!
Midnight hears the welcome voices,
And at the thrilling cry rejoices:
  Come forth, ye virgins, night is past!
    The Bridegroom comes, awake;
    Your lamps with gladness take:
      Hallelujah!

And for His marriage-feast prepare,
For ye must go to meet Him there.

Zion hears the watchmen singing,
And all her heart with joy is springing,
  She wakes, she rises from her gloom;
For her Lord comes down all-glorious,
The strong in grace, in truth victorious:
  Her Star is risen, her Light is come!
    Ah, come, Thou blessèd Lord,
      O Jesus, Son of God,
        Hallelujah!
We follow till the halls we see
Where Thou hast bid us sup with Thee.

Now let all the heavens adore Thee,
And men and angels sing before Thee
  With harp and cymbal's clearest tone;
Of one pearl each shining portal,
Where we are with the choir immortal
  Of angels round Thy dazzling throne:
    Nor eye hath seen, nor ear
      Hath yet attained to hear
        What there is ours;
But we rejoice, and sing to Thee
Our hymn of joy eternally.

REJOICE, ALL YE BELIEVERS!

(*Ermuntert euch, ihr Frommen!*)

FROM the German of LAURENTIUS LAURENTI, 1700. His best hymn. The original has ten stanzas (SCHAFF's "G. H. B.," No. 158). Translated by JANE BORTHWICK, in "Hymns from the Land of Luther," Edin. 1853. Adjusted by the Editor to the measure of the original. ALFORD has given three verses of it a place in his "Year of Praise," 1867, No. 11. The Lutheran "Church-Book," Philad. 1868, No. 116, gives four verses, altered.

REJOICE, all ye believers,
  And let your lights appear!
The evening is advancing,
And darker night is near:

The Bridegroom is arising,
   And soon will He draw nigh.
Up! pray and watch and wrestle:
   At midnight comes the cry.

See that your lamps are burning,
   Replenish them with oil;
Look now for your salvation,
   The end of earthly toil.
The watchers on the mountain
   Proclaim the Bridegroom near;
Go meet Him as He cometh,
   With Hallelujahs clear!

Ye wise and holy virgins,
   Now raise your voices higher,
Until, in songs of triumph,
   They meet the angel-choir.
The marriage-feast is waiting,
   The gates wide open stand;
Up! up! ye heirs of glory:
   The Bridegroom is at hand!

Ye saints who here in patience
   Your cross and sufferings bore,
Shall live and reign for ever,
   When sorrow is no more.
Around the throne of glory,
   The Lamb ye shall behold;
In triumph cast before Him
   Your diadems of gold!

There flourish palms of victory;
   There radiant garments are;
There stands the peaceful harvest,
   Beyond the reach of war.
There, after stormy winter,
   The flowers of earth arise,
And from the grave's long slumber
   Shall meet again our eyes.

Our Hope and Expectation,
   O Jesus! now appear;
Arise, Thou Sun, so longed for,
   O'er this benighted sphere!

With hearts and hands uplifted,
  We plead, O Lord ! to see
The day of our redemption,
  That brings us unto Thee !

LO ! HE COMES WITH CLOUDS DESCENDING.

BY CHARLES WESLEY, 1758. This hymn, the English "Dies Iræ," was originally part second of a hymn in three parts, entitled "Thy Kingdom come," published in Wesley's "Hymns of Intercession for all Mankind," 1758. A somewhat similar hymn, in the same metre, was published by the Rev. JOHN CENNICK (first a Methodist, then a Moravian, d. 1755), in 1752, commencing :—

"Lo, He cometh ! countless trumpets
 Blow before the bloody sign."

In 1760, the Rev. MARTIN MADAN amalgamated, with some alterations, these hymns of Wesley and Cennick, adopting the first, second, and fourth stanzas of Wesley, the third and fifth stanzas of Cennick, and substituting one of his own for the third of Wesley. About 1758, THOMAS OLIVERS composed, in the same metre, a judgment-hymn of twenty stanzas, to which he afterwards added sixteen more. Sir ROUNDELL PALMER, Nos. XC. and XCI., gives Madan's compilation (six stanzas), and eleven out of the thirty-six stanzas of Olivers. I prefer the original form of Wesley. There is much confusion about the text and authorship of these hymns. Compare the note of ROGERS, "Lyra Brit.," p. 675.

LO ! He comes with clouds descending,
  Once for favoured sinners slain !
Thousand, thousand saints attending,
  Swell the triumph of His train :
    Hallelujah !
  God appears on earth to reign !

Every eye shall now behold Him
  Robed in dreadful majesty ;
Those who set at nought and sold Him,
  Pierced, and nailed Him to the tree,
    Deeply wailing,
  Shall the true Messiah see.[1]

---

[1] After this, MADAN inserts two stanzas from Cennick, with some variations, as follows :—

"Every island, sea, and mountain,
  Heaven and earth, shall flee away ;

CHRIST JUDGING THE WORLD.

The dear tokens of His passion
  Still His dazzling body bears,
Cause of endless exultation
  To His ransomed worshippers ;
    With what rapture
  Gaze we on those glorious scars !

Yea, Amen ! let all adore Thee,
  High on Thine eternal throne !
Saviour, take the power and glory,
  Claim the kingdom for Thine own :
    Jah, Jehovah ![1]
  Everlasting God, come down !

          All who hate Him must, confounded,
            Hear the trump proclaim the day ;
              Come to judgment!
            Come to judgment, come away !
[CENNICK, orig.: " Stand before the Son of Man."]
             " Now redemption, long expected,
             See in solemn pomp appear !
             All His saints, by man rejected,
             Now shall meet Him in the air :
               Hallelujah !
             See the day of God appear ! "
[CENNICK ; " Now the promised kingdom's come."]
Then follows, in MADAN's compilation, a stanza which seems to be own :—
             " Answer Thine own Bride and Spirit ;
             Hasten, Lord, the general doom ;
             The new heaven and earth t' inherit,
             Take Thy pining exiles home :
               All creation
             Travails, groans, and bids Thee come ! "

[1] MADAN changed this line into—
               " O come quickly."

PALMER adopted this alteration ; but, in the other stanzas, he retained the original readings of Wesley.

DAY OF JUDGMENT!

JOHN NEWTON, 1725-1807 ("Olney Hymns"). Likewise on the basis of the "Dies Iræ."

DAY of judgment! Day of wonders!
    Hark, the trumpet's awful sound,
Louder than a thousand thunders,
    Shakes the vast creation round!
        How the summons
    Will the sinner's heart confound!

See the Judge, our nature wearing,
    Clothed in majesty Divine!
You, who long for His appearing,
    Then shall say, "This God is mine."
        Gracious Saviour,
    Own me in that day for Thine.

At His call the dead awaken,
    Rise to life from earth and sea;
All the powers of nature, shaken
    By His looks, prepare to flee.
        Careless sinner,
    What will then become of thee?

Horrors past imagination
    Will surprise your trembling heart,
When you hear your condemnation:—
    "Hence, accursed wretch, depart!
        Thou with Satan
    And his angels have thy part."

Satan, who now tries to please you,
    Lest you timely warning take,
When that word is past, will seize you,—
    Plunge you in the burning lake.
        Think, poor sinner,
    Thy eternal all's at stake.

But to those who have confessèd,
    Loved, and served the Lord below,
He will say, "Come near, ye blessed,
    See the kingdom I bestow.
        You for ever
    Shall My love and glory know."

Under sorrows and reproaches,
  May this thought your courage raise:
Swiftly God's great Day approaches,
  Sighs shall then be changed to praise;
    We shall triumph
  When the world is in a blaze.

THE LORD WILL COME.

By Bishop REGINALD HEBER, D.D.; d. at Calcutta, 1826. From his "Poetical Works." London, 1854, p. 43. For Second Sunday in Advent.

THE Lord will come! the earth shall quake,
  The hills their fixèd seat forsake;
  And, withering, from the vault of night
The stars withdraw their feeble light.

The Lord will come! but not the same
As once in lowly form He came,
A silent Lamb to slaughter led,
The bruised, the suffering, and the dead.

The Lord will come! a dreadful form,
With wreath of flame, and robe of storm;
On cherub wings, and wings of wind,
Anointed Judge of human-kind!

Can this be He, who wont to stray
A pilgrim on the world's highway,
By power oppressed, and mocked by pride?
O God! is this the Crucified?

Go, tyrants! to the rocks complain!
Go, seek the mountains' cleft in vain!
But faith, victorious o'er the tomb,
Shall sing for joy, the Lord is come!

JESUS, THY CHURCH WITH LONGING EYES.

WILLIAM HILEY BATHURST, a clergyman of the Church of England; b. near Bristol, 1796. See notice in ROGERS's " Lyra Brit." p. 40.

JESUS, Thy Church with longing eyes,
    For Thy expected coming waits;
  When will the promised light arise,
    And glory beam from Zion's gates?

E'en now, when tempests round us fall,
    And wintry clouds o'ercast the sky,
Thy words with pleasure we recall,
    And deem that our redemption's nigh.

Come, gracious Lord, our hearts renew,
    Our foes repel, our wrongs redress;
Man's rooted enmity subdue,
    And crown Thy gospel with success.

O come and reign o'er every land!
    Let Satan from his throne be hurled,
All nations bow to Thy command,
    And grace revive a dying world.

Yes, Thou wilt speedily appear;
    The smitten earth already reels;
And, not far off, we seem to hear
    The thunder of Thy chariot wheels.

Teach us, in watchfulness and prayer,
    To wait for the appointed hour,
And fit us by Thy grace to share
    The triumphs of Thy conquering power.

THE CHARIOT! THE CHARIOT!

BY DR. H. H. MILMAN, Dean of St. Paul's; b. in London, 1791; d. 1868.

THE chariot! the chariot! its wheels roll on fire,
As the Lord cometh down in the pomp of His
    ire;
Self-moving, it drives on its pathway of cloud,
And the heavens with the burden of Godhead are bowed.

The glory! the glory! By myriads are poured
The hosts of the angels to wait on their Lord;
And the glorified saints, and the martyrs are there,
And all who the palm-wreath of victory wear.

The trumpet! the trumpet! The dead have all heard.
Lo! the depths of the stone-covered charnels are stirred;
From the sea, from the land, from the south and the
    north,
The vast generations of man are come forth!

The judgment! the judgment! The thrones are all set,
Where the Lamb and the white-vested elders are met;
All flesh is at once in the sight of the Lord,
And the doom of eternity hangs on His word!

Oh, mercy! oh, mercy! look down from above,
Creator! on us, Thy sad children, with love;
When beneath to their darkness the wicked are driven,
May our sanctified souls find a mansion in heaven!

THE THRONE OF HIS GLORY.

"THEN shall He sit upon the throne of His Glory." By Dr. W. A.
MUHLENBERG, New York, 1839.

THE Throne of His Glory!—as snow it is white,
Upborne in the air by the legions of Light;
And, startled to life by the trumpet's last sound,
The hosts of the nations stand waiting around.

The Throne of His Glory !—there lieth unsealed
The Life-roll, the Death-roll, of names ne'er revealed,
Now secret no longer: the millions divide
To the right and the left, on the Throne's either side.

The Throne of His Glory !—and glorious there stand
The elect of His love, and the sheep of His hand;
While dark on His left, shrunk away from His face,
The lost ones that sought not the Throne of His grace.

The Throne of His Glory !—my poor trembling soul !
Oh what, when arraigned there, thy dread shall control,
Of that doom of the exiled, " Ye cursed depart !"
For ever and ever to toll on the heart.

From thy Father an exile ? Thy home never see ?
No, child of His mercy, unchanging and free,
Ere creation began, in the councils of love,
He wrote thee an heir of His kingdom above.

LATE, LATE, SO LATE!

THE foolish virgins. Matt. xxv. 11, 12. By ALFRED TENNYSON, poet laureate. From "Idylls of the King" (the Legends of King Arthur), first published 1859 (from the last poem, entitled "Guinevere," which has been called his highest effort).

LATE, late, so late ! and dark the night, and chill !
Late, late, so late! but we can enter still.
   " Too late, too late ! ye cannot enter now."

No light had we: for that we do repent;
And, learning this, the Bridegroom will relent.
   " Too late, too late ! ye cannot enter now."

No light, so late ! and dark and chill the night !
O let us in, that we may find the light!
   " Too late, too late ! ye cannot enter now."

Have we not heard the Bridegroom is so sweet?
O let us in, though late, to kiss His feet !
   " No, no; too late ! ye cannot enter now."

COME, LORD, AND TARRY NOT.

By HORATIUS BONAR, D.D. From his "Hymns of Faith and Hope," First Series.

"Senuit mundus."—AUGUSTINE.

COME, Lord, and tarry not:
   Bring the long-looked-for Day;
   O why these years of waiting here,
These ages of delay?

Come, for Thy saints still wait:
   Daily ascends their sigh;
The Spirit and the Bride say, Come;
   Dost Thou not hear the cry?

Come, for creation groans,
   Impatient of Thy stay,
Worn out with these long years of ill,
   These ages of delay.

Come, for Thy Israel pines,
   An exile from Thy fold;
O call to mind Thy faithful word,
   And bless them as of old!

Come, for Thy foes are strong;
   With taunting lip they say,
"Where is the promised Advent now,
   And where the dreaded Day?"

Come, for the good are few;
   They lift the voice in vain:
Faith waxes fainter on the earth,
   And love is on the wane.

Come, for the truth is weak,
   And error pours abroad
Its subtle poison o'er the earth,—
   An earth that hates her God.

Come, for love waxes cold;
   Its steps are faint and slow:
Faith now is lost in unbelief,
   Hope's lamp burns dim and low.

COME, LORD, AND TARRY NOT.

Come, for the grave is full;
  Earth's tombs no more can hold:
The sated sepulchres rebel,
  And groans the heaving mould.

Come, for the corn is ripe;
  Put in Thy sickle now,
Reap the great harvest of the earth,—
  Sower and reaper Thou!

Come, in Thy glorious might,
  Come with the iron rod,
Scattering Thy foes before Thy face,
  Most mighty Son of God!

Come, spoil the strong man's house,
  Bind him and cast him hence;
Show Thyself stronger than the strong,
  Thyself Omnipotence.

Come, and make all things new;
  Build up this ruined earth,
Restore our faded Paradise,
  Creation's second birth.

Come, and begin Thy reign
  Of everlasting peace;
Come, take the kingdom to Thyself,
  Great King of righteousness!

HOPE OF OUR HEARTS.

"THE Church waiting for the Son from Heaven." By Sir EDWARD DENNY. Bart., a writer on prophetic topics. From his "Hymns and Poems," London [1863].

HOPE of our hearts, O Lord! appear:
  Thou glorious Star of day,
Shine forth, and chase the dreary night,
  With all our fears, away!

Strangers on earth, we wait for Thee:
  Oh! leave the Father's throne;
Come with the shout of victory, Lord,
  And claim us for Thine own!

Oh! bid the bright archangel now
    The trump of God prepare,
To call Thy saints—the quick, the dead—
    To meet Thee in the air.

No resting-place we seek on earth,
    No loveliness we see;
Our eye is on the royal crown
    Prepared for us and Thee.

But, dearest Lord, however bright
    That crown of joy above,
What is it to the brighter hope
    Of dwelling in Thy love?

What to the joy—the deeper joy,
    Unmingled, pure, and free—
Of union with our Living Head,
    Of fellowship with Thee?

This joy e'en now on earth is ours:
    But only, Lord, above,
Our hearts, without a pang, shall know
    The fulness of Thy love.

There, near Thy heart, upon the throne,
    Thy ransomed bride shall see
What grace was in the bleeding Lamb
    Who died to make her free.

BRIDE OF THE LAMB, AWAKE!

"The Church cheered with the Hope of her Lord's Return." By Sir EDWAR DENNY [1863].

BRIDE of the Lamb, awake! awake!
    Why sleep for sorrow now?
The hope of glory, Christ, is thine,
    A child of glory thou.

Thy spirit, through the lonely night,
    From earthly joy apart,
Hath sighed for one that's far away,
    The Bridegroom of thy heart.

But see! the night is waning fast,
　The breaking morn is near;
And Jesus comes, with voice of love,
　Thy drooping heart to cheer.

He comes—for oh! His yearning heart
　No more can bear delay—
To scenes of full, unmingled joy,
　To call His bride away.

This earth, the scene of all His woe,
　A homeless wild to thee,
Full soon, upon His heavenly throne,
　Its rightful King shall see.

Thou, too, shalt reign,—He will not wear
　His crown of joy alone;
And earth His royal bride shall see
　Beside Him, on the throne.

Then weep no more: 'tis all thine own,
　His crown, His joy divine;
And, sweeter far than all beside,
　He, He Himself, is thine!

END OF PART FIRST.

PART SECOND.

CHRISTUS IN NOBIS.

THE LOVE AND LOVELINESS OF CHRIST.

"I AM the good Shepherd: the good Shepherd giveth His life for the sheep."
—*John* x. 11.

"Hereby perceive we the love of God, because He laid down His life for us."—1 *John* iii. 16.

"Unto Him that loved us, and washed us from our sins in His own blood, and hath made us kings and priests unto God and His Father,—to Him be glory and dominion for ever and ever. Amen."—*Rev.* i. 5, 6.

ALMIGHTY GOD, our Heavenly Father, who didst so love the world as to give Thine only-begotten Son, that whosoever believeth on Him should not perish, but have everlasting life: mercifully grant unto us, we beseech Thee, that Christ may dwell in our hearts by faith, so that we, being rooted and grounded in love, may be able to comprehend, with all saints, what is the breadth and length and depth and height, and to know the love of Christ, which passeth knowledge; to whom, with Thee and the Holy Ghost, be glory in the Church throughout all ages, world without end. Amen.

> JESU, dulcedo cordium,
> Fons vivus, lumen mentium,
> Excedens omne gaudium,
> Et omne desiderium.
>
> Nec lingua valet dicere,
> Nec litera exprimere,
> Expertus potest credere
> Quid sit Jesum diligere.
> ST. BERNARD.

CHRIST is both Loveliness and Love immense,
And loves to be re-loved with love the most intense.

NOT all the music of the spheres
Sounds half so sweet in angels' ears,
    As when to hearts contrite
      We Jesus' name recite.
That Name with sweetness overflows,
Creates full joys, and damps our woes.
              From BISHOP KEN'S " *Christian Year.*"

THE LOVE AND LOVELINESS OF CHRIST.

JESU, NAME ALL NAMES ABOVE.

('Ἰησοῦ γλυκύτατε.)

FROM the Greek of THEOCTISTUS OF THE STUDIUM, about A.D. 890. A cento from his "Suppliant Canon to Jesus," the only thing known of him, but it is perhaps the most tender and evangelical of Greek hymns, and might almost have been written by PAUL GERHARDT or ZINZENDORF. Translated by Dr. J M. NEALE, of Sackville College, 1862.

JESU, name all names above,
 Jesu, best and dearest,
 Jesu, Fount of perfect love,
  Holiest, tenderest, nearest !
Jesu, source of grace completest,
Jesu truest, Jesu sweetest,
 Jesu, Well of power divine,
 Make me, keep me, seal me Thine !

Jesu, open me the gate
 Which the sinner entered,
Who in his last dying state
 Wholly on Thee ventured.
Thou whose wounds are ever pleading,
And Thy passion interceding,
 From my misery let me rise
 To a home in Paradise !

Thou didst call the prodigal ;
 Thou didst pardon Mary :
Thou whose words can never fall,
 Love can never vary,

Lord, amidst my lost condition
Give—for Thou canst give—contrition!
  Thou canst pardon all mine ill:
  If Thou wilt, O say, "I will"!

Woe, that I have turned aside
  After fleshly pleasure!
Woe, that I have never tried
  For the heavenly treasure!
Treasure, safe in homes supernal;
Incorruptible, eternal!
  Treasure no less price hath won
  Than the Passion of the Son!

Jesu, crowned with thorns for me,
  Scourged for my transgression!
Witnessing, through agony,
  That Thy good confession;
Jesu, clad in purple raiment,
For my evils making payment;
  Let not all Thy woe and pain,
  Let not Calvary be in vain!

When I reach Death's bitter sea,
  And its waves roll higher,
Help the more forsaking me,
  As the storm draws nigher:
Jesu, leave me not to languish,
Helpless, hopeless, full of anguish!
  Tell me,—" Verily, I say,
  Thou shalt be with me to-day!"

JESU! THE VERY THOUGHT OF THEE.

(Jesu, dulcis memoria.)

"JUBILUS rhythmicus de nomine Jesu," the sweetest and most evangelical (as the "Dies Iræ" is the grandest, and the "Stabat Mater" the most pathetic) hymn of the middle ages, though somewhat monotonous, and wanting in progress, by ST. BERNARD, of Clairvaux (called "Doctor mellifluus," flowing with honey), d. 1153. The original has 192 or 200 lines, in the "Works" of BERNARD, ed. Mabillon, 1719, vol. ii. pp. 914, *seq.* (forty-eight quatrains); DANIEL, I. pp. 227-230; WACKERNAGEL, I. pp. 117-120 (fifty quatrains). TRENCH, p. 246, gives a selection of fifteen quatrains, with the remark, "Where all was beautiful, the task of selection was a hard one." The Roman Breviary has abridged and divided the hymn into three distinct hymns ("Jesu, dulcis memoria;" "Jesu, Rex admirabilis;" and "Jesu, decus angelicum"), which are here given in the smooth translation of E. CASWALL (from the "Lyra Catholica"). The first part has also been translated by NEALE ("Hymnal Noted:" "Jesu! the very thought is sweet"), R. PALMER ("Jesus, Thou joy of loving hearts!"), J. W. ALEXANDER ("Jesus, how sweet Thy memory is!"), Mrs. CHARLES ("O, Jesus! Thy sweet memory"), and others, and into German by MÜLLER, ZINZENDORF, SAILER, KÖNIGSFELD, &c. (see SCHAFF'S "G. H. B." No. 160).

I.

(Jesu, dulcis memoria.)

JESU! the very thought of Thee
   With sweetness fills my breast;
But sweeter far Thy face to see,
   And in Thy presence rest.

Nor voice can sing, nor heart can frame,
   Nor can the memory find,
A sweeter sound than Thy blest name,
   O Saviour of mankind!

O Hope of every contrite heart,
   O Joy of all the meek!
To those who fall, how kind Thou art!
   How good to those who seek!

But what to those who find? Ah! this
   Nor tongue nor pen can show;
The love of Jesus, what it is,
   None but His loved ones know.[1]

---

[1] CASWALL has taken the liberty of making two fine stanzas out of the third, which reads in Latin:

    "Jesu, spes pœnitentibus
    Quam pius es petentibus!
    Quam bonus Te quærentibus!
    Sed quid invenientibus?"

The "Hymnal Noted" renders this verse more faithfully thus:—

    "Jesu! the hope of souls forlorn!
    How good to them for sin that mourn!
    To them that seek Thee, oh, how kind!
    But what art Thou to them that find?"

Jesu ! our only joy be Thou,
  As Thou our prize shalt be ;
Jesu ! be Thou our glory now,
  And through eternity.

II.

(Jesu, Rex admirabilis.)

JESU ! King most wonderful !
  Thou Conqueror renowned !
Thou Sweetness most ineffable,
  In whom all joys are found !

When once Thou visitest the heart,
  Then truth begins to shine ;
Then earthly vanities depart ;
  Then kindles love divine.

O Jesu ! Light of all below !
  Thou Fount of life and fire !
Surpassing all the joys we know,
  All that we can desire :

May every heart confess Thy name,
  And ever Thee adore ;
And seeking Thee, itself inflame
  To seek Thee more and more.

Thee may our tongues for ever bless ;
  Thee may we love alone ;
And ever in our lives express
  The image of Thine own.

III.

(Jesu, decus angelicum.)

JESU ! Thou the beauty art
  Of angel worlds above ;
Thy name is music to the heart,
  Enchanting it with love.

Celestial sweetness unalloyed !
　Who eat Thee hunger still ;
Who drink of Thee still feel a void,
　Which nought but Thou can fill.

O my sweet Jesu ! hear the sighs
　Which unto Thee I send ;
To Thee mine inmost spirit cries,
　My being's hope and end !

Stay with us, Lord, and with Thy light
　Illume the soul's abyss ;
Scatter the darkness of our night,
　And fill the world with bliss.

O Jesu ! spotless virgin-flower !
　Our love and joy ! to Thee
Be praise, beatitude, and power,
　Through all eternity.

JESUS, HOW SWEET THY MEMORY IS !

ANOTHER version, in part, of ST. BERNARD'S " Jesu, dulcis memoria," by Dr. JAMES W. ALEXANDER (d. 1859), first published in SCHAFF'S " Kirchenfreund," for April, 1859.

JESUS, how sweet Thy memory is !
　Thinking of Thee is truest bliss ;
　Beyond all honeyed sweets below
Thy presence is it here to know.

Tongue cannot speak a lovelier word,
Nought more melodious can be heard,
Nought sweeter can be thought upon,
Than Jesus Christ, God's only Son.

Jesus, Thou hope of those who turn,
Gentle to those who pray and mourn,
Ever to those who seek Thee, kind,—
What must Thou be to those who find !

Jesus, Thou dost true pleasures bring,
Light of the heart, and living spring;
Higher than highest pleasures roll,
Or warmest wishes of the soul.

Lord in our bosoms ever dwell,
And of our souls the night dispel,
Pour on our inmost mind the ray,
And fill our earth with blissful day.

If Thou dost enter to the heart,
Then shines the truth in every part;
All worldly vanities grow vile,
And charity burns bright the while.

This love of Jesus is most sweet,
This laud of Jesus is most meet,
Thousand and thousand times more dear
Than tongue of man can utter here.

Praise Jesus, all with one accord,
Crave Jesus, all, your love and Lord,
Seek Jesus, warmly, all below,
And seeking into rapture glow!

Thou art of heavenly grace the fount,
Thou art the true Sun of God's mount,
Scatter the saddening cloud of night!
And pour upon us glorious light!

HEART OF CHRIST MY KING!

(Summi regis cor, aveto.)

ONE of the seven passion-hymns of ST. BERNARD (compare pp. 130 and 142), addressed to the heart of Christ ("Ad Cor Christi"); faithfully translated (for the first time, I believe) by the Rev. Dr. E. A. WASHBURN, of New York, June, 1868. Contributed. See the Latin in BERNARD's "Works," and in DANIEL, IV. p. 227; WACKERNAGEL, I. p. 123.

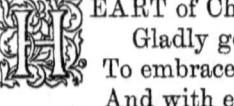EART of Christ my King! I greet Thee:
    Gladly goes my heart to meet Thee;
To embrace Thee now it burneth,
And with eager thirst it yearneth,

Spirit blest, to talk with Thee.
Oh! what love divine compelling!
With what grief Thy breast was swelling!
All Thy soul for us o'erflowing,
All Thy life on us bestowing,
   Sinful men from death to free!

Oh, that death! in bitter anguish,
Cruel, pitiless to languish!
To the inmost cell it entered,
Where the life of man was centred,
   Gnawing Thy sweet heartstrings there.
For that death which Thou hast tasted,
For that form by sorrow wasted,
Heart to my heart ever nearest,
Kindle in me love the dearest;
   This, O Lord, is all my prayer.

O sweet Heart! my choicest blessing,
Cleanse my heart, its sin confessing;
Hardened in its worldly folly,
Make it soft again, and holy,
   Melting all its icy ground.
To my heart's core come, and quicken
Me a sinner, conscience-stricken;
Be Thy grace my soul renewing,
All its powers to Thee subduing,
   Languishing with love's sweet wound.

Open flower, with blossom fairest,
As a rose of fragrance rarest;
Knit to Thee mine inmost feeling;
Pierce, then pour the oil of healing;
   What to love of Thee is pain?
Naught he fears, whom Thy love calleth,
No self-sacrifice appalleth;
Love divine can have no measure,
Every death to him is pleasure,
   Where such holy love doth reign.

Cries my heart with living voices:
In Thee, heart of Christ, rejoices;

Draw Thou nigh with gracious motion,
Knit it, till in full devotion
   Thou its every power employ.
Love be all my life; no slumber
E'er my drowsy thought incumber;
To Thee praying, Thee imploring,
Thee aye praising, Thee adoring,
   Thee my sempiternal joy!

Heart Rose, in thy fulness blossom,
Shed Thy perfume o'er my bosom;
Be Thy beauty in me growing;
Light the fires for ever glowing
   On the altar of my heart.
Aid me, Thy dear image wearing,
E'en Thy wounds, my Jesu, sharing,
Till Thy very form I borrow,
When my bosom feels Thy sorrow,
   Piercing with its keenest dart.

To Thy holy heart, oh, take me!
Thy companion, Jesu, make me,
In that sorrow joy exceeding,
In that beauty scarred and bleeding,
   Till my heart be wholly Thine.
Rest, my soul! now naught shall sever;
After Thee it follows ever;
Here its thirst finds glad fulfilling;
Jesu! be Thou not unwilling,
   Take this loving heart of mine!

FAIREST LORD JESUS.

(Schönster Herr Jesu.)

FROM an old German hymn of the 12th century (see WICHERN's Collection of popular songs for his " Rough House," near Hamburg, entitled : " Unsere Lieder," No. 207 ; and SCHAFF's " German S. S. Hymn-Book," No. 44,) which was sung by the Crusaders, and then forgotten, until it was recently brought to light again, and soon acquired a new popularity.

    FAIREST Lord Jesus,
        Ruler of nature !
    Jesus, of God and of Mary the Son !
        Thee will I cherish,
        Thee will I honour ;
Thee, my delight and my glory and crown !

        Fair are the meadows,
        Fairer the woodlands,
Robed in the flowery vesture of spring :
        Jesus is fairer,
        Jesus is purer,
Making my sorrowful spirit to sing.

        Fair is the moonshine,
        Fairer the sunlight,
Than all the starry, celestial host :
        Jesus shines brighter,
        Jesus shines purer,
Than all the angels that heaven can boast.

O LOVE, WHO FORMEDST ME.

(Liebe, die Du mich zum Bilde.)

FROM the German of JOHANN SCHEFFLER, called "Angelus Silesius," 1657, (SCHAFF's " G. H. B." No. 312) ; translated by C. WINKWORTH. Another version, by JOHN CHRISTIAN JACOBI (1722) : " Lord, Thine image Thou hast lent me."

    LOVE, who formedst me to wear
        The image of Thy Godhead here ;
    Who soughtest me with tender care
  Through all my wanderings wild and drear ;
O Love, I give myself to Thee,
Thine ever, only Thine to be.

O Love, who e'er life's earliest dawn
  On me Thy choice hast gently laid;
O Love, who here as man wast born
  And wholly like to us wast made;
O Love, I give myself to Thee,
Thine ever, only Thine to be.

O Love, who once in time wast slain,
  Pierced through and through with bitter woe;
O Love, who wrestling thus didst gain,
  That we eternal joy might know;
O Love, I give myself to Thee,
Thine ever, only Thine to be.

O Love, of whom is truth and light,
  The Word and Spirit, life and power,
Whose heart was bared to them that smite,
  To shield us in our trial hour;
O Love, I give myself to Thee,
Thine ever, only Thine to be.

O Love, who thus hath bound me fast,
  Beneath that gentle yoke of Thine;
Love, who hast conquered me at last
  And rapt away this heart of mine;
O Love, I give myself to Thee,
Thine ever, only Thine to be.

O Love, who lovest me for aye,
  Who for my soul dost ever plead;
O Love, who didst my ransom pay,
  Whose power sufficeth in my stead;
O Love, I give myself to Thee,
Thine ever, only Thine to be.

O Love, who once shall bid me rise
  From out this dying life of ours;
O Love, who once o'er yonder skies
  Shalt set me in the fadeless bowers;
O Love, I give myself to Thee,
Thine ever, only Thine to be.

ONE THING'S NEEDFUL.

(Eins ist noth: ach Herr, diess Eine.)

JOHANN HEINRICH SCHRÖDER, 1697. Based on Luke x. 38-42 ("One thing is needful; and Mary hath chosen that good part"); 1 Cor. i. 30 ("Christ Jesus who of God is made unto us wisdom, and righteousness, and sanctification, and redemption"). One of the most popular German hymns (SCHAFF's "G. H. B." No. 314). This translation, by FRANCES ELIZABETH COX ("Sacred Hymns from the German," Lond. 1841, p. 137), strictly preserves the metre of the original, and is more faithful than that of Miss CATHERINE WINKWORTH: "One thing is needful! Let me deem" ("Lyra Germ." I. 183).

ONE thing's needful: then, Lord Jesus,
    Keep this one thing in my mind;
    All beside, though first it please us,
    Soon a grievous yoke we find.
Beneath it, the heart is still fretting and striving;
No true, lasting happiness ever deriving:
The gain of this one thing all loss can requite,
And teach me in all things to find some delight.

    Soul, wilt thou this one thing find thee?
    Seek it in no earthly end;
    Leave all Nature far behind thee,
    High above the world ascend:
For, where God and man both in one are united,
With God's perfect fulness the heart is delighted;
There, there, is the worthiest lot and the best,
My one and my all, and my joy and my rest.

    How were Mary's thoughts devoted,
    Her eternal joy to find,
    As intent each word she noted,
    At her Saviour's feet reclined!
How kindled her heart, how devout was its feeling,
While hearing the lessons that Christ was revealing!
For Jesus all earthly concerns she forgot,
And all was repaid in that one happy lot.

    Thus my longings, heavenward tending,
    Jesu, rest alone on Thee:
    Help me, thus on Thee depending,
    Saviour! come and dwell in me.

Although all the world should forsake and forget Thee,
In love I will follow Thee, ne'er will I quit Thee:
For, Jesus, both spirit and life is Thy word;
And is there a joy which Thou dost not afford?

    Wisdom's highest, noblest treasure,
    Jesu! lies concealed in Thee;
    Grant that this may still the measure
    Of my will and actions be.
Humility there, and simplicity, reigning,
My steps shall in wisdom for ever be training;
Oh! if I of Christ have this knowledge divine,
The fulness of heavenly *wisdom* is mine.[1]

    Christ, Thou art the sole oblation
    That I'll bring before my God:
    In His sight, I've acceptation
    Only through Thy streaming blood.
Immaculate *righteousness* now I've acquired,
Since Thou on the tree of the Cross hast expired:
The robe of Salvation for ever is mine;
In this shall my faith through eternity shine.

    Let my soul, in full exemption,
    Wake up in Thy likeness now:
    Thou art made to me redemption,
    My *sanctification* Thou.
What though, all through life, in good works I had striven,
For Thy sake alone my reward should be given:
Oh, let me all perishing pleasures forego,
And Thy life, O Jesus! alone let me know!

    Where should else my hopes be centred?
    Grace o'erwhelms me with its flood;
    Thou, my Saviour, once hast entered
    Holiest heaven through Thy blood.
Eternal *redemption* for sinners there finding,
From hell's dark dominion my spirit unbinding,
To me perfect freedom Thy entrance has brought,
And childlike to cry, "Abba, Father," I'm taught.

---

[1] The last two lines are often quoted in German devotional books:—
    "*Wenn ich nur Jesum recht kenne und weiss,*
    So hab ich der Weisheit vollkommenen Preis."

Christ Himself, my Shepherd, feeds me;
Peace and joy my spirit fill:
In a pasture green, He leads me
Forth beside the waters still.
Oh! nought to my soul is so sweet and reviving,
As thus unto Jesus alone to be living:
True happiness this, and this only supplies,
Through faith on my Saviour, to fasten mine eyes.

Therefore, Jesus my Salvation,
Thou my One, my All, shalt be!
Prove my fixed determination,
Root out all hypocrisy.
Look well if on sin's slippery paths I am hasting,
And lead me, O Lord! in the way everlasting:
This one thing is needful, all others are vain;
I count all but loss that I Christ may obtain.

DEAREST OF ALL THE NAMES ABOVE.

By Isaac Watts, D.D.

DEAREST of all the names above,
  My Jesus and my God,
Who can resist Thy heavenly love,
  Or trifle with Thy blood?

'Tis by the merits of Thy death
  Thy Father smiles again;
'Tis by Thine interceding breath
  The Spirit dwells with men.

Till God in human flesh I see,
  My thoughts no comfort find:
The holy, just, and sacred Three
  Are terror to my mind.

But if Immanuel's face appear,
  My hope, my joy, begins:
His name forbids my slavish fear,
  His grace removes my sins.

While Jews on their own law rely,
  And Greeks of wisdom boast,
I love th' incarnate Mystery,
  And there I fix my trust.

LOVE DIVINE, ALL LOVES EXCELLING.

CHARLES WESLEY, 1746. From "Hymns for those that seek, and those that have, Redemption in the Blood of Jesus Christ," 5th ed. 1756.

LOVE Divine, all loves excelling,
  Joy of heaven, to earth come down,
Fix in us Thy humble dwelling,
  All Thy faithful mercies crown.
Jesus, Thou art all compassion,—
  Pure, unbounded love Thou art:
Visit us with Thy salvation,
  Enter every trembling heart.

Breathe, O breathe Thy loving Spirit
  Into every troubled breast!
Let us all in Thee inherit,
  Let us find that second rest.
Take away the love of sinning;[1]
  Alpha and Omega be;
End of faith, as its beginning,
  Set our hearts at liberty.

Come, Almighty to deliver!
  Let us all Thy life receive;
Suddenly return, and never,
  Never more Thy temples leave.
Thee we would be always blessing,
  Serve Thee as Thy host above;
Pray, and praise Thee without ceasing,
  Glory in Thy perfect love.

Finish, then, Thy new creation;
  Pure and spotless let us be;

---

[1] Others read, less aptly: "our *power* of sinning."

Let us see Thy great salvation
　Perfectly secured by Thee,—
Changed from glory into glory,
　Till in heaven we take our place,—
Till we cast our crowns before Thee,
　Lost in wonder, love, and praise!

HOW WONDROUS ARE THE WORKS OF GOD!

JOSEPH HART, an Independent minister; b. in London, 1712; d. 1768. He published a "Hymn-Book," 1759, with an account of his former sinful life, and the blessed change wrought by the grace of God in his heart.

HOW wondrous are the works of God,
　Displayed through all the world abroad!
　Immensely great, immensely small,
Yet one strange work exceeds them all.

He formed the sun, fair fount of light,
The moon and stars, to rule the night;
But night and stars and moon and sun
Are little works compared with one.

He rolled the seas, and spread the skies;
Made valleys sink, and mountains rise;
The meadows clothed with native green,
And bade the rivers glide between.

But what are seas or skies or hills,
Or verdant vales or gliding rills,
To wonders man was born to prove?
The wonders of redeeming love!

'Tis far beyond what words express,
What saints can feel, or angels guess.
Angels, that hymn the great *I Am*,
Fall down and veil before the Lamb.

The highest heavens are short of this;
'Tis deeper than the vast abyss;
'Tis more than thought can e'er conceive,
Or hope expect, or faith believe.

Almighty God sighed human breath;
The Lord of life experienced death;
How it was done, we can't discuss:
But this we know, 'twas done for us.

Blest with this faith, then let us raise
Our hearts in love, our voice in praise;
All things to us must work for good,
For whom the Lord hath shed His blood.

Trials may press of every sort;
They may be sore,—they must be short;
We now *believe*, but soon shall *view*
The greatest glories God can show.

THE SAVIOUR! O, WHAT CHARMS!

MISS ANNE STEELE, daughter of a Baptist clergyman in England, 1717-1778. The following hymn, which, in this abridged form (or rather only five verses), has received wide currency, is a mere extract (verses 2, 3, 6, 7, 8, 37, 39) from a hymn on the life of Christ, in thirty-nine stanzas, too long for insertion in full. It begins :—

"Come, Heavenly Dove, inspire my song
  With Thy immortal flame,
And teach my heart and teach my tongue
  The Saviour's lovely name."

THE Saviour! O, what endless charms
    Dwell in that blissful sound!
  Its influence every fear disarms,
    And spreads sweet comfort round.

Here pardon, life, and joys divine
    In rich effusion flow
For guilty rebels, lost in sin,
    And doomed to endless woe.

Wrapped in the gloom of dark despair
    We helpless, hopeless lay:
But sov'reign mercy reached us there,
    And smiled despair away.

God's only Son, stupendous grace!
    Forsook His throne above,
And, swift to save our wretched race,
    He flew on wings of love.

The almighty Former of the skies
  Stooped to our vile abode;
While angels viewed with wondering eyes,
  And hailed the incarnate God.

O the rich depths of love divine!
  Of bliss a boundless store!
Dear Saviour, let me call Thee mine;
  I cannot wish for more.

On Thee alone my hope relies;
  Beneath Thy cross I fall;
My Lord, my Life, my Sacrifice,
  My Saviour, and my All.

HARK, MY SOUL! IT IS THE LORD.

"LOVEST thou Me?"—John xxi. 16. By WILLIAM COWPER (1731-1800).
"Olney Hymns," Book I. No. 118.

HARK, my soul! it is the Lord;
'Tis thy Saviour, hear His word;
Jesus speaks, and speaks to thee:
"Say, poor sinner, lov'st thou Me?

"I delivered thee when bound,
And, when bleeding, healed thy wound;
Sought thee wandering, set thee right,
Turned thy darkness into light.

"Can a woman's tender care
Cease towards the child she bare?
Yes: she may forgetful be,
Yet will I remember thee.

"Mine is an unchanging love,
Higher than the heights above;
Deeper than the depths beneath;
Free and faithful, strong as death.

"Thou shalt see My glory soon,
When the work of grace is done;
Partner of My throne shalt be;
Say, poor sinner, lov'st thou Me?"

Lord, it is my chief complaint,
That my love is cold and faint;
Yet I love Thee and adore:
O for grace to love Thee more!

HOW SWEET THE NAME OF JESUS!

The Rev. John Newton, d. 1807. "Olney Hymns," 1779, Book I. No. 57.
One of the best hymns in the English language.

HOW sweet the name of Jesus sounds
  In a believer's ear!
It soothes his sorrows, heals his wounds,
  And drives away his fear.

It makes the wounded spirit whole,
  And calms the troubled breast;
'Tis manna to the hungry soul,
  And to the weary rest.

Dear name! the rock on which I build
  My shield and hiding-place;
My never-failing treasury, filled
  With boundless stores of grace.

By Thee, my prayers acceptance gain,
  Although with sin defiled;
Satan accuses me in vain,
  And I am owned a child.

Jesus! my Shepherd, Husband,[1] Friend;
  My Prophet, Priest, and King;
My Lord, my Life, my Way, my End,
  Accept the praise I bring.

Weak is the effort of my heart,
  And cold my warmest thought;
But when I see Thee as Thou art,
  I'll praise Thee as I ought.

---

[1] Many hymn-books substitute "Guardian" for "Husband."

Till then I would Thy love proclaim,
  With every fleeting breath;
And may the music of Thy name
  Refresh my soul in death!

ONE THERE IS, ABOVE ALL OTHERS.

"A FRIEND that sticketh closer than a brother."—Prov. xviii. 24. By the Rev. JOHN NEWTON, 1779 ("Olney Hymns," B. I. No. 53).

ONE there is, above all others,
  Well deserves the name of friend;
His is love beyond a brother's,
  Costly, free, and knows no end:
They who once His kindness prove,
Find it everlasting love,

Which of all our friends to save us,
  Could or would have shed their blood?
But our Jesus died to have us
  Reconciled in Him to God:
This was boundless love indeed,
Jesus is a friend in need.

Men, when raised to lofty stations,
  Often know their friends no more;
Slight and scorn their poor relations,
  Though they valued them before:
But our Saviour always owns
Those whom He redeemed with groans.

When He lived on earth abasèd,
  Friend of sinners was His name;
Now, above all glory raisèd,
  He rejoices in the same:
Still He calls them brethren, friends,
And to all their wants attends.

Could we bear from one another
  What He daily bears from us?
Yet this glorious Friend and Brother
  Loves us, though we treat Him thus:
Though for good we render ill,
He accounts us brethren still.

Oh! for grace our hearts to soften;
 Teach us, Lord, at length to love.
We, alas! forget too often
 What a Friend we have above;
But, when home our souls are brought,
We will love Thee as we ought.

I WAS A WANDERING SHEEP.

HORATIUS BONAR, D.D. of Kelso. First Series of " Hymns of Faith and Hope." "Lost, but found." 1857.

 " Arte mirâ, miro consilio,
  Quærens ovem suam summus opilio,
  Ut nos revocaret ab exilio."
   OLD HYMN.

I WAS a wandering sheep,
 I did not love the fold;
I did not love my Shepherd's voice,
 I would not be controlled.
I was a wayward child,
 I did not love my home;
I did not love my Father's voice,
 I loved afar to roam.

The Shepherd sought His sheep,
 The Father sought His child;
They followed me o'er vale and hill,
 O'er deserts waste and wild.
They found me nigh to death,
 Famished and faint and lone;
They bound me with the bands of love,
 They saved the wandering one!

They spoke in tender love,
 They raised my drooping head;
They gently closed my bleeding wounds,
 My fainting soul they fed.
They washed my filth away,
 They made me clean and fair:
They brought me to my home in peace,—
 The long-sought wanderer!

Jesus my Shepherd is,
  'Twas He that loved my soul;
'Twas He that washed me in His blood,
  'Twas He that made me whole.
'Twas He that sought the lost,
  That found the wandering sheep;
'Twas He that brought me to the fold,
  'Tis He that still doth keep.

I was a wandering sheep,
  I would not be controlled;
But now I love my Shepherd's voice,—
  I love, I love the fold.
I was a wayward child,
  I once preferred to roam;
But now I love my Father's voice,—
  I love, I love His home!

JESUS, HOW MUCH THY NAME UNFOLDS!

Mrs. Mary Peters; died 1856, at Clifton, England.

JESUS, how much Thy name unfolds
  To every opened ear!
The pardoned sinner's memory holds
  None other half so dear.

"Jesus!"—it speaks a life of love,
  And sorrows meekly borne;
It tells of sympathy above,
  Whatever makes us mourn.

It speaks of righteousness complete,
  Of holiness to God;
And, to our ears, no tale so sweet
  As His atoning blood.

Jesus, the one who knew no sin,
  Made sin to make us just,
Worthy art Thou our love to win,
  And worthy all our trust.

Thy name encircles every grace
  That God as man could show;
There only can the Spirit trace
  A perfect life below.

The mention of Thy name shall bow
  Our hearts to worship Thee:
The chiefest of ten thousand, Thou;
  The chief of sinners, we.

STILL ON THY LOVING HEART.

(Still an Deinem liebevollen Herzen.)

From the German of C. J. P. Spitta ("Psaltery and Harp," 1836). "Comfort in Jesus' Love." Translated by R. Massie ("Lyra Dom," 1860.)

STILL on Thy loving heart let me repose,
  Jesus, sweet Author of my joy and rest;
  O let me pour my sorrows, cares, and woes,
Into Thy true and sympathizing breast!
Thy love grows never cold, but its pure flame
  Seems every day more strong and bright to glow:
Thy truth remains eternally the same,
  Pure and unsullied as the mountain snow.

O what is other love compared with Thine,
  Of such high value, such eternal worth!
What is man's love compared with love divine,
  Which never changes in this changing earth,—
Love, which in this cold world grows never cold;
  Love, which decays not with the world's decay;
Love, which is young when all things else grow old,
  Which lives when heaven and earth shall pass away?

How little love unchangeable and fixed
  In this dark valley doth to man remain!
With what unworthy motive is it mixed!
  How full of grief, uncertainty, and pain!
Love is the object which attracts all eyes:
  We win it, and already fear to part;
A thousand rivals watch to seize the prize,
  And tear the precious idol from our heart.

But Thou, in spite of our offences past,
  And those, alas! which still in us are found,
Hast loved us, Jesus, with a love so vast,
  No span can reach it, and no plummet sound.
Though the poor love we give Thee in return
  Should be extinguished, Thine is ever true;
Its vestal fire eternally doth burn,
  Though everlasting, always fresh and new.

Thou, who art ever ready to embrace
  All those who truly after Thee inquire;
Thou who hast promised in Thy heart a place
  To all who love Thee, and a place desire,—
O Lord, when I am anxious and deprest,
  And dim with tears, mine eyes can hardly see,
O let me lean upon Thy faithful breast,
  Rejoicing that e'en I am loved by Thee!

OUR LOT IS FALLEN.

(*Ein lieblich Loos ist uns gefellen.*)

"THE Happy Lot." From the German of SPITTA, 1833. Translated by MASSIE, 1860.

OUR lot is fall'n in pleasant places,
    A goodly heritage is ours:
  To Him, whence come all gifts and graces,
    Let us give praise with all our powers;
  He chooses us of His free grace,
  And makes us His peculiar race.

He undertook our soul's salvation,
    Our sad condition moved Him so;
  And came to us from pure compassion,
    To raise us from our depths of woe:
  O wonderful, surpassing love,
  Which brought Him to us from above!

He saw in us no real beauty,
    No virtue, nor intrinsic worth:

Not one there was that did his duty,
    For all were sinners from their birth;
Nor was there one, in such distress,
Who could our misery redress.

Then, moved at heart with deep compassion,
    The Lord stretched out His arm to save;
And His own life for our salvation,
    And therewith all things, freely gave,—
Adoption, sonship, and with this
A whole eternity of bliss.

O Lord of goodness so amazing,
    Not one is worthy, no! not one;
We stand in shame and wonder gazing
    At the great things which Thou hast done:
Thy crowning grace and precious blood
Have reconciled us with our God.

We feel quite certain of obtaining
    Nothing but goodness from Thy hand,
And wend our way without complaining,
    Through dreary mist and barren land,
With heaven in view, where we shall be
Joined through eternity to Thee.

The lines are fall'n in pleasant places,
    A goodly heritage is ours;
And gladly would we share the graces
    Which God's great goodness richly showers:
We offer them alike to all
Who will obey the gracious call.

It grieves us sore when men refuse them,
    And treat our offers with disdain,
Or by neglect for ever lose them,
    And make the grace of God in vain:
All ye who thirst, come here and buy;
And Christ will all your wants supply.

BENEATH THE SHADOW.

SAMUEL LONGFELLOW, a Unitarian clergyman in Massachusetts; brother of the celebrated poet, Henry Wadsworth Longfellow; published, in conjunction with the Rev. S. Johnson, " Hymns of the Spirit," 1846.

BENEATH the shadow of the Cross,
 As earthly hopes remove,
His new commandment Jesus gives,
 His blessed word of love.

O bond of union strong and deep!
 O bond of perfect peace!
Not e'en the lifted cross can harm,
 If we but hold to this.

Then, Jesus, be Thy Spirit ours!
 And swift our feet shall move
To deeds of pure self-sacrifice,
 And the sweet tasks of love.

JESUS' NAME SHALL EVER BE.

"THE Blessed Name Jesus: an Evangelical Rosary." By the Rev. Dr. W. A. MUHLENBERG, of New York, 1842. Revised by the author, Aug. 1868, for this Collection.

JESUS' name shall ever be
 For my heart its Rosary.
 I will tell it o'er and o'er,
Always dearer than before.

Ave Mary may not be
For my heart its Rosary;
Jesus, Saviour, all in all,—
Other name why should I call?

Morning hymns and evening lays,
Noontide prayer and midnight praise,
Heart and voice, and tune and time,
Jesus' name they all shall chime.

Ever new and fresh the strain;
Of all themes, the sweet refrain:
Time bring what it may along,
Jesus still the unchanging song.

Redolent with healing balm,
Pleasure's charm and trouble's calm;
All of Heaven my hope and claim,
Grace on grace in Jesus' name.

In my soul each deepest chord
Ring it out, One Saviour Lord;
Jesus, the eternal hymn
Forth from saint and seraphim.

Breathe it, then, my every breath;
Linger on my last in death;
Jesus — Rest in paradise;
Jesus — Glory in the skies!

IN THE SILENT MIDNIGHT WATCHES.

CHRIST knocking at the door. By A. CLEVELAND COXE, b. 1818; Bishop of the Protestant Episcopal diocese of Western New York (since 1865).

IN the silent midnight watches,
   List,—thy bosom door!
How it knocketh, knocketh, knocketh,
   Knocketh evermore!
Say not 'tis thy pulse is beating:
   'Tis thy heart of sin;
'Tis thy Saviour knocks, and crieth,
   Rise, and let Me in!

Death comes down, with reckless footstep,
   To the hall and hut:
Think you death will stand a-knocking
   Where the door is shut?
Jesus waiteth, waiteth, waiteth;
   But thy door is fast!
Grieved, away thy Saviour goeth:
   Death breaks in at last.

Then 'tis thine to stand entreating
  Christ to let thee in;
At the gate of heaven beating,
  Wailing for thy sin.
Nay, alas! thou foolish virgin,
  Hast thou then forgot?
Jesus waited long to know thee,
  But He knows thee not!

THERE IS NO LOVE LIKE JESUS' LOVE.

W. E. LITTLEWOOD.

THERE is no love like the love of Jesus,
  Never to fade or fall,
Till into the fold of the peace of God
  He has gathered us all.

There is no heart like the heart of Jesus,
  Filled with a tender lore:
Not a throb or throe our hearts can know
  But he suffered before.

There is no eye like the eye of Jesus,
  Piercing far away:
Never out of the sight of its tender light
  Can the wanderer stray!

There is no voice like the voice of Jesus:
  Ah! how sweet its chime,
Like the musical ring of some rushing spring
  In the summer-time!

O might we listen that voice of Jesus!
  O might we never roam,
Till our souls should rest, in peace on His breast,
  In the heavenly home!

SOULS OF MEN, WHY WILL YE SCATTER?

"Come to Jesus." By Frederick William Faber, D.D.; b. 1815;
died 1863. From his "Hymns," Lond. 1862, p. 289.

SOULS of men! why will ye scatter
    Like a crowd of frightened sheep?
Foolish hearts! why will ye wander
    From a love so true and deep?

Was there ever kindest shepherd
    Half so gentle, half so sweet,
As the Saviour who would have us
    Come and gather round His feet?

It is God: His love looks mighty,
    But is mightier than it seems.
'Tis our Father; and His fondness
    Goes far out beyond our dreams.

There's a wideness in God's mercy,
    Like the wideness of the sea;
There's a kindness in His justice,
    Which is more than liberty.

There is no place where earth's sorrows
    Are more felt than up in heaven;
There is no place where earth's failings
    Have such kindly judgment given.

There is welcome for the sinner,
    And more graces for the good;
There is mercy with the Saviour;
    There is healing in His blood.

There is grace enough for thousands
    Of new worlds as great as this;
There is room for fresh creations
    In that upper home of bliss.

For the love of God is broader
    Than the measures of man's mind;
And the Heart of the Eternal
    Is most wonderfully kind.

But we make His love too narrow
    By false limits of our own;
And we magnify His strictness
    With a zeal He will not own.

There is plentiful redemption
    In the blood that has been shed;
There is joy for all the members
    In the sorrows of the Head.

'Tis not all we owe to Jesus:
    It is something more than all,—
Greater good because of evil,
    Larger mercy through the fall.

Pining souls! come nearer Jesus;
    And, oh, come not doubting thus,
But with faith that trusts more bravely
    His huge tenderness for us.

If our love were but more simple,
    We should take Him at His word;
And our lives would be all sunshine
    In the sweetness of our Lord.

I BORE WITH THEE.

"THE Love of Christ, which passeth knowledge." By CHRISTINA G. ROSSETTI. From "Goblin Market and other Poems," 1856 (Boston ed., pp. 81, 82). The best of her "Devotional Pieces," if not of all her poems.

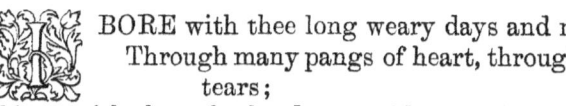 BORE with thee long weary days and nights,
    Through many pangs of heart, through many tears;
I bore with thee, thy hardness, coldness, slights,
    For three and thirty years.

Who else had dared for thee what I have dared?
    I plunged the depth most deep from bliss above;
I not My flesh, I not my spirit spared:
    Give thou Me love for love.

For thee I thirsted in the daily drought,
    For thee I trembled in the nightly frost:
Much sweeter thou than honey to My mouth;
    Why wilt thou still be lost?

I bore thee on my shoulders, and rejoiced,
    Men only marked upon My shoulders borne
The branding cross; and shouted hungry-voiced,
    Or wagged their heads in scorn.

Thee did nails grave upon My hands; thy name
    Did thorns for frontlets stamp between Mine eyes:
I, Holy One, put on thy guilt and shame;
    I, God, Priest, Sacrifice.

A thief upon My right hand and My left;
    Six hours alone, athirst, in misery:
At length in death one smote My heart, and cleft
    A hiding-place for thee.

Nailed to the racking cross, than bed of down
    More dear, whereon to stretch Myself and sleep:
So did I win a kingdom,—share My crown;
    A harvest,—come and reap.

LISTEN TO THE WONDROUS STORY.

ELLIN ISABELLE TUPPER, daughter of Martin F. Tupper, the author of "Proverbial Philosophy." Contributed to ROGERS'S "Lyra Brit.," 1867. On John iii. 16.

LISTEN to the wondrous story,
    How, upon the Christmas morn,
Jesus left the realms of glory,
    As a little babe was born;
Left those bright and happy regions,
    Of His Father's home above,
And the glorious angel legions,
    In His great and boundless love!

Came into a lowly manger,
    Dwelt beneath a humble shed,

And, among His own a stranger,
   Knew not where to lay His head;
Went from city unto city,
   All His life was doing good,
Weeping o'er His friend with pity,
   When beside the grave he stood.

Love all human love exceeding
   Brought Him to a cruel death;
Even then, though hanging bleeding
   On the cross, His latest breath
Spent He for His murderers, praying
   To His Father to forgive;
To the thief repentant saying,
   "Thou in Paradise shalt live!"

Oh, what love in God the Father
   To bestow His only Son!
Oh, what love in Christ, who rather
   Than the world should be undone,
Came Himself to seek and save us,
   Came to claim us for His own;
Freely all our sins forgave us,
   Raised us to His glorious throne!

THERE WAS NO ANGEL.

THE Divine Deliverer. John x. 30. By Mrs. GRACE WEBSTER HINSDALE, of Brooklyn, N.Y., April, 1868. Written for this Collection.

THERE was no angel 'midst the throng
   Which stood around the throne,
Who could God's justice satisfy,
   Or for man's sin atone.

Nor could Jehovah's love endure
   A messenger to send,
To bear the sinner's punishment,
   The guilty to befriend.

Not e'en the bursting floods of wrath
    Could quench the flames of love,
Which shining hid the flashing sword
    The law unsheathed above.

The gracious Father spoke a word
    Into His dear Son's ear,
Which, echoing o'er the trembling earth,
    Dismissed our anxious fear.

And, when the weary ages passed,
    God to the world appeared;
And in the Babe of Bethlehem
    His glory was ensphered.

No creature whom His hand had made,
    Came with that word of hope;
Nor was a creature's strength required
    With Satan's power to cope.

For God Himself in Mary's Son
    Brought grace and truth to light,
And in the face of Jesus Christ
    We read His love aright.

Jesus, Thou art my Lord, my God,
    Kneeling I bow to Thee;
For on Thy brow, though bruised with thorns,
    A crown divine I see.

And I can trust the mighty work
    Which must be done for me,
To those dear hands of love and power,
    Now fastened to the tree.

If Thou wert less than one divine,
    My soul would be dismayed;
But through Thy human lips God speaks,—
    "'Tis I, be not afraid."

Yet, bruised and bleeding on the cross,
    I see Thy form divine;
And, though upon the accursed tree,
    I joy to call Thee mine.

The sword which should have pierced my life
  Has entered Thy dear breast,
And in God's faithfulness to Thee
  My trusting heart shall rest.

Death and the tomb no power had
  To hide Thy glory, Lord;
For Thou didst rise 'midst heavenly hosts,
  By whom Thou wert adored.

And after men were comforted
  By sight of Thee again,
Thou didst ascend to God's right hand,
  Their greater good to gain.

Thou wilt not leave my soul alone,
  To struggle to Thy side,
But in my spirit's helplessness
  Shall strength divine abide.

And, when I stand on Jordan's waves,
  Thou shalt my weakness hold,
Until at last my weary feet
  Shall walk the streets of gold.

There, in that cloudless light serene,
  Before the shining throne
I'll worship at the feet of Him
  Who did for me atone.

CHRIST OUR REFUGE AND STRENGTH.

"COME unto Me, all ye that labour and are heavy laden, and I will give you rest."—*Matt.* xi. 28.

"Lord, to whom shall we go? Thou hast the words of eternal life. And we believe, and are sure, that thou art that Christ, the Son of the living God."—*John* vi. 68, 69.

BLESSED Jesus! who dost invite all that labour and are heavy laden to come unto Thee, that they may find rest for their souls: mercifully enable us, we beseech Thee, so to cleave to Thee, that, in all the trials and temptations of this mortal life, we may do Thy will, and enjoy Thy peace, which the world cannot give nor take away. Amen.

"O DOMINE DEUS!
Speravi in Te;
O care mi Jesu!
Nunc libera me.
In dura catena,
In misera pœna,
Desidero Te.
Languendo, gemend
Et genuflectendo,
Adoro, imploro,
Ut liberes me."

From the Prayer-Book of QUEEN MARY STUART (?)

THE SHADOW OF THE ROCK.

THE Shadow of the Rock
Stay, Pilgrim, stay!
Night treads upon the heels of day;
There is no other resting-place this way;
The Rock is near,
The well is clear—
Rest in the Shadow of the Rock!

The Shadow of the Rock!
Abide! abide!
This Rock moves ever at thy side,
Pausing to welcome thee at eventide.
Ages are laid
Beneath its shade—
Rest in the Shadow of the Rock!

The Shadow of the Rock!
To angel's eyes
This Rock its shadows multiplies,
And at this hour in countless places lies.
One Rock, one shade,
O'er thousands laid—
Rest in the Shadow of the Rock!

From Dr. FABER.

CHRIST OUR REFUGE AND STRENGTH.

FIERCE WAS THE WILD BILLOW.

(Ζοφερᾶς τρικυμίας.)

FROM the Greek of ANATOLIUS, Patriarch of Constantinople (d. 458), by J. M. NEALE, 1862. Christ in the tempest. Mark iv. 37-39.

FIERCE was the wild billow,
    Dark was the night;
Oars laboured heavily,
    Foam glimmered white;
Mariners trembled,
    Peril was nigh;
Then said the God of God:[1]
    "Peace! it is I!"

Ridge of the mountain-wave,
    Lower thy crest!
Wail of the stormy wind,[2]
    Be thou at rest!
Peril can none be,
    Sorrow must fly,
Where saith the Light of Light;
    "Peace! it is I!"

---

[1] The terms "God of God," and "Light of Light," are used of Christ in the Nicene Creed against the Arian heresy. Anatolius was a member of the fourth general Council which met at Chalcedon, 451.

[2] Orig.: Euroclydon, or Euryclydon, a heavy wind.

Jesu, Deliverer!
  Come Thou to me!
Soothe Thou my voyaging
  Over life's sea!
Thou, when the storm of death,
  Roars, sweeping by,
Whisper, O Truth of Truth!
  "Peace! it is I!"

ART THOU WEARY?

(Κόπον τε καὶ κάματον.)

By St. Stephen, called the Sabaite, from the monastery of St. Sabas or Sabbas, near Jerusalem, a nephew of John of Damascus, d. about 794. The following sweet stanzas were translated by Dr. Neale, not from the Office-Books of the Greek Church, but from a dateless Constantinopolitan book. ("Hymns of the Eastern Church," p. 83.)

ART thou weary, art thou languid,
  Art thou sore distrest?
"Come to me," saith One, "and coming
  Be at rest!"

Hath He marks to lead me to Him,
  If He be my Guide?
"In His feet and hands are wound-prints,
  And His side."

Is there diadem, as Monarch,
  That His brow adorns?
"Yea, a crown in very surety,
  But of thorns!"

If I find Him, if I follow,
  What His guerdon here?
"Many a sorrow, many a labour,
  Many a tear."

If I still hold closely to Him,
  What hath He at last?
"Sorrow vanquished, labour ended,
  Jordan past!"

If I ask Him to receive me,
  Will He say me nay?
"Not till earth, and not till heaven
  Pass away!"

Finding, following, keeping, struggling,
  Is He sure to bless?
"Angels, martyrs, prophets, virgins,
  Answer, Yes!"

LORD JESUS CHRIST, IN THEE ALONE.

(Allein zu Dir, Herr Jesu Christ.)

From the German of JOHANN SCHNEESING, 1522. "Lyra Germ." II. 175 (SCHAFF, No. 277).

LORD Jesus Christ, in Thee alone
  My hope on earth I place;
  For other comforter is none,
Nor help save in Thy grace.
There is no man nor creature here,
No angel in the heavenly sphere,
Who at my need can succour me:
  I cry to Thee,
For Thou canst end my misery.

My sin is very sore and great,
  I mourn its load beneath:
O free me from this heavy weight,
  Through Thy most precious death!
And with Thy Father for me plead,
That Thou hast suffered in my stead,
The burden then from me is rolled:
  Lord, I lay hold
On Thy dear promises of old.

And of Thy grace on me bestow
  True Christian faith, O Lord!
That all the sweetness I may know
  That in Thy cross is stored,—

Love Thee o'er earthly pride or pelf,
And love my neighbour as myself;
And when at last is come my end,
   Be Thou my friend,
From all assaults my soul defend.

Glory to God in highest heaven,
   The Father of all love!
To His dear Son, for sinners given,
   Whose grace we daily prove!
To God the Holy Ghost we cry,
That we may find His comfort nigh,
And learn how, free from sin and fear,
   To please Him here,
And serve Him in the sinless sphere.

COURAGE, MY TEMPTED HEART!

(Brich durch, mein angefocht'nes Herz.)

From the German of J. H. Böhmer, 1704. Translated by Miss Catherine Winkworth ("Lyra Germ." II. 192).

Courage, my sorely-tempted heart!
   Break through thy woes, forget their smart;
   Come forth, and on Thy Bridegroom gaze,
The Lamb of God, the Fount of grace;
   Here is thy place!

His arms are open; thither flee!
There rest and peace are waiting thee,
The deathless crown of righteousness,
The entrance to eternal bliss;
   He gives thee this!

Then combat well, of naught afraid,
For thus His follower thou art made:
Each battle teaches thee to fight,
Each foe to be a braver knight,
   Armed with His might.

If storms of fierce temptations rise,
Unmoved we'll face the frowning skies;

If but the heart is true indeed,
Christ will be with us in our need,—
   His own could bleed.

I flee away to Thy dear cross,
For hope is there for every loss,
Healing for every wound and woe;
There all the strength of love I know,
   And feel its glow.

Before the Holy One I fall,
The Eternal Sacrifice for all;
His death has freed us from our load,
Peace on the anguished soul bestowed,
   Brought us to God.

How then should I go mourning on?
I look to Thee,—my fears are gone;
With Thee is rest that cannot cease,
For Thou hast wrought us full release,
   And made our peace.

Thy word hath still its glorious powers,
The noblest chivalry is ours;
O Thou for whom to die is gain,
I bring Thee here my all! oh, deign
   To accept and reign!

NOW I HAVE FOUND THE GROUND.

(Ich habe nun den Grund gefunden.)

FROM the German of JOH. ANDR. ROTHE (a Moravian), composed for Zinzendorf's birthday, 1728. Freely reproduced by JOHN WESLEY, 1740. (See the German, ten verses, with a note, in SCHAFF'S "G. H. B." No. 290.) Charles Wesley, to whom it is sometimes attributed, was probably ignorant of the German language. His brother John made all the translations from Zinzendorf, Tersteegen and others.

NOW I have found the ground wherein
   Sure my soul's anchor may remain;
   The wounds of Jesus, for my sin
Before the world's foundation slain;
Whose mercy shall unshaken stay,
When heaven and earth are fled away.

Jesus, Thine everlasting grace
  Our scanty thought surpasses far:
Thy heart still melts with tenderness;
  Thine arms of love still open are,
Returning sinners to receive,
That mercy they may taste, and live.

O Love, thou bottomless abyss!
  My sins are swallowed up in Thee;
Covered is my unrighteousness,
  No spot of guilt remains in me;
While Jesus' blood, through earth and skies,
Mercy, free, boundless mercy, cries.

By faith I plunge me in this sea;
  Here is my hope, my joy, my rest;
Hither, when hell assails, I flee,
  And look unto my Saviour's breast:
Away, sad doubt and anxious fear!
Mercy is all that's written here.

Though waves and storms go o'er my head,
  Though strength and health and friends be gone;
Though joys be withered all, and dead,
  And every comfort be withdrawn,—
On this my steadfast soul relies,
Jesus, Thy mercy never dies.

Fixed on this ground will I remain,
  Though my heart fail, and flesh decay,
This anchor shall my soul sustain,
  When earth's foundations melt away:
Mercy's full power I then shall prove,
Loved with an everlasting love.

JESU, LOVER OF MY SOUL.

Rev. Charles Wesley. From his "Hymns and Sacred Poems," 1740. One of the sweetest and most popular hymns in the English language, a worthy companion of Toplady's "Rock of Ages." Judged by æsthetic rules, the hymn, like St. Bernard's "Jesu dulcis memoria," is a string of pearls, but lacks progress of ideas, and is somewhat repetitious. The last lines of the first stanza would form an appropriate conclusion. The third stanza, "Wilt Thou not regard my call," is generally omitted.

JESU, lover of my soul,
    Let me to Thy bosom fly,
    While the waters near me roll,[1]
While the tempest still is high;
Hide me, O my Saviour! hide,
    Till the storm of life is past;
Safe into the haven guide,
    O receive my soul at last!

Other refuge have I none;
    Hangs my helpless soul on Thee:
Leave, ah! leave me not alone;
    Still support and comfort me:
All my trust on Thee is stayed;
    All my help from Thee I bring;
Cover my defenceless head
    With the shadow of Thy wing.

Wilt Thou not regard my call?
    Wilt Thou not accept my prayer?
Lo! I sink, I faint, I fall;
    Lo! on Thee I cast my care.
Reach me out Thy gracious hand,
    While I of Thy strength receive;
Hoping against hope I stand,
    Dying, and behold I live![2]

Thou, O Christ! art all I want:
    More than all in Thee I find:
Raise the fallen, cheer the faint,
    Heal the sick, and lead the blind.

---

[1] Originally:—
    "While the nearer waters roll."

[2] This beautiful verse makes it plain that the hymn was suggested by the story of Peter's peril and deliverance on the lake, Matt. xiv. 26-31.

Just and holy is Thy name;
 I am all unrighteousness :
False, and full of sin I am ;
 Thou art full of truth and grace.

Plenteous grace with Thee is found,—
 Grace to cover all my sin:
Let the healing streams abound ;
 Make and keep me pure within.
Thou of life the Fountain art;
 Freely let me take of Thee:
Spring Thou up within my heart ;
 Rise to all eternity.

ROCK OF AGES, CLEFT FOR ME.

By Augustus Montague Toplady, Vicar of Broadhembury, in Devonshire (d. 1778, in his 38th year). First published in "The Gospel Messenger," March, 1776, signed "A. T." under the title "A prayer, living and dying, for the holiest believer in the world." We give the text from Toplady's "Works." One of the most deeply evangelic and touching hymns in any language, the favourite of many Christians (*e.g.* of Prince Albert of England, in his dying hour). Faith in Christ, as the only and all-sufficient Saviour, has never found a more melting expression. It is one of those classic lyrics which sink at once into the heart, and can never be forgotten. As compared with the hymn of Charles Wesley, "Jesu, lover of my soul," it affords a striking illustration of the unity of Christian life, notwithstanding the diversity of theological conviction. The Calvinism of Toplady and the Arminianism of Wesley, which were arrayed against each other in fierce controversy, are here melted together into one common love to the Saviour, as the only refuge and comfort of the sinner in life and in death. Toplady's polemical tracts, (against Methodism), and Wesley's polemical verses (against the Calvinistic doctrine of predestination), are now mere matters of history ; but the devotional hymns of both will be sung to the end of time by Christians of all creeds. We mention, as a curiosity, that even the "Lyra Catholica" contains, alongside of the hymns of the Romish Breviary and Missal, this hymn of Toplady, but gives it as a translation from the Latin, "Jesus, pro me perforatus." See the next hymn.

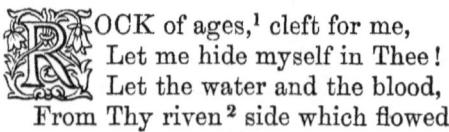

ROCK of ages,[1] cleft for me,
 Let me hide myself in Thee !
Let the water and the blood,
 From Thy riven[2] side which flowed,

---

[1] Comp. Isa. xxvi. 4 ("in Jehovah is everlasting strength," lit. "rock of ages," *zur olamim*); Ps. xviii. 3 ; xix. 14; Cant. ii. 14 ("in the clefts of the rock," *i e.* the wounds of Christ); 1 Cor. x. 4, ("And that Rock was Christ").

[2] Hymn-books generally change *riven* into *wounded.*

Be of sin the double cure,[1]
Cleanse me from its guilt and power.

Not the labours of my hands,
Can fulfil Thy law's demands:
Could my zeal no respite know,
Could my tears for ever flow,
All for sin could not atone,
Thou must save, and Thou alone.

Nothing in my hand I bring,
Simply to Thy cross I cling;
Naked come to Thee for dress,
Helpless look to Thee for grace:
Foul I to the fountain fly,
Wash me, Saviour, or I die.

While I draw this fleeting breath;
When my eyelids close in death;[2]
When I soar through tracts unknown,[3]
See Thee on Thy judgment throne,
Rock of ages, cleft for me,
Let me hide myself in Thee!

JESUS, PRO ME PERFORATUS.

(Rock of ages, cleft for me.)

THE "Rock of Ages" in Latin. Translated, A.D. 1848, by the distinguished statesman, W. E. GLADSTONE (b.1809). From "Translations by Lord Lyttelton and the Right Hon. W. E. Gladstone," Lond. 1861, p. 142; a Collection of translations of choice poems of Milton, Dryden, Tennyson, Gray, Goldsmith, Heber, and Toplady into Greek or Latin, and of several selections from

---

[1] Many hymn-books substitute "*perfect* cure," thus destroying the obvious reference to the *guilt* and *power* of sin.

[2] Originally: "When *my eye-strings break* in death." The above change, though not strictly correct, is one of the very rare instances in which compilers of hymn-books have improved upon the author. Generally, the endless alterations of English and German hymns are changes for the worse, or, as the Germans say, *Verschlimmbesserungen*. Even this invaluable hymn has been subjected to ruthless mutilations.

[3] Usually changed: "*to worlds* unknown."

Homer, Æschylus, Horace, Dante, Manzoni, and Schiller into English. The volume was published in commemoration of the double marriage of the two authors to two sisters (July 25, 1839).

JESUS, pro me perforatus,
   Condar intra Tuum latus.
   Tu per lympham profluentem,
Tu per sanguinem tepentem,
In peccata mi redunda,
Tolle culpam, sordes munda.

Coram Te, nec justus forem,
Quamvis totâ vi laborem,
Nec si fide nunquam cesso,
Fletu stillans indefesso:
Tibi soli tantum munus;
Salva me, Salvator unus!

Nil in manu mecum fero,
Sed me versus crucem gero;
Vestimenta nudus oro,
Opem debilis imploro;
Fontem Christi quæro immundus,
Nisi laves, moribundus.

Dum hos artus vita regit;
Quando nox sepulchro tegit;
Mortuos cum stare jubes,
Sedens Judex inter nubes;
Jesus, pro me perforatus,
Condar intra Tuum latus.

AWAKE, SWEET HARP OF JUDAH.

"The Hiding-place." By Henry Kirke White; b. 1785, at Nottingham; d. 1806. His remains, with a memoir, have been edited by Southey.

AWAKE, sweet harp of Judah, wake!
   Retune thy strings for Jesus' sake;
   We sing the Saviour of our race,
The Lamb, our shield and hiding-place.

When God's right arm is bared for war,
And thunders clothe His cloudy car;
Where, where, oh where shall man retire,
To escape the horrors of His ire?

'Tis He, the Lamb; to Him we fly,
While the dread tempest passes by;
God sees His well-beloved's face,
And spares us, in our hiding-place.

Thus, while we dwell in this low scene,
The Lamb is our unfailing screen;
To Him, though guilty, still we run,
And God still spares us for His Son.

While yet we sojourn here below,
Pollutions still our hearts o'erflow;
Fallen, abject, mean, a sentenced race,
We deeply need a hiding-place.

Yet, courage; days and years will glide,
And we shall lay these clods aside;
Shall be baptized in Jordan's flood,
And washed in Jesus' cleansing blood.

Then pure, immortal, sinless, freed,
We, through the Lamb, shall be decreed:
Shall meet the Father face to face,
And need no more a hiding-place.

WHEN THROUGH THE TORN SAIL.

By Bishop REGINALD HEBER, of Calcutta (d. 1826). "Help, Lord, or we perish!"

WHEN through the torn sail the wild tempest is streaming,
When o'er the dark wave the red lightning is gleaming,
Nor hope lends a ray, the poor seaman to cherish,
We fly to our Maker: "Help, Lord, or we perish!"

O Jesus! once tossed on the breast of the billow,
Aroused by the shriek of despair from Thy pillow,
Now seated in glory the mariner cherish,
Who cries in his danger: "Help, Lord, or we perish!"

And oh! when the whirlwind of passion is raging,
When hell in our heart his wild warfare is waging,
Arise in Thy strength, Thy redeemèd to cherish;
Rebuke the destroyer: "Help, Lord, or we perish!"

FROM EVERY STORMY WIND.

The Mercy-seat. Rev. Hugh Stowell, b. 1799; graduated at Oxford, 1822; Rural Dean of Salford; d. 1865. He published "A Collection of Psalms and Hymns," 1831.

FROM every stormy wind that blows,
   From every swelling tide of woes,
   There is a calm, a sure retreat:
'Tis found beneath the mercy-seat.

There is a place where Jesus sheds
"The oil of gladness" on our heads;
A place than all beside more sweet:
It is the blood-bought mercy-seat.

There is a spot where spirits blend,
Where friend holds fellowship with friend,
Though sundered far, by faith they meet
Around one common mercy-seat.

Ah! whither could we flee for aid,
When tempted, desolate, dismayed!
Or how the hosts of hell defeat,
Had suffering saints no mercy-seat?

There! there on eagle wings we soar,
And sin and sense molest no more;[1]
And heaven comes down, our souls to greet,
Where glory crowns the mercy-seat.

---

[1] Charles Rogers ("Lyra Britannica," p. 532) reads:—
"And time and sense seem all no more."

O may my hand forget her skill,
My tongue be silent, cold, and still,
This bounding heart forget to beat,
If I forget the mercy-seat!

SAVIOUR! WHEN, IN DUST, TO THEE.

A POETIC litany, by Sir ROBERT GRANT, an eminent philanthropist and statesman; b. 1785; d. 1838, as Governor of Bombay. He wrote twelve sacred lyrics. This is his best, and one of the best in the English language.

SAVIOUR! when, in dust, to Thee
Low we bow the adoring knee;
When, repentant, to the skies
Scarce we lift our weeping eyes:
Oh! by all the pains and woe
Suffered once for man below,
Bending from Thy throne on high,
Hear our solemn Litany!

By Thy helpless infant years,
By Thy life of want and tears;
By Thy days of sore distress
In the savage wilderness;
By the dread mysterious hour
Of the insulting tempter's power:
Turn, oh! turn a favouring eye,
Hear our solemn Litany!

By the sacred griefs that wept
O'er the grave where Lazarus slept;
By the boding tears that flowed
Over Salem's loved abode;
By the anguished sigh that told
Treachery lurked within Thy fold:
From Thy seat above the sky,
Hear our solemn Litany!

By Thine hour of dire despair
By Thine agony of prayer;
By the cross, the nail, the thorn,
Piercing spear, and torturing scorn;

By the gloom that veiled the skies
O'er the dreadful sacrifice:
Listen to our humble cry,
Hear our solemn Litany!

By Thy deep expiring groan;
By the sad sepulchral stone;
By the vault, whose dark abode
Held in vain the rising God:
O! from earth to heaven restored,
Mighty re-ascended Lord,
Listen, listen to the cry
Of our solemn Litany!

WHEN GATHERING CLOUDS.

Sir Robert Grant, 1838.

WHEN gathering clouds around I view,
And days are dark, and friends are few,
On Him I lean, who not in vain
Experienced every human pain:
He sees my wants, allays my fears,
And counts and treasures up my tears.

If aught should tempt my soul to stray
From heavenly wisdom's narrow way,
To fly the good I would pursue,
Or do the sin I would not do,
Still He, who felt temptation's power,
Shall guard me in that dangerous hour.

If wounded love my bosom swell,
Deceived by those I prized too well,
He shall His pitying aid bestow,
Who felt on earth severer woe;
At once betrayed, denied, or fled,
By those who shared His daily bread.

If vexing thoughts within me rise,
And sore dismayed my spirit dies,

Still He, who once vouchsafed to bear
The sickening anguish of despair,
Shall sweetly soothe, shall gently dry,
The throbbing heart, the streaming eye.

When sorrowing o'er some stone I bend,
Which covers all that was a friend,
And from his voice, his hand, his smile,
Divides me for a little while,
Thou, Saviour, seest the tears I shed,
For Thou didst weep o'er Lazarus dead.

And O! when I have safely past,
Through every conflict but the last,
Still, still unchanging, watch beside
My painful bed, for Thou hast died!
Then point to realms of endless day,
And wipe the latest tear away!

WHEN OUR HEADS ARE BOWED.

Dr. H. H. MILMAN, Dean of St. Paul's (d. 1868), author of "History of Latin Christianity," and other works. 1839.

WHEN our heads are bowed with woe,
When our bitter tears o'erflow,
When we mourn the lost, the dear,—
Gracious Son of Mary, hear!

Thou our throbbing flesh hast worn;
Thou our mortal griefs hast borne;
Thou hast shed the human tear:
Gracious Son of Mary, hear!

When the sullen death-bell tolls
For our own departed souls;
When our final doom is near,—
Gracious Son of Mary, hear!

Thou hast bowed the dying head,
Thou the blood of life hast shed;
Thou hast filled a mortal bier:
Gracious Son of Mary, hear!

When the heart is sad within,
With the thought of all its sin ;
When the spirit shrinks with fear,—
Gracious Son of Mary, hear !

Thou the shame, the grief, hast known,
Though the sins were not Thine own ;
Thou hast deigned their load to bear :
Gracious Son of Mary, hear !

WITH TEARFUL EYES I LOOK AROUND.

HUGH WHITE, 1841. From " The Invalid's Hymn-Book," and Sir R. PALMER'S " Book of Praise."

WITH tearful eyes I look around ;
   Life seems a dark and stormy sea ;
   Yet 'midst the gloom I hear a sound,
A heavenly whisper, " Come to Me ! "

It tells me of a place of rest,
   It tells me where my soul may flee :
Oh ! to the weary, faint, opprest,
   How sweet the bidding, " Come to Me ! "

When the poor heart with anguish learns
   That earthly props resigned must be,
And from each broken cistern turns,
   It hears the accents, " Come to Me ! "

When against sin I strive in vain,
   And cannot from its yoke get free,
Sinking beneath the heavy chain,
   The words arrest me, " Come to Me ! "

When nature shudders, loath to part
   From all I love, enjoy, and see ;
When a faint chill steals o'er my heart,
   A sweet voice utters, " Come to Me !

" Come, for all else must fail and die ;
   Earth is no resting-place for thee ;
Heavenward direct thy weeping eye ;
   I am thy portion ; Come to me ! "

O voice of mercy, voice of love !
 In conflict, grief, and agony,
Support me, cheer me from above,
 And gently whisper, " Come to Me ! "

JUST AS I AM,—WITHOUT ONE PLEA.

MISS CHARLOTTE ELLIOTT (1836), daughter of the Rev. Henry Venn Elliott, of St. Mary's, Brighton (d. 1841), and sister of the Rev. Edward B. Elliott, the author of " Horæ Apocalypticæ." She has written several volumes, contributed one hundred and seventeen hymns to " The Invalid's Hymn-Book," and edited the last edition of that compilation. The following hymn is, perhaps, the most popular, certainly one of the best, from her pen.

JUST as I am,—without one plea,
 But that Thy blood was shed for me,
 And that Thou bidst me come to Thee,
  O Lamb of God, I come !

Just as I am,—and waiting not
To rid my soul of one dark blot,
To Thee, whose blood can cleanse each spot,
 O Lamb of God, I come !

Just as I am,—though tossed about,
With many a conflict, many a doubt,
Fightings and fears within, without,
 O Lamb of God, I come !

Just as I am,—poor, wretched, blind ;
Sight, riches, healing of the mind,
Yea, all I need in Thee to find,
 O Lamb of God, I come !

Just as I am,—Thou wilt receive,
Wilt welcome, pardon, cleanse, relieve ;
Because Thy promise I believe,
 O Lamb of God, I come !

Just as I am,—Thy love unknown
Has broken every barrier down ;
Now to be Thine, yea, Thine alone,
 O Lamb of God, I come !

Just as I am,—of that free love
"The breadth, length, depth, and height" to prove,—
Here for a season, then above,—
   O Lamb of God, I come!

JUST AS THOU ART.

Rev. Russell S. Cook, Secretary of the "American Tract Society," afterwards of the "New York Sabbath Committee;" d. Sept. 4, 1864. This hymn, the counterpart of the preceding, was sent by the author to Miss Elliott, and printed anonymously in tract form. It found a place in Sir R. Palmer's "Book of Praise," No. 326, but without the second and last stanzas, which are here supplied from the author's copy.

JUST as thou art,—without one trace
  Of love, or joy, or inward grace,
  Or meetness for the heavenly place,
    O guilty sinner, come!

Thy sins I bore on Calvary's tree;
The stripes thy due were laid on Me,
That peace and pardon might be free,—
    O wretched sinner, come!

Burdened with guilt, wouldst thou be blest?
Trust not the world; it gives no rest:
I bring relief to hearts opprest,—
    O weary sinner, come!

Come, leave thy burden at the cross;
Count all thy gains but empty dross;
My grace repays all earthly loss,—
    O needy sinner, come!

Come, hither bring thy boding fears,
Thy aching heart, thy bursting tears:
'Tis mercy's voice salutes thine ears;
    O trembling sinner, come!

"The Spirit and the Bride say, Come;"
Rejoicing saints re-echo, Come;
Who faints, who thirsts, who will, may come;
    Thy Saviour bids thee come.

WHERE IS MERCY AND COMPASSION?
(*Wo ist göttliches Erbarmen.*)

THE fulness of Christ. C. J. P. SPITTA (died 1859). Second Series, 1843; seventeenth ed., Leipzig, 1866, p. 83. Translated by RICHARD MASSIE, " Lyra Domestica," Second Series, Lond. 1864, p. 69.

WHERE is mercy and compassion
 For the sinner that repents?
 Love, which offers free salvation
To returning penitents?
Where is crimson guilt forgiven?
 Who, when death and hell affright,
Sets before us joy in heaven,
 Everlasting life and light?
 Christ, in whom all fulness is,
 Can alone bestow all this.

Where is balsam which assuages
 Grief or pain's acutest smart?
Where is counsel for all ages,
 Comfort for the broken heart?
Who revives the faint and weary?
 Who brings back the sheep that stray?
Who, when long the way and dreary,
 Is our Guide, Support, and Stay?
 Christ, in whom all fulness is
 Can alone bestow all this.

Who gives joy in tribulation?
 Who enables us to bless
God in every dispensation,
 And in all to acquiesce?
Who the trust of children gives us,
 Lays us on our Father's breast,
From all needless care relieves us,
 Shows us all is for the best?
 Christ in whom all fulness is,
 Can alone bestow all this.

Who gives us a childlike meekness,
 And humility of mind?
Calm endurance, strength in weakness,
 Gentleness to all mankind?

Love, which shuns no sacrifices,
  Prompt to answer every call,
And a heart which sympathises
  In the joy and grief of all?
    Ah! thank Him who will and can
    Give such grace to every man.

Who to us a life hath given
  Over which death hath no power?
Who makes us the heirs of heaven,
  And of joys for evermore?
Who will raise again in glory
  What is here in weakness sown,
And the frail and transitory
  Clothe with beauty like His own?
    Ah! rejoice, for Jesus is
    He who can alone do this.

Thou who with the Father livest,
  And whose presence all things fills,
Who to all men all things givest,
  And in whom all fulness dwells,
Oh, how large the invitation
  Which Thou giv'st to all our race,
To accept a free salvation,
  And partake of Thy rich grace!
    Happy he who thus can taste
    All Thou art, and all Thou hast!

LONG HAST THOU WEPT AND SORROWED.

(Herz, du hast viel geweinet.)

By Mrs. META HEUSSER, Hirzel, Canton Zurich, Switzerland. Written 1837; first printed anonymously 1858 (then with the name of the authoress in SCHAFF's "G. H. B." No. 479). Translated by Miss JANE BORTHWICK, 1863.

LONG hast thou wept and sorrowed,
  Poor mourner; dry thy tears!
Behold, with light and comfort,
  Jesus Himself appears!

All other hopes must perish,
　　All earthly props decay;
Then let the seed be buried,
　　The husk be blown away.

Yet think not, God has granted
　　But to recall again,
His gifts of love and goodness,
　　Shall ever thine remain.

The seed, before it flourish,
　　Must low in darkness lie;
And love to live for ever,
　　Must for a season die.

But those like thee, bereaved,
　　Within earth's darkened home,
Are rich in many a promise
　　And pledge of joys to come.

"Trust in My mercy ever,
　　My people," saith the Lord;
Hold fast in deepest sorrow,
　　That soul-sustaining word.

The harvest day is hasting,
　　The rest from toil and pain,
When those who sleep in Jesus
　　Shall come with Him again.

And, more than all the treasures
　　That morning shall restore,
Himself, Himself, shall meet thee,
　　Thy portion evermore!

Then rest, sad heart, in patience,
　　With this petition still,
" Lord, all these vacant places
　　With thine own fulness fill!"

I HEARD THE VOICE OF JESUS SAY.

HORATIUS BONAR, D.D.; b. in Edinburgh, 1808; minister of the Free Church of Scotland, 1856. "Come unto Me."

HEARD the voice of Jesus say,
"Come unto Me and rest;
Lay down, thou weary one, lay down
Thy head upon My breast."
I came to Jesus as I was,
Weary and worn and sad;
I found in Him a resting-place,
And He has made me glad.

I heard the voice of Jesus say,
"Behold! I freely give
The living water: thirsty one,
Stoop down, and drink and live."
I came to Jesus, and I drank
Of that life-giving stream;
My thirst was quenched, my soul revived,
And now I live in Him.

I heard the voice of Jesus say,
"I am this dark world's light;
Look unto Me, thy morn shall rise,
And all thy day be bright."
I looked to Jesus, and I found
In Him my Star, my Sun;
And in that light of life I'll walk
Till travelling days are done.

A SINFUL MAN AM I.

HORATIUS BONAR. "Hymns of Faith and Hope," Third Series, 1868. "Come unto Me."

A SINFUL man am I,
Therefore I come to Thee,—
To Thee, the holy and the just,
That Thou mayst pity me.

Wert Thou not holy, Lord,
　Why should I come to Thee?
It is Thy holiness that makes
　Thee, Lord, so meet for me.

Wert Thou not gracious, Lord,
　I must in dread depart:
It is the riches of Thy grace
　That win and draw my heart.

Wert Thou not righteous, Lord,
　I dare not come to Thee:
It is a righteous pardon, Lord,
　Alone that suiteth me.

Our God is love,—we come;
　Our God is light, we stay;
Abiding ever in His word,
　And walking in His way.

Mercy and truth are His,
　Unchanging faithfulness;
The cross is all our boast and trust;
　And Jesus is our peace.

We give Thee glory, Lord;
　Thy Majesty adore.
Thee, Father, Son, and Holy Ghost,
　We bless for evermore.

LO! THE STORMS OF LIFE.

DR. HENRY ALFORD; b. 1810. Written 1845. From his "Year of Praise,"
Lond. 1867, No. 48.

LO! the storms of life are breaking;
　Faithless fears our hearts are shaking;
　For our succour undertaking,
　　Lord and Saviour, help us!

Lo! the world from Thee rebelling,
Round Thy Church in pride is swelling;
With Thy word their madness quelling,
　Lord and Saviour, help us!

On Thine own command relying,
We our onward task are plying;
Unto Thee for safety sighing,
    Lord and Saviour, help us!

By Thy birth, Thy cross, and passion,
By Thy tears of deep compassion,
By Thy mighty intercession,
    Lord and Saviour, help us!

THERE IS AN EVERLASTING HOME.

"Latus Salvatoris." MATTHEW BRIDGES. 1852.

THERE is an everlasting home,
    Where contrite souls may hide;
Where death and danger dare not come,—
    The Saviour's side.

It was a cleft of matchless love,
    Opened when He had died,
When mercy hailed in worlds above
    That wounded side.

Hail! Rock of Ages, pierced for me,
    The grave of all my pride;
Hope, peace, and heaven are all in Thee,
    Thy sheltering side.

There issued forth the double flood,
    The sin-atoning tide,
In streams of water and of blood,
    From that dear side.

There is the only Fount of Bliss,
    In joy and sorrow tried;
No refuge for the heart like this,—
    A Saviour's side.

Thither the Church, through all her days,
    Points as a faithful guide,
And celebrates with ceaseless praise
    That spear-pierced side.

TOSSED WITH ROUGH WINDS.

"It is I: be not afraid."—Matt. xiv. 27. By Mrs. ANDREW PATON CHARLES, *née* ELIZABETH RUNDELL. She published several books anonymously. The following poem was revised by her for ROGERS' "Lyra Brit.," 1867, p. 138.

TOSSED with rough winds, and faint with fear,
Above the tempest, soft and clear,
What still small accents greet mine ear?—
    'Tis I: be not afraid.

'Tis I who wash thy spirit white;
'Tis I who gave thy blind eyes sight;
'Tis I, thy Lord, thy Life, thy Light.
    'Tis I: be not afraid.

These raging winds, this surging sea,
Bear not a breath of wrath to thee;
That storm has all been spent on Me.
    'Tis I: be not afraid.

This bitter cup, I drank it first;
To thee it is no draught accurst;
The hand that gives it thee is pierced.
    'Tis I: be not afraid.

Mine eyes are watching by thy bed;
My arms are underneath thy head;
My blessing is around thee shed.
    'Tis I: be not afraid.

When on the other side thy feet
Shall rest,—'mid thousand welcomes sweet,
One well-known voice thy heart shall greet,—
    'Tis I: be not afraid.

From out the dazzling majesty,
Gently He'll lay His hand on thee,
Saying, "Belovèd, lovest thou Me?
'Twas not in vain I died for thee.
    'Tis I: be not afraid."

MY SAVIOUR, 'MID LIFE'S SCENE.

"Save, Lord, or I perish."   Mrs. Eliz. A. E. Godwin.   [1867.]

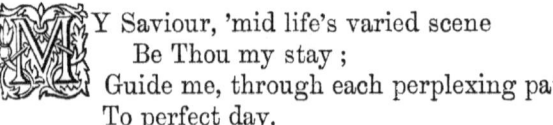Y Saviour, 'mid life's varied scene
    Be Thou my stay;
Guide me, through each perplexing path,
    To perfect day.
In weakness and in sin I stand;
Still faith can clasp Thy mighty hand,
And follow at Thy dear command.

My Saviour, I have nought to bring
    Worthy of Thee;
A broken heart Thou wilt not spurn:
    Accept of me.
I need Thy righteousness divine,
I plead Thy promises as mine,
I perish if I am not Thine.

My Saviour, wilt Thou turn away
    From such a cry?
My refuge, and wilt Thou forget,
    And must I die?
Faith trembles; but her glance of light
Has pierced through regions dark as night,
And entered into realms of light.

My Saviour, 'mid heaven's glorious throng
    I see Thee there,
Pleading with all Thy matchless love,
    And tender care,
Not for the angel-forms around,
But for lost souls in fetters bound,
That they may hear salvation's sound.

My Saviour, thus I find my rest
    Alone with Thee,
Beneath Thy wing I have no fear
    Of what may be.
Strengthened with Thy all-glorious might,
I shall be conqueror in the fight,
Then give to Thee my crown of light.

THE WAY IS LONG AND DREARY.

ADELAIDE ANNE PROCTER; b. in Bedford Square, London, 1825: contributor to Dickens' "Household Words;" author of "Legends and Lyrics," 1858, 1860, and other works; joined the Roman Catholic Church; d. 1864.

THE way is long and dreary,
    The path is bleak and bare,
Our feet are worn and weary;
    But we will not despair.
More heavy was Thy burthen,
    More desolate Thy way:
O Lamb of God, who takest
    The sin of the world away,
        Have mercy on us!

The snows lie thick around us
    In the dark and gloomy night,
And the tempest wails above us,
    And the stars have hid their light.
But blacker was the darkness
    Round Calvary's cross that day.
O Lamb of God, that takest
    The sin of the world away,
        Have mercy on us!

Our hearts are faint with sorrow,
    Heavy and sad to bear;
For we dread the bitter morrow,
    But we will not despair.
Thou knowest all our anguish,
    And Thou wilt bid it cease.
O Lamb of God, who takest
    The sin of the world away,
        Give us Thy peace!

IN THE HOURS OF PAIN AND SORROW.

By Mrs. HELEN L. PARMELEE, of Albany, New York; d. 1864. From her " Poems, Religious and Miscellaneous," New York, 1865, p. 108 (a posthumous publication).

 IN the hours of pain and sorrow,
  When the world brings no relief,
  When the eye is dim and heavy,
  And the heart oppressed with grief,
   While blessings flee,
  Saviour, Lord, we trust in Thee!

When the snares of earth surround us,—
 Pride, ambition, love of ease;
Mammon with her false allurements;
 Words that flatter, smiles that please,—
  Then, ere we yield,
 Saviour, Lord, be Thou our shield!

When forsaken, in distress,
 Poor, despised, and tempest-tost,
With no anchor here to stay us,
 Drifting, sail and rudder lost,—
  Then save us, Thou
 Who trod this earth with weary brow!

Thou, the hated and forsaken!
 Thou, the bearer of the cross!
Crowned of thorns, and mocked, and smitten,
 Counting earthly gain but loss;
  When scorned are we,
 We joy to be the more like Thee!

Thou, the Father's best belovèd!
 Thou, the throned and sceptred King!
Who but Thee should we, adoring,
 All our prayers and praises bring?
  Thrice blessed are we,
 Saviour, Lord, in loving Thee!

WATCHER, WHO WATCHEST BY THE BED OF PAIN.

Mrs. Lydia Huntley Sigourney; born in Norwich, Connecticut, 1791; died at Hartford, Connecticut, 1865; one of the most fertile American writers.

Watcher, who watchest by the bed of pain,
    While the stars sweep on in their midnight train;
Stifling the tear for Thy loved one's sake;
Holding Thy breath, lest his sleep should break;
In Thy loneliest hours, there's a helper nigh,
    "Jesus of Nazareth passeth by."

Stranger, afar from thy native land,
Whom no one takes with a brother's hand;
Table and hearthstone are glowing free,
Casements are sparkling, but not for thee;
There is one who can tell of a home on high,
    "Jesus of Nazareth passeth by."

Sad one, in secret, bending low,
A dart in Thy breast, that the world may not know,
Striving the favour of God to win,—
Asking His pardon for days of sin,—
Press on, press on, with thy earnest cry,
    "Jesus of Nazareth passeth by."

Mourner, who sits in the churchyard lone,
Scanning the lines on that marble stone;
Plucking the weeds from Thy children's bed,
Planting the myrtle, the rose instead,—
Look up, look up, with thy tearful eye,
    "Jesus of Nazareth passeth by."

Fading one, with the hectic streak,
With thy vein of fire, and thy burning cheek,
Fear'st thou to tread the darken'd vale,
Look unto One who can never fail.
He hath trod it Himself, He will hear thy sigh,
    "Jesus of Nazareth passeth by."

THUS FAR THE LORD HAS LED US ON.

EBENEZER; 1 Sam. vii. 12. By Miss JANE BORTHWICK, of Edinburgh. From "Thoughtful Hours," a collection of her poems, original and translated, London, 1867, 3rd edition. Miss J. Borthwick is the translator in part of the "Hymns from the Land of Luther."

THUS far the Lord has led us on,—in darkness and in day,
Through all the varied stages of the narrow homeward way.
Long since, He took that journey, He trod that path alone ;
Its trials and its dangers full well Himself hath known.

Thus far the Lord hath led us,—the promise has not failed,
The enemy encounter'd oft has never quite prevailed :
The shield of faith has turned aside or quenched each fiery dart ;
The Spirit's sword in weakest hands has forced Him to depart.

Thus far the Lord hath led us,—the waters have been high,
But yet in passing through them we felt that He was nigh.
A very present helper in trouble we have found,
His comforts most abounded when our sorrows did abound.

Thus far the Lord hath led us,—our need has been supplied,
And mercy has encompassed us about on every side;
Still falls the daily manna, the pure rock-fountains flow,
And many flowers of love and hope along the wayside grow.

Thus far the Lord hath led us,—and will He now forsake
The feeble ones whom for His own it pleaseth Him to take.
Oh, never, never! earthly friends may cold and faithless prove,
But His is changeless pity and everlasting love.

Calmly we look behind us, on joys and sorrows past;
We know that all is mercy now, and shall be well at last.
Calmly we look before us,—we fear no future ill;
Enough for safety and for peace, if Thou art with us still.

Yes, "They that know Thy name, O Lord, shall put their trust in Thee,"
While nothing in themselves but sin and helplessness they see.
The race Thou hast appointed us, with patience we can run;
Thou wilt perform unto the end the work Thou hast begun.

AMID THE DARKNESS.

"THE Voice of Christ." "Peace be still."—*Mark* iv. 39.   Dr. RAY PALMER. Written 1867, and first published in his "Hymns of my Holy Hours," New York, 1867.

AMID the darkness, when the storm,
   Swept fierce and wild o'er Galilee,
   Was seen of old, dear Lord, Thy form,
All calmly walking on the sea;
And raging elements were still,
Obedient to Thy sovereign will.

So on life's restless, heaving wave,
   When night and storm my sky o'ercast,
Oft hast Thou come to cheer and save,
   Hast changed my fear to joy at last.
Thy voice hath bid the tumult cease,
And soothed my throbbing heart to peace.

But ah! too soon my fears return,
   And dark mistrust disturbs anew :
What smothered fires within yet burn !
   My days of peace, alas, how few !
These heart-throes,—shall they ne'er be past ?
These strifes,—shall they for ever last ?

I heed not danger, toil, nor pain,
   Care not how hard the storm may beat,
If in my heart Thy peace may reign,
   And faith and patience keep their seat ;
If strength divine may nerve my soul,
And love my every thought control.

O may that voice that quelled the sea,
   And laid the surging waves to rest,
Speak in my spirit, set me free
   From passions that disturb my breast.
Jesus, I yield me to Thy will,
And wait to hear Thy " Peace, be still !"

I NEED THEE, PRECIOUS JESUS.

From the " People's Hymnal," Lond. 1867, No. 499, where it is ascribed to F. Whitfield.

I NEED Thee, precious Jesus,
   For I am full of sin ;
My soul is dark and guilty,
   My heart is dead within :
I need the cleansing fountain
   Where I can always flee,
The blood of Christ most precious,
   The sinner's perfect plea.

I need Thee, blessèd Jesus,
   For I am very poor ;
A stranger and a pilgrim,
   I have no earthly store :
I need the love of Jesus
   To cheer me on my way,
To guide my doubting footsteps,
   To be my strength and stay.

I need Thee, blessèd Jesus ;
   I need a friend like Thee,—
A friend to soothe and pity,
   A friend to care for me.

I need the Heart of Jesus
  To feel each anxious care,
To tell my every trial
  And all my sorrows share.

I need Thee, blessèd Jesus,
  And hope to see Thee soon,
Encircled with the rainbow,
  And seated on Thy throne !
There, with Thy blood-bought children,
  My joy shall ever be,
To sing Thy praise, Lord Jesus,
  To gaze, my Lord, on Thee.

CHRIST OUR PEACE.

" PEACE I leave with you, My peace I give unto you : not as the world giveth give I unto you. Let not your heart be troubled, neither let it be afraid."—*John* xiv. 27.

" He is our peace."—*Eph.* ii. 14.

" The peace of God, which passeth all understanding, shall keep your hearts and minds through Jesus Christ."—*Phil.* iv. 7.

BLESSED Saviour ! who, by the shedding of Thy precious blood on the Cross, and by Thy glorious triumph over death and hell, hast procured for us the remission of sins, and the peace with God which passeth all understanding : grant unto us, we humbly beseech Thee, such an abiding sense of Thy presence, that, amidst the trials and tribulations of this mortal life, our hearts may be at peace in the enjoyment of Thy favour, and in hopeful anticipation of the glory of the saints in light, who praise Thee, with the Father and the Holy Ghost, for ever and ever.   Amen.

> WITHOUT Thy presence, wealth is bags of cares;
>   Wisdom, but folly ; joy, disquiet, sadness;
> Friendship is treason, and delights are snares ;
>   Pleasure's but pain, and mirth but pleasing madness.
> Without Thee, Lord, things be not what they be ;
> Nor have they being, when compared with Thee.
>
> In having all things, and not Thee, what have I !
>   Not having Thee, what have my labours got ?
> Let me enjoy but Thee, what further crave I ?
>   And, having Thee alone, what have I not !
> I wish nor sea, nor land ; nor would I be
> Possessed of heaven, heaven unpossessed of Thee.
>
>   FRANCIS QUARLES.

"Thro' life and death, thro' sorrow and thro' sinning
 Christ shall suffice me, for He hath sufficed;
Christ is the end, for Christ is the beginning,
 Christ the beginning, for the end is Christ."

CHRIST OUR PEACE.

JESUS, MY CHIEF PLEASURE.

(Jesu, meine Freude.)

BY JOHANN FRANCK, burgomaster in Guben, Saxony: b. 1618; d. 1677. Translated from the German by R. MASSIE. ("Lyra Domestica," second series, Lond. 1864, p. 132.) The original (in SCHAFF's "G. H. B.," No. 162) is a transformation of an erotic song : " Flora, meine Freude, Meine Augenweide," and became soon popular all over Germany. A Russian translation was made by order of Peter the Great, 1724.

JESUS, my chief pleasure,
   Jesus, my heart's treasure,
     Matchless pearl of grace !
   Long my heart hath panted.
   And hath well nigh fainted,
     To behold Thy face.
Lamb, who died, behold Thy bride !
O what tie can e'er be nearer?
Who than Jesus dearer?

   When the tempest rages,
   In the Rock of Ages
     I will safely hide;
   Tho' the earth be shaking,
   And all hearts be quaking,
     Christ is at my side.
Lightnings flash, and thunders crash ;
Yea, tho' sin and hell assail me,
Jesus will not fail me.

Hence, deluding pleasure!
Jesus is the treasure
  To my heart most dear.
Hence, vain pomp and glories!
To your flattering stories
  I will lend no ear.
Grief and loss, shame, death, the cross,
Though they may afflict, shall never
Me from Jesus sever.

Hence, ye empty bubbles,
Self-inflicted troubles,
  Vanish from my sight!
Sins, which once could bind me,
Get ye all behind me,
  Come not to the light.
Pomp and pride, your faces hide!
Hence, ye brood of sin and folly,
I renounce you wholly.

Flee, ye shades of sadness!
Christ, the Prince of gladness,
  Comes with me to sup.
He may joy discover,
Who is Christ's true lover,
  In the bitterest cup.
Welcome cross, reproach, and loss,
Thou art still my consolation
In all tribulation.

O FRIEND OF SOULS! HOW BLEST THE TIME.

(Wie wohl ist mir, o Freund der Seelen.)

FROM the German of WOLFGANG CHRISTOPH DESSLER, 1692. Song of Solomon, viii. 5: "Who is this that cometh up from the wilderness, leaning upon her beloved?" The original (in SCHAFF's "G. H. B." No. 301) is very sweet, but difficult to translate. A closer version in "Lyra Germ." I. 346: "O Friend of souls, how well is me!" Another, abridged, in the "Moravian H. B." No. 389: "How blest am I, most gracious Saviour!"

FRIEND of souls! how blest the time
    When in Thy love I rest,
When from my weariness I climb
    E'en to Thy tender breast!
The night of sorrow endeth there,
    Thy rays outshine the sun,
And in Thy pardon and Thy care
    The heaven of heavens is won.

The world may call itself my foe,
    Or flatter and allure:
I care not for the world,—I go
    To this tried Friend and sure.
And when life's fiercest storms are sent
    Upon life's wildest sea,
My little bark is confident,
    Because it holdeth Thee.

The law may threaten endless death
    Upon the dreadful hill;
Straightway from its consuming breath
    My soul mounts higher still.
She hastes to Jesus, wounded, slain,
    And finds in Him her home,
Whence she shall not go forth again,
    And where no death can come.

I do not fear the wilderness
    Where Thou hast been before:
Nay! rather would I daily press
    After Thee, near Thee, more!
Thou art my strength, on Thee I lean;
    My heart Thou makest sing,
And to Thy pastures green at length
    Thy chosen flock wilt bring.

To others, death seems dark and grim,
    But not, O Lord! to me:
I know Thou ne'er forsakest him
    Who puts his trust in Thee.
Nay, rather, with a joyful heart
    I welcome the release
From this dark desert, and depart
    To Thy eternal peace.

THOU HIDDEN SOURCE.

"Jesus All, and in All." By Charles Wesley, b. 1708, d. 1788.

THOU hidden Source of calm repose,
    Thou all-sufficient Love Divine,
My help and refuge from my foes,
    Secure I am while Thou art mine:
And lo! from sin and grief and shame,
I hide me, Jesus, in Thy name.

Thy mighty name salvation is,
    And keeps my happy soul above:
Comfort it brings, and power and peace
    And joy, and everlasting love:
To me, with Thy dear name, are given
Pardon and holiness and heaven.

Jesus, my All in All Thou art;
    My rest in toil; my ease in pain;
The med'cine of my broken heart;
    In war, my peace: in loss, my gain;
My smile beneath the tyrant's frown;
In shame, my glory and my crown;

In want, my plentiful supply;
    In weakness, my almighty power;
In bonds, my perfect liberty.
    My light in Satan's darkest hour;
In grief, my joy unspeakable;
My life in death, my All in All.[1]

---

[1] Originally: "my heaven in hell."

THE WORLD CAN NEITHER GIVE NOR TAKE.

SELINA, COUNTESS OF HUNTINGDON; "the most extraordinary woman of her age;" b. 1707, d. 1791. This cento was composed by her, 1780, from two of JOHN MASON'S "Songs of Praise" (1683). Sir R. Palmer omits the last two stanzas.

THE world can neither give nor take,
    Nor can they comprehend,
That peace of God, which Christ hath bought,
    That peace which knows no end.

The burning bush was not consumed
    Whilst God remainèd there;
The three, when Jesus made the fourth,
    Found fire as soft as air.

God's furnace doth in Zion stand;
    But Zion's God sits by,
As the refiner views his gold
    With an observant eye.

His thoughts are high, His love is wise,
    His wounds a cure intend;
And, though He doth not always smile,
    He loves unto the end.

His love is constant as the sun,
    Though clouds come oft between;
And, could my faith but pierce these clouds,
    It might be always seen.

Yet I shall ever, ever sing,
    And Thou for ever shine:
I have Thine own dear pledge for this;
    Lord, Thou art ever mine.

COME, WEARY SOULS.

Miss ANNE STEELE; b. at Broughton, 1717; d. 1778. A lady of delicate health, who spent her life in works of piety and benevolence. She published, under the name of "Theodosia," two volumes of poems, 1760; a third volume appeared after her death. Republished in Boston, 1808, 2 vols. This poem is based on Matt. xi. 28.

COME, weary souls, with sin distressed,
The Saviour offers heavenly rest;
The kind, the gracious call obey,
And cast your gloomy fears away.

Oppressed with guilt, a painful load,
Oh come and spread your woes abroad!
Divine compassion, mighty love,
Will all the painful load remove.

Here mercy's boundless ocean flows,
To cleanse your guilt and heal your woes;
Pardon and life and endless peace,—
How rich the gift, how free the grace!

Lord, we accept with thankful heart
The hope Thy gracious words impart;
We come with trembling, yet rejoice,
And bless the kind inviting voice.

Dear Saviour, let Thy powerful love
Confirm our faith, our fears remove,
And sweetly influence every breast,
And guide us to eternal rest.

JESUS, MY LORD.

(Ach mein Herr Jesu, Dein Nahesein.)

CHRISTIAN GREGOR, a Moravian bishop, 1778. One of the sweetest hymns from the holy of holies of the believer's personal communion with his Saviour, and very characteristic of Moravian piety in its best form. Translated by EDWARD REYNOLDS, M.D., of Boston (from an unpublished translation of SCHAFF's "G. H. B."). Contributed. Other translations, by C. WINK-

WORTH, "Ah, dearest Lord! to feel that Thou art near" ("Lyra Germ." II. 224); and by Dr. H. MILLS, "Jesus, our Lord, when Thou art near" ("Horæ Germ." p. 87).

JESUS, my Lord, Thy nearness does impart
 Sweet peace and gladness to the longing heart,
 Thy gracious smile infuse a joyous thrill,
And soul and body with sweet pleasure fill,
  And thankfulness.

We see not with our eyes Thy friendly face,
So full of kindness, love, and gentle grace;
But in our hearts we know that Thou art here,
For Thou canst make us feel Thy presence near,
  Although unseen.

Whoever makes it life's chief aim and end
To have his happiness on Thee depend,
In him a well of joy for ever springs,
And all day long his heart is glad, and sings:
  Who is like Thee?

To meet us ever with a friendly face,
In mercy, patience, and the kindest grace,
Daily Thy rich forgiveness to bestow,
To comfort, heal, in peace to bid us go,—
  Is Thy delight.

Lord, for Thy rich salvation, hear our prayer,
And daily give us an abounding share;
And let our souls, in all their poverty,
From deep-felt love be looking unto Thee,
  Till life's last end.

In sorrowing hours may our o'erflowing eyes
For comfort look to Thy dear sacrifice;
And, with Thy cross before us, may we find
Thy genuine image stamped upon our mind,
  In constant view!

Lord, at all times mayst Thou within us find
A loving spirit and a childlike mind;
And from Thy wounds may we receive the power,
Through all life's weal and woe, in every hour,
  To cling to Thee.

Thus, till the heavens receive us, shall we be
Like children, finding all our joys in Thee;
And though the tears of sorrow oft must fall,
Yet, if Thou to our hearts art All in All,
    Sweet peace will come.

Thy wounded hand, dear Saviour, as a friend,
Thou dost to us in faithfulness extend;
At the sad sight our tears of grief must flow,
And conscious shame come o'er us as we go,
    With thankful praise.

O FOR A CLOSER WALK WITH GOD.

WILLIAM COWPER, 1779. "Olney Hymns," First Book, No. 3. Gen. v. 24:
"And Enoch walked with God: and he was not; for God took him."

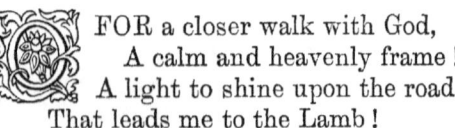FOR a closer walk with God,
    A calm and heavenly frame!
A light to shine upon the road
    That leads me to the Lamb!

Where is the blessedness I knew
    When first I saw the Lord!
Where is the soul-refreshing view
    Of Jesus and His word?

What peaceful hours I once enjoyed!
    How sweet their memory still!
But they have left an aching void,
    The world can never fill.

Return, O holy Dove! return,
    Sweet messenger of rest!
I hate the sins that made Thee mourn,
    And drove Thee from my breast.

The dearest idol I have known,
    Whate'er that idol be,
Help me to tear it from Thy throne,
    And worship only Thee!

So shall my walk be close with God,
Calm and serene my frame;
So purer light shall mark the road
That leads me to the Lamb.

WHY SHOULD I FEAR?

"JESUS my all." By the Rev. JOHN NEWTON, 1779. "Olney Hymns,"
Book III. No. 46.

WHY should I fear the darkest hour,
Or tremble at the tempter's power?
Jesus vouchsafes to be my tower.

Though hot the fight, why quit the field,
Why must I either flee or yield,
Since Jesus is my mighty shield?

When creature comforts fade and die,
Worldlings may weep, but why should I?
Jesus still lives, and still is nigh.

Though all the flocks and herds were dead,
My soul a famine need not dread,
For Jesus is my living bread.

I know not what may soon betide,
Or how my wants shall be supplied;
But Jesus knows, and will provide.

Though sin would fill me with distress,
The throne of grace I dare address,
For Jesus is my righteousness.

Though faint my prayers, and cold my love,
My steadfast hope shall not remove,
While Jesus intercedes above.

Against me earth and hell combine,
But on my side is power divine:
Jesus is all, and He is mine.

JESUS, MY LORD! MY LIFE! MY ALL!

By Samuel Medley, a Baptist minister at Liverpool, b. 1738, d. 1799. He was converted in consequence of a severe wound which he received, as a midshipman, in a naval engagement with the French, off Cape Lagos, 1759.

JESUS, my Lord! my life! my all!
Prostrate before Thy throne I fall;
Fain would my soul look up and see
My hope, my heaven, my all, in Thee.

Here, in this world of sin and woe,
I'm filled with tossings to and fro,
Burdened with sin, with fear oppressed;
And nothing here can give me rest.

In vain from creatures help I seek:
Thou, only Thou, the word canst speak,
To heal my wounds and calm my grief,
Or give my mournful heart relief.

Lord, I am vile and poor and weak,
Yet will I for Thy mercy seek:
I therefore cannot turn away,
But wait to hear what Thou wilt say.

Oh speak and bid my soul rejoice!
I long to hear Thy pardoning voice:
Say, "Peace, be still! look up and live;
Life, peace, and heaven are Mine to give."

Without Thy peace and presence, Lord,
Not all the world can help afford:
Oh, do not frown my soul away!
Lord, smile my darkness into day!

Then, filled with grateful, holy love,
My soul in praise shall soar above,
And with delightful joy record
The wondrous goodness of my Lord.

IF I ONLY HAVE THEE.

(Wenn ich Ihn nur habe.)

FROM the German of NOVALIS (or HARDENBERG, of Moravian connections, author of several glowing hymns; d., prematurely, 1801), by Dr. GEORGE W. BETHUNE, 1847. Another translation (four stanzas) in "Hymns from the Land of Luther," p. 96 ("If only He is mine").

  IF I only have Thee,
   If only mine Thou art,
    And to the grave
  Thy power to save
 Upholds my faithful heart,—
Naught can then my soul annoy,
Lost in worship, love, and joy.

  If I only have Thee,
  I gladly all forsake.
   To follow on
   Where Thou hast gone,
 My pilgrim staff I take;
Leaving other men to stray
In the bright, broad, crowded way.

  If I only have Thee,
  If only Thou art near,
   In sweet repose
   My eyes shall close,
 Nor Death's dark shadow fear;
And Thy heart's flood through my breast,
Gently charm my soul to rest.

  If I only have Thee,
  Then all the world is mine;
   Like those who gaze
   Upon the rays
 That from Thy glory shine,
Rapt in holy thought of Thee,
Earth can have no gloom for me.

  Where I only have Thee,
  There is my fatherland;

For everywhere
The gifts I share
From Thy wide-spreading hand;
And in all my human kind,
Long-lost brothers dear I find.

TREMBLING BEFORE THY THRONE.

FORGIVENESS of sins, a joy unknown to angels. 1822. The only hymn of AUGUSTUS LUCAS HILLHOUSE (brother of James Abraham H., who is commonly called " the poet Hillhouse"); b., 1792, at New Haven, Conn.; graduated, in Yale College, 1810; d., near Paris, 1859. This hymn was written in Paris, after 1816, and first published in the " Christian Spectator," New Haven, April, 1822. Dr. L. BACON (in the " New-Englander," Aug. 1860) praises it rather extravagantly, as being " unsurpassed in the English or any other language, and as near perfection as an uninspired composition can be. The thought, the feeling, the imagery, the diction, and the versification are all exquisite." It certainly has rare merit. Verse three is the gem of the hymn.

TREMBLING before Thine awful throne,
O Lord! in dust my sins I own:
Justice and Mercy for my life
Contend!—O smile, and heal the strife!

The Saviour smiles! Upon my soul
New tides of hope tumultuous roll:
His voice proclaims my pardon found,
Seraphic transport wings the sound!

Earth has a joy unknown in heaven—
The new-born peace of sin forgiven!
Tears of such pure and deep delight,
Ye angels! never dimmed your sight.

Ye saw of old on chaos rise
The beauteous pillars of the skies;
Ye know where morn exulting springs,
And evening folds her drooping wings.

Bright heralds of the Eternal Will,
Abroad His errands ye fulfil;
Or, throned in floods of beamy day,
Symphonious in His presence play.

Loud is the song,—the heavenly plain
Is shaken with the choral strain;
And dying echoes, floating far,
Draw music from each chiming star.[1]

But I amid your choirs shall shine,
And all your knowledge shall be mine:
Ye on your harps must lean to hear
A secret chord that mine will bear!

YES! OUR SHEPHERD LEADS.

(Ja fürwahr! uns führt mit sanfter Hand.)

Ps. xxiii.; Ezek. xxiv. 15. From the German of Fr. Adolph Krummacher, D.D.; b. 1767; d. 1845, as Reformed pastor in Bremen; author of the "Parables," &c.; a man of genius and lovely character. The translator in "Hymns from the Land of Luther," p. 49, seems to confound him with his son Friedrich Wilhelm, the celebrated orator and court-preacher at Potsdam, who is better known, in England and America, from his "Elijah," "Elisha," "The Suffering Saviour," "King David," &c.

YES! our Shepherd leads with gentle hand,
    Through the dark pilgrim-land,
    His flock, so dearly bought,
So long and fondly sought.
    Hallelujah!

When in clouds and mist the weak ones stray,
    He shows again the way,
    And points to them afar
A bright and guiding star.
    Hallelujah!

Tenderly He watches from on high
    With an unwearied eye;
    He comforts and sustains,
In all their fears and pains.
    Hallelujah!

---

[1] The Andover "Sabbath H. B.," No. 614, substitutes for vv. 4-6 of the original, which certainly needs no improvement, the following stanza :—

"Ye know where morn exulting springs,
And evening folds her drooping wings;
Loud is your song; the heavenly plain
Is shaken by your choral strain."

Through the parched, dreary desert He will guide
    To the green fountain-side ;
Through the dark, stormy night,
    To a calm land of light.
        Hallelujah !

Yes ! His " little flock " are ne'er forgot ;
    His mercy changes not :
Our home is safe above,
    Within His arms of love.
        Hallelujah !

LONG DID I TOIL.

"I AM His, and He is mine." By HENRY FRANCIS LYTE. 1833.

LONG did I toil, and knew no earthly rest ;
    Far did I rove, and found no certain home ;
    At last I sought them in His sheltering breast,
Who spreads His arms and bids the weary come.
With Him I found a home, a rest divine ;
And I since then am His, and He is mine.

Yes, He is mine ! and naught of earthly things,
    Not all the charms of pleasure, wealth, or power,
The fame of heroes, or the pomp of kings,
    Could tempt me to forego His love an hour.
" Go, worthless world," I cry, " with all that's thine ;
Go ! I my Saviour's am, and He is mine."

The good I have is from His store supplied ;
    The ill is only what He deems the best ;
With Him my Friend, I'm rich with naught beside,
    And poor without Him, though of all possessed.
Changes may come,—I take, or I resign,—
Content while I am His, while He is mine.

Whate'er may change, in Him no change is seen !
    A glorious Sun that wanes not, nor declines,
Above the clouds and storms He walks serene,
    And sweetly on His people's darkness shines.
All may depart,—I fret not, nor repine,
While I my Saviour's am, while He is mine.

He stays me falling; lifts me up when down;
  Reclaims me wandering; guards from every foe;
Plants on my worthless brow the victor's crown,
  Which, in return, before His feet I throw,
Grieved that I cannot better grace His shrine,
Who deigns to own me His, as He is mine.

While here, alas! I know but half His love,
  But half discern Him, and but half adore;
But, when I meet Him in the realms above,
  I hope to love Him better, praise Him more,
And feel and tell, amid the choir divine,
How fully I am His, and He is mine.

O BLESSED SUN, WHOSE SPLENDOUR.

(*O Jesu, meine Sonne.*)

C. J. P. SPITTA. "Life and Contentment in Jesus." From his "Psalter und Harfe," 1833. Translated by R. MASSIE, 1860.

BLESSED Sun, whose splendour
  Dispels the shades of night;
O Jesus, my defender,
  My soul's supreme delight,—
All day I hear resounding
  A voice with silver tone,
Which speaks of grace abounding
  Through God's eternal Son.

A deep and heavenly feeling
  Oft seizes on my breast,
Ah! here is balm for healing,
  Here only is true rest!
Though fortune should bereave me
  Of all I love the best,
If Christ His love still leave me,
  I freely give the rest.

To win this precious treasure
  And matchless pearl, I would
Give honour, wealth, and pleasure,
  And every earthly good;

I gladly would surrender
  The dearest thing which might
Obscure my Sun's bright splendour,
  And rob me of His light.

I know no life divided,
  O Lord of life! from Thee;
In Thee is life provided
  For all mankind and me.
I know no death, O Jesus
  Because I live in Thee:
Thy death it is which frees us
  From death eternally.

I fear no tribulation,
  Since, whatsoe'er it be,
It makes no separation
  Between my Lord and me.
If Thou, my God and teacher,
  Vouchsafe to be my own,
Though poor, I shall be richer
  Than monarch on his throne.

If, while on earth I wander,
  My heart is light and blest,
Ah! what shall I be yonder
  In perfect peace and rest?
O blessed thought in dying!
  We go to meet the Lord,
Where there shall be no sighing,
  A kingdom our reward.

Lord, with this truth impress me,
  And write it on my heart,
To comfort, cheer, and bless me,
  That Thou my Saviour art;
Without Thy love to guide me,
  I should be wholly lost;
The floods would quickly hide me,
  On life's wide ocean tost.

Thy love it was which sought me,
  Thyself unsought by me,
And to the haven brought me
  Where I would gladly be.

The things which once distrest me,
My heart no longer move,
Since this sweet truth imprest me,—
That I possess Thy love.

NOW I HAVE FOUND A FRIEND.

HENRY HOPE; born at Belfast; bookbinder in Dublin. The following hymn was printed by Mr. Hope, in 1852, for private circulation. Like other popular hymns, it has been unscrupulously and needlessly altered by editors of hymn-books and popular collections. It is here printed from a copy supplied by the author to ROGERS's "Lyra Brit." 1867.

NOW I have found a friend,
   Jesus is mine;
His love shall never end,
   Jesus is mine.
Though earthly joys decrease,
Though earthly friendships cease,
Now I have lasting peace,
   Jesus is mine.

Though I grow poor and old,
   Jesus is mine;
Though I grow faint and cold,
   Jesus is mine;
He shall my wants supply,
His precious blood is nigh,
Nought can my hope destroy,
   Jesus is mine.

When death is sent to me,
   Jesus is mine;
Welcome eternity,
   Jesus is mine.
He my redemption is,
Wisdom and righteousness,
Life, light, and holiness,
   Jesus is mine.

When earth shall pass away,
  Jesus is mine.
In the great judgment-day,
  Jesus is mine.
Oh! what a glorious thing,
Then to behold my King,—
On tuneful harp to sing,
  Jesus is mine.

Father, Thy name I bless,
  Jesus is mine;
Thine was the sovereign grace,
  Praise shall be Thine.
Spirit of holiness,
Sealing the Father's grace,
Thou mad'st my soul embrace
  Jesus as mine.

TELL ME NOT OF EARTHLY LOVE.

(Saget mir von keinem Lieben.)

FROM the German of an unknown author (see KNAPP's "Liederschatz," 2nd ed., No. 1762), translated by Miss JANE BORTHWICK, in her fourth series of "Hymns from the Land of Luther," Edinburgh, p. 70.

TELL me not of earthly love,
Bid me not its sweetness prove,
If it doth not heavenward tend,
And in Jesus find its end.

Tell me not of earthly bliss,
Bright, alluring as it is,
If its source I cannot see
In Thy love, my Lord, for me.

Tell me not of mental peace,
Till the sinner's conflicts cease;
Till that peace possess the heart
Jesus can alone impart.

Tell me not of knowledge high,
Roaming over earth and sky,—
This I know, worth all beside,
Jesus, and Him crucified.

Tell me not of earthly gain,
Earthly pleasures to obtain ;—
I the priceless Pearl have found,—
I have all things, and abound.

Tell me not of earthly glory,
Wild ambition's wondrous story,—
Higher far my hopes can rise,
To a kingdom in the skies.

Tell me not of life below,
With its changing joy and woe;
Hid with God doth mine remain,
Life is Christ, and death is gain.

Not where death and change can come,
Is my portion or my home!
Jesus! all my bliss shall be
Sought and found alone in Thee!

THROUGH THE LOVE OF GOD.

Mrs. Mary Peters; d. at Clifton, England, 1856 (Rogers's "Lyra Brit." p. 461). Sir R. Palmer (p. 437) attributes this hymn to Mary Bowly (the maiden name of the authoress). 1847.

THROUGH the love of God our Saviour,
    All will be well ;
Free and changeless is His favour,
    All, all is well.
Precious is the blood that healed us ;
Perfect is the grace that sealed us ;
Strong the hand stretched forth to shield us :
    All must be well !

Though we pass through tribulation,
    All will be well ;
Ours is such a full salvation,
    All, all is well !

Happy still, to God confiding;
Fruitful, if in Christ abiding;
Holy through the Spirit's guiding,—
    All must be well!

We expect a bright to-morrow,
    All will be well;
Faith can sing, through days of sorrow,
    All, all is well!
On our Father's love relying,
Jesus every need supplying,
Or in living or in dying,
    All must be well.

THOU KNOWEST, LORD.

By Miss JANE BORTHWICK, translator (in part) of " Hymns from the Land of Luther." Hence her assumed name, " H. L. L." From "Thoughtful Hours " (Edin. 1859, 3rd ed. London, 1867, p. 12), a collection of original poems and translations from the German of Mrs. META HEUSSER and others.

THOU knowest, Lord, the weariness and sorrow
    Of the sad heart that comes to Thee for rest:
  Cares of to-day, and qurdens for to-morrow,
    Blessings implored, and sins to be confessed,
I come before Thee at Thy gracious word,
And lay them at Thy feet,—Thou knowest, Lord.

Thou knowest all the past,—how long and blindly,
    On the dark mountains the lost wanderer strayed;
How the Good Shepherd followed, and how kindly
    He bore it home, upon His shoulders laid,
And healed the bleeding wounds, and soothed the pain,
And brought back life, and hope, and strength again.

Thou knowest all the present,—each temptation,
    Each toilsome duty, each foreboding fear;
All to myself assigned of tribulation,
    Or to beloved ones, than self more dear!
All pensive memories, as I journey on,
Longings for vanished smiles and voices gone!

Thou knowest all the future,—gleams of gladness
  By stormy clouds too quickly overcast,
Hours of sweet fellowship, and parting sadness,
  And the dark river to be crossed at last.—
Oh, what could confidence and hope afford
To tread that path, but this,—Thou knowest, Lord.

Thou knowest, not alone as God all-knowing—
  As Man, our mortal weakness Thou hast proved;
On earth, with purest sympathies o'erflowing,
  Oh, Saviour! Thou hast wept, and Thou hast loved!
And love and sorrow, still to Thee may come,
And find a hiding-place, a rest, a home.

Therefore I come, Thy gentle call obeying,
  And lay my sins and sorrows at Thy feet,
On everlasting strength my weakness staying,
  Clothed in Thy robe of righteousness complete:
Then rising and refreshed, I leave Thy throne,
And follow on to know as I am known.

REST, WEARY SOUL!

By Miss Jane Borthwick. From "Thoughts for Thoughtful Hours," By H. L. L. Edin. 1859, 3rd ed. 1867, p. 51. This poem passed, without a name, into Sir R. Palmer's "Book of Praise," No. CCCCIX. p. 438.

REST, weary soul!
  The penalty is borne, the ransom paid,
  For all thy sins full satisfaction made,
Strive not thyself to do what Christ has done;
Claim the free gift, and make the joy thine own;
No more by pangs of guilt and fear distrest,
    Rest, sweetly rest!

  Rest, weary heart,
From all thy silent griefs and secret pain,
Thy profitless regrets and longings vain;
Wisdom and love have ordered all the past,
All shall be blessedness and light at last;
Cast off the cares that have so long opprest:
    Rest, sweetly rest!

        Rest, weary head!
Lie down to slumber in the peaceful tomb;
Light from above has broken through its gloom:
Here, in the place where once thy Saviour lay,
Where He shall wake thee on a future day,
Like a tired child upon its mother's breast,
        Rest, sweetly rest!

        Rest, spirit free!
In the green pastures of the heavenly shore,
Where sin and sorrow can approach no more,
With all the flock by the Good Shepherd fed,
Beside the streams of life eternal led,
For ever with thy God and Saviour blest,
        Rest, sweetly rest!

I'VE FOUND A JOY IN SORROW.

"PILGRIM Discoveries." By Mrs. JANE CREWDSON (*née* FOX); b. 1809; d., near Manchester, England, 1863. She wrote, during a protracted period of illness, four volumes of genuine poetry. "Many felt that her sick-room was the highest place to which they could resort for refreshment of spirit, and even for mental recreation." From CHARLES ROGERS'S "Lyra Brit." p. 649.

I'VE found a joy in sorrow,
  A secret balm for pain.
A beautiful to-morrow
  Of sunshine after rain.
I've found a branch of healing
  Near every bitter spring;
A whispered promise stealing
  O'er every broken string.
I've found a glad hosanna
  For every woe and wail,
A handful of sweet manna
  When grapes from Eshcol fail.
I've found a Rock of Ages
  When desert wells were dry;
And, after weary stages,
  I've found an Elim nigh,—

An Elim, with its coolness,
  Its fountains, and its shade!

A blessing in its fulness,
　　When buds of promise fade!
O'er tears of soft contrition,
　　I've seen a rainbow light;
A glory and fruition,
　　So near!—yet out of sight.

My Saviour! Thee possessing,
　　I have the joy, the balm,
The healing and the blessing,
　　The sunshine and the psalm;
The promise for the fearful,
　　The Elim for the faint,
The rainbow for the tearful,
　　The glory for the saint.

LET NOT YOUR HEART BE FAINT.

Rev. John A. Latrobe, a native of London. 1863. His father was Secretary of the Moravian Church Missions. He published several poetic volumes.

LET not your heart be faint:
　　My peace I give to you,—
Such peace as reason never planned,
　　As worldlings never knew.

'Tis not the noiseless calm
　　That bodes a tempest nigh,
Or lures the heedless mariner
　　Where rocks and quicksands lie.

'Tis not fallen nature's sleep,
　　The stupor of the soul
That knows not God, nor owns His hand,
　　Though wide His thunders roll.

'Tis not the sleep of death,
　　Low in the darksome grave,
Where the worm spreads its couch, and feeds,—
　　No hand put forth to save.

It speaks a ransomed world,
   A Father reconciled,
A sinner to a saint transformed,
   A rebel to a child.

It tells of joys to come;
   It soothes the troubled breast;
It shines, a star amid the storm,—
   The harbinger of rest.

Then murmur not, nor mourn,
   My people faint and few:
Though earth to its foundation shake,
   My peace I leave with you.

REST OF THE WEARY.

By the Rev. JOHN S. B. MONSELL, LL.D.; b. at St. Columbs, Derry, 1811; a gifted and fertile living hymn writer, and author of several volumes of sacred lyrics. From his "Hymns of Love and Praise," Lond. 1863, p. 128. On Cant. v. 6 ("This is my Beloved, and this is my Friend"), and Isa. xliii. 3.

REST of the weary,
   Joy of the sad,
Hope of the dreary,
   Light of the glad;
Home of the stranger,
   Strength to the end,
Refuge from danger,
   Saviour and Friend!

Pillow where, lying,
   Love rests its head;
Peace of the dying,
   Life of the dead;
Path of the lowly,
   Prize at the end,
Breath of the holy,
   Saviour and Friend!

When my feet stumble,
   I'll to Thee cry;
Crown of the humble,
   Cross of the high.

When my steps wander,
   Over me bend,
Truer and fonder,
   Saviour and Friend!

Ever confessing
   Thee, I will raise
Unto Thee blessing,
   Glory, and praise;
All my endeavour,
   World without end,
Thine to be ever,
   Saviour and Friend!

JESUS, MY LORD, 'TIS SWEET TO REST.

From Savile's "Lyra Sacra" (3rd ed., Lond. 1865), where it bears the initials "H. B."

JESUS, my Lord, 'tis sweet to rest
Upon Thy tender, loving breast,
Where deep compassions ever roll
Towards my helpless, weary soul.

Thy love, my Saviour, dries my tears,
Expels my griefs, and calms my fears;
Sheds light and gladness o'er my heart,
And bids each anxious thought depart.

Blest foretaste this of joys to come
In Thy eternal, heavenly home;
Where I shall see Thy smiling face,
And know Thy rich, unfathomed grace.

That grace sustains my spirit now,
Though still a pilgrim here below;
That grace suffices, comforts, guides,
Upholds, defends, preserves, provides.

Yes, Thou art with me, O my God!
To bear me on to Thine abode;
Where I shall never cease to prove
Thy deep, divine, unfailing love.

Help me to praise Thee day by day,
Till earth's dark scenes are passed away,
Till in Thine own unclouded light
Thy glory satisfies my sight.

WHEN ACROSS THE HEART.

From the "Canterbury Hymnal," 1863.

WHEN across the heart deep waves of sorrow
    Break, as on a dry and barren shore;
When hope glistens with no bright to-morrow,
    And the storm seems sweeping evermore;

When the cup of every earthly gladness
    Bears no taste of the life-giving stream;
And high hopes, as though to mock our sadness,
    Fade and die as in some fitful dream,—

Who shall hush the weary spirit's chiding?
    Who the aching void within shall fill?
Who shall whisper of a peace abiding,
    And each surging billow calmly still?

Only He whose wounded heart was broken
    With the bitter cross and thorny crown;
Whose dear love glad words of joy had spoken;
    Who His life for us laid meekly down.

Blessed Healer! all our burdens lighten;
    Give us peace, Thine own sweet peace, we pray;
Keep us near Thee till the morn shall brighten,
    And all mists and shadows flee away.

SWEET WAS THE HOUR, O LORD!

THE well of Sychar. By Sir EDWARD DENNY, Bart. From his "Hymns and Poems," published in London, by U. H. Broom, 8, Athol Place (without date, probably 1863). Sir E. D. is a millenarian, and writer on prophetic themes.

SWEET was the hour, O Lord! to Thee,
   At Sychar's lonely well,
When a poor outcast heard Thee there
   Thy great salvation tell.

Thither she came; but oh! her heart,
   All filled with earthly care,
Dreamed not of Thee, nor thought to find
   The Hope of Israel there.

Lord! 'twas Thy power, unseen, that drew
   The stray one to that place,
In solitude to learn of Thee
   The secrets of Thy grace.

There Jacob's erring daughter found
   Those streams, unknown before,
The water-brooks of life, that make
   The weary thirst no more.

And, Lord, to us, as vile as she,
   Thy gracious lips have told
That mystery of love, revealed
   At Jacob's well of old.

In spirit, Lord, we've sat with Thee
   Beside the springing well
Of life and peace, and heard Thee there
   Its healing virtues tell.

Dead to the world, we dream no more
   Of earthly pleasures now;
Our deep, divine, unfailing spring
   Of grace and glory Thou!

No hope of rest in aught beside,
   No beauty, Lord, we see;
And, like Samaria's daughter, seek
   And find our all in Thee.

WHEN WINDS ARE RAGING.

"THE Secret." By Mrs. HARRIET BEECHER STOWE; b. at Litchfield, Conn., 1812; residing at Hartford, Connecticut. From her "Religious Poems," Boston, 1867, p. 32.

WHEN winds are raging o'er the upper ocean,
 And billows wild contend with angry roar,
'Tis said, far down beneath the wild commotion,
 That peaceful stillness reigneth evermore.

Far, far beneath, the noise of tempest dieth,
 And silver waves chime ever peacefully;
And no rude storm, how fierce soe'er it flieth,
 Disturbs the sabbath of that deeper sea.

So to the heart that knows Thy love, O Purest!
 There is a temple sacred evermore,
And all the babble of life's angry voices
 Dies in hushed stillness at its sacred door.

Far, far away, the roar of passion dieth,
 And loving thoughts rise calm and peacefully;
And no rude storm, how fierce soe'er it flieth,
 Disturbs that deeper rest, O Lord! in Thee.

O Rest of rests! O Peace serene, eternal!
 Thou ever livest, and Thou changest never;
And in the secret of Thy presence dwelleth
 Fulness of joy, for ever and for ever.

ALONE WITH THEE.

"ALONE with Christ." "I will come to you."—*John* xiv. 18. By RAY PALMER, D.D. Written 1867, and first published in his "Hymns of my Holy Hours." New York, 1867.

ALONE with Thee! alone with Thee!
  O Friend divine!
 Thou Friend of friends, to me most dear,
Though all unseen, I feel Thee near;
And, with the love that knows no fear,
  I call Thee mine.

ALONE WITH THEE.

Alone with Thee ! alone with Thee !
    Now through my breast
There steals a breath like breath of balm
That healing brings and holy calm,
That soothes like chanted song or psalm,
    And makes me blest.

Alone with Thee ! alone with Thee !
    Thy grace more sweet
Than music in the twilight still,
Than airs that groves of spices fill,
More fresh than dews on Hermon's hill,
    My soul doth greet.

Alone with Thee ! alone with Thee !
    In Thy pure light
The splendid pomps and shows of time,
The tempting steeps that pride would climb,
The peaks where glory rests sublime,
    Pale on my sight.

Alone with Thee ! alone with Thee !
    My softened heart
Floats on the flood of love divine,
Feels all its wishes drowned in Thine,
Content that every good is mine
    Thou canst impart.

Alone with Thee ! alone with Thee !
    I want no more
To make my earthly bliss complete,
Than oft my Lord unseen to meet ;
For sight I wait till tread my feet
    Yon glistering shore.

Alone with Thee ! alone with Thee !
    There not alone,
But with all saints, the mighty throng,
My soul unfettered, pure, and strong,
Her high communings shall prolong
    Before Thy throne.

JESUS! THE RAYS DIVINE.

"My Heavenly Friend." By Mrs. GRACE WEBSTER HINSDALE, Brooklyn, New York, July, 1868. Contributed.

JESUS! the rays divine,
  Which from Thy presence shine,
  Cast light o'er depths profound,
Which in Thy word are found,
    And lead me on!

The love within Thine eye
Oft checks the rising sigh;
The touch of Thy dear hand
Answers my heart's demand,
    And comforts me!

Yes, Lord, in hours of gloom,
When shadows fill my room,
When pain breathes forth its groans,
And grief its sighs and moans,
    Then Thou art near!

Oh! will it always be
That Thou wilt comfort me?
When friends are far away,
Wilt Thou, my Saviour, stay,
    And soothe my pain?

Jesus, Thou art my life!
No more I dread the strife,—
The rays of light divine,
Which from Thy presence shine,
    Fall o'er my heart!

ABIDE WITH ME!

REV. HENRY FRANCIS LYTE; b. 1793; graduated at Trinity College, Dublin; d. at Nice, 1847; author of "Religious Poems;" "Tales on the Lord's Prayer;" "The Spirit of the Psalms," &c. This beautiful hymn has passed into several recent Anglican hymn-books; e.g., "Hymns Ancient and Modern," and "The People's Hymnal," but only five stanzas of it. I have borrowed the text from Sir R. PALMER, No. CCCCV.

ABIDE with me! fast falls the eventide:
The darkness deepens; Lord, with me abide!
When other helpers fail, and comforts flee,
Help of the helpless, O abide with me!

Swift to its close ebbs out life's little day;
Earth's joys grow dim, its glories pass away;
Change and decay in all around I see;
O Thou who changest not, abide with me!

Not a brief glance I beg, a passing word;
But, as Thou dwell'st with Thy disciples, Lord,
Familiar, condescending, patient, free,—
Come, not to sojourn, but abide, with me!

Come not in terrors, as the King of kings;
But kind and good, with healing in Thy wings;
Tears for all woes, a heart for every plea;
Come, Friend of sinners, and thus 'bide with me!

Thou on my head, in early youth, didst smile;
And, though rebellious and perverse meanwhile,
Thou hast not left me, oft as I left Thee:
On to the close, O Lord, abide with me!

I need Thy presence every passing hour;
What but Thy grace can foil the Tempter's power?
Who like Thyself my guide and stay can be?
Through cloud and sunshine, Lord, abide with me!

I fear no foe, with Thee at hand to bless;
Ills have no weight, and tears no bitterness;
Where is Death's sting? where Grave, thy victory?
I triumph still, if Thou abide with me!

Hold, then, Thy cross before my closing eyes!
Shine through the gloom, and point me to the skies!
Heaven's morning breaks, and earth's vain shadows flee;
In life, in death, O Lord, abide with me!

THE CHILDREN OF THE WORLD HAVE MANY FRIENDS.

From the Danish of Timm. From the "Literary Churchman," Sept. 19, 1868.

THE children of the world have many friends,—
    The children of the light seek only One;
But He knows all thy faults and needs, and sends
    Amendment, succour, ere thou art undone.
Steals timidly to Him thy lonely sigh,
He heeds it quicker than the loudest cry;
Where pious souls in saddest silence weep,
The solaces of Christ are prompt and deep.

The children of the world have many ways,
    The children of the light seek only one;
But grace's corner-stone is there,—oh, gaze
    Boldly on terror grim thou fain wouldst shun!
Thorns crown and cumber the wild, flinty track,
Let them not, weary pilgrim, drive thee back,
Thy brother, Jesus, took this path of pain,
Before Him, as He marched, gleamed grandest gain.

The children of the world have many joys;
    The children of the light seek only one:
But like a stream, with flowery banks that toys,
    The living waters of my rapture run.
The fountain of my gladness manifold,
Of valours, strengths, resolves, and hopes untold,
Is my dear Saviour's rich and yearning breast;
Faith is the pledge and prelude of my rest.

FAITH IN CHRIST.

"LET not your heart be troubled: ye believe in God, believe also in Me.—*John* xiv. 1.

"The life which I now live in the flesh, I live by the faith of the Son of God, who loved me and gave Himself for me."—*Gal.* ii. 20.

"Looking unto Jesus, the author and finisher of our faith."—*Heb.* xii. 2.

"Lord, I believe; help Thou mine unbelief."—*Mark* ix. 24.

ALMIGHTY GOD, who hast revealed Thyself, in Thy Son Jesus Christ, as a God of infinite love and wisdom, and who dost offer us in Him complete salvation and everlasting bliss: work in us, by Thy Holy Spirit, a hearty, constant, and abiding faith in Thee and in Thy Son, that we may never be ashamed to confess Him before men, and, following His holy example, may overcome the world, abound in fruits of righteousness, and, having fought the good fight of faith, carry away at last the crown of life; through Jesus Christ our Lord, to whom, with Thee and the Holy Spirit, be honour and glory, world without end. Amen.

"ETERNAL God of earth and air!
Unseen, yet seen in all around,
Remote, but dwelling everywhere,
Though silent, heard in every sound,—

If e'er Thine ear in mercy bent
When wretched mortals cried to Thee;
And if, indeed, Thy Son was sent
To save lost sinners such as me:

Then hear me now, while, kneeling here,
I lift to Thee my heart and eye,
And all my soul ascends in prayer,
Oh, give me, give me faith! I cry.

Without some glimmering in my heart,
I could not raise this fervent prayer:
But, oh! a stronger light impart,
And in Thy mercy fix it there."

My Lord, Thy Love be praised,
Thou by the doubt which Thomas raised,
Our doubting didst prevent,
We without sight give firm assent,
With joy Thy benediction we receive,
They blessed are, who see not, yet believe.
BISHOP KEN.

Oh, gift of gifts! oh grace of faith
  My God! how can it be
That Thou, who hast discerning love,
  Should'st give that gift to me?

The crowd of cares, the weightiest cross,
  Seem trifles less than light,
Earth looks so little and so low
  When faith shines full and bright.

Oh, happy, happy that I am!
  If thou canst be, O faith,
The treasure that thou art in life,
  What wilt thou be in death!

FAITH IN CHRIST.

WHEN SINS AND FEARS.

Miss Anne Steele, died 1778. John xiv. 19. The poems of this pious and deservedly popular authoress were first published in England, 1760, in 2 vols., with an additional volume after her death, 1780; and republished in Boston. 1808 (by Munroe, Francis, & Parker, 4, Cornhill), in 2 vols. The text is from the Boston ed., I. p. 137.

HEN sins and fears prevailing rise,
    And fainting hope almost expires.
Jesus, to Thee I lift mine eyes,
    To Thee I breathe my soul's desires.

Art Thou not mine, my dearest Lord?
    And can my hope, my comfort die,
Fixed on Thy everlasting word,
    That word which built the earth and sky?

If my immortal Saviour lives,
    Then my immortal life is sure;
This word a firm foundation gives,
    Here let me build, and rest secure.

Here let my faith unshaken dwell;
    Immoveable the promise stands;
Not all the powers of earth or hell
    Can e'er dissolve the sacred bands.

Here, O my soul! thy trust repose;
    Since Jesus is for ever mine,
Not death itself, that last of foes,
    Shall break a union so divine.

SEE A POOR SINNER, DEAREST LORD.

Samuel Medley, a Baptist minister at Liverpool, d. 1799.

SEE a poor sinner, dearest Lord,
Whose soul, encouraged by Thy word,
At mercy's footstool would remain,
And then would look, "and look again."

How oft, deceived by self and pride,
Has my poor heart been turned aside;
And, Jonah-like, has fled from Thee,
Till Thou hast looked again on me!

Ah! bring a wretched wanderer home,
And to Thy footstool let me come,
And tell Thee all my grief and pain,
And wait and look, and look again.

Do fears and doubts thy soul annoy,
Do thundering tempests drown thy joy?
And canst thou not one smile obtain?
Yet wait and look, and look again.

Take courage then, my trembling soul;
One look from Christ will make Thee whole:
Trust thou in Him, 'tis not in vain,
But wait and look, and look again.

Look to the Lord, His word, His throne;
Look to His grace, and not your own:
There wait and look, and look again;
You shall not wait nor look in vain.

Ere long that happy day will come,
When I shall reach my blissful home;
And when to glory I attain,
O then I'll look, and look again.

AMID LIFE'S WILD COMMOTION.

(Aus irdischem Getümmel.)

FROM the German of CARL JULIUS ASSCHENFELD (b. at Kiel, Holstein, 1792). 1819. John xiv. 6. (SCHAFF, No. 102.) Translator unknown.

AMID life's wild commotion,
   Where nought the heart can cheer,
Who points beyond its ocean
   To heaven's brighter sphere?
Our feeble footsteps guiding,
   When from the path we stray,
Who leads to bliss abiding?
   Christ is our only Way.

When doubts and fears distress us,
   And all around is gloom,
And shame and fear oppress us,
   Who can our souls illume?
Heaven's rays are round us gleaming,
   And making all things bright,
The sun of Truth is beaming
   In glory on our sight.

Who fills our hearts with gladness
   That none can take away?
Who shows us, 'midst our sadness,
   The distant realms of day?
'Mid fears of death assailing,
   Who stills the heart's wild strife?
'Tis Christ! our Friend unfailing,
   The Way, the Truth, the Life.

I KNOW IN WHOM I PUT MY TRUST.

(Ich weiss, an wen ich glaube.)

ERNST MORITZ ARNDT. 1819. (SCHAFF'S "German Hymn Book," No. 295)
Translated by C. WINKWORTH. The author († 1860) was one of the noblest
German patriots, and at the same time a sincere, childlike Christian. His
"Was ist des Deutschen Vaterland," is one of the most popular German
songs.

I KNOW in whom I put my trust,
   I know what standeth fast,
When all things here dissolve like dust
   Or smoke before the blast:
I know what still endures, howe'er
   All else may quake and fall,
When lies the prudent men ensnare,
   And dreams the wise inthrall.

It is the Dayspring from on high,
   The adamantine Rock,
Whence never storm can make me fly,
   That fears no earthquake's shock;
My Jesus Christ, my sure Defence,
   My Saviour, and my Light,
That shines within, and scatters thence
   Dark phantoms of the night;

Who once was borne, betrayed and slain,
   At evening to the grave;
Whom God awoke, who rose again,
   A Conqueror strong to save:
Who pardons all my sin, who sends
   His Spirit pure and mild;
Whose grace my every step befriends,
   Who ne'er forgets His child!

Therefore I know in whom I trust,
   I know what standeth fast,
When all things formed of earthly dust
   Are whirling in the blast;
The terrors of the final foe
   Can rob me not of this;
And this shall crown me once, I know,
   With never-fading bliss.

MY FAITH LOOKS UP TO THEE.

THE REV. RAY PALMER, D. D.; b. 1808, in Rhode Island; now of New York. This is his most popular hymn, written (as the author informs me) 1830, and first published 1833; translated into Arabic, and sung in many missionary stations; one of the very few American hymns that have been naturalized in England. The text is taken from his " Hymns and Sacred Pieces," New York, 1865.

MY faith looks up to Thee,
Thou Lamb of Calvary,
   Saviour divine !
Now hear me while I pray,
Take all my guilt away,
O let me from this day
   Be wholly Thine.

May Thy rich grace impart
Strength to my fainting heart,
   My zeal inspire;
As Thou hast died for me,
O may my love to Thee,
Pure, warm, and changeless be, —
   A living fire.

While life's dark maze I tread,
And griefs around me spread,
   Be Thou my guide;
Bid darkness turn to day,
Wipe sorrow's tears away,
Nor let me ever stray
   From Thee aside.

When ends life's transient dream,
When death's cold, sullen stream,
   Shall o'er me roll;
Blest Saviour, then in love
Fear and distrust remove;
O, bear me safe above, —
   A ransomed soul.

HALLELUJAH! I BELIEVE!

(Ich glaube, Hallelujah.)

FROM the German of HEINRICH MÖWES, a devoted clergyman near Magdeburg, Prussia; d 1831, after severe afflictions, which he bore with heroic faith. Translated, by JANE BORTHWICK, in "Hymns from the Land of Luther," p. 114.

HALLELUJAH! I believe!
  Now the giddy world stands fast,
  Now my soul has found an anchor
Till the night of storm is past.
All the gloomy mists are rising,
  And the clue is in my hand,
Through earth's labyrinth to guide me
  To a bright and heavenly land.

Hallelujah! I believe!
Sorrow's bitterness is o'er,
And affliction's heavy burden
  Weighs my spirit down no more.
On the cross the mystic writing
  Now revealed before me lies,
And I read the words of comfort,
  "As a father, I chastise."

Hallelujah! I believe!
Now no longer on my soul
All the debt of sin is lying:
  One great Friend has paid the whole!
Ice-bound fields of legal labour
  I have left with all their toil,
While the fruits of love are growing
  From a new and genial soil.

Hallelujah! I believe!
Now life's mystery is gone;
Gladly through its fleeting shadows,
  To the end I journey on.
Through the tempest or the sunshine,
  Over flowers or ruins led,
Still the path is *homeward* hasting,
  Where all sorrow shall have fled.

Hallelujah! I believe!
Now, O Love! I know Thy power;
Thine no false or fragile fetters,
　　Not the rose-wreaths of an hour!
Christian bonds of holy union
　　Death itself does not destroy;
Yes, to live and love for ever,
　　Is our heritage of joy!

O HOLY SAVIOUR, FRIEND UNSEEN!

Miss Charlotte Elliott, authoress of "Just as I am," and a large number of other hymns. 1836.

 HOLY Saviour, Friend unseen!
The faint, the weak, on Thee may lean;
Help me, throughout life's varying scene,
　　By faith to cling to Thee.

Blest with communion so divine,
Take what Thou wilt, shall I repine,
When, as the branches to the vine,
　　My soul may cling to Thee?

Far from her home, fatigued, opprest,
Here she has found a place of rest;
An exile still, yet not unblest,
　　While she can cling to Thee.

Without a murmur I dismiss
My former dreams of earthly bliss:
My joy, my recompense, be this,—
　　Each hour to cling to Thee.

What though the world deceitful prove,
And earthly friends and joys remove;
With patient, uncomplaining love,
　　Still would I cling to Thee.

Oft when I seem to tread alone
Some barren waste, with thorns o'ergrown,
A voice of love, in gentlest tone,
　　Whispers, "Still cling to Me."

Though faith and hope awhile be tried,
I ask not, need not, aught beside:
How safe, how calm, how satisfied,
    The souls that cling to Thee!

They fear not life's rough storms to brave,
Since Thou art near, and strong to save;
Nor shudder e'en at death's dark wave;
    Because they cling to Thee!

Blest is my lot, whate'er befall:
What can disturb me, who appal,
While, as my Strength, my Rock, my All,
    Saviour! I cling to Thee?

I ONCE WAS A STRANGER.

ROBERT MURRAY MCCHEYNE; b. at Edinburgh, 1813; pastor at Dundee; d. 1843. The following hymn is inscribed, "Jehovah Tsidkenu, 'The Lord our Righteousness.'"

ONCE was a stranger to grace and to God,
I knew not my danger, and felt not my load;
Though friends spoke in rapture of Christ on the tree,
Jehovah Tsidkenu was nothing to me.

I oft read with pleasure, to soothe or engage,
Isaiah's wild measure and John's simple page;
But, e'en when they pictured the blood-sprinkled tree,
Jehovah Tsidkenu seemed nothing to me.

Like tears from the daughters of Sion that roll,
I wept when the waters went over His soul;
Yet thought not that my sins had nailed to the tree
Jehovah Tsidkenu,—'twas nothing to me.

When free grace awoke me by light from on high,
Then legal fears shook me: I trembled to die;
No refuge, no safety, in self could I see;
Jehovah Tsidkenu my Saviour must be.

My terrors all vanished before the sweet name;
My guilty fears banished, with boldness I came
To drink at the fountain, life-giving and free:
Jehovah Tsidkenu is all things to me.

Jehovah Tsidkenu! my treasure and boast;
Jehovah Tsidkenu! I ne'er can be lost;
In Thee I shall conquer by flood and by field,
My cable, my anchor, my breast-plate, and shield!

Even treading the valley, the shadow of death,
This watchword shall rally my faltering breath;
For, while from life's fever my God sets me free,
Jehovah Tsidkenu my death-song shall be.

WHILE FAITH IS WITH ME.

ANNE BRONTE. A prayer for faith. Abridged I found this poem in a newspaper, and cannot vouch for a correct text.

WHILE Faith is with me I am blest;
   It turns my darkest night to day;
But while I clasp it to my breast
   I often feel it slide away.

Then, cold and dark, my spirit sinks,
   To see my light of life depart;
And every friend of hell, methinks,
   Enjoys the anguish of my heart.

What shall I do, if all my love,
   My hopes, my toil, are cast away,
And if there be no God above
   To hear and bless me when I pray?—

If this be vain delusion all,
   If death be an eternal sleep,
And none can hear my secret call,
   Or see the silent tears I weep?

Oh, help me, God! for Thou alone
   Canst my distracted soul relieve;
Forsake it not; it is Thine own,
   Though weak, yet longing to believe.

Oh, drive these cruel doubts away,
  And make me know that Thou art God!
A faith that shines by night and day
  Will lighten every earthly load.

If I believed that Jesus died,
  And, waking, rose to reign above,
Then, surely, sorrow, sin, and pride,
  Must yield to peace and hope and love.

And all the blessed words He said
  Will strength and holy joy impart;
A shield of safety o'er my head,
  A spring of comfort in my heart.

WE WALK BY FAITH, AND NOT BY SIGHT.

By HENRY ALFORD, D.D., Dean of Canterbury. 1845. From his
"Year of Praise," 1867, No. 249.

WE walk by faith and not by sight;
  No gracious words we hear
From Him who spoke as never man,
  But we believe Him near.

We may not touch His hands and side,
  Nor follow where He trod;
But in His promise we rejoice,
  And cry, "My Lord and God!"

Help Thou, O Lord, our unbelief:
  And may our faith abound,
To call on Thee when Thou art near,
  And seek where Thou art found:

That, when our life of faith is done,
  In realms of clearer light
We may behold Thee as Thou art,
  With full and endless sight.

STRONG SON OF GOD.

ALFRED TENNYSON, poet laureate of England. Introductory to his "In Memoriam," 1849. Abridged.

STRONG Son of God, immortal Love,
  Whom we, that have not seen Thy face,
  By faith, and faith alone, embrace,
Believing where we cannot prove!

Thine are these orbs of light and shade;
  Thou madest life in man and brute;
  Thou madest Death; and, lo! Thy foot
Is on the skull which Thou hast made.

Thou wilt not leave us in the dust:
  Thou madest man, he knows not why;
  He thinks he was not made to die;
And Thou hast made him: Thou art just.

Thou seemest human and divine
  The highest, holiest manhood Thou:
  Our wills are ours, we know not how;
Our wills are ours, to make them Thine.

Our little systems have their day;
  They have their day, and cease to be;
  They are but broken lights of Thee,
And Thou, O Lord! art more than they.

We have but faith: we cannot know,
  For knowledge is of things we see;
  And yet we trust it comes from Thee,
A beam in darkness: let it grow.

Let knowledge grow from more to more,
  But more of reverence in us dwell;
  That mind and soul, according well,
May make one music, as before.

WE WERE NOT WITH THE FAITHFUL.

FROM the "Canterbury Hymnal," 1863. John, xx. 29 : " Blessed are they that have not seen, and yet have believed."

WE were not with the faithful few
   Who stood Thy bitter cross around,
   Nor heard Thy prayer for those that slew,
Nor felt that earthquake rock the ground;
We saw no spear-wound pierce Thy side:
Yet we believe that Thou hast died.

No angel's message met our ear
   On that first glorious Easter day,—
"The Lord is risen. He is not here:
   Come, see the place where Jesus lay!"
But we believe that Thou didst quell
The banded powers of death and hell.

We saw Thee not return on high;
   And now, our longing sight to bless,
No ray of glory from the sky
   Shines down upon our wilderness:
Yet we believe that Thou art there,
And seek Thee, Lord, in praise and prayer.

LIFE'S MYSTERY.

"THE Mystery of Life." A poem of rare beauty. By Mrs. HARRIET BEECHER STOWE; b. 1812; authoress of "Uncle Tom's Cabin," &c. From her "Religious Poems," Boston, 1867, p. 74.

"Let my heart calm itself in Thee. Let the great sea of my heart, that swelleth with waves, calm itself in Thee."—ST. AUGUSTINE.

LIFE'S mystery—deep, restless, as the ocean—
   Hath surged and wailed for ages to and fro;
   Earth's generations watch its ceaseless motion
As in and out its hollow moanings flow.
Shivering and yearning by that unknown sea,
Let my soul calm itself, O Christ, in Thee!

LIFE'S MYSTERY.

Life's sorrows, with inexorable power,
  Sweep desolation o'er this mortal plain ;
And human loves and hopes fly as the chaff
  Borne by the whirlwind from the ripened grain.
Ah ! when before that blast my hopes all flee,
Let my soul calm itself, O Christ, in Thee !

Between the mysteries of death and life
  Thou standest, loving, guiding, not explaining ;
We ask, and Thou art silent; yet we gaze,
  And our charmed hearts forget their drear complaining.
No crushing fate, no stony destiny,
O Lamb that hast been slain, we find in Thee !

The many waves of thought, the mighty tides,
  The ground-swell that rolls up from other lands,
From far-off worlds, from dim, eternal shores,
  Whose echo dashes on life's wave-worn strands,—
This vague, dark tumult of the inner sea
Grows calm, grows bright, O risen Lord, in Thee !

Thy piercèd hand guides the mysterious wheels ;
  Thy thorn-crowned brow now wears the crown of power ;
And, when the dread enigma presseth sore,
  Thy patient voice saith, "Watch with Me one hour."
As sinks the moaning river in the sea
In silver peace, so sinks my soul in Thee !

YES !—MY REDEEMER LIVES.

(Ich weiss, dass mein Erlöser lebet.)

By Mrs. META HEUSSER, of Switzerland. Written, 1859, for SCHAFF'S "G. H. B." (No. 359). Translated by the late Rev. Dr. HENRY MILLS, of Auburn, N.Y., and here published for the first time, from a written copy sent to the Editor.

YES !—my Redeemer lives, to save us,
  And ever faithful will abide :
When Time shall mar what good it gave us,
  What once was ours in dust shall hide ;

When stars in darkness veil their gleaming,
   When Death's dread form shall louder moan,
Amid the gloom—with glory beaming—
   He'll then appear, and save His own.

What else, but trials, here is granted?
   Safe from the ordeal—who can come?
A wintry field with gravestones planted,
   Such is on earth our dreary home:
We see, like soon-forgotten story
   Form after form away has pass'd,—
Yet One, when all that's transitory
   Is gone, our life and light shall last.

We now move on, in fetters grievous,
   At ev'ry step drawn tighter round:
On ev'ry side fresh lures deceive us,
   E'en in our holiest things are found:
But He who, 'gainst all ill-abettors
   How we should strive example gives,
He has the strength to loose our fetters—
   We know that our Redeemer lives.

And, living, may He love and guide us!
   Thus changing darkness into day:
Tho' Death may chill our hearts, beside us
   His heart, our source of life shall stay:
This shames all human riddles—Dying
   Is turn'd to life and happiness!
Sin's wages our best good supplying,
   While He shall crown His saints with bliss!

Haste onward then, ye hours, to meet it!
   Ye ages, that on earth shall be
Our Rock of hope, ye mortals greet it—
   A Saviour for eternity.
Now Faith her flight is upward winging,
   Borne on by Him new life that gives,
And, as she soars, is ever singing—
   "I know that my Redeemer lives!"

WHEN TIME SEEMS SHORT.

By the Rev. GEORGE W. BETHUNE, D.D., minister of the Reformed Dutch Church, New York. This touching poem was found in his portfolio, and was written on the day before his death, which took place on the Lord's Day, April 27, 1862, at Florence, in Italy, the same day on which he preached his last sermon, on Matt. ix. : " Son, be of good cheer : thy sins be forgiven thee." (Dr. VAN NEST, " Memoir of Dr. Bethune," 1867, p. 409.)

WHEN time seems short and death is near,
And I am pressed by doubt and fear,
And sins, an overflowing tide,
Assail my peace on every side,
This thought my refuge still shall be,
I know the Saviour died for me.

His name is Jesus, and He died,
For guilty sinners crucified;
Content to die that He might win
Their ransom from the death of sin :
No sinner worse than I can be,
Therefore I know He died for me.

If grace were bought, I could not buy;
If grace were coined, no wealth have I;
By grace alone I draw my breath,
Held up from everlasting death;
Yet, since I know His grace is free,
I know the Saviour died for me.

I read God's holy Word, and find
Great truths which far transcend my mind;
And little do I know beside
Of thoughts so high, so deep and wide:
This is my best theology,
I know the Saviour died for me.

My faith is weak, but 'tis Thy gift;
Thou canst my helpless soul uplift,
And say, " Thy bonds of death are riven,
Thy sins by Me are all forgiven;
And thou shalt live from guilt set free,
For I, Thy Saviour, died for thee."

EVER IS MY PERIL NEAR.

Trial and Faith. From the Danish of Kingo. See "Literary Churchman," Sept. 19, 1868.

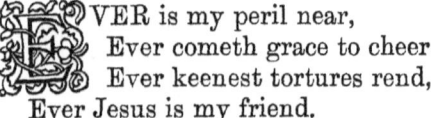VER is my peril near,
  Ever cometh grace to cheer;
  Ever keenest tortures rend,
Ever Jesus is my friend.

Ever sin enslaves, ensnares;
Ever Christ my burden bears;
Ever tread I sorrow's way;
Ever, ever sing and pray.

Joyful, woeful are my cries;
Now I fall, and now I rise;
Now I wrestle with unrest,
Now I lean on Jesus' breast.

Thus I grief and gladness link,
And the mystic cup I drink,—
Sweet and bitter, bitter-sweet;
Strange and sad life's contrasts meet.

But, oh Christ, the more I weep,
Send the more faith strong and deep;
Sin may tempt and sorrow wail,—
Never let them, Christ, prevail!

UNION WITH CHRIST.

"ABIDE in Me, and I in you."—*John* xv 4.
"We are members of His body, of His flesh, and of His bones."—*Eph.* v. 30.
"God hath given to us eternal life, and this life is in His Son. He that hath the Son, hath life."—1 *John* v. 11, 12.

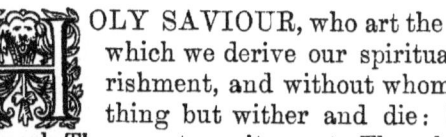OLY SAVIOUR, who art the true Vine from which we derive our spiritual life and nourishment, and without whom we can do nothing but wither and die: be pleased, we beseech Thee, so to unite us to Thee, by the power of the Holy Ghost and through the bond of a living faith, that, being partakers of Thy divine nature, we may bring forth much fruit, and for ever abide in Thee, as Thou dost abide in us, until we shall see Thee as Thou art, and glorify and enjoy Thee, with the Father and the Holy Spirit, for ever and ever. Amen.

> My blessed Saviour, Lord Divine,
> I am Thine own, and Thou art mine.
> I am Thine own; for Thou didst give
> Thy precious life, that I might live.
> And Thou art mine: with all my heart,
> I cleave to Thee, my chosen part.
> How dearly didst Thou purchase me!
> Oh, let me never part from Thee!
>
> P. S.

UNION WITH CHRIST.

HOW LOVELY SHINES THE STAR!

(*Wie schön leuchtet der Morgenstern.*)

FROM the German of PHILIPP NIKOLAI, a Lutheran minister at Unna, Westphalia. A favourite German hymn, written in a time of prevailing pestilence, 1597. It celebrates the union of a believing soul with Christ, her heavenly Bridegroom, according to Psalm xlv. and the Song of Solomon. A. Knapp pronounces this the sweetest and most excellent of all German hymns, and compares it with the 17th chapter of John. It has a rich and blessed history. The tune is one of the noblest German chorals. Translated 1860, from the text in SCHAFF'S "G. H. B.," No. 311, in the metre of the original, by the Rev. Dr. H. HARBAUGH (d. 1867).

HOW lovely shines the Morning Star!
The nations see and hail afar
The light in Judah shining.
Thou David's Son of Jacob's race,
My Bridegroom, and my King of grace,
For Thee my heart is pining!
Lowly, holy,
Great and glorious, Thou victorious
Prince of graces,
Filling all the heavenly places!

O highest joy by mortals won!
Of Mary and of God, the Son!
Thou high-born King of ages,
Thou art my heart's best, sweetest flower,
And Thy blest gospel's saving power
My raptured soul engages.
Thou mine, I Thine;
Sing Hosanna! Heavenly manna
Tasting, eating,
Whilst Thy love in songs repeating.

Now richly to my waiting heart,
O Thou, my God, deign to impart
   The grace of love undying.
In Thy blest Body let me be,
E'en as the branch is in the tree;
   Thy life my life supplying.
      Sighing, crying,
   For the savour of Thy favour;
      Resting never,
   Till I rest in Thee for ever.

Token of peace from God I see,
When Thy pure eyes are turned to me
   With heavenly enliving;
Jesus, Thy Spirit and Thy Word,
Thy body and Thy blood, afford
   My soul the best reviving.
      Take me kindly,
   To Thy favour, O my Saviour!
      Thou wilt cheer me,
   Since Thy word invites me near Thee.

My Father God, in mercy's plan,
Before creation's work began,
   Thy love in Christ foresaw me.
Thy Son has called me to His side;
He is my Friend, I am His bride,
   From Him no power can draw me.
      Praise be to Thee!
   Thou hast given life of heaven!
      I shall never
   Die, but praise Thy love for ever.

Wake, wake, your harps to sweetest songs!
In praise of Him, to whom belongs
   All praise, join hearts and voices.
For evermore, O Christ! in Thee,
Thee all in all of love to me,
   My grateful heart rejoices.
      With joy, employ,
   Hymns victorious, glad and glorious;
      E'er be given
   Honour to the King of heaven.

O joy! to know that Thou, my Friend,
Art Lord, Beginning without end,
　　The First and Last,—Eternal!
And Thou at length—O glorious grace!—
Wilt take me to that holy place,
　　The home of joys supernal.
　　　　Amen, Amen!
Come and meet me, quickly greet me;
　　　Draw me ever
　　Nearer to Thyself for ever!

LORD, THOU ART MINE.

By the Rev. GEORGE HERBERT, Rector of Bemerton, d. 1632.

LORD, Thou art mine, and I am Thine,
　　If mine I am: and Thine much more,
　　Than I or ought, or can be mine.
　Yet to be Thine, doth me restore;
So that again I now am mine,
　And with advantage mine the more.
Since this being mine, brings with it Thine,
　And Thou with me dost Thee restore.
If I without Thee would be mine,
I neither should be mine nor Thine.

Lord, I am Thine, and Thou art mine:
　So mine Thou art, that something more
I may presume Thee mine, then Thine;
　For Thou didst suffer to restore
Not Thee, but me, and to be mine:
　And with advantage mine the more,
Since Thou in death wast none of Thine,
　Yet then as mine didst me restore.
O be mine still! still make me Thine;
Or rather make no Thine and mine!

I LEAVE THEE NOT.

(Ich lass Dich nicht, Du musst mein Jesus bleiben.)

FROM the German of WOLFGANG CHRISTOPH DESSLER (b. 1660, d. 1722, author of fifty-six hymns), by Dr. JAMES W. ALEXANDER (d. 1859).

LEAVE Thee not: Thou art my Jesus ever,
  Though earth rebel,
  And death and hell
Would, from its steadfast hold, my faith dissever.
  Ah, no! I ever will
  Cling to my Helper still,
Hear what my love is taught;
  Thou art my Jesus ever,
I leave Thee not, I leave Thee not!

I leave Thee not, O Love! of love the highest,
  Though doubt display
  Its battle-day;
I own the power which Thou my Lord appliest:
  Thou didst bear guilt and woe;
  Shall I to torment go,
When into judgment brought?
  O Love! of love the highest,
I leave Thee not, I leave Thee not!

I leave Thee not, O Thou who sweetly cheerest!
  Whose fresh supplies,
  Cause strength to rise,
Just in the hour when faith's decay is nearest.
  If sickness chill the soul,
  And nights of languor roll,
My heart one hope hath caught:
  O Thou who sweetly cheerest,
I leave Thee not, I leave Thee not!

I leave Thee not, Thou help in tribulation;
  By stroke on stroke,
  Though almost broke,
I hope, when all seems near to desolation.
  Do what Thou wilt with me,
  I still must cling to Thee;

Thy grace I have besought;
    Thou help in tribulation,
I leave Thee not, I leave Thee not!

I leave Thee not: shall I forsake salvation?
    No, Jesus, no!
    Thou shalt not go;
Mine still Thou art, to free from condemnation.
    After this fleeting night,
    Thy presence brings me light,
Whose ray my soul hath sought;
    Shall I forsake salvation?
I leave Thee not, I leave Thee not!

I leave Thee not: Thy word my way shall brighten:
    With Thee I go
    Through weal and woe,
Thy precept wise shall every burden lighten.
    My Lord, on Thee I hang,
    Nor heed the journey's pang,
Though thorny be my lot:
    Let but Thy word enlighten,
I leave Thee not, I leave Thee not!

I leave Thee not, even in the lap of pleasure;
    For, when I stray,
    Without Thy ray,
My richest joy must cease to be a treasure.
    I shudder at the glee,
    When no delight from Thee
Has heartfelt peace begot:
    Even in the lap of pleasure,
I leave Thee not, I leave Thee not!

I leave Thee not, my God, my Lord, my Heaven!
    Nor death shall rend
    From Thee, my Friend,
Who for my soul Thyself to death hast given.
    For Thou didst die for me,
    And love goes back to Thee;
My heart has but one thought:
    My God, my Life, my Heaven,
I leave Thee not, I leave Thee not!

MY SAVIOUR! I AM THINE.

DR. PHILIP DODDRIDGE. 1755. On 1 Cor. vi. 17, "Being joined to Christ, and one spirit with Him."

MY Saviour! I am Thine,[1]
    By everlasting bands;
My name, my heart, I would resign;
    My soul is in Thy hands.

To Thee I still would cleave
    With ever-growing zeal;
Let millions tempt me Christ to leave,
    They never shall prevail!

Thy Spirit shall unite
    My soul to Thee, my Head;
Shall form me to Thine image bright,
    And teach Thy paths to tread.

Death may my soul divide
    From this abode of clay;
But love shall keep me near Thy side,
    Through all the gloomy way.

Since Christ and we are one,
    Why should we doubt or fear?
If He in heaven has fixed His throne,
    He'll fix His members there.

JESUS, IMMUTABLY THE SAME.

By the Rev. AUGUSTUS M. TOPLADY, B.A., Vicar of Broadhembury, Devon. 1776. "The Vine and the Branches." John xv. 1-8.

JESUS, immutably the same,
    Thou true and living vine,
Around Thy all-supporting stem,
    My feeble arms I twine.

---

[1] This is the original form in Doddridge's Hymns, edited, from the author's MS., by Job Orton. Nearly all the hymn-books, however, read, "*Dear Saviour, we are Thine*," and substitute the plural throughout for the singular.

JESUS, IMMUTABLY THE SAME.

Quickened by Thee, and kept alive,
   I flourish and bear fruit;
My life I from Thy sap derive,
   My vigour from Thy root.

Grafted in Thee by grace alone,
   In growth I daily rise;
And, raised on this foundation-stone,
   My top shall reach the skies.

I can do nothing without Thee:
   My strength is wholly Thine;
Withered and barren should I be,
   If severed from the vine.

Upon my leaf, when parched with heat,
   Refreshing dew shall drop:
The plant, which Thy right hand hath set,
   Shall ne'er be rooted up.

Till Thou hast led me to the place
   Of pure, immortal joy,
The riches of Thy glorious grace
   Shall all my need supply.

Who from eternity decreed
   To glorify His own,
Will not forsake the holy seed,
   Nor take away their crown.

The righteous shall hold on their way,
   Nor miss the promised land:
Jesus shall guard them night and day,
   And hide them in His hand.

Each moment watered by Thy care,
   And fenced with power divine,
Fruit to eternal life shall bear
   The feeblest branch of Thine.

JESUS, LEAD US WITH THY POWER.

WILLIAM WILLIAMS, a Calvinistic Methodist, who preached with great effect in Wales, and composed several hymns, chiefly in the Welsh language; d. 1791.

JESUS, lead us with Thy power
    Safe into the promised rest;
Hide our souls within Thy bosom;
    Let us slumber on Thy breast;
Feed us with the heavenly manna,
    Bread that angels eat above:
Let us drink from the holy fountain
    Draughts of everlasting love.

Throughout the desert wild conduct us,
    With a glorious pillar bright;
In the day a cooling comfort,
    And a cheering fire by night;
Be our guide in every peril;
    Watch us hourly, night and day;
Otherwise we'll err and wander
    From Thy Spirit far away.

In Thy presence we are happy;
    In Thy presence we're secure;
In Thy presence all afflictions
    We will easily endure;
In Thy presence we can conquer,
    We can suffer, we can die;
Far from Thee, we faint and languish;
    Lord, our Saviour, keep us nigh.

SUN OF MY SOUL.

FROM the Evening Hymn of Dr. JOHN KEBLE (d. 1866), the second in his "Christian Year" (first published 1827), commencing:—

    "'Tis gone, that bright and orbèd blaze,
    Fast fading from our wistful gaze."

Sir R. PALMER (No. CCLIX.), the compilers of "Hymns Ancient and Modern," and other editors, omit the first two stanzas; and, in this abridged

SUN OF MY SOUL.

form, the hymn is likely to pass into general use, as equal in merit to Bishop Ken's well-known evening-hymn. Alford, in his "Year of Praise," 1867, No. 314, gives only three verses.

SUN of my soul, Thou Saviour dear,
It is not night if Thou be near;
Oh! may no earth-born cloud arise
To hide Thee from Thy servant's eyes!

When round Thy wondrous works below
My searching rapturous glance I throw,
Tracing out wisdom, power, and love,
In earth or sky, in stream or grove;

Or, by the light Thy words disclose,
Watch time's full river as it flows,
Scanning Thy gracious providence,
Where not too deep for mortal sense;

When with dear friends sweet talk I hold,
And all the flowers of life unfold,—
Let not my heart within me burn,
Except in all I Thee discern!

When the soft dews of kindly sleep
My wearied eyelids gently steep,
Be my last thought, how sweet to rest
For ever on my Saviour's breast!

Abide with me from morn till eve,
For without Thee I cannot live!
Abide with me when night is nigh,
For without Thee I dare not die!

Thou Framer of the light and dark,
Steer through the tempest Thine own ark!
Amid the howling wintry sea
We are in port if we have Thee.

The rulers of this Christian land,
'Twixt Thee and us ordained to stand,
Guide Thou their course, O Lord! aright;
Let all do all as in Thy sight!

Oh! by Thine own sad burthen, borne
So meekly up the hill of scorn,
Teach Thou Thy priests their daily cross
To bear as Thine, nor count it loss!

If some poor wandering child of Thine
Have spurned, to-day, the voice divine ;
Now, Lord, the gracious work begin ;
Let him no more lie down in sin !

Watch by the sick, enrich the poor
With blessings from Thy boundless store !
Be every mourner's sleep to-night
Like infant's slumbers, pure and light !

Come near and bless us when we wake,
Ere through the world our way we take :
Till, in the ocean of Thy love,
We lose ourselves in Heaven above !

AH! JESUS, LET ME HEAR THY VOICE.

ANDREW REED, D.D. ; 1787-1862 ; Independent minister at London, founder of several orphan asylums, and author of popular works. In 1841, he published a Collection of hymns, with twenty-seven compositions of his own.

AH ! Jesus, let me hear Thy voice
    Fall gently on mine ear ;
  Thy voice alone can soothe my grief,
    And charm away my fear.

Ah ! Jesus, let me see Thy face
    Beaming with truth and love ;
I ask no other heaven below,
    No other heaven above.

Ah ! Jesus, let me feel Thy grace ;
    Now hear my earnest cry :
If Thou art absent, oh ! behold
    I droop, I faint, I die !

" I come, I come ! " the Saviour cries,
    " To give you full repose ;
My presence shall revive your joys,
    My frown confound your foes."

I hear His voice! I see His face!
　I feel His present grace!
'Tis life, 'tis heaven, 'tis transport, thus
　To rest in His embrace.

※

WHEN IN THE HOUR OF LONELY WOE

JOSIAH CONDER, an author and publisher; b. in London, 1789; d. 1855. One of the best modern hymn-writers. From the revised edition of his "Hymns of Praise, Prayer, and Devout Meditation," 1855.

WHEN in the hour of lonely woe,
　I give my sorrow leave to flow,
　And anxious fear and dark distrust
Weigh down my spirit to the dust;

When not e'en friendship's gentle aid
Can heal the wounds the world has made,—
Oh! this shall check each rising sigh,
That Jesus is for ever nigh.

His counsels and upholding care
My safety and my comfort are;
And He shall guide me all my days,
Till glory crown the work of grace.

Jesus! in whom but Thee above
Can I repose my trust, my love?
And shall an earthly object be
Loved in comparison with Thee?

My flesh is hastening to decay,
Soon shall the world have passed away;
And what can mortal friends avail,
When heart and strength and life shall fail?

But oh! be Thou, my Saviour, nigh,
And I will triumph while I die;
My strength, my portion, is divine,
And Jesus is for ever mine!

IN THY SERVICE WILL I EVER.

(Bei Dir, Jesu, will ich bleiben.)

"I WILL abide with thee." From the German of SPITTA, 1833, by RICHARD MASSIE, 1860.

IN Thy service will I ever,
    Jesus, my Redeemer, stay;
Nothing me from Thee shall sever,
    Gladly would I go Thy way.
Life in me Thy life produces,
    And gives vigour to my heart,
As the vine doth living juices
    To the purple grape impart.

Could I be in other places
    Half so happy as with Thee,
Who so many gifts and graces
    Hast Thyself prepared for me?
No place could be half so fitted
    To impart true joy, I ween,
Since to Thee, O Lord! committed
    Power in heaven and earth hath been.

Where shall I find such a Master,
    Who hath done my soul such good,
And retrieved the great disaster
    Sin first caused, by His own blood?
Is not He my rightful owner,
    Who for me His own life gave?
Were it not a foul dishonour
    Not to love Him to the grave?

Yes, Lord Jesus, I am ever
    Thine in sorrow and in joy;
Death the union shall not sever,
    Nor eternity destroy.
I am waiting, yea, am sighing
    For my summons to depart;
He is best prepared for dying
    Who in life is Thine in heart.

Let Thy light on me be shining
  When the day is almost gone,
When the evening is declining,
  And the night is drawing on:
Bless me, O my Saviour! laying
  Thy hands on my weary head;
"Here thy day is ended," saying,
  "Yonder live the faithful dead."

Stay beside me, when the stillness
  And the icy touch of death
Fills my trembling soul with chilness,
  Like the morning's frosty breath;
As my failing eyes grow dimmer,
  Let my spirit grow more bright,
As I see the first faint glimmer
  Of the everlasting light.

O HAPPY HOUSE!

(*O selig Haus, wo man Dich aufgenommen.*)

FROM the German of C. J. PH. SPITTA (d. 1859), " Psalter und Harfe," Leipzig, 1833, p. 100. A beautiful description of a Christian household, from the personal experience of the lovely author, on the words, "Salvation is come to this house" (Luke xix. 9). Translated by Miss JANE BORTHWICK, in " Hymns from the Land of Luther," p. 121, but slightly altered, in conformity to the original. Another translation by R. MASSIE; "O happy house! O home supremely blest!"

HAPPY house! where Thou art loved the best,
  Dear Friend and Saviour of our race,
Where never comes such welcome, honoured
    Guest,
  Where none can ever fill Thy place;
Where every heart goes forth to meet Thee,
  Where every ear attends Thy word,
Where every lip with blessing greets Thee,
  Where all are waiting on their Lord.

O happy house! where man and wife in heart,
  In faith, and hope are one,
That neither life nor death can ever part
  The holy union here begun;

Where both are sharing one salvation,
    And live before Thee, Lord, always,
In gladness or in tribulation,
    In happy or in evil days.

O happy house! whose little ones are given
    Early to Thee, in faith and prayer,—
To Thee, their Friend, who from the heights of heaven
    Guards them with more than mother's care.
O happy house! where little voices
    Their glad hosannas love to raise;
And childhood's lisping tongue rejoices
    To bring new songs of love and praise.

O happy house! and happy servitude!
    Where all alike one Master own;
Where daily duty, in Thy strength pursued,
    Is never hard nor toilsome known;
Where each one serves Thee, meek and lowly,
    Whatever Thine appointment be,
Till common tasks seem great and holy,
    When they are done as unto Thee.

O happy house! where Thou art not forgot
    When joy is flowing full and free;
O happy house! where every wound is brought—
    Physician, Comforter—to Thee.
Until at last, earth's day's work ended,
    All meet Thee in that home above,
From whence Thou camest, where Thou hast ascended,
    Thy heaven of glory and of love!

CHIEF OF SINNERS THOUGH I BE.

WILLIAM McCOMB (b. 1793), a bookseller in Belfast. His poetical works were published 1864.

CHIEF of sinners though I be,
    Jesus shed His blood for me;
    Died, that I might live on high;
Lived, that I might never die.
As the branch is to the vine,
I am His and He is mine.

Oh! the height of Jesus' love!
Higher than the heavens above,
Deeper than the depths of sea,
Lasting as eternity;
Love that found me, wondrous thought!
Found me when I sought Him not.

Jesus only can impart
Balm to heal the smitten heart;
Peace that flows from sin forgiven,
Joy that lifts the soul to heaven;
Faith and hope to walk with God,
In the way that Enoch trod.

Chief of sinners though I be,
Christ is all in all to me:
All my wants to Him are known,
All my sorrows are His own;
Safe with Him from earthly strife,
He sustains the hidden life.

O my Saviour, help afford,
By Thy Spirit and Thy Word!
When my wayward heart would stray.
Keep me in the narrow way;
Grace in time of need supply,
While I live, and when I die.

ON THEE, O JESUS!

DR. HORATIUS BONAR. From his "Hymns of Faith and Hope," Third Series, 1868. "Fellowship with Christ."

IN Thee, O Jesus! strongly leaning,
  I calmly onward go;
No cloud, no coldness, intervening,
  To damp love's blessed glow.
In Thee for ever, Lord, abiding,
  I feel that all is well;
Within Thy love for ever hiding,
  Who can my gladness tell?

True Light of light, for ever shining,
   I hail Thy happy ray;
Bright Sun of suns, still undeclining,
   'Tis Thou who mak'st my day!
Without Thee life and time are sadness,
   No fragrance breathes around;
But with Thee even grief is gladness,
   My heart its home hath found.

In Thee my soul is sweetly resting,
   My hand takes hold of Thine;
My hope is ever upward hasting,—
   And Thou, and Thou, art mine!
My refuge from each storm that rages,
   From wind and wave and war,
My home throughout eternal ages,
   Above yon sparkling star!

My hope, my joy, my peace, my glory,
   My first, my last, my all,
Great theme of the unending story
   In yon celestial hall!
Great theme above of song and wonder
   In ages yet to come,
True theme below while here we wander,
   Alas, how cold and dumb!

LORD! LET MY HEART.

Lady Powerscourt. From Savile's "Lyra Sacra," third ed. Lond. 1865.

LORD! let my heart still turn to Thee,
   In all my hours of waking thought,
   Nor let this heart e'er wish to flee,
Or think, or feel, where Thou art not.

In every hour of pain and woe,
   When nought on earth this heart can cheer,
When sighs will burst and tears will flow,
   Lord, hush the sigh and chase the tear.

In every dream of earthly bliss,
  Do Thou, dear Jesus, present be;
Nor let a thought of happiness
  On earth intrude, apart from Thee!

To my last lingering thought at night,
  Do Thou, Lord Jesus, still be near;
And ere the dawn of opening light
  In still small accents wake mine ear,

Whene'er I read Thy sacred word,
  Bright on the page of glory shine;
And let me say, "This precious Lord
  In all His full salvation's mine."

And when before the throne I kneel,
  Hear from that throne of grace my prayer,
And let each hope of heaven I feel
  Burn with the thought to meet Thee there.

Thus teach me, Lord, to look to Thee
  In every hour of waking thought;
Nor let me ever wish to be,
  Or think, or feel, where Thou art not.

THAT MYSTIC WORD OF THINE.

THE soul's answer to the words of Christ: "Abide in Me, and I in you" (John xv. 4). By Mrs. HARRIET BEECHER STOWE. From her "Religious Poems," p. 30, Boston, 1867, with an additional verse.

THAT mystic word of Thine, O sovereign Lord,
  Is all too pure, too high, too deep for me;
Weary of striving, and with longing faint,
  I breathe it back again in prayer to Thee.

Abide in me, I pray, and I in Thee!
From this good hour, O, leave me nevermore!
Then shall the discord cease, the wound be healed,
  The life-long bleeding of the soul be o'er.

Abide in me; o'ershadow by Thy love
  Each half-formed purpose and dark thought of sin
Quench, e'er it rise, each selfish, low desire,
  And keep my soul as Thine, calm and divine.

As some rare perfume in a vase of clay
    Pervades it with a fragrance not its own,
So, when Thou dwellest in a mortal soul,
    All heaven's own sweetness seems around it thrown.

The soul alone, like a neglected harp,
    Grows out of tune, and needs that Hand divine:
Dwell Thou within it, tune and touch the chords,
    Till every note and string shall answer thine.[1]

Abide in me: there have been moments blest,
    When I have heard Thy voice and felt Thy power;
Then evil lost its grasp; and passion, hushed,
    Owned the divine enchantment of the hour.

These were but seasons, beautiful and rare;
    Abide in me, and they shall ever be;
Fulfil at once Thy precept and my prayer,
    Come, and abide in me, and I in Thee.

STILL, STILL WITH THEE.

"When I awake, I am still with Thee." By Mrs. HARRIET BEECHER STOWE, "Religious Poems," p. 88, Boston, 1867.

STILL, still with Thee, when purple morning breaketh,
    When the bird waketh, and the shadows flee;
Fairer than morning, lovelier than the daylight,
    Dawns the sweet consciousness, I am with Thee!

Alone with Thee, amid the mystic shadows,
    The solemn hush of nature newly born;
Alone with Thee in breathless adoration,
    In the calm dew and freshness of the morn.

---

[1] This verse, though omitted in the volume of Mrs. STOWE's collected "Poems," and in the "Plymouth Collection," belongs to the poem as originally written. So the authoress informed the Editor, in response to an inquiry, Sept. 11, 1868, in which she kindly permits him to use several of her compositions, as "attempts at that great harmony in which one day all shall be one."

As in the dawning o'er the waveless ocean
  The image of the morning star doth rest,
So in this stillness Thou beholdest only
  Thine image in the waters of my breast.

Still, still with Thee! as to each new-born morning
  A fresh and solemn splendour still is given,
So doth this blessed consciousness, awaking,
  Breathe, each day, nearness unto Thee and heaven.

When sinks the soul, subdued by toil, to slumber,
  Its closing eye looks up to Thee in prayer;
Sweet the repose beneath the wings o'ershading,
  But sweeter still to wake, and find Thee there.

So shall it be at last, in that bright morning
  When the soul waketh and life's shadows flee;
O, in that hour, fairer than daylight dawning,
  Shall rise the glorious thought, I am with Thee!

JESUS! I LIVE TO THEE.

By Dr. HENRY HARBAUGH, Professor of Theology, at Mercersburg, Pa.; b. 1818; d. Dec. 27, 1867, in the midst of his strength and usefulness. His last intelligible words, on waking from a slumber, were: "You have called me back from the golden gates, from the verge of my heavenly home." Rom. xiv. 8; "Whether we live, we live unto the Lord; and whether we die, we die unto the Lord. Whether we live, therefore, or die, we are the Lord's."

JESUS! I live to Thee,
  The loveliest and best!
My life in Thee, Thy life in me,
  In Thy blest love I rest.

Jesus! I die to Thee,
  Whenever death shall come;
To die in Thee is life to me,
  In my eternal home.

Whether to live or die,
  I know not which is best;
To live in Thee is bliss to me,
  To die is endless rest.

UNION WITH CHRIST.

  Living or dying, Lord,
   I ask but to be Thine:
  My life in Thee, Thy life in me,
   Makes heaven for ever mine.

O BLESSED LORD!

"FAR off, yet near." By A. D. F. RANDOLPH; b. 1820; publisher and bookseller in New York; written 1864, published 1868.

 BLESSED Lord!
Once more, as at the opening of the day,
   I read Thy word;
And now, in all I read, I hear Thee say,
"To those who love, I will be ever near;"
   And yet, while this I hear,
To me, O Lord, Thou seemest far away!

   Thou Sovereign One,
Greater than mightiest kings, can it be fear
   Or blinding sun
Made by Thy glory, so if Thou art here
I cannot see Thee; yet this Word declares
   That whoso loves and bears
Thy Holy Name, shall have Thee ever near!

   I bear Thy name:
That love, dear Lord, have I not long confessed?
   Thy love's the same,
As when, like John, I leaned upon Thy breast,
And knew I loved; oh, which of us has changed?
   Am I from Thee estranged?
O Lord, Thou changest not: I know the rest!

   My doubting heart
Trembles with its own weakness, and afraid
   I dwell apart
From Thee, on whom alone my hope is stayed:
I would, and yet I do not know Thy will
   And perfect love; am still
Trusting myself, to be by self betrayed.

O blessed Lord!
Far off, yet near, on me new grace bestow
 As on Thy Word
I go to meet Thee; even now I know
Thou nearer art than when my quest began;
 One cry, and Thy feet ran
To meet me; Lord, I will not let Thee go!

THE HOLY COMMUNION.

"I AM the living Bread which came down from heaven : if any man eat of this Bread he shall live for ever."—*John* vi. 51.
"The blood of Jesus Christ cleanseth us from all sin."—1 *John* i. 7.
"Take, eat : this is My body."—*Matt.* xxvi. 26.
"The cup of blessing which we bless, is it not the communion of the blood of Christ ? The bread which we break, is it not the communion of the body of Christ ?"—1 *Cor.* x. 16.

LORD JESUS CHRIST, who didst ordain, in the blessed sacrament, a perpetual memorial of Thy bitter passion and atoning death, and dost invite us to Thy table, that our souls may be nourished by Thee, the Bread of eternal life : grant unto us, we beseech Thee, such faith in Thy promise, and such discernment of Thy holy mysteries, that we may receive the full fruition of Thy redeeming love, and attain at last, with all saints, to the marriage supper of the Lamb, in the kingdom of glory above, where Thou livest and reignest, with the Father and the Holy Ghost, one God, world without end. Amen.

"HERE, in figure represented,
  See the Passion once again ;
Here behold the Lamb most Holy,
  As for our redemption slain ;
Here the Saviour's Body, broken,
  Here the Blood which Jesus shed,
Mystic Food of life eternal,
  See for our refreshment spread.
Here shall highest praise be offered,
  Here shall meekest prayers be poured ;
Here, with body, soul, and spirit,
  God Incarnate be adored.
Holy Jesu ! for Thy coming
  May Thy love our hearts prepare ;
Thine we fain would have them wholly ;
  Enter, Lord, and tarry there."
                    From J. W. HEWETT. 1865.

PANGUE, lingua, gloriosi
　　Corporis mysterium,
Sanguinisque pretiosi,
　　Quem in mundi pretium
Fructus ventris generosi,
　　Rex effudit gentium.
　　　　　　　THOMAS AQUINAS.　1274.

O QUAM sanctus panis iste!
Tu solus es, JESU CHRISTE,
Caro, cibus, sacramentum,
Quo non maius est inventum.

Salutare medicamen,
Peccatorum relevamen,
Pasce nos, a malis leva,
Duc nos, ubi est lux Tua.
　　From JOANNIS HUSSI, "*Carmen de Cœna Sacra*"
　　　　(DANIEL, II. 370).　1414.

HERE would I feed upon the Bread of God ;
　Here drink with Thee the royal Wine of Heaven ;
Here would I lay aside each earthly load,
　Here taste afresh the calm of sin forgiven.

This is the hour of banquet and of song,
　This is the heavenly Table spread for me ;
Here let me feast, and feasting, still prolong
　The brief, bright hour of fellowship with Thee.
　　　　　　　　HORATIUS BONAR.　1856.

THE HOLY COMMUNION.

O LAMB OF GOD WHO, BLEEDING.

(O Lamm Gottes unschuldig.)

A POPULAR German communion hymn of NIKOLAUS DECIUS, written 1523; based on John i. 29, and upon the old Latin mass-song, "Agnus Dei qui tollis peccata mundi, miserere nobis" (SCHAFF's "G. H. B." No. 107). Translated by Prof. THOMAS C. PORTER, Easton, Pa. Contributed.

LAMB of God who, bleeding,
    Upon the cross didst languish,
Nor scorn nor malice heeding,
    So patient in Thine anguish,
On Thee our guilt was lying ;
Thou savedst us by dying:
    Have mercy on us, Lord Jesus ! [1]

SING, MY TONGUE, THE MYSTERY TELLING.

(Pange, lingua, gloriosi corporis mysterium.)

ST. THOMAS AQUINAS, the greatest divine of the Middle Ages, called the "Angelic Doctor;" d. 1274, forty-eight years old, on a journey from Paris to Lyons. DANIEL, I. 251; WACKERNAGEL, I. 145. This is the shorter of his two famous eucharistic hymns (the other being "Lauda, Sion, Salvatorem,"

---

[1] " O Lamm Gottes unschuldig,
  Am Stamm des Kreuzes geschlachtet,
    Allzeit funden geduldig,
      Wiewohl Du warst verachtet,
  All' Sünd' hast Du getragen ;
  Sonst müssten wir verzagen :
    Erbarm' Dich unser, o Jesu !"

see Daniel, II. 97), which are used in the Roman Catholic Church on the feast of *Corpus Christi* and in solemn masses. Although it strongly savours of transubstantiation (ver. 4), it could not be omitted in this Collection. It "contests the second place, among the hymns of the Western Church, with the 'Vexilla Regis,' the 'Stabat Mater,' the 'Jesu dulcis Memoria,' and a few others, leaving the 'Dies Iræ' in its unapproachable glory" (Neale). The translation is based upon that of Dr. Neale ("Mediæval Hymns," p. 178), which commences: "Of the glorious Body telling," and which, with various modifications, has passed into some recent Anglican hymn-books, as the "Hymns Ancient and Modern," No. 203, and "The People's Hymnal," No. 166. There are other translations, by Dr. Pusey, Wackerbarth, Caswall Erastus C. Benedict, &c. The "Lauda, Sion, Salvatorem" (which we must omit, on account of its length) has also been repeatedly rendered into German and English, more recently by E. C. Benedict (in the "Hymn of Hildebert," &c., New York, 1868, p. 93). Neale (l. c. p. 176) gives a version of a third eucharistic hymn of St. Thomas: "Adoro Te devote, latens Deitas," which, however, never passed into public use. I quote from it the following verse:—

> " O most sweet memorial of His death and woe,
> Living Bread, which givest life to man below,
> Let my spirit ever eat of Thee, and live,
> And the blest fruition of Thy sweetness give!"

SING, my tongue, the mystery telling,
 Of the glorious Body sing,
And the Blood, all price excelling,
 Which the world's eternal King,
In a noble womb once dwelling,
 Shed for this world's ransoming.

Of a Virgin condescending
 To be born for us below,
He, with men in converse blending,
 Dwelt the seed of truth to sow;
Then He closed, with wondrous ending,
 His appointed course of woe.

At the last Great Supper lying,
 Circled by His chosen band,
Jesus, with the law complying,
 Meekly finished its command;
Then, immortal food supplying,
 Gave Himself with His own hand.

God incarnate, bread He maketh
 By His word His flesh to be;
Who by faith that cup partaketh,
 Tastes the Blood of Calvary:

Though the carnal sense forsaketh,
Faith beholds the mystery.[1]

Therefore at the altar bending,
We this sacrament revere,
Ancient shadows have their ending,
Where the substance doth appear;
Faith, her aid to vision lending,
Tells that Christ unseen is here.

Glory let us give, and blessing
To the Father and the Son;

---

[1] This stanza must, of course, be taken with considerable allowance by the Protestant reader. I have taken some liberty, and inserted "by faith," which is not in the original. It has severely tried the skill of translators. See the interesting note in NEALE, pp. 180, 181. I append the Latin, with the two closest versions :—

"Verbum caro, panem verum verbo carnem efficit,
Fitque sanguis Christi merum ; etsi sensus deficit,
Ad firmandum cor sincerum sola fides sufficit."

CASWALL :
"Word made Flesh, the bread of nature
By His word to Flesh He turns ;
Wine into His blood He changes :
What though sense no change discerns?
Only be the heart in earnest,
Faith her lesson quickly learns."

NEALE :
"Word made Flesh, by Word He maketh
Very Bread His Flesh to be ;
Man in wine Christ's Blood partaketh ;
And, if senses fail to see,
Faith alone the true heart waketh
To behold the Mystery."

In "Lauda, Sion, Salvatorem," THOMAS AQUINAS expresses, with equal clearness, his belief in the mystery of the real presence, which Protestants can adopt only in a spiritual (though none the less real) sense, and divested of all materialistic conceptions (John vi. 63) :—

"Dogma datur Christianis,
Quod in carnem transit panis,
  Et vinum in sanguinem.
Quod non capis, quod non vides,
Animosa firmat fides,
  Præter rerum ordinem.

"A sumente non concisus,
Non confractus, non divisus,
  Integer accipitur.
Sumit unus, sumunt mille,
Quantum isti, tantum ille,
  Nec sumptus consumitur."

"Wondrous truth to Christians given,
Bread becomes His Flesh from heaven,
  To His Blood is turned the Wine.
Sight hath failed, nor thought conceiveth
But a dauntless faith believeth,
  Resting on a power Divine.

"Whoso of this Food partaketh
Rendeth not the Lord, nor breaketh :
  Christ is whole to all that taste.
Thousands are, as one, receivers ;
One, as thousands of believers,
  Eats of Him who cannot waste."

Honour, might, and praise addressing,
    While eternal ages run:
Holy Ghost, from both progressing,
    Equal praise to Thee be done!

SING, AND THE MYSTERY DECLARE.

(Pange, lingua, gloriosi.)

ANOTHER version, or transfusion rather, of the preceding hymn of THOMAS AQUINAS, kindly prepared for this Collection by the Rev. Dr. RAY PALMER, New York, Aug. 19, 1868.

SING, and the mystery declare;
    Sing of the glorious Body slain;
And of the Blood beyond compare,—
    Price of the world,—that not in vain
He, sole of men pure born, hath shed;
He, of the nations King and Head.

To us was born the Christ of God;
    A Virgin's Son to us was given;
And, while the earth His footsteps trod,
    Abroad He sowed the seed of heaven;
Then, when drew near His destined hour,
Ordained this rite of wondrous power.

'Twas on the last night of the feast,
    Reclining with His faithful few,
Of ancient laws, e'en to the least,
    Each word obeyed with service true;
Himself He gave with His own hand
The Bread of Life to all the band.

The incarnate Word, in broken bread,
    His body broken there did show;
And in the wine His blood, once shed
    From guilt to cleanse, to save from woe;
Where falters sense, faith trusts His word,
And souls sincere receive the Lord.[1]

---

[1] Here the doctrinal difficulty of the original is happily overcome: the form is changed, without sacrificing the substance (i.e. the *spiritual* real presence, and the *spiritual* real fruition of the Lord by faith).

Before this noblest sacrifice,
   In reverent love we lowly bow;
No more the appointed victim dies,
   But shadow yields to substance now;
While faith, that want of sight supplies,
Lifts to the Cross her trustful eyes!

Now to the Father and the Son,
   And Spirit sent by each, shall be
All worship, honour, homage done,
   By all that live, eternally;
Unto the Three in One be given
An equal praise, in earth and heaven.

O BREAD OF LIFE FROM HEAVEN!

(O esca viatorum, O panis angelorum, O manna cœlitum.)

FROM an anonymous mediæval hymn "De sanctissimo Sacramento," in DANIEL, II. 369. Translated by the Editor. A less literal version, by Dr. RAY PALMER, "O Bread to pilgrims given" (in the Andover "Sabbath Hymn-Book," No. 1051, where the original is, without good reason, ascribed to THOMAS AQUINAS). Another in SHIPLEY'S "Lyra Eucharistica" (p. 174), "O Food that weary pilgrims love!"

BREAD of Life from heaven
To saints and angels given,
   O Manna from above!
The souls that hunger feed Thou,
The hearts that seek Thee lead Thou,
   With Thy sweet, tender love.

O Fount of grace redeeming,
O River ever streaming
   From Jesu's holy side!
Come Thou, Thyself bestowing
On thirsting souls, and flowing
   Till all are satisfied.

Jesu, this feast receiving
Thy word of truth believing,
   We Thee unseen adore;

Grant, when the veil is rended,
That we, to heaven ascended,
May see Thee evermore.[1]

DECK THYSELF, MY SOUL.

(*Schmücke dich, o liebe Seele.*)

JOHANN FRANK (a lawyer; d., at Guben, Prussia, 1677). 1650. One of the richest German communion-hymns. SCHAFF, "G. H. B.," No. 262. Translated by C. WINKWORTH ("Lyra Germ.," II. 133).

DECK thyself, my soul, with gladness;
Leave the gloomy haunts of sadness,
Come into the daylight's splendour;
There with joy thy praises render
Unto Him, whose boundless grace
Grants thee at His feast a place;
He whom all the heavens obey
Deigns to dwell in thee to-day.

Hasten as a bride to meet Him,
And with loving reverence greet Him,
Who with words of life immortal
Now is knocking at thy portal;
Haste to make for Him a way,
Cast thee at His feet, and say:
Since, O Lord! Thou com'st to me,
Never will I turn from Thee.

Ah, how hungers all my spirit,
For the love I do not merit!
Ah, how oft with sighs fast thronging
For this food have I been longing!

---

[1] "O Jesu, tuum vultum,
Quem colimus occultum
Sub panis specie,
Fac, ut, remoto velo,
Aperta nos in cœlo
Cernamus acie."

How have thirsted in the strife
For this draught, O Prince of Life!
Wished, O Friend of man! to be
Ever one with God through Thee!

Here I sink before Thee, lowly,
Filled with joy most deep and holy,
As with trembling awe and wonder
On Thy mighty works I ponder;
On this banquet's mystery,
On the depths we cannot see;
Far beyond all mortal sight
Lie the secrets of Thy might.

Sun, who all my life dost brighten,
Light, who dost my soul enlighten,
Joy, the sweetest man e'er knoweth,
Fount, whence all my being floweth!
Here I fall before Thy feet:
Grant me worthily to eat
Of this blessed heavenly food,
To Thy praise and to my good.

Jesus, Bread of Life from Heaven,
Never be Thou vainly given,
Nor I to my hurt invited;
Be Thy love with love requited;
Let me learn its depths indeed,
While on Thee my soul doth feed;
Let me here, so richly blest,
Be hereafter, too, Thy guest.

SUFFERING SAVIOUR, LAMB OF GOD.

ANONYMOUS. From an old hymn-book.

SUFFERING Saviour, Lamb of God,
    How hast Thou been usèd!
  With the Almighty's wrathful rod
Soul and body bruisèd!

We, for whom Thou once wast slain,
  We, whose sins did pierce Thee,
Now commemorate Thy pain,
  And implore Thy mercy.

We would with Thee sympathize
  In Thy bitter passion;
With soft hearts and weeping eyes
  See Thy great salvation.

Thine's an everlasting love:
  We have dearly tried Thee.
Whom have we in heaven above,
  Whom on earth, beside Thee?

What can helpless sinners do,
  When temptations seize us?
Nought have we to look unto
  But the blood of Jesus.

Pardon all our baseness, Lord,
  All our weakness pity;
Guide us safely by Thy word
  To the heavenly city.

Oh! sustain us on the road
  Through this desert dreary;
Feed us with Thy flesh and blood,
  When we're faint and weary.

Bid us call to mind Thy cross
  Our hard hearts to soften;
Often, Saviour, feed us thus;
  For we need it often.

'TWAS ON THAT DARK, THAT DOLEFUL NIGHT.

By Dr. Isaac Watts; b. at Southampton, 1674; d. in London, 1748. 1 Cor. xi. 23. The hymn has seven verses, but verse four and five are usually omitted.

'TWAS on that dark, that doleful night,
  When powers of earth and hell arose
Against the Son of God's delight,
  And friends betrayed Him to His foes:

Before the mournful scene began,
  He took the bread, and blessed and brake;
What love through all His actions ran!
  What wondrous words of grace He spake!

"This is My Body, broke for sin;
  Receive and eat the living food."
Then took the cup and blessed the wine:
  "This the new covenant in My Blood.

"Do this," He cried, "till time shall end,
  In memory of your dying Friend;
Meet at My Table, and record
  The love of your departed Lord."

Jesus! Thy feast we celebrate;
  We show Thy death, we sing Thy name,
Till Thou return, and we shall eat
  The marriage Supper of the Lamb.

IN MEMORY OF THE SAVIOUR'S LOVE.

ANONYMOUS [1813]. From Sir R. PALMER's "Book of Praise," No. CCXCIII.

IN memory of the Saviour's love,
  We keep the sacred feast,
Where every humble contrite heart
  Is made a welcome guest.

By faith we take the Bread of Life,
  With which our souls are fed;
The Cup, in token of His Blood
  That was for sinners shed.

Under His banner thus we sing
  The wonders of His love,
And thus anticipate by faith
  The heavenly feast above.

BODY OF JESUS, O SWEET FOOD!

By A. C. Coxe, D.D.; b. 1818; bishop of the Protestant Episcopal diocese of Western New York. This piece was written in 1858, at St. James's College, Maryland (which was broken up, by the civil war, in 1864), and printed on a slip of paper, with the text, " Arise and eat, because the journey is too great for thee " (1 Kings xix. 7).

BODY of Jesus, O sweet food!
Blood of my Saviour, precious Blood!
On these Thy gifts, Eternal Priest,
Grant Thou my soul in faith to feast.

Weary and faint I thirst and pine
For Thee my Bread, for Thee my Wine,
Till strengthened, as Elijah trod,
I journey to the mount of God.

There clad in white, with crown and palm,
At the great Supper of the Lamb,
Be mine with all Thy saints to rest,
Like him that leaned upon Thy breast.

Saviour, till then, I fain would know
That feast above by this below,
This Bread of Life, this wondrous food,
Thy Body and Thy precious Blood.

O GOD, UNSEEN, YET EVER NEAR!

Anonymous [1836]. From Sir R. Palmer's " Book of Praise," No. 294. Also in " Hymns Ancient and Modern," London, No. 207.

O GOD, unseen, yet ever near,
 Thy presence may we feel!
And thus, inspired with holy fear,
 Before Thine altar kneel.

Here may Thy faithful people know
 The blessings of Thy love,
The streams that through the desert flow,
 The manna from above.

We come, obedient to Thy word,
  To feast on heavenly food;
Our meat, the Body of the Lord,
  Our drink, His precious Blood.

Thus may we all Thy words obey,
  For we, O God! are Thine;
And go rejoicing on our way,
  Renewed with strength divine.

To Father, Son, and Holy Ghost,
  The God whom we adore,
Be glory as it was, is now,
  And shall be evermore.

JESU, TO THY TABLE LED.

The Rev. ROBERT HALL BAYNES; b. at Wellington, Somerset, England, 1831; studied at Oxford; editor of " Lyra Anglicana," and the " Canterbury Hymnal." 1863.

JESU, to Thy Table led,
  Now let every heart be fed
  With the true and living Bread.

While in penitence we kneel,
Thy sweet presence let us feel,
All Thy wondrous love reveal!

While on Thy dear cross we gaze,
Mourning o'er our sinful ways,
Turn our sadness into praise!

When we taste the mystic wine,
Of Thine outpoured blood the sign,
Fill our hearts with love divine!

Draw us to Thy wounded side,
Whence there flowed the healing tide;
There our sins and sorrows hide!

From the bonds of sin release,
Cold and wavering faith increase,
Lamb of God, grant us Thy peace!

Lead us by Thy piercèd hand,
Till around Thy throne we stand,
In the bright and better land.

BY CHRIST REDEEMED.

1 Cor. xi. 26: "As often as ye eat this bread, and drink this cup, ye do show the Lord's death till He come." Anonymous, from Shipley's "Lyra Eucharistica," Lond. 1863, p. 249.

Y Christ redeemed, in Christ restored,
We keep the memory adored,
And show the death of our dear Lord,
  Until He come.

His Body, broken in our stead,
Is here in this Memorial Bread;
And so our feeble love is fed,
  Until He come.

His fearful drops of agony,
His life-blood shed for us we see:
The wine shall tell the mystery,
  Until He come.

And thus that dark betrayal-night
With the last Advent we unite—
The shame, the glory—by this rite,
  Until He come.

Until the trump of God be heard,
Until the ancient graves be stirred,
And with the great, commanding word,
  The Lord shall come.

O blessed hope! with this elate,
Let not our hearts be desolate,
But strong in faith, in patience wait,
  Until He come.

LO, THE FEAST IS SPREAD TO-DAY!

DR. HENRY ALFORD, Dean of Canterbury. 1845. From his "Year of Praise," Lond. 1867, No. 152.

LO, the feast is spread to-day!
Jesus summons, come away!
From the vanity of life,
From the sounds of mirth or strife,
To the feast by Jesus given,
Come and taste the Bread of Heaven.

Why, with proud excuse and vain,
Spurn His mercy once again?
From amidst life's social ties,
From the farm and merchandise,
Come, for all is now prepared;
Freely given, be freely shared.

Blessèd are the lips that taste
Our Redeemer's marriage feast;
Blessèd who on Him shall feed,
Bread of Life, and drink indeed.
Blessèd, for their thirst is o'er,
They shall never hunger more.

Make, then, once again your choice,
Hear to-day His calling voice;
Servants, do your Master's will;
Bidden guests, His table fill;
Come, before His wrath shall swear:
Ye shall never enter there.

LOVE AND GRATITUDE TO CHRIST.

"WE love Him, because He first loved us."—1 *John,* iv. 19.

"The love of Christ constraineth us ... He died for all, that they which live should not henceforth live unto themselves, but unto Him which died for them, and rose again."—2 *Cor.* v. 14, 15.

BLESSED SAVIOUR, whose love to sinners passeth the comprehension of men and of angels, and will be the theme of grateful praise throughout the ages of eternity: impress upon us, we beseech Thee, such a deep and abiding sense of our indebtedness for Thy great salvation, that we may wholly live to Thy glory, and serve Thee in holiness and righteousness all our days, until we join in the songs of Thy redeemed army in heaven where, with the Father and the Holy Ghost, Thou art worshipped and glorified world without end. Amen.

> " I cannot love Thee as I would,
> Yet pardon me, O Highest Good !
> My life, and all I call mine own,
> I lay before Thy mercy-throne :
> And if a thousand lives were mine,
> O sweetest Lord! they should be Thine.
> And scanty would the offering be,
> So richly hast thou lovèd me."
> *From the German.*

XAVIER'S HYMN.

O Deus, ego amo Te,
Nec amo Te, ut salves me,
Aut quia non amantes Te
Æterno punis igne.

Tu, Tu, mi Jesu, totum me
Amplexus es in cruce;
Tulisti clavos, lanceam,
Multamque ignominiam.

Innumeros dolores,
Sudores, et angores,
Ac mortem, et hæc propter me,
Ac pro me peccatore.

Cur igitur non amem Te,
O Jesu amantissime!
Non, ut in cœlo salves me,
Aut ne æternum damnes me;

Nec præmii ullius spe,
Sed sicut Tu amasti me;
Sic amo et amabo Te,
Solum, quia Rex meus es.

Daniel, II. 335.

LOVE AND GRATITUDE TO CHRIST.

JESUS, THOU JOY OF LOVING HEARTS.

(Jesus, dulcedo cordium.)

A FREE and happy transfusion of selected stanzas from St. BERNARD'S "Jesu dulcis memoria," 1153, by the Rev. Dr. RAY PALMER, prepared, 1858, for the Andover "Sabbath Hymn-book." The first verse corresponds to the fourth in the Latin : " Jesus, dulcedo cordium, Fons veri, Lumen mentium," &c. Sir R. PALMER has given this hymn a place in his collection (No. 296) among the communion-hymns, with the note, "Anonymous [1860]. From St. Bernard."

ESUS, Thou Joy of loving hearts!
 Thou Fount of Life! Thou Light of men!
 From the best bliss that earth imparts,
  We turn unfilled to Thee again.

Thy truth unchanged hath ever stood;
 Thou savest those that on Thee call;
To them that seek Thee, Thou art good,
 To them that find Thee, All in All!

We taste Thee, O Thou Living Bread!
 And long to feast upon Thee still;
We drink of Thee, the Fountain Head,
 And thirst our souls from Thee to fill.

Our restless spirits yearn for Thee,
 Where'er our changeful lot is cast;
Glad when Thy gracious smile we see,
 Blest when our faith can hold Thee fast.

O Jesus! ever with us stay,
 Make all our moments calm and bright;
Chase the dark night of sin away,
 Shed o'er the world Thy holy light!

I GIVE MY HEART TO THEE.

(Cor meum Tibi dedo, Jesu dulcissime.)

FROM a charming Latin poem, of uncertain date and authorship, in DANIEL'S "Thes." II. 370, freely and happily reproduced by the Rev. Dr. RAY PALMER, for this Collection, Aug. 20, 1868. I know of no other English version.

    I GIVE my heart to Thee,
        O Jesus most desired!
    And heart for heart the gift shall be,
        For Thou my soul hast fired:
        Thou hearts alone would'st move;
        Thou only hearts dost love.
I would love Thee as Thou lov'st me,
        O Jesus most desired!

    What offering can I make,
        Dear Lord, to love like Thine?
    That Thou, the God, didst stoop to take
        A human form like mine!
        "Give me thy heart, My son:"
        Behold my heart,—'tis done!
I would love Thee as Thou lov'st me,
        O Jesus most desired!

    Thy heart is opened wide,
        Its offered love most free,
    That heart to heart I may abide,
        And hide myself in Thee:[1]
        Ah, how Thy love doth burn,
        Till I that love return!
I would love Thee as Thou lov'st me,
        O Jesus most desired!

    Here finds my heart its rest,
        Repose that knows no shock,
    The strength of love that keeps it blest:
        In Thee, the riven Rock,[2]

---

[1] Cor Tuum est apertum ut intrem libere,
    Ut cordi cor insertum condatur intime."

[2] "In petræ hoc foramine," an allusion to Cant. ii. 14, in its allegorical sense; to which, also, Toplady's "Rock of ages, cleft for me," may be re-

My soul, as girt around,
  Her citadel hath found.
I would love Thee as Thou lov'st me,
  O Jesus most desired!

JESUS, I LOVE THEE.

(O Deus, ego amo Te, Nec amo Te ut salves me.)

A FREE translation of the "Suspirium amoris" of FRANCIS XAVIER, "the apostle of the Indies;" b. in Spain, 1506; d. in China, 1552; one of the most devoted and successful missionaries of the Roman-Catholic Church, burning with the love of Christ and the love of souls, which is the essence of true piety, whether Catholic or Protestant. The translation is substantially that of E. CASWALL (" Lyra Catholica," p. 338): "My God, I love Thee,—not because," with a few changes and an additional verse. The poem was written in Latin, but soon translated into the Spanish, from which DIEPENBROCK'S German version (DANIEL, IV. 347) was made. See the Latin on p. 480; and in DANIEL, II. p. 335, without name—the authorship of Xavier being doubtful.

JESUS, I love Thee,—not because
  I hope for heaven thereby,
  Nor yet because, if I love not,
I must for ever die.

I love Thee, Saviour dear, and still
  I ever will love Thee,
Solely because my God Thou art,
  Who first hast lovèd me.

For me to lowest depths of woe
  Thou didst Thyself abase;
For me didst bear the cross and shame
  And manifold disgrace.

---

ferred. St. Bernard says: "Foramina petræ, vulnera Christi." In the anonymous hymn, "Ecquis binas columbinas" (DANIEL, II. 344; TRENCH, p. 150), the following beautiful stanza occurs:—

" Et profunde me reconde
  Intra sacra vulnera;
In supernâ me cavernâ
  Colloca maceriæ.
Hic viventi, quiescenti
  Finis est miseriæ."

For me didst suffer pains unknown,
  Blood-sweat and agony,
Yea, death itself,—all, all for me,
  Who was Thine enemy.

Then why, O blessed Saviour mine!
  Should I not love Thee well?
Not for the sake of winning heaven,
  Nor of escaping hell;

Not with the hope of gaining aught,
  Nor seeking a reward,—
But freely, fully, as Thyself
  Hast lovèd me, O Lord!

Even so I love Thee and will love,
  And in Thy praise will sing;
Solely because Thou art my God,
  And my eternal King.

JESUS, I LOVE THEE EVERMORE.

(O Deus, ego amo Te, Nam prior Tu amasti me.)

FROM an anonymous Latin poem in DANIEL'S Collection, II. 335, similar to the preceding one of Xavier, translated by the Hon. E. C. BENEDICT, New York, August, 1868. Contributed.

JESUS, I love Thee evermore,
  For Thou hast loved me, Lord, before;
  I have no freedom but to be
A willing slave, dear Lord, to Thee.

Let memory, then, no thought retain,
Except the glory of Thy reign;
Nor let my mind desire below
Aught but the love of Christ to know.

I cannot have a wish or thought,
Except to love Thee as I ought;
What, by Thy gracious gift, is mine,
With joy I freely make it Thine.

From Thee I have, to Thee I give,
In Thy commands, oh, let me live!
My wants will then be all supplied,
For all are only dreams beside.

O LORD! I LOVE THEE.

(Herzlich lieb hab ich Dich, o Herr.)

MARTIN SCHALLING, a pupil of Melancthon, and pastor in the Palatinate. 1571. Based on Ps. 18 and 73; a favourite hymn of Spener, Gellert, the Duchess of Orleans (daughter of Louis Philippe), and others. See the German original in SCHAFF'S " G. H. B." No. 310. Other versions, by MILLS (" Horæ Germ." p. 80): " I love Thee, Lord, with love sincere;" C. WINKWORTH (" Lyra Germ." II. 218): " Lord, all my heart is fixed on Thee." The following preserves the measure of the original.

LORD! I love Thee from my heart;
I pray Thee never more depart,
   With help and grace to cheer me.
I scorn the richest earthly lot;
E'en heaven itself attracts me not,
   If I can feel Thee near me.
Through all my heart's severest pains,
In Thee my confidence remains;
That Saviour shall my comfort be
Who by His blood hath purchased me.
   O Jesus Christ, my God and Lord,
     My God and Lord!
   Be near, according to Thy Word.

Yea, Lord, 'twas Thy free bounty gave
My body, soul, and all I have
   In this poor life of mine;
That I may spend them in Thy praise,
And use, and service all my days,
   Give me Thy grace divine!
Guard me when heresies arise,
And shield from Satan's murderous lies:
For all my crosses strengthen me;
Then shall I bear them patiently.
   O Jesus Christ, my Lord and God,
     My Lord and God!
   Comfort my soul beneath its load.

Ah! Lord, let Thy dear angels fly,
At last, and bear my soul on high,
  On Abraham's breast to stay;
My flesh, in its dark sleeping-room,
Rest softly where no ill shall come
  Until the Judgment-day.
Then from the dead awaken me,
That these glad eyes may look on Thee,
O Jesus, God's eternal Son!
My Saviour! on Thy glorious throne.
  Lord Jesus Christ my prayer attend,
    My prayer attend,
  And I will praise Thee without end.

JESUS, THY BOUNDLESS LOVE TO ME.

(O Jesu Christ, mein schönstes Licht.)

FREELY condensed from a German hymn of PAUL GERHARDT, 1653, which is based on a meditation and prayer in JOHN ARNDT'S "Paradiesgärtlein." See the original in WACKERNAGEL'S ed. of P. GERHARDT'S "Geistliche Lieder," 1855, p. 174 (sixteen stanzas, of eight lines each), and partly in KNAPP'S "Liederschatz," 3rd ed. No. 1813 (twelve stanzas). The translation is by JOHN WESLEY, 1739. Four stanzas are omitted. See the whole in WESLEY'S "Sacred Poetry," N. Y. 1864, p. 679.

JESUS, Thy boundless love to me
    No thought can reach, no tongue declare.
  O knit my thankful heart to Thee,
  And reign without a rival there!
Thine wholly, Thine alone, I am;
Be Thou alone my constant flame!

O grant that nothing in my soul
  May dwell but Thy pure love alone;
O may Thy love possess me whole,
  My joy, my treasure, and my crown:
Strange flames far from my heart remove;
May every act, word, thought, be love!

O Love, how cheering is Thy ray!
  All pain before Thy presence flies:

Care, anguish, sorrow, melt away,
  Where'er Thy healing beams arise.
O Jesus, nothing may I see,
Nothing desire or seek, but Thee!

Still let Thy love point out my way!
  What wondrous things Thy love hath wrought!
Still lead me, lest I go astray;
  Direct my word, inspire my thought;
And if I fall, soon may I hear
Thy voice, and know that love is near.

In suffering, be Thy love my peace;
  In weakness, be Thy love my power;
And when the storms of life shall cease,
  Jesus, in that dark, final hour
Of death, be Thou my guide and friend,
That I may love Thee without end.[1]

I PLACE AN OFFERING AT THY SHRINE.

"THE perfect sacrifice." From the French of Madame JEANNE MARIE BAUVIER DE LA MOTHE GUYON, by WILLIAM COWPER. Madame G. was born 1648, d. 1717: one of the most interesting characters in the history of mysticism and religious enthusiasm; devoted to the system of quietism and the principle of disinterested love to God; much defamed, persecuted, and imprisoned for heresy and eccentricity, but defended by Fénélon. She wrote many works, and a large number of hymns distinguished for graceful composition, and exquisite sensibility, though not free from pious extravagance. Some of the latter were admirably translated by Cowper. We select the best.

I PLACE an offering at Thy shrine
    From taint and blemish clear,
  Simple and pure in its design,
    Of all that I hold dear.

I yield Thee back Thy gifts again,
  Thy gifts which most I prize;
Desirous only to retain
  The notice of Thine eyes.

---

[1] Originally:—

  " In death as life be Thou my guide,
  And save me who for me hast died.'

But if, by Thine adored decree,
   That blessing be denied,
Resigned and unreluctant, see
   My every wish subside.

Thy will in all things I approve,
   Exalted or cast down;
Thy will in every state I love,
   And even in Thy frown.

THE LORD OF ALL THINGS.

From the French of Madame DE LA MOTHE GUYON, by WILLIAM COWPER. Select lines from her poem on the "Nativity," arranged in stanzas by the Editor.

THE Lord of all things, in His humble birth,
   Makes mean the proud magnificence of earth;
   The straw, the manger, and the mouldering wall
Eclipse its lustre; and I scorn it all.

All, all have lost the charms they once possessed;
An infant God reigns sovereign in my breast:
From Bethlehem's bosom I no more will rove;
There dwells the Saviour, and there rests my love.

But I am poor, oblation I have none,
None for a Saviour but Himself alone:
Whate'er I render Thee, from Thee it came;
And, if I give my body to the flame,

My patience, love, and energy divine
Of heart and soul and spirit, all are Thine.
Ah, vain attempt to expunge the mighty score!
The more I pay, I owe Thee still the more.

The more I love Thee, I the more reprove
A soul so lifeless, and so slow to love;
Till, on a deluge of Thy mercy tossed,
I plunge into that sea, and there am lost.

YES: I WILL ALWAYS LOVE.

FROM the French of Madame GUYON, translated by COWPER. Part of a poem commencing: "Ye linnets, let us try beneath this grove." We must omit the poem from her prison, "O Thou! by long experience tried," where the beautiful passage occurs:—

> "My country, Lord, art Thou alone:
> No other can I claim my own:
> The point where all my wishes meet,
> My law, my love, life's only sweet."

YES: I will always love; and, as I ought,
    Tune to the praise of love my ceaseless voice;
    Preferring love too vast for human thought,
In spite of erring men, who cavil at my choice.

Why have I not a thousand thousand hearts,
    Lord of my soul! that they might all be Thine?
If Thou approve,—the zeal Thy smile imparts,
    How should it ever fail? Can such a fire decline?

Love, pure and holy, is a deathless fire;
    Its object heavenly, it must ever blaze;
Eternal love a God must needs inspire,
    When once He wins the heart, and fits it for His praise.

Self-love dismissed,—'tis then we live indeed;
    In her embrace, death, only death is found:
Come, then, one noble effort, and succeed;
    Cast off the chain of self with which thy soul is bound.

O, I would cry, that all the world might hear,
    Ye self-tormentors, love your God alone;
Let His unequalled excellence be dear,
    Dear to your inmost souls, and make Him all your own!

O LOVE DIVINE, HOW SWEET THOU ART.

CHARLES WESLEY. "Desiring to Love." First printed in Lamp's " Hymns on the Great Festivals," &c., 1746, and next in Charles Wesley's " Hymns and Sacred Poems," 1749.

LOVE divine, how sweet Thou art!
When shall I find my willing heart
   All taken up by Thee?
I thirst and faint and die to prove
The greatness of redeeming love,
   The love of Christ to me!

Stronger His love than death or hell;
Its riches are unsearchable:
   The first-born sons of light
Desire in vain its depth to see;
They cannot reach the mystery,
   The length and breadth and height.

God only knows the love of God:
O that it now were shed abroad
   In this poor stony heart!
For love I sigh, for love I pine:
This only portion, Lord, be mine,
   Be mine this better part!

O that I could for ever sit
With Mary at the Master's feet!
   Be this my happy choice:
My only care, delight, and bliss,
My joy, my heaven on earth, be this,
   To hear the Bridegroom's voice!

O that, with humbled Peter, I
Could weep, believe, and thrice reply,
   My faithfulness to prove:
Thou know'st (for all to Thee is known),
Thou know'st, O Lord! and Thou alone,
   Thou know'st that Thee I love.

O that I could, with favoured John,
Recline my weary head upon
   The dear Redeemer's breast!

From care and sin and sorrow free,
Give me, O Lord! to find in Thee
  My everlasting rest.

Thy only love do I require,
Nothing in earth beneath desire,
  Nothing in heaven above;
Let earth and heaven and all things go;
Give me Thy only love to know,
  Give me Thy only love.

JESUS, I LOVE THY NAME.

Dr. Ph. Doddridge, d. 1751. "Christ precious to the Believer." 1 Peter ii. 7.

JESUS, I love Thy charming name,
  'Tis music to mine ear;
Fain would I sound it out so loud
  That earth and heaven should hear.

Yes: Thou art precious to my soul,
  My transport and my trust;
Jewels to Thee are gaudy toys,
  And gold is sordid dust.

All my capacious powers can wish,
  In Thee doth richly meet;
Nor to mine eyes is light so dear
  Nor friendship half so sweet.

Thy grace still dwells upon my heart,
  And sheds its fragrance there;
The noblest balm of all its wounds,
  The cordial of its care.

I'll speak the honours of Thy name
  With my last labouring breath;
Then, speechless, clasp Thee in mine arms,
  The antidote of death.

COMPARED WITH CHRIST.

By Augustus Montague Toplady. 1772. "Christ all in all."

COMPARED with Christ, in all beside
    No comeliness I see;
The one thing needful, dearest Lord,
    Is to be one with Thee.
The sense of Thy expiring love
    Into my soul convey;
Thyself bestow; for Thee alone
    I absolutely pray.

Whatever else Thy will withholds,
    Here grant me to succeed:
O let Thyself my portion be,
    And I am blest indeed!
Less than Thyself will not suffice
    My comfort to restore:
More than Thyself I cannot have;
    And Thou canst give no more.

Loved of my God, for Him again
    With love intense I burn;
Chosen of Thee ere time began,
    I choose Thee in return.
Whate'er consists not with Thy love,
    Oh teach me to resign;
I'm rich to all the intents of bliss,
    If Thou, O God! art mine.

WHEN THIS PASSING WORLD IS DONE.

The Rev. Robert Murray McCheyne; b. 1813, d. 1843; one of the most earnest of modern Scottish preachers. "Our Indebtedness to Christ." The text from Rogers, p. 381.

WHEN this passing world is done,
    When has sunk yon glaring sun,
    When we stand with Christ in glory,
Looking o'er life's finished story,
Then, Lord, shall I fully know,—
Not till then,—how much I owe.

When I hear the wicked call
On the rocks and hills to fall;
When I see them start and shrink,
On the fiery deluge brink,—
Then, Lord, shall I fully know,—
Not till then,—how much I owe.

When I stand before the throne,
Dressed in beauty not my own;
When I see Thee as Thou art,
Love Thee with unsinning heart,—
Then, Lord, shall I fully know,—
Not till then,—how much I owe.

When the praise of heaven I hear,
Loud as thunder to the ear,
Loud as many waters' noise,
Sweet as harp's melodious voice,
Then, Lord, shall I fully know,—
Not till then,—how much I owe.

Even on earth, as through a glass,
Darkly let Thy glory pass,
Make forgiveness feel so sweet,
Make Thy Spirit's help so meet,
Even on earth, Lord, make me know
Something of how much I owe.

Chosen not for good in me,
Wakened up from wrath to flee,
Hidden in the Saviour's side,
By the Spirit sanctified!
Teach me, Lord, on earth to show,
By my love, how much I owe.

Oft I walk beneath the cloud,
Dark as midnight's gloomy shroud;
But, when fear is at the height,
Jesus comes, and all is light.
Blessèd Jesus! bid me show
Doubting saints how much I owe.

When in flowery paths I tread,
Oft by sin I'm captive led;

Oft I fall, but still arise;
The Spirit comes—the tempter flies;
Blessèd Spirit! bid me show
Weary sinners all I owe.

Oft the nights of sorrow reign,
Weeping, sickness, sighing, pain:
But a night Thine anger burns;
Morning comes and joy returns;
God of comforts! bid me show
To Thy poor how much I owe.

OH HOW COULD I FORGET HIM?

(Wie könnt' ich Sein vergessen.)

FROM the German of GOTTLOB CHRISTIAN KERN, a highly accomplished and deeply pious Evangelical pastor in the kingdom of Württemberg, d. 1835. Translated by CATHERINE WINKWORTH. This beautiful hymn was written in 1820 for the holy communion. See verse 4.

OH how could I forget Him
  Who ne'er forgetteth me?
Or tell the love that let Him
  Come down to set me free?
I lay in darkest sadness,
  Till He made all things new;
And still fresh love and gladness
  Flow from that heart so true.

Oh how could I e'er leave Him
  Who is so kind a Friend?
Or how could ever grieve Him
  Who thus to me doth bend?
Have I not seen Him dying
  For us on yonder tree?
Do I not hear Him crying:
  Arise and follow Me!

For ever will I love Him
  Who saw my hopeless plight,
Who felt my sorrows move Him,
  And brought me life and light:

Whose arm shall be around me
    When my last hour is come,
And suffer none to wound me,
. Though dark the passage home.

He gives me pledges holy,
    His body and His blood.
He lifts the scorned, the lowly,
    He makes my courage good;
For He will reign within me,
    And shed His graces there:
The heaven He died to win me
    Can I then fail to share?

In joy and sorrow ever
    Shine through me, Blessed Heart,
Who bleeding for us never
    Didst shrink from sorest smart!
Whate'er I've loved or striven
    Or borne, I bring to Thee;
Now let Thy heart and heaven
    Stand open, Lord, to me!

O ABIDE, ABIDE IN JESUS!

(*Bleibt bei Dem, der euretwillen.*)

"ABIDE in Jesus." By PH. SPITTA, d. 1859. From "Psalter und Harfe,"
1833. Translated by R. MASSIE, 1860.

ABIDE, abide in Jesus,
    Who for us bare griefs untold,
And Himself, from pain to ease us,
    Suffered pangs a thousand-fold!
Bide with Him who still abideth
    When all else shall pass away,
And as Judge supreme presideth
    In that dread and awful day.

All is dying: hearts are breaking,
    Which to ours were once fast bound;
And the lips have ceased from speaking,
    Which once uttered such sweet sound;

And the arms are powerless lying,
   Which were our support and stay;
And the eyes are dim and dying,
   Which once watched us night and day.

Every thing we love and cherish
   Hastens onward to the grave,
Earthly joys and pleasures perish,
   And whate'er the world e'er gave:
All is fading, all is fleeing,
   Earthly flames must cease to glow;
Earthly beings cease from being,
   Earthly blossoms cease to blow.

Yet unchanged, while all decayeth,
   Jesus stands upon the dust;
" Lean on Me alone," He sayeth,
   " Hope and love and firmly trust!"
O abide, abide with Jesus,
   Who Himself for ever lives,
Who from death eternal frees us,
   Yea, who life eternal gives!

WE ARE THE LORD'S.

(Wir sind des Herrn, wir leben oder sterben.)

FROM the German of Dr. SPITTA, one of the sweetest modern hymnists, d. 1859. Second Series of his " Psaltery and Harp," 1843. Translated by RICHARD MASSIE, 1864. The sainted author, in a letter to a friend, says: " To the Lord I consecrate my life, my love, and likewise my song. His love is the one great theme of all my hymns; to praise and exalt it worthily is the aim and longing desire of the Christian poet. He gave me song, and I give it back to Him."

WE are the Lord's, whether we live or die;
   We are the Lord's, who for us all hath died;
   We are the Lord's, and heirs of the Most High;
We are the Lord's, and shall the Lord's abide.

We are the Lord's—to Him, then, let us live,
   With soul and body, both with deeds and words,
While heart, and tongue, and life assurance give
   Of this most precious truth: we are the Lord's!

We are the Lord's,—so shall our hearts ne'er fail,
  For one bright star its steady light affords,
To cheer and guide us thro' the gloomy vale,
  It is the blessed word: we are the Lord's!

We are the Lord's, who will preserve us still,
  When none beside Him help to us accords;
In death's last conflict we will fear no ill,
  Thy word abideth true: we are the Lord's.

MORE THAN ALL, ONE THING MY HEART IS CRAVING.

(*Eines wünsch ich mir vor allem andern.*)

THE best hymn of ALBERT KNAPP, one of the most fertile of German poets (d. at Stuttgart, 1864); written, 1823, for a catechumen; first published 1829, and since introduced intos everal hymn-books (SCHAFF's "G. H. B." No. 170). Translated, at the request of the editor, for the first time, by Prof. THOS. C. PORTER, Lafayette College, Easton, Pa., April 13, 1868.

MORE than all, one thing my heart is craving,
    As my food by night or day;
    With it blessèd and all trials braving,
  Through this wilderness we stray:
Ever on the Man to gaze adoring,
Who, with bloody sweat and tears, imploring,
    On His face submissive sank,
    And the Father's chalice drank.

Ever shall mine eyes, His form retaining,
  View the Lamb once slain for me,
As He yonder, pale and uncomplaining,
  Hangs upon the bitter tree;
As He thirsting, wrestled in His anguish,
That in hell my soul might never languish,—
    Of me thinking, when His cry,
    "It is finished!" rose on high.

O my Saviour! never shall Thy kindness,
  Nor my guilt, forgotten be:
When I sat a stranger in my blindness,
  Thou didst still remember me;

For Thy sheep Thou long hadst interceded,
Ere the Shepherd's gentle voice was heeded,
   And—a costly ransom-price !—
   Bought me with Thy sacrifice.

I am Thine! Say Thou, "Amen, for ever !"
   Blessed Jesus, mine Thou art !
Let Thy precious name escape me never ;
   Stamp it burning on my heart.
With Thee all things bearing and achieving ;
In Thee both to live and die, believing :
   This our solemn covenant be,
   Till my spirit rest in Thee !

LOVEST THOU ME?

JAMES MONTGOMERY. 1853.

"LOVEST thou Me?" I hear my Saviour say :
   Would that my heart had power to answer
      "Yea !
Thou knowest all things, Lord, in heaven above
And earth beneath : Thou knowest that I love."

But 'tis not so : in word, in deed, in thought,
I do not, cannot, love Thee as I ought ;
Thy love must give that power, Thy love alone ;
There's nothing worthy of Thee but Thine own :
Lord, with the love wherewith Thou lovest me,
Reflected on Thyself, I would love Thee.

JESU, MY LORD, MY GOD, MY ALL.

From "Hymns Ancient and Modern," No. 178, and "The People's Hymnal," No. 508. This hymn is evidently suggested by a eucharistic hymn, "Corpus Christi," of F. W. Faber (p. 107 in the last ed. of his "Hymns," Lond. 1862), commencing,—

> "Jesus! my Lord, my God, my All!
> How can I love Thee as I ought?
> And how revere this wondrous gift,
> So far surpassing hope or thought?
> Sweet *Sacrament*, we Thee adore!
> Oh make us love Thee more and more!"

JESU, my Lord, my God, my all,
Hear me, blest Saviour, when I call:
Hear me, and from Thy dwelling-place
Pour down the riches of Thy grace.
Jesu, my Lord, I Thee adore;
Oh make me love Thee more and more!

Jesu, too late I Thee have sought:
How can I love Thee as I ought;
And how extol Thy matchless fame,
The glorious beauty of Thy name?
Jesu, my Lord, I Thee adore;
Oh make me love Thee more and more!

Jesu, what didst Thou find in me,
That Thou hast dealt so lovingly?
How great the joy that Thou hast brought,
So far exceeding hope or thought!
Jesu, my Lord, I Thee adore;
Oh make me love Thee more and more!

Jesu, of Thee shall be my song:
To Thee my heart and soul belong;
All that I have or am is Thine,
And Thou, blest Saviour, Thou art mine.
Jesu, my Lord, I Thee adore;
Oh make me love Thee more and more!

JESUS, THESE EYES HAVE NEVER SEEN.

The Rev. Dr. Ray Palmer. Christ loved unseen. 1 Peter i. 8. From "Hymns and Sacred Pieces." New York, 1865. Written 1858, for the Andover "Sabbath Hymn-Book."

JESUS, these eyes have never seen
    That radiant form of Thine;
The veil of sense hangs dark between
    Thy blessed face and mine.

I see Thee not, I hear Thee not,
    Yet art Thou oft with me;
And earth hath ne'er so dear a spot
    As where I meet with Thee.

Like some bright dream that comes unsought,
    When slumbers o'er me roll,
Thine image ever fills my thought,
    And charms my ravished soul.

Yet though I have not seen, and still
    Must rest in faith alone,
I love Thee, dearest Lord,—and will,
    Unseen, but not unknown.

When death these mortal eyes shall seal,
    And still this throbbing heart,
The rending veil shall Thee reveal,
    All glorious as Thou art.

THAT HOLY ONE.

"Consider Him." By A. D. F. Randolph. Written Sept. 1867. Contributed.

THAT Holy One,
    Who came to earth for thee,—
    Oh strangest thing beneath the sun,
That He, by any mortal one,
    Forgotten e'er should be!

The Son of God,
  Who pity had on thee;
Who turned aside the smiting rod,
And all alone the Garden trod,—
  Forgotten shall He be?

The blessed Lord,
  Who came to die for thee;
Whom Jew and Gentile then abhorred,
While heavenly hosts His name adored,—
  Forgotten can he be?

That Brother, Friend,
  Who daily waits on Thee;
Who every want doth comprehend
With love divine that has no end,—
  Forgotten can He be?

O Patient One!
  Thou speakest thus to me:
"Oh strangest thing beneath the sun,
That thou, for whom so much is done,
  Shouldst oft forgetful be!"

My Lord, I know
  What truth Thou say'st to me:
Forgive my sin, on me bestow
Such grace, as hence to all will show
  I do consider Thee.

FOR EVER WITH CHRIST.

"In My Father's house are many mansions. . . . I go to prepare a place for you."—*John* xiv. 2.
"Where I am, there shall also My servant be."—*John* xii. 26.
"And so shall we ever be with the Lord."—1 *Thess.* iv. 17.
"Eye hath not seen, nor ear heard, neither have entered into the heart of man the things which God hath prepared for them that love Him."—1 *Cor.* ii. 9.
"We shall be like Him; for we shall see Him as He is."—1 *John* iii. 2.

> WHAT no human eye hath seen,
>   What no mortal ear hath heard,
> What on thought hath never been,
>   In its noblest flights, conferred,—
> This hath God prepared in store
> For His people evermore.
>
> Jesus reigns, the Life, the Sun,
>   Of that wondrous world above;
> All the clouds and storms are gone,
>   All is light, and all is love.
> All the shadows melt away
> In the blaze of perfect day!
>   Dr. LANGE (*Germany*).

> For ever with the Lord!
>   Amen! so let it be!
> Life from the dead is in that word,
>   And immortality.
>   JAMES MONTGOMERY (*England*).

> "I WOULD not live alway!" no longer I sing;
> Live alway I shall, whilst Jesus is King!
> United to Him, his righteousness mine,
> My life bound in His, no fate shall untwine,
> Ne'er till sin enters heaven, and Death wields his rod,
> Defiant, enthroned in the palace of God;
> Not till heaven's a graveyard, and Christ lies there slain,—
> Shall I cease in His glory, and with Him to reign.
>   Dr. MUHLENBERG. *Postscript to his "I would not live alway."* 1868. (*America*).

"Let not your heart be troubled," Jesus said,
  "My Father's house hath mansions large and fair;
I go before you to prepare your place;
  I will return to take you with Me there."
H. BEECHER STOWE.

    I THANK Thee, Lord, that Thou hast kept
      The best in store:
  We have enough, yet not too much
      To long for more,—
  A yearning for a deeper peace,
      Not known before.

  I thank Thee, Lord, that here our souls,
      Though amply blest,
  Can never find, although they seek,
      A perfect rest;
  Nor ever shall, until they lean
      On Jesus' breast.
ADELAIDE A. PROCTER.

  Yet one pang, searching and sore,
  And then heaven for ever more;
  Yet one moment awful and dark,
  Then safety within the Veil and the Ark;
  Yet one effort by Christ, His Grace,
  Then Christ for ever face to face.
CHRISTINA G. ROSSETTI.

FOR EVER WITH CHRIST.

MY HOME IN HEAVEN ALONE.

(Μούνη μοι πάτρη περιλείπετο.)

TRANSLATED from the Greek of Bishop GREGORY OF NAZIANZEN (d. 390), a great pulpit orator and divine, who divided his life between the silence of monastic seclusion and the tumult of public usefulness. He was one of the ablest defenders of the Divinity of Christ, and presided over the second Ecumenical Council, at Constantinople, 381, but voluntarily resigned. Deeply lamenting the evils and distractions of the Church of his age, he longed for eternal rest in Christ. He wrote a large number of verses, mostly descriptive of his own life and the time in which he lived, also odes, and a drama on the Suffering Saviour. In the following poem, he struggles, from the depth of his complaints and 'fears, after the loss of father, mother, brother, and sister, into the light of God. It commences: Ποῦ δὲ λόγοι πτερόεντες; εἰς ἀέρα, "Where are the winged words? Lost in the air." The first six lines are omitted. See the Greek in GREGORY's "Opera," I. 77, and in Daniel, iii. 11. Another English version, by Mrs. CHARLES.

MY home in heaven alone to me remains,
The floods of faction o'er my country sweep;
For my uncertain feet, the land retains
No resting-place, no friend to weep;
No child to soothe the homeless poor forlorn;
I wander day by day with trembling limbs and torn.

What lot awaits me? What my mortal doom?
Where shall this jaded body find its rest?
Shall this poor trembling flesh e'er find a tomb?
By whom shall these dim eyes in death be blest?
Will any watch? Will any pity me?
Will they be Christian watchers? Or shall sinners see?

Or shall no grave inclose this mortal frame,
  When laid a heavy breathless corpse of clay?
Cast on the rock uncovered and in shame,
  Or tossed in scorn to birds and beasts of prey?
Or burnt to ashes, given to the air?
Or thrown into the weedy deep to perish there?

Thy will be done, O Lord! That day shall spring,
  When at Thy word this clay shall reappear!
No death I dread but that which sin will bring;
  No fire or flood without Thy wrath I fear;
For Thou, O Christ, my Lord! art fatherland to me,
My wealth and might and rest; my all I find in Thee.[1]

CEASE, YE TEARFUL MOURNERS!

(Jam mœsta quiesce querela.)

THE celebrated funeral-hymn of PRUDENTIUS CLEMENS, of Spain (d. 405); his masterpiece; originally the concluding part of his tenth "Catheme- rinŏn," but complete as an independent poem, which, after lying dormant to the sixteenth century, arose to new life, and became (in the version, "Hört auf mit Trauern und Klagen") a favourite funeral-hymn in Protestant Germany. See the original in full in PRUD. "Opera," ed. Obbarius (1845) p. 41, and in part in Daniel, i. p. 137; "Wackernagel," i. 40 and 329; "Trench," p. 281. It reminds one of the worship in the catacombs, whose gloom was lit up with the hope of a glorious resurrection in Christ. Freely translated by E. CASWALL. German translations by Knapp, Puchta, Königsfeld, Bässler, Schaff. Another English version, without rhymes, by Mrs. CHARLES (in "Voice of Christian Life in Song," p. 110): "Ah! hush now your mournful complainings;" and one, on the basis of a German version (in BUNSEN'S "Gesangbuch," No. 288), by Miss CATHERINE WINKWORTH: "Oh weep not, mourn not, over this bier!"

The conception of the resurrection contained in this poem, and taught by several of the ancient Fathers, especially Jerome, is rather materialistic. Paul teaches the resurrection of the body, not of the flesh (1 Cor. xv. 50). Lazarus was raised in the flesh, but to die again: the resurrection body will be immortal.

---

[1] Χριστὲ ἄναξ, σὺ δέ μοι πάτρη, σθένος, ὄλβος ἄπαντα,
Σοὶ δ' ἄρ' ἀναψύξαιμι βίον καὶ κῆδε' ἀμείψας.

"Thus," says Mrs. CHARLES of this poem (in "The Voice of Christian Life in Song," p. 66), "in the old Ionic tongue, the wail of feeble mortality went forth once more, but with a close the old Ionic music never knew; for Christ had died, and risen from the dead, and the other world was a region of melancholy shades no longer, for He is there."

CEASE, YE TEARFUL MOURNERS.

CEASE, ye tearful mourners,
    Thus your hearts to rend:
Death is life's beginning
    Rather than its end.[1]

All the grave's adornments,
    What do they declare,
Save that the departed
    Are but sleeping there?

What though now to darkness
    We this body give;
Soon shall all its senses
    Re-awake and live.

Soon shall warmth revisit
    These poor bones again,
And the blood meander
    Through each tingling vein;

And from its corruption
    This same body soar,
With the selfsame spirit
    That was here of yore.

E'en as duly scattered
    By the sower's hand
In the fading autumn
    O'er the fallow land,

Nature's seed, decaying,
    First in darkness dies,
Ere it can in glory
    Renovated rise.

Earth, to thy fond bosom
    We this pledge intrust;
Oh! we pray, be careful
    Of the precious dust.

---

[1] A more literal rendering, in the measure of the original:—
    "Each sorrowful mourner be silent!
    Fond mothers, give over your weeping!
    None grieve for those pledges as perished:
    This dying is life's reparation."

FOR EVER WITH CHRIST.

This was once the mansion
  Of a soul endowed
With sublimest powers,
  By the breath of God.

Here eternal Wisdom
  Lately made His home;
And again will claim it
  In the days to come;

When thou must this body,
  Bone for bone, restore,—
Every single feature
  Perfect as before.

O divinest period!
  Speed upon thy way;
O eternal Justice!
  Make no more delay.

When shall love in glory
  Its fruition see?
When shall hope be lost in
  Immortality?

NO MORE, AH, NO MORE.

(Jam mæsta quiesce querela.)

ANOTHER, and more faithful, version of the resurrection hymn of PRUDENTIUS, by the Rev. Dr. E. A. WASHBURN, New York, 1865; revised, Oct. 1868. See the note on the preceding hymn.

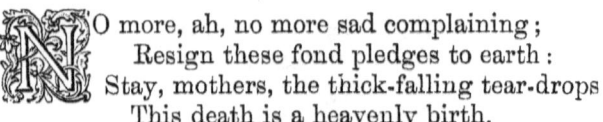O more, ah, no more sad complaining;
  Resign these fond pledges to earth:
Stay, mothers, the thick-falling tear-drops;
  This death is a heavenly birth.

What mean these still caverns of marble,
  Fair shrines that the dear ashes keep?
How sweetly they tell of the loved ones,
  Not dead, but soft resting in sleep!

NO MORE, AH, NO MORE.

What though, on the pale, icy forehead,
   No gleam of the intellect break?
A moment it slumbers, till nobler
   Its powers in their beauty awake.

Soon, soon, through the motionless body,
   The warm, loving life-tide shall pour,
And, blushing with joy, shall revisit
   The home it has dwelt in before.

These clods, 'neath the hillock reposing,
   Long wasting in silent decay,
Shall follow the souls that have loved them.
   On wingèd winds soaring away.

So, green from the seed springs the blossom,
   Long perished, long hid in the mould;
And, fresh from the turf, it remembers
   The wide-waving harvests of old.

Take, Earth, to thy bosom so tender,—
   Take, nourish this body. How fair,
How noble in death! we surrender
   These relics of man to thy care.

This, this was the home of the spirit,
   Once built by the breath of our God;
And here, in the light of His wisdom,
   Christ, Head of the risen, abode.

Guard well the dear treasure we lend thee:
   The Maker, the Saviour of men
Shall never forget His belovèd,
   But claim His own likeness again.

Speed on, perfect year, to the morning;
   God's fulness shall dawn on the just,
And thou, open Grave, shalt restore us
   The glorified form from the dust.

WITH TERROR THOU DOST STRIKE.

(Gravi me terrore pulsas, vitæ dies ultima.)

"DE DIE MORTIS." By PETER DAMIANI, cardinal-bishop of Ostia (1002-1072); friend of Hildebrand (afterwards Pope Gregory VII.), whom, "with a marvellous insight into the heights and depths of his character," he called his "Holy Satan" (Sanctus Satanas); promoter of his hierarchical reforms; died 1072, after a season of retirement and prayer, as abbot of Santa Croce d'Avellano; the author of several poems, among which that on the "Glory and Delights of Paradise" ("Ad perennis vitæ fontem mens sitivit arida") is best known and appreciated. The following comes next in merit. Dr. NEALE calls it an "awful hymn, the 'Dies Iræ' of individual life" ("Mediæval Hymns," p. 52). Translated by the Hon. ERASTUS C. BENEDICT, of New York, August, 1868. Contributed. An older translation, by Dr. NEALE: "O what terror in thy forethought, ending scene of mortal life!" See the Latin in Daniel i. p. 224; KÖNIGSFELD "Lat. Hymnen I." p. 112; fifteen stanzas, with a German version); and in "Trench," p. 278, who also gives Damiani's epitaph, written by himself.

WITH terror thou dost strike me now,
    Life's fearful dying day!
My heart is sad, my loins are weak,
    My spirit faints away;
While to my saddened soul, thy sight
    My anxious thoughts display.

Who can that dreadful sight describe,
    Or without trembling see!
When, from the ended course of life,
    The weary soul would flee;
And, sick of all the bonds of flesh,
    It struggles to be free.

The senses fail, the tongue is stiff,
    The eyes uncertain stray;
The panting breath and gasping throat
    The coming end betray;
From palsied limbs and pallid lips
    All charm has fled away.

Now spring at once to view past thoughts
    And words and deeds and life,
Before unwilling eyes they come,
    All crowding fresh and rife,
And stand revealed before the mind
    That shrinks with timid strife.

And biting conscience tortures now
   The trembling guilty breast,
And weeps the loss of perished hours,
   That might have given rest:
Too late repentance, full of grief,
   No proper fruit has blessed.

Of the false sweetness of the flesh,
   What bitterness remains,
When the brief pleasure of this life
   Is turned to endless pains,
And all life's idols here below
   The dying hour disdains.

I pray Thee, Jesus, grant me, then,
   Thine own almighty aid,
When I shall enter, at the last,
   In death's dark valley shade;
Let not the tyrant foe, I pray,
   My trembling soul invade.

Oh from the prince of darkness, then,
   And hell's dark prison save!
And take me ransomed to Thy home,
   Good Shepherd, now I crave,
Where I may live in endless life,
   With Thee, beyond the grave.

THE HEAVENLY JERUSALEM.

(Hora novissima.)

THIS glowing description of the celestial country is the sweetest of all the New-Jerusalem hymns of heavenly home-sickness, which have taken their inspiration from the last two chapters of Revelation; composed, about 1145, by BERNARD, a monk of Cluny, in France (b. of English parents, at Morlaix, in Bretagne), and contemporary of the more illustrious St. Bernard, of Clairvaux; very freely, but most happily, reproduced, and first made available for popular use, by Dr. JOHN M. NEALE, 1859, and more fully 1867; arranged, by the Editor, in three separate hymns. (Similar divisions in "Hymns Ancient and Modern," No. 142, and in "The People's Hymnal," Nos. 465-469.) The original, entitled "De Contemptu Mundi," and dedicated to Peter the Venerable, Abbot of Cluny (1122-1156), is in great part a bitter satire on the corruptions of the age, but opens, by way of contrast, with this exquisite description of the peace and glory of heaven. It comprises nearly three thousand lines, of dactylic hexameters, with the leonine (sometimes a trisyllabic or dactylic) and tailed rhyme, each line being broken up in three equal parts,—a most difficult metre, which only a special grace and inspiration enabled the author, as he believed, to master. I quote the first lines:—

> Hōră novīssĭmă ‖ tēmpŏră pēssĭmă ‖ sūnt : vĭgĭlēmŭs!
> Ecce! mina*citer* ‖ imminet ar*biter* ‖ ille sup*remus*!
> Imminet, im*minet*, ‖ ut mala ter*minet* ‖ æqua cor*onet*.
> Recta remu*neret*, ‖ anxia li*beret*, ‖ æthera *donet*.

It was first published by Matthias Flacius, with other poems calling for a reformation of ecclesiastical abuses, at Basle, 1557: and about five times since, more recently by "Trench," though only in part (96 lines, pp. 304-310); but first naturalized in English by the admirable transfusion (based upon "Trench's" extracts) of Dr. NEALE, portions of which, especially "Jerusalem the golden" (Part III.), have at once been adopted as "a priceless acquisition" to the hymns of the Church universal.

Dr. A. COLES, of Newark, New Jersey, the well known translator of "Dies Iræ," published, in 1866, a more literal version, preserving the leonine and tailed rhymes, but substituting anapests for dactyls:

> "The last of the hours, iniquity towers,
>   The times are the worst, let us vigils be keeping!
> Lest the Judge, who is near, and soon to appear,
>   Shall us at His coming find slumbering and sleeping.
> He is nigh, He is nigh! He descends from the sky,
>   For the ending of evil, and the right's coronation,
> The just to reward, relief to afford,
>   And the heavens bestow for the saints' habitation."

S. W. DUFFIELD has gone still further, and attempted a version in the inimitable measure of the original (New York, 1867), commencing:

> "These are the latter times, these are not better times:
>   Let us stand waiting.
> Lo! how with awfulness, He, first in lawfulness,
>   Comes arbitrating.
>   .   .   .   .   .   .
> Land of delightfulness, safe from all spitefulness,
>   Safe from all trouble,
> Thou shalt be filled again, Israel built again;
>   Joy shall redouble."

PART I.

BRIEF LIFE IS HERE OUR PORTION.

(*Hic breve vivitur, hic breve plangitur, hic breve fletur.*[1])

BRIEF life is here our portion,
  Brief sorrow, short-lived care;
  The life that knows no ending,
  The tearless life, is *there*.

---

[1] Briefly we tarry here, briefly are hurried here,
  Here is brief sorrow.

O happy retribution!
  Short toil, eternal rest;
For mortals and for sinners
  A mansion with the blest!

There grief is turned to pleasure;
  Such pleasure, as below
No human voice can utter,
  No human heart can know.

Then all the halls of Sion
  For aye shall be complete,
And in the land of beauty
  All things of beauty meet.

The Saviour whom we trust in
  Shall then be seen and known,
And they that know and see Him
  Shall have Him for their own.

There Jesus shall embrace us,
  There Jesus be embraced,
That spirit's food and sunshine
  Whence earthly love is chased.

Yes! Christ my King and Portion,
  In fulness of His grace,
I then shall see for ever,
  And worship face to face.

PART II.

FOR THEE, O DEAR, DEAR COUNTRY!

(O bona patria, lumina sobria te speculantur.)

FOR thee, O dear, dear Country!
  Mine eyes their vigils keep;
For very love, beholding
  Thy happy name, they weep.

The mention of thy glory
  Is unction to the breast,
And medicine in sickness,
  And love and life and rest.

FOR EVER WITH CHRIST.

O come, O onely Mansion!
   O Paradise of Joy!
Where tears are ever banished,
   And smiles have no alloy.

The Lamb is all thy splendour,
   The Crucified thy praise:
His laud and benediction
   Thy ransomed people raise.

Jesus, the Gem of Beauty,
   True God and Man! they sing;
The never-failing Garden,
   The ever-golden Ring!

The Shepherd and the Husband,
   The Guardian of His Court;
The Day-star of Salvation,
   The Porter and the Port!

Thou hast no shore, fair ocean!
   Thou hast no time, bright day!
Dear fountain of refreshment
   To pilgrims far away!

Thou feel'st in mystic rapture,
   O Bride, that know'st no guile,
The Prince's sweetest kisses,
   The Prince's loveliest smile.

Unfading lilies, bracelets
   Of living pearl thine own:
The Lamb is ever near thee,
   The Bridegroom thine alone.

And all thine endless leisure
   In sweetest accents sings
The ill that was thy merit,
   The wealth that is thy King's!

PART III.

JERUSALEM THE GOLDEN.

(Urbs Syon aurea, patria, lactea, cive decora.)

JERUSALEM the golden,
    With milk and honey blest!
Beneath thy contemplation
    Sink heart and voice oppressed.

I know not, O I know not,
    What holy joys are there!
What radiancy of glory,
    What light beyond compare!

They stand, those halls of Sion,
    Conjubilant with song,
And bright with many an angel,
    And all the martyr throng.

The Prince is ever in them;
    The daylight is serene:
The pastures of the blessed
    Are decked in glorious sheen.

There is the throne of David,
    And there, from care released,
The song of them that triumph,
    The shout of them that feast.

And they, who, with their Leader,
    Have conquered in the fight,
For ever and for ever
    Are clad in robes of white!

And there the Sole-Begotten
    Is Lord in regal state;
He, Judah's mystic Lion,
    He, Lamb immaculate.

O fields that know no sorrow!
    O state that fears no strife!
O princely bowers! O land of flowers!
    O realm and home of life!

Exult, O dust and ashes!
    The Lord shall be thy part:
His only, His for ever,
    Thou shalt be and thou art!

Jesus, in mercy bring us
    Soon to that land of rest;
Who art, with God the Father,
    And Spirit, ever blest!

REGION OF LIFE AND LIGHT.

The Life of the Blessed. From the Spanish of LUIS PONCE DE LEON; b. at Granada, 1527: bred in the solitude of a cloister, but free from the intolerant fanaticism of his age and country; died 1590, as General and Provincial Vicar of Salamanca. Translated by W. CULLEN BRYANT, 1836.

REGION of life and light!
    Land of the good whose earthly toils are o'er!
      Nor frost nor heat may blight,
    Thy vernal beauty, fertile shore,
Yielding thy blessed fruits for evermore!

    There, without crook or sling,
Walks the Good Shepherd; blossoms white and red
      Round His meek temples cling;
      And, to sweet pastures led,
His own loved flock beneath His eye is fed.

    He guides, and near Him they
Follow delighted; for He makes them go
      Where dwells eternal May,
      And heavenly roses blow,
Deathless, and gathered but again to grow.

    He leads them to the height
Named of the infinite and long-sought Good,
      And fountains of delight;
      And where His feet have stood,
Springs up, along the way, their tender food.

    And when in the mid skies,
The climbing sun has reached his highest bound,
      Reposing as He lies,
      With all His flock around,
He witches the still air with numerous sound.

From His sweet lute flow forth
Immortal harmonies, of power to still
   All passions born of earth,
   And draw the ardent will
Its destiny of goodness to fulfil.

   Might but a little part,
A wandering breath, of that high melody
   Descend into my heart,
   And change it till it be
Transformed and swallowed up, O love! in Thee:

   Ah! then my soul should know,
Beloved! where Thou liest at noon of day;
   And from this place of woe
   Released, should take its way
To mingle with Thy flock, and never stray.

THE LIFE ABOVE, THE LIFE ON HIGH.

(Vivo sin vivir en mi.)

PART of a post-communion hymn of ST. TERESA, of Spain (d. 1582), one of the greatest saints of the Roman-Catholic Church. Translated by E. CASWALL. (From SHIPLEY's "Lyra Eucharistica," p. 201.) This poem is not free from a morbid asceticism, which, like the extravagant passion of Ignatius for martyrdom, differs widely from the calm resignation of the healthy Christian life, as exhibited in St. Paul, Phil. ii. 21-26; yet it is full of burning love to Christ, and represents a phase of Christian experience, in favourable contrast to the secularized Christianity of the day, which feels too much at home in this world.

THE Life above, the Life on high,
   Alone is Life in verity;
      Nor can we Life at all enjoy,
   Till this poor life is o'er;
Then, O sweet Death! no longer fly
From me, who, ere my time to die,
   Am dying evermore;
For evermore I weep and sigh,
Dying, because I do not die.

To Him, who deigns in me to live,
What better gift have I to give,

O my poor earthly life, than thee?
  Too glad of Thy decay,
So but I may the sooner see
That Face of sweetest majesty,
  For which I pine away;
While evermore I weep and sigh,
Dying, because I do not die.

Absent from Thee, my Saviour dear,
I call not Life this living here,
  But a long dying agony,
    The sharpest I have known;
  And I myself, myself to see
  In such a rack of misery,
    For very pity moan;
And ever, ever weep and sigh,
Dying, because I do not die.

Ah! Lord, my Light and living Breath,
Take me, oh, take me from this death,
  And burst the bars that sever me
    From my true Life above!
  Think how I die Thy Face to see,
  And cannot live away from Thee,
    O my eternal Love!
And ever, ever, weep and sigh,
Dying, because I do not die.

I weary of this endless strife;
I weary of this dying life,
  This living death, this heavy chain,
    This torment of delay,
  In which her sins my soul detain.
  Ah! when shall it be mine? Ah! when,
    With my last breath to say,—
No more I weep, no more I sigh;
I'm dying of desire to die.

LORD, IT BELONGS NOT TO MY CARE.

RICHARD BAXTER: b. 1615, d. 1691; the model pastor of Kidderminster: author of the "Saint's Rest," and other excellent works. The following verses are taken from a longer poem, entitled: "The Covenant and Confidence of Faith" (see ROGERS, p. 47). They form a Protestant pendant to the preceding poem of Saint Teresa.

LORD, it belongs not to my care
    Whether I die or live;
To love and serve Thee is my share,
    And this Thy grace must give.

If life be long, I will be glad,
    That I may long obey;
If short, yet why should I be sad,
    That shall have the same pay?[1]

Christ leads me through no darker rooms
    Than He went through before;
He that unto God's kingdom comes,
    Must enter by this door.[2]

Come, Lord, when grace has made me meet
    Thy blessèd face to see;
For if Thy work on earth be sweet,
    What will Thy glory be!

Then shall I end my sad complaints,
    And weary, sinful days,
And join with the triumphant saints
    To sing Jehovah's praise.

My knowledge of that life is small,
    The eye of faith is dim;
But it's enough that Christ knows all,
    And I shall be with Him.

---

[1] Improved in the Andover "Sabbath Hymn Book," No. 763:—
    "To soar to endless day?"

The "Marylebone Collection," 1851, and Alford's "Year of Praise," 1867, change the whole verse thus:

    "If life be long, my days are blest, When they are spent for Thee;
    If short my course, I sooner rest, From sin and trouble free."

[2] Andover "Sabbath Hymn-Book:"
    "No one into His kingdom comes,
    But through His opened door."

THOU SHALT RISE!

(Auferstehn, ja auferstehn wirst du.)

FRIEDRICH GOTTLIEB KLOPSTOCK (the German Milton, though not quite equal to him in genius); b. 1724; d. at Hamburg, 1803. Translated in "Hymns from the Land of Luther," slightly altered by the Editor, according to the original. A closer version in BASKERVILLE'S "Poetry of Germany," "Arise, yes, yes, arise, O thou my dust, From short repose thou must."

THOU shalt rise! my dust, thou shalt arise!
Not always closed thine eyes:
    Thy life's first Giver
    Will give thee life for ever.
        Hallelujah!

Sown in darkness, but to bloom again,
When, after winter's reign,
    Jesus is reaping
    The seed now quietly sleeping.
        Hallelujah!

Day of praise! for thee, thou wondrous day,
In my quiet grave I stay;
    And, when I number
    My days and nights of slumber,
        Thou wakest me!

Then, as they who dream, we shall arise
With Jesus to the skies,
    And find that morrow,
    The weary pilgrim's sorrow,
        All past and gone!

Then shall I the Holy of Holiest tread,
By my Redeemer led,
    Through heaven soaring,
    His holy name adoring
        Eternally!

GUIDE ME, O THOU GREAT JEHOVAH.

The Christian Pilgrim's Hymn. By the Rev. WILLIAM WILLIAMS, a Calvinistic Methodist, who laboured as a travelling preacher in Wales; b. 1717, d. 1791. This hymn was originally written in Welsh, and translated, either by himself or by Wm. Evans. Sir R. Palmer omits the last stanza.

GUIDE me, O Thou great Jehovah,
  Pilgrim thro' this barren land:
  I am weak, but Thou art mighty;
Hold me with Thy powerful hand:
    Bread of heaven! bread of heaven!
    Feed me now and evermore.

Open now the crystal fountain
  Whence the healing streams do flow;
Let the fiery cloudy pillar
  Lead me all my journey through:
    Strong Deliverer! strong Deliverer!
    Be Thou still my strength and shield.

When I tread the verge of Jordan,
  Bid my anxious fears subside;
Death of deaths, and hell's destruction,
  Land me safe on Canaan's side.
    Songs of praises, songs of praises,
    I will ever give to Thee.

Musing on my habitation,
  Musing on my heav'nly home,
Fills my soul with holy longing;
  Come, my Jesus, quickly come.
    Vanity is all I see;
    Lord, I long to be with Thee!

ASLEEP IN JESUS.

Mrs. MARGARET MACKAY. This popular lyric appeared first in "The Amethyst," at Edinburgh, 1832. ROGERS, p. 389.

ASLEEP in Jesus! blessèd sleep,
  From which none ever wakes to weep,
  A calm and undisturbed repose,
Unbroken by the last of foes!

Asleep in Jesus! oh, how sweet
To be for such a slumber meet!
With holy confidence to sing
That death hath lost his venomed sting.

Asleep in Jesus! peaceful rest,
Whose waking is supremely blest;
No fear, no woe, shall dim that hour,
That manifests the Saviour's power.

Asleep in Jesus! oh for me
May such a blissful refuge be;
Securely shall my ashes lie,
Waiting the summons from on high!

Asleep in Jesus! time nor space
Debars this precious "hiding-place;"
On Indian plains, or Lapland snows,
Believers find the same repose.

Asleep in Jesus! far from thee
Thy kindred and their graves may be;
But thine is still a blessèd sleep,
From which none ever wakes to weep!

LET ME BE WITH THEE.

Miss Charlotte Elliott. 1836. Compare John xvii. 24.

LET me be with Thee where Thou art,
  My Saviour, my eternal Rest!
Then only will this longing heart,
  Be fully and for ever blest!

Let me be with Thee where Thou art,
  Thy unveiled glory to behold;
Then only will this wandering heart
  Cease to be treacherous, faithless, cold!

Let me be with Thee where Thou art,
  Where spotless saints Thy Name adore;
Then only will this sinful heart
  Be evil and defiled no more!

Let me be with Thee where Thou art,
  Where none can die, where none remove;
There neither death nor life will part
  Me from Thy presence and Thy love!

WE SPEAK OF THE REALMS.

ANONYMOUS. Often ascribed to a Mrs. WILSON. 1837. ROGERS, p. 633.

WE speak of the realms of the blessed,
  Of that country so bright and so fair,
And oft are its glories confessed;
  But what must it be to be there?

We speak of its pathways of gold,
  Of its walls decked with jewels so rare,
Of its wonders and treasures untold;
  But what must it be to be there?

We speak of its freedom from sin,
  From sorrow, temptation, and care,
From trials without and within;
  But what must it be to be there?

We speak of its service of love,
  Of the robes which the glorified wear,
The Church of the first-born above;
  But what must it be to be there?

Do Thou, Lord, midst pleasure and woe,
  Still for heaven my spirit prepare;
And shortly I also shall know
  And feel what it is to be there.

FOREVER WITH THE LORD!

JAMES MONTGOMERY; a Moravian, b. 1771 : d. at Sheffield, 1854.
1 *Thess*. iv. 17.

FOREVER with the Lord!
  Amen! so let it be!
Life from the dead is in that word,
  And immortality!

FOR EVER WITH CHRIST.

Here in the body pent,
    Absent from Him I roam,
Yet nightly pitch my moving tent
    A day's march nearer home.

My Father's house on high,
    Home of my soul! how near,
At times, to faith's foreseeing eye,
    Thy golden gates appear!

Ah! then my spirit faints
    To reach the land I love,
The bright inheritance of saints,
    Jerusalem above!

Yet clouds will intervene,
    And all my prospect flies;
Like Noah's dove, I flit between
    Rough seas and stormy skies.

Anon the clouds depart,
    The winds and waters cease;
While sweetly o'er my gladdened heart
    Expands the bow of peace!

Beneath its glowing arch,
    Along the hallowed ground,
I see cherubic armies march
    A camp of fire around.

I hear at morn and even,
    At noon and midnight hour,
The choral harmonies of Heaven
    Earth's Babel tongues o'erpower.

Then, then I feel, that He,
    Remembered or forgot,
The Lord, is never far from me,
    Though I perceive Him not.

I WOULD NOT LIVE ALWAY.

JOB, vii. 16. Rev. W. A. MÜHLENBERG, D.D., St. Luke's Hospital, New York. This beautiful lyric was written 1824, and, in an abridged and somewhat altered form, commencing, "I would not live alway, I asked not to stay" (ver. 2), it was adopted, without the agency of the author, by a Commission of the Protestant Episcopal Church to prepare an Appendix of Hymns to the Book of Common Prayer. From this it passed into many collections, and has justly become one of the most popular hymns in all American churches. We give it here in its original shape, as finally revised by the venerable author in 1859, although the abridged form of the Prayer Book will probably always retain its hold upon the Christian public.

WOULD not live alway—live alway below!
Oh no, I'll not linger when bidden to go:
The days of our pilgrimage granted us here,
Are enough for life's woes, full enough for its cheer:
Would I shrink from the path which the prophets of God,
Apostles, and martyrs, so joyfully trod?
Like a spirit unblest, o'er the earth would I roam,
While brethren and friends are all hastening home?

I would not live alway: I ask not to stay,
Where storm after storm rises dark o'er the way;
Where seeking for rest we but hover around,
Like the patriarch's bird, and no resting is found;
Where Hope when she paints her gay bow in the air,
Leaves its brilliance to fade in the night of despair,
And joy's fleeting angel ne'er sheds a glad ray,
Save the gleam of the plumage that bears him away.

I would not live alway—thus fettered by sin,
Temptation without and corruption within;
In a moment of strength if I sever the chain,
Scarce the victory is mine, ere I'm captive again;
E'en the rapture of pardon is mingled with fears,
And the cup of thanksgiving with penitent tears:
The festival trump calls for jubilant songs,
But my spirit her own *miserere* prolongs.

I would not live alway—no, welcome the tomb,
Since Jesus hath lain there, I dread not its gloom;

Where he deigned to sleep, I'll too bow my head,
All peaceful to slumber on that hallowed bed.
Then the glorious daybreak, to follow that night,
The orient gleam of the angels of light,
With their clarion call for the sleepers to rise
And chant forth their matins, away to the skies.

Who, who would live alway? away from his God.
Away from yon heaven, that blissful abode
Where the rivers of pleasure flow o'er the bright plains,
And the noon-tide of glory eternally reigns;
Where the saints of all ages, in harmony meet
Their Saviour and brethren, transported to greet,
While the songs of salvation exultingly roll,
And the love of the Lord is the bliss of the soul.[1]

That heavenly music! hark, sweet in the air
The notes of the harpers how clear ringing there!
And see, soft unfolding those portals of gold,
The King all arrayed in His beauty behold!
Oh give me, Oh give me, the wings of a dove
To adore Him—be near Him—enrapt with His love;
I but wait for the summons, I list for the word—
Alleluia—Amen—evermore with the Lord.

SINCE O'ER THY FOOTSTOOL.

REV. W. A. MUHLENBERG, D.D. of New York. 1824.

SINCE o'er Thy footstool here below
    Such radiant gems are strewn,
Oh, what magnificence must glow,
    My God, about Thy throne!
So brilliant here those drops of light,—
There the full ocean rolls, how bright!

---

[1] Or, as in the form now in common use:

"While the anthems of rapture unceasingly roll,
And the smile of the Lord is the feast of the soul."

If night's blue curtain of the sky
  With thousand stars inwrought,
Hung like a royal canopy
  With glittering diamonds fraught,
Be, Lord, Thy temple's outer veil,
What splendour at the shrine must dwell!

The dazzling sun, at noontide hour,
  Forth from his flaming vase,
Flinging o'er earth the golden shower,
  Till vale and mountain blaze,
But shows, O Lord! one beam of Thine:
What, then, the day where Thou dost shine!

Ah! how shall these dim eyes endure
  That noon of living rays,
Or how my spirit so impure
  Upon Thy glory gaze?
Anoint, O Lord! anoint my sight,
And robe me for that world of light!

WHAT SHALL WE BE?

(Wie wird uns sein, wenn endlish narh dem schweren.)

PH. SPITTA, "Psalter und Harfe," 1833. Translated by R. MASSIE. 1860.
Compare the translation in the "Hymns from the Land of Luther:" "What shall I be, my Lord, when I behold Thee?"

WHAT shall we be, and whither shall we go,
  When the last conflict of our life is o'er,
  And we return from wandering to and fro
To our dear home through heaven's eternal door!
When we shake off the last dust from our feet,
  When we wipe off the last drop from our brow,
And our departed friends once more shall greet,
  The hope which cheers and comforts us below!

What shall we be, when we ourselves shall see
  Bathed in the flood of everlasting light,
And from all guilt and sin entirely free,
  Stand pure and blameless in our Maker's sight;

No longer from His holy presence driven,
   Conscious of guilt, and stung with inward pain,
But friends of God and citizens of heaven,
   To join the ranks of His celestial train!

What shall we be, when we drink in the sound
   Of heavenly music from the spheres above,
When golden harps to listening hosts around
   Declare the wonders of redeeming love;
When far and wide through the resounding air
   Loud hallelujahs from the ransomed rise,
And holy incense, sweet with praise and prayer,
   Is wafted to the Highest through the skies!

What shall we be, when the freed soul can rise
   With unrestrained and bold aspiring flight
To Him, who by His wondrous sacrifice
   Hath opened heaven, and scattered sin's dark night;
When from the eye of faith the thin veil drops,
   Like wreaths of mist before the morning's rays,
And we behold, the end of all our hopes,
   The Son of God in full refulgent blaze!

What shall we be, when we shall hear Him say:
   "Come, O ye blessed," when we see Him stand,
Robed in the light of everlasting day,
   Before the throne of God at His right hand;
When we behold the eyes from which once flowed
   Tears o'er the sin and misery of man,
And the deep wounds from which the precious blood,
   That made atonement for the world, once ran;

What shall we be, when hand in hand we go
   With blessed spirits risen from the tomb,
Where streams of living water softly flow,
   And trees still flourish in primeval bloom;
Where in perpetual youth no cheek looks old
   By the sharp tooth of cruel time imprest,
Where no bright eye is dimm'd, no heart grows cold,
   No grief, no pain, no death invades the blest!

What shall we be, when every glance we cast
   At the dark valley underneath our feet,
And every retrospect of troubles past
   Makes heaven brighter and its joys more sweet;

When the remembrance of our former woe
  Gives a new relish to our present peace,
And draws our heart to Him, to whom we owe
  Our past deliverance and our present bliss!

What shall we be, who have in Christ believed,
  What through His grace will be our sweet reward!
Eye hath not seen, ear heard, or heart conceived,
  What God for those who love Him hath prepared:
Let us the steep ascent then boldly climb,
  Our toil and labour will be well repaid;
Let us haste onward, till in God's good time
  We reap the fruit, a crown that doth not fade.

OH, PARADISE MUST FAIRER BE!

(Das Paradies muss schöner sein.)

FRIEDRICH RÜCKERT, 1789-1866. "Das Paradies." A free and abridged translation, taken from "Heavenward: Hymns and Poems of Consolation," New York, 1867, p. 184, where it is given without the name of the translator. This beautiful poem is true only on the basis of a vital union with Him who is the Resurrection and the Life.

OH, Paradise must fairer be
    Than any spot below!
  My spirit pines for liberty;
Now let me thither go!

In Paradise, for ever clear
    The stream of love is flowing;
  For every tear that I've shed here
    A pearl therein is glowing.

In Paradise alone is rest;
    Joy breathing, woe dispelling;
  A heavenly wind fans every breast
    Within that happy dwelling.

For every wounding thorn below
    A rose shall blossom there;
  And sweeter flowers than earth can show
    Shall twine around my hair.

M M

And every joy, that, budding, died,
  Shall open there in bloom;
And Spring, in all her flowery pride,
  Shall waken from the tomb.

And all the joys shall meet me there
  For which my heart was pining,
Like golden fruit in gardens fair,
  And flowers for ever shining.

My youth, that fled so soon away,
  And left me sad, decaying,
Shall there be with me every day
  With bright wings round me playing.

All hopes, all wishes, all the love
  I sighed for, pined for, ever,
Shall bloom around me there above,
  And last with me for ever!

O PARADISE! O PARADISE!

F. W. Faber, D.D.; b. 1815. From the last edition of his "Hymns," Lond. 1862, p. 423. The last two verses are omitted, and the third has been put last. Some British collections give only three stanzas.

PARADISE! O Paradise!
  Who doth not crave for rest?
Who would not seek the happy land,
  Where they that loved are blest;
    Where loyal hearts, and true,
      Stand ever in the light,
    All rapture through and through,
      In God's most holy sight?

O Paradise! O Paradise!
  The world is growing old:
Who would not be at rest and free
  Where love is never cold;
    Where loyal hearts, and true,
      Stand ever in the light,
    All rapture through and through,
      In God's most holy sight?

O Paradise! O Paradise!
'Tis weary waiting here;
I long to be where Jesus is,
To feel, to see Him near;
Where loyal hearts, and true,
Stand ever in the light,
All rapture through and through,
In God's most holy sight.

O Paradise! O Paradise!
I want to sin no more;
I want to be as pure on earth
As on thy spotless shore;
Where loyal hearts, and true,
Stand ever in the light,
All rapture through and through,
In God's most holy sight.

O Paradise! O Paradise!
Wherefore doth death delay?—
Bright death, that is the welcome dawn
Of our eternal day;
Where loyal hearts, and true,
Stand ever in the light,
All rapture through and through,
In God's most holy sight.

NO, NO, IT IS NOT DYING.

(Non, ce n'est pas mourir.)

FROM the French of the Rev. Dr. CÆSAR MALAN; b. 1785; d. 1864; pastor of an Independent Reformed Church at Geneva; a man of genius and striking individuality; author of "Chants de Sion, ou Recueil de Cantiques," Paris, 1841 (No. 233). The following excellent translation was made by the Rev. Dr. R. P. DUNN, late professor of rhetoric and English literature in Brown University, Providence, R. I. (d. Aug. 28, 1867), not directly from the French, but from an admirable German version of A. KNAPP: "Nein, nein, das ist kein Sterben" (in SCHAFF's "G. H. B.," No. 464).

O, no, it is not dying,
    To go unto our God;
    This gloomy earth forsaking,
Our journey homeward taking
    Along the starry road.

No, no, it is not dying,
  Heaven's citizen to be;
A crown immortal wearing,
And rest unbroken sharing,
  From care and conflict free.

No, no, it is not dying,
  To hear this gracious word;
" Receive a Father's blessing,
For evermore possessing
  The favour of thy Lord."

No, no, it is not dying,
  The Shepherd's voice to know;
His sheep He ever leadeth,
His peaceful flock He feedeth,
  Where living pastures grow.

No, no, it is not dying,
  To wear a lordly crown;
Among God's people dwelling,
The glorious triumph swelling,
  Of Him whose sway we own.

Oh, no, this is not dying,
  Thou Saviour of mankind!
There streams of love are flowing,
No hindrance ever knowing;
  Here drops alone we find.

IT IS NOT DEATH TO DIE.

(Non, ce n'est pas mourir.)

FREE, from the French of Dr. MALAN (see the preceding hymn), by Dr. GEORGE W. BETHUNE ("Lays of Love and Faith," Phila. 1847). This hymn was sung, by his own direction, at Bethune's funeral, in New York, Sept. 1862.

IT is not death to die,
  To leave this weary road,
  And, 'midst the brotherhood on high,
To be at home with God.

IT IS NOT DEATH TO DIE.

It is not death to close
  The eye long dimmed by tears,
And wake in glorious repose,
  To spend eternal years.

It is not death to bear
  The wrench that sets us free
From dungeon-chain, to breathe the air
  Of boundless liberty.

It is not death to fling
  Aside this sinful dust,
And rise, on strong, exulting wing,
  To live among the just.

Jesus, Thou Prince of Life!
  Thy chosen cannot die!
Like Thee, they conquer in the strife,
  To reign with Thee on high.

O SWEET HOME-ECHO!

(" *Wir werden bei dem Herrn sein allezeit.*)

"And so shall we ever be with the Lord."—1 *Thess.* iv. 17. By Mrs. META HEUSSER-SCHWEIZER, the sweet evangelical singer of Switzerland; b. 1797; residing at Hirzel, Canton Zurich. Written, 1845, for a friend in America. Translated by JANE BORTHWICK, 1853, in "Hymns from the Land of Luther."

SWEET home-echo on the pilgrim's way,
  Thrice welcome message from a land of light!
As through a clouded sky the moonbeams stray,
  So on eternity's deep shrouded night
Streams a mild radiance, from that cheering word:
  "So shall we be for ever with the Lord."

At home with Jesus? He who went before,
  For His own people mansions to prepare;
The soul's deep longings stilled, its conflicts o'er,
  All rest and blessedness with Jesus there.
What home like this can the wide earth afford?
  "So shall we be for ever with the Lord."

With Him all gathered ! to that blessed home,
    Through all its windings, still the pathway tends ;
While ever and anon bright glimpses come
    Of that fair city where the journey ends.
Where all of bliss is centred in one word :
    " So shall we be for ever with the Lord."

Here, kindred hearts are severed far and wide,
    By many a weary mile of land and sea,
Or life's all varied cares and paths divide ;
    But yet a joyful gathering shall be,
The broken links repaired, the lost restored,
    " So shall we be for ever with the Lord."

And is there ever perfect union here ?
    Ah ! daily sins, lamented and confessed,
They come between us and the friends most dear,
    They mar our blessedness and break our rest.
With life we leave the evils long deplored :
    " So shall we be for ever with the Lord."

All prone to error, none set wholly free
    From the old serpent's soul-ensnaring chain,
The truths one child of God can clearly see,
    He seeks to make his brother feel in vain ;
But all shall harmonize in heaven's full chord ;
    " So shall we be for ever with the Lord."

O blessed promise ! mercifully given,
    Well may it hush the wail of earthly woe ;
O'er the dark passage to the gates of heaven
    The light of hope and resurrection throw !
Thanks for the blessed, life-inspiring word :
    " So shall we be for ever with the Lord."

JESUS! WHEN MY SOUL IS PARTING.

"JESUS First and Jesus Last." By THOMAS MACKELLAR, stereotyper, Philadelphia, author of a volume of poems.

JESUS ! when my soul is parting
 From this body frail and weak,
And the deathly dew is starting
 Down this pale and wasted cheek,—
  Thine, my Saviour,
 Be the name I last shall speak,

Jesus ! when my memory wanders
 Far from loved ones at my side,
And in fitful dreaming ponders
 Who are they that near me glide,—
  Last, my Saviour,
 Let my thoughts on Thee abide,

When the morn in all its glory
 Charms no more mine ear nor eye,
And the shadows closing o'er me
 Warn me of the time to die,—
  Last, my Saviour,
 Let me see Thee standing by.

When my feet shall pass the river,
 And upon the farther shore
I shall walk, redeem'd for ever—
 Ne'er to sin—to die no more,—
  First, Lord Jesus!
 Let me see Thee, and adore.

GO AND DIG MY GRAVE TO-DAY!

(Geht nun hin und grabt mein Grab.)

FROM the German of ERNST MORITZ ARNDT: b. 1769; d. 1860; professor of history in the University of Bonn (where a fine statue is erected to his memory); a German patriot, a friend of liberty, and a childlike Christian. This is his "Schwanengesang." See the German in Knapp's "Liederschatz," 3rd ed., No. 2936.

Go and dig my grave to-day!
    Weary of these wanderings all,
    Now from earth I pass away,
For the Prince of Peace doth call:
Angel voices from above
Call me to their rest and love.

Go and dig my grave to-day!
    Homeward doth my journey tend,
And I lay my staff away
    Here, where all things earthly end;
And I lay my weary head
In the only painless bed.

What is there I yet should do,
    Lingering in this darksome vale?
Proud and mighty, fair to view,
    Are our schemes, and yet they fail
Like the sand before the wind,
That no power of man can bind.

Farewell, earth, then, I am glad
    That in peace I now depart!
For thy very joys are sad,
    And thy hopes deceive the heart;
Fleeting is thy beauty's gleam,
False and changing as a dream.

And to you a last good-night,
    Sun and moon and stars so dear,
Farewell all your golden light!
    I am travelling far from here,
To the splendours of that day
Where ye all must fade away.

Weep not that I take my leave
  Of the world,—that I exchange
Errors that too closely cleave,
  Shadows, empty ghosts that range
Through this world of naught and night,
For a land of truth and light.

Weep not, dearest to my heart,
  For I find my Saviour near,
And I know that I have part
  In the pains He suffered here,
When He shed His precious blood
For each sinner's highest good.

Weep not, my Redeemer lives!
  Heavenward springing from the dust,
Clear-eyed Hope her comfort gives;
  Faith, Heaven's champion, bids me trust;
Love eternal whispers nigh,
" Child of God, fear not to die."

THERE IS A BLESSED HOME.

REV. Sir HENRY WILLIAMS BAKER, Bart. 1861. Born, in London, 1821; son of a vice-admiral in the Royal Navy; graduated at Cambridge, 1844; vicar of Monkland; one of the editors of "Hymns Ancient and Modern," to which the following piece was contributed (No. 182).

THERE is a blessèd home
    Beyond this land of woe,
  Where trials never come,
    Nor tears of sorrow flow;
  Where faith is lost in sight,
    And patient hope is crowned,
  And everlasting light
    Its glory throws around.

There is a land of peace,
  Good angels know it well;
Glad songs that never cease
  Within its portals swell;

Around its glorious throne
  Ten thousand saints adore
Christ, with the Father One,
  And Spirit, evermore.

O joy all joys beyond,
  To see the Lamb who died,
And count each sacred wound
  In hands and feet and side!
To give to Him the praise
  Of every triumph won,
And sing through endless days
  The great things He hath done.

Look up, ye saints of God,
  Nor fear to tread below
The path your Saviour trod
  Of daily toil and woe;
Wait but a little while
  In uncomplaining love,
His own most gracious smile
  Shall welcome you above.

STAR OF MORN AND EVEN.

ἀώϊον ἀεροφοίταν
᾿Αστέρα μείναμεν· ᾿Αελίου λευκοπτέρυγα πρόδρομον.

"THE Daystar." By FRANCIS TURNER PALGRAVE, late Scholar of Balliol, and Fellow of Exeter College, Oxford. 1862. From his "Hymns," 2nd ed. 1868.

STAR of morn and even,
  Sun of Heaven's heaven,
    Saviour high and dear,
  Toward us turn Thine ear;
  Through whate'er may come,
  Thou canst lead us home.

Though the gloom be grievous,
Those we leant on leave us,
  Though the coward heart
  Quit its proper part,
  Though the tempter come,
  Thou wilt lead us home.

Saviour pure and holy,
Lover of the lowly,
  Sign us with Thy sign,
  Take our hands in Thine;
  Take our hands and come,
  Lead Thy children home!

Star of morn and even,
Shine on us from Heaven;
  From Thy glory-throne
  Hear Thy very own!
  Lord and Saviour, come,
  Lead us to our home!

O HEAVEN! SWEET HEAVEN!

REV. EDWIN H. NEVIN; b. 1814, at Shippensburg, Pa.; pastor of St. Paul's German Reformed Church, Lancaster, Pa. (since 1868). The following hymn, as the author kindly informs us, was written and first printed in 1862, after the death of a beloved son, which made heaven nearer and dearer from the conviction that now a member of his family was one of its inhabitants.

HEAVEN! Sweet Heaven! the home of the blest,
Where hearts once in trouble are ever at rest;
Where eyes that could see not rejoice in the light,
And beggars made princes are walking in white.

O Heaven! Sweet Heaven! the mansion of love,
Where Christ in His beauty shines forth from above,
The Lamb with his sceptre, to charm and control,
And love is the sea that encircles the whole.

O Heaven! Sweet Heaven! where purity reigns,
Where error disturbs not, and sin never stains;
Where holiness robes in its garments so fair
The great multitude that is worshipping there.

O Heaven! Sweet Heaven! where music ne'er dies,
But rich pealing anthems of glory arise;
Where saints with one feeling of rapture are stirred,
And loud hallelujahs for ever are heard.

O Heaven! Sweet Heaven! where friends never part,
But cords of true friendship bind firmly the heart;
Where farewell shall never more fall on the ear,
Nor eyes that have sorrowed be dimmed with a tear.

OH FOR THE ROBES OF WHITENESS.

C̲H̲A̲R̲I̲T̲I̲E̲ L̲E̲E̲S̲ S̲M̲I̲T̲H̲, daughter of the Rev. Sidney Smith, D.D., rector of Aghalurcher, Ireland. This hymn, entitled "Heavenly Anticipations," is a favourite in Sunday Schools in England. From R̲O̲G̲E̲R̲S̲' "Lyra Brit." 1867, p. 511.

OH for the robes of whiteness!
   Oh for the tearless eyes!
Oh for the glorious brightness
   Of the unclouded skies!

Oh for the no more weeping
   Within the land of love,
The endless joy of keeping
   The bridal feast above!

Oh for the bliss of dying,
   My risen Lord to meet!
Oh for the rest of lying
   For ever at His feet!

Oh for the hour of seeing
   My Saviour face to face,
The hope of ever being
   In that sweet meeting-place!

Jesus, Thou King of glory,
   I soon shall dwell with Thee;
I soon shall sing the story
   Of Thy great love to me.

Meanwhile my thoughts shall enter,
   E'en now, before Thy throne,
That all my love may centre
   On Thee, and Thee alone.

OH FOR THE PEACE WHICH FLOWETH!

"WHAT is this that He saith, A little while?"—*John* xvi. 18. By Mrs. JANE CREWDSON (daughter of George Fox): b. 1809; d. 1863, near Manchester, after a long period of illness, during which she wrote her poems, breathing the rich flavour of sanctified affliction.

OH for the peace which floweth as a river,
    Making life's desert places bloom and smile!
Oh for the faith to grasp heaven's bright "for ever,"
    Amid the shadows of earth's "little while."

"A little while," for patient vigil-keeping,
    To face the stern, to wrestle with the strong;
"A little while," to sow the seed with weeping,
    Then bind the sheaves, and sing the harvest-song.

"A little while," to wear the weeds of sadness,
    To pace with weary step through miry ways;
Then to pour forth the fragrant oil of gladness,
    And clasp the girdle round the robe of praise.

"A little while," 'midst shadow and illusion,
    To strive, by faith, love's mysteries to spell;
Then read each dark enigma's bright solution,
    Then hail sight's verdict, "He doth all things well."

"A little while," the earthen pitcher taking
    To wayside brooks, from far-off fountains fed;
Then the cool lip its thirst for ever slaking
    Beside the fulness of the Fountain Head.

"A little while," to keep the oil from failing,
    "A little while," faith's flickering lamp to trim;
And then, the Bridegroom's coming footsteps hailing,
    To haste to meet Him with the bridal hymn.

And He, who is Himself the Gift and Giver,
    The future glory and the present smile,
With the bright promise of the glad "for ever"
    Will light the shadows of the "little while."

'SOON AND FOR EVER.'

BY JOHN S. B. MONSELL, Vicar of Egham; b. 1811. From his "Hymns of Love and Praise for the Church's Year." Lond. 1863, p. 167. Comp. Ps. xc. 10, "It is *soon* cut off, and we fly away," and, Thess. iv. 17, "So shall we *ever* be with the Lord."

"SOON and for ever,"
   Such promise our trust,
   Though ashes to ashes
  And dust unto dust;
"Soon and for ever"
  Our union shall be
Made perfect, our glorious
  Redeemer, in Thee:
When the sins and the sorrows
  Of time shall be o'er,
Its pangs and its partings
  Remembered no more,
Where life cannot fail, and where
  Death cannot sever,
Christians with Christ shall be
  "Soon and for ever."

"Soon and for ever,"
  The breaking of day
Shall drive all the night-clouds
  Of sorrow away;
"Soon and for ever"
  We'll see as we're seen,
And learn the deep meaning
  Of things that have been:
When fightings without us,
  And fears from within,
Shall weary no more in
  The warfare of sin;
Where fears, and where tears, and where
  Death shall be never,
Christians with Christ shall be
  "Soon and for ever."

"Soon and for ever"
  The work shall be done,

The warfare accomplished,
  The victory won;
"Soon and for ever"
  The soldier lays down
His sword for a harp, and
  His cross for a crown:
Then droop not in sorrow,
  Despond not in fear,
A glorious to-morrow
  Is brightening and near;
When (blessed reward
  Of each faithful endeavour)
Christians with Christ shall be
  "Soon and for ever."

WE SHALL SEE HIM IN OUR NATURE.

SELECTED from a longer poem of unknown authorship. 1868. "We shall see Him as He is."—1 *John* iii. 2.

"WE shall see Him," in our nature,
  Seated on His lofty Throne,
Loved, adored, by every creature,
  Owned as God, and God alone!

There the hosts of shining spirits
  Strike their harps, and loudly sing
To the praise of Jesus' merits,
  To the glory of their King.

When we pass o'er death's dark river,
  "We shall see Him as He is,"
Resting in His love and favour,
  Owning all the glory His.

There to cast our crowns before Him,
  Oh, what bliss the thought affords!
There for ever to adore Him,
  King of kings and Lord of lords!

PRAISE AND ADORATION OF CHRIST.

"My Lord and my God."—*John* **xx**. 28.
"That at the name of Jesus every knee should bow, of things in heaven and things in earth and things under the earth."—*Phil.* ii. 10.
"Worthy is the Lamb that was slain, to receive power, and riches, and wisdom, and strength, and honour, and glory, and blessing."—*Rev.* v. 12.

LORD JESUS CHRIST, in whom the whole fulness of the Godhead and Manhood, without sin, dwelleth in one Person for ever, who, for us men and for our salvation, didst die and rise again, and now sittest at the right hand of the Father Almighty, as our Prophet, Priest, and King, able and willing to save to the uttermost all that come unto God by Thee:—Thou art worthy to receive the grateful homage of all ages and creeds and tongues; and with the glorious company of the apostles, with the goodly fellowship of the prophets, with the noble army of martyrs, with the holy Church throughout all the world, with the heavenly Jerusalem, the joyful assembly of the first-born on high, with the innumerable host of angels around Thy throne, the heaven of heavens, and all the powers therein, we worship and adore Thy glorious name, saying, with a loud voice: Blessing and honour and glory and power be unto Him that sitteth upon the throne, and unto the Lamb, for ever and ever! Amen.

> "Lauda, Sion, Salvatorem,
> Lauda Ducem et Pastorem
>   In hymnis et canticis;
> Quantum vales, tantum aude,
> Quia major omni laude,
>   Nec laudare sufficis."

"To Him who loved the souls of men,
   And washed us in His blood,
To royal honours raised our head,
   And made us priests to God,—

To Him let every tongue be praise,
   And every heart be love;
All grateful honours paid on earth,
   And nobler songs above!

Thou art the First, and Thou the Last:
   Time centres all in Thee,—
The mighty Lord, who was, and is,
   And evermore shall be!"

PRAISE AND ADORATION OF CHRIST.

SHEPHERD OF TENDER YOUTH.

(Στόμιον πώλων ἀδαῶν.)

A FREE transfusion, by an unknown author, of the oldest Christian hymn extant (next to the "Gloria in Excelsis"), composed by CLEMENT of Alexandria, about A.D. 200. A sublime but somewhat turgid song of praise to the Logos, as the divine Educator and Leader of the human race. The Greek in the works of Clement (at the close of his "Pedagogue," p. 311, edit. Potter), and in DANIEL, III. p. 3. German versions by |Münter, Dorner, Hagenbach, Fortlage ; closer English versions by Mrs. CHARLES, and in the "Ante-Nicene Christian Library," vol. v. p. 343. A very learned article on the contents and structure of this hymn, by Professor PIPER, in his "Evangel. Kalender" for 1868, pp. 17-39.

SHEPHERD of tender youth,
  Guiding in love and truth
    Through devious ways;
  Christ, our triumphant King,
We come Thy name to sing,
And here our children bring
    To shout Thy praise!

  Thou art our Holy Lord,
  The all-subduing Word,
    Healer of strife!
  Thou didst Thyself abase,
  That from sin's deep disgrace
  Thou mightest save our race,
    And give us life.

  Thou art the great High Priest;
  Thou hast prepared the feast
    Of heavenly love.

While in our mortal pain,
None calls on Thee in vain;
Help Thou dost not disdain,
   Help from above.

Ever be Thou our Guide,
Our Shepherd, and our Pride,
   Our Staff and Song!
Jesus, Thou Christ of God,
By Thy perennial word
Lead us where Thou hast trod,
   Make our faith strong.

So now, and till we die,
Sound we Thy praises high,
   And joyful sing!
Let all the holy throng
Who to Thy Church belong,
Unite and swell the song
   To Christ our King!

THEE WE ADORE, ETERNAL LORD!

Part of "Te Deum Laudamus" (400), adapted to Christ. Anonymous [1842]. Slightly altered. Compare Sir R. Palmer, No. V.

THEE we adore, eternal Lord!
We praise Thy Name with one accord;
Thy saints, who here Thy goodness see,
Through all the world do worship Thee.

To Thee aloud all angels cry,
And ceaseless raise their songs on high;
Both cherubim and seraphim,
The heavens and all the powers therein.

The apostles join the glorious throng;
The prophets swell the immortal song;
The martyrs' noble army raise
Eternal anthems to Thy praise.

Thee, holy Prophet, Priest, and King!
Thee, Saviour of mankind, they sing:
Thus earth below, and heaven above,
Resound Thy glory and Thy love.

I GREET THEE.

(Je Te salue, mon certain Rédempteur.)

"SALUTATION to Jesus Christ." By JOHN CALVIN, the great Reformer; b.1509; d., at Geneva, 1564. This hymn, together with eleven others (mostly translations of Psalms), written in French, was recently discovered by Felix Bovet, of Neuchatel, in an old Genevese prayer-book, and first published in the sixth volume of the new edition of the works of Calvin by Baum, Cunitz, and Reuss, 1868. It reveals a poetic vein, and a devotional fervour and tenderness, which one could hardly have suspected in the severe logician. (His "Epinicion Christo Cantatum," A.D. 1537, is not devotional, but a controversial poem against popery.) German translation by Dr. E. Stähelin, of Basel (author of a biography of Calvin, in 2 vols.) English translation by Mrs. Professor H. B. SMITH, of New York, 1868. Contributed.

GREET Thee, who my sure Redeemer art,
My only Trust, and Saviour of my heart!
Who so much toil and woe
And pain didst undergo,
For my poor, worthless sake;
And pray Thee, from our hearts,
All idle griefs and smarts,
And foolish cares to take.[1]

Thou art the King of mercy and of grace,
Reigning omnipotent in every place;
So come, O King! and deign
Within our hearts to reign,

---

[1] We give the first stanza in the original old French:

"Je Te salue, mon certain Rédempteur,
Ma vraye fianc' et mon seul Salvateur,
Qui tant de labeur,
D'ennuys et de douleur
As enduré pour moy:
Oste de noz cueurs
Toutes vaines langueurs,
Fol soucy et es moy."

And our whole being sway;
  Shine in us by Thy light,
  And lead us to the height
Of Thy pure, heavenly day.

Thou art the Life by which alone we live,
And all our substance and our strength receive:
  Comfort us by Thy faith
  Against the pains of death;
Sustain us by Thy power;
  Let not our fears prevail,
  Nor our hearts faint or fail,
When comes the trying hour.

Thou art the true and perfect gentleness,
No harshness hast Thou, and no bitterness:
  Make us to taste and prove,
  Make us adore and love
The sweet grace found in Thee;
  With longing to abide
  Ever at Thy dear side,
In Thy sweet unity.

Our hope is in no other save in Thee,
Our faith is built upon Thy promise free;
  Come, and our hope increase,
  Comfort and give us peace,
Make us so strong and sure,
  That we shall conquerors be,
  And well and patiently
Shall every ill endure.

Poor, banished exiles, wretched sons of Eve,
Full of all sorrows, unto Thee we grieve!
  To Thee we bring our sighs,
  Our groanings, and our cries:
Thy pity, Lord, we crave;
  We take the sinner's place,
  And pray Thee, of Thy grace,
To pardon and to save.

Turn Thy sweet eyes upon our low estate,
Our Mediator and our Advocate,
  Propitiator best!
  Give us that vision blest,

The God of gods most High!
  And let us, by Thy right,
  Enter the blessèd light
And glories of the sky!

Oh, pitiful and gracious as Thou art,
The lovely Bridegroom of the holy heart,
    Lord Jesus Christ, meet Thou
      The Antichrist our foe,
    In all his cruel ruth!
      Thy Spirit give, that we
      May, in true verity,
    Follow Thy word of truth.

COME, LET US JOIN.

ISAAC WATTS. 1709. "Christ Jesus, the Lamb of God, worshipped by all the creation." Rev. v. 11-13. I reluctantly omit, from want of space, his "Join all the glorious names" (twelve stanzas).

COME, let us join our cheerful songs
  With angels round the throne;
Ten thousand thousand are their tongues,
  But all their joys are one.

" Worthy the Lamb that died," they cry,
  " To be exalted thus!"
" Worthy the Lamb!" our lips reply,
  " For He was slain for us."

Jesus is worthy to receive
  Honour and power divine;
And blessings more than we can give,
  Be, Lord, for ever Thine!

Let all that dwell above the sky,
  And air and earth and seas,
Conspire to lift Thy glories high,
  And speak Thine endless praise.

The whole creation join in one,
  To bless the sacred name
Of Him who sits upon the throne,
  And to adore the Lamb!

O FOR A THOUSAND TONGUES!

CHARLES WESLEY. 1740. Based on Isa. xii. 2; xxxv. 5, 6; xlv. 22; John i. 29; Matt. xi. 5; xxiv. 14. Originally eighteen verses. The last four are generally omitted in hymn books, also in Sir R. PALMER's "Book of Praise." ROGERS gives eight, PALMER only five verses.

FOR a thousand tongues to sing
    My great Redeemer's praise!
The glories of my God and King,
    The triumphs of His grace!

My gracious Master and my God,
    Assist me to proclaim,
To spread through all the earth abroad,
    The honours of Thy name.

Jesus! the name that charms[1] our fears,
    That bids our sorrows cease;
'Tis music in the sinner's ears;
    'Tis life and health and peace!

He breaks the power of cancelled sin;[2]
    He sets the prisoner free;
His blood can make the foulest clean;
    His blood availed for me.

He speaks; and, listening to His voice,
    New life the dead receive;
The mournful, broken hearts rejoice;
    The humble poor believe.

Hear Him, ye deaf! His praise, ye dumb,
    Your loosened tongues employ!
Ye blind, behold your Saviour come;
    And leap, ye lame, for joy!

Look unto Him, ye nations! own
    Your God, ye fallen race!
Look, and be saved through faith alone,
    Be justified by grace!

---

[1] Popular collections substitute "*calms*."
[2] Usually changed into "*reigning* sin."

See all your sins on Jesus laid:
  The Lamb of God was slain;
His soul was once an offering made
  For every soul of man.

Awake from guilty nature's sleep,
  And Christ shall give you light;
Cast all your sins into the deep,
  And wash the Ethiop white.

With Me, your chief, ye then shall know,
  Shall feel, your sins forgiven;
Anticipate your heaven below,
  And own that love is heaven.

YE SERVANTS OF GOD.

Charles Wesley. 1740.

YE servants of God,
    Your Master proclaim,
  And publish abroad
    His wonderful name:
  The name, all victorious,
    Of Jesus extol;
  His kingdom is glorious,
    And rules over all.

God ruleth on high
  Almighty to save;
And still He is nigh;
  His presence we have:
The great congregation
  His triumph shall sing,
Ascribing salvation
  To Jesus, our King.

Salvation to God,
  Who sits on the throne,
Let all cry aloud,
  And honour the Son:

Our Saviour's high praises
  The angels proclaim,—
Fall down on their faces
  And worship the Lamb.

Then let us adore,
  And give Him his right—
All glory and power
  And wisdom and might;
All honour and blessing,
  With angels above,
And thanks never ceasing,
  And infinite love!

AWAKE, AND SING THE SONG.

WILLIAM HAMMOND, a Calvinistic Methodist preacher, afterwards a Moravian; d. 1783, at Chelsea. His "Psalms, Hymns, and Spiritual Songs" were published at London, 1745. Abridged. By condensation, this fine but somewhat repetitious hymn is made more effective. PALMER gives Madan's variation of 1760, eight verses.

AWAKE, and sing the song
  Of Moses and the Lamb;
Tune every heart and every tongue,
  To praise the Saviour's name.

Sing of His dying love;
  Sing of His rising power;
Sing how He intercedes above
  For those whose sins He bore.

Tell, in seraphic strains,
  What Christ has done for you;
How He has taken off your chains,
  And formed your hearts anew.

Are you in deep distress?
  Then sing to ease the smart.
Are you rejoiced? let psalms express
  The gladness of your heart.

When Paul and Silas sung,
  The earth began to quake;
The prison doors were open flung,
  Her firm foundations shake.

Sing, till you feel your hearts
  Ascending with your tongues;
Sing, till the love of sin departs,
  And grace inspires your songs.

Sing on your heavenly way:
  Ye ransomed sinners, sing!
Sing on, rejoicing every day,
  In Christ the eternal King.

Soon shall our raptured tongue
  In heaven His praise proclaim,
And sweeter voices tune the song
  Of Moses and the Lamb.

HAIL, THOU ONCE DESPISED JESUS!

JOHN BAKEWELL, b. 1721; d 1819; a Wesloyan minister. His gravestone records: "He adorned the doctrine of God our Saviour eighty years, and preached his glorious gospel about seventy years" The following hymn appeared first in Madan's Collection, in 1760; then in Toplady's Collection, in 1776, with an additional stanza, borrowed from James Allen. We give the original text from ROGERS, p. 29. Sir R. Palmer follows Toplady's Collection.

HAIL, Thou once despisèd Jesus!
  Hail, Thou Galilean King!
Who didst suffer to release us;
  Who didst free salvation bring:
Hail, Thou universal Saviour,[1]
  Who hast borne our sin and shame!
By whose merits we find favour;
  Life is given through Thy name.

---

[1] Toplady's Collection and R. Palmer substitute "*agonizing* Saviour," which is certainly no improvement.

Paschal Lamb, by God appointed,
   All our sins were on Thee laid;
By almighty love appointed,
   Thou hast full atonement made:
Every sin may be forgiven
   Through the virtue of Thy blood;
Opened is the gate of heaven;
   Peace is made 'twixt man and God.

Jesus, hail! enthroned in glory,
   There for ever to abide;
All the heavenly hosts adore Thee,
   Seated at Thy Father's side:
There for sinners Thou art pleading;
   " Spare them yet another year;"[1]
Thou for saints art interceding,
   Till in glory they appear.

Worship, honour, power, and blessing,
   Christ is worthy to receive;
Loudest praises, without ceasing,
   Meet it is for us to give.
Help, ye bright angelic spirits!
   Bring your sweetest, noblest lays!
Help to sing our Jesu's merits;
   Help to chant Immanuel's praise.

NOW LET US JOIN.

JOHN NEWTON, 1779. From the "Olney Hymns," Book ii. No 39.
Palmer omits verse 3.

NOW let us join with hearts and tongues,
   And emulate the angels' songs;
Yea, sinners may address their King
   In songs that angels cannot sing.

---

[1] Toplady's Collection and Palmer:—
   " There thou dost our place prepare."

They praise the Lamb who once was slain;
But we can add a higher strain;
Not only say: " He suffered thus,"
But that " He suffered all for us."

When angels by transgression fell,
Justice consigned them all to hell;
But mercy formed a wondrous plan,
To save and honour fallen man.

Jesus, who passed the angels by,
Assumed our flesh to bleed and die;
And still He makes it His abode:
As Man He fills the throne of God.

Our next of kin, our Brother now,
Is He to whom the angels bow;
They join with us to praise His Name,
And we the nearest interest claim.

But ah! how faint our praises rise!
Sure 'tis the wonder of the skies,
That we, who share His richest love,
So cold and unconcerned should prove.

O glorious hour! it comes with speed,
When we, from sin and darkness freed,
Shall see the God who died for man,
And praise Him more than angels can.

AWAKE, MY SOUL, IN JOYFUL LAYS.

SAMUEL MEDLEY, a Baptist minister at Liverpool, d. 1799; author of 232 hymns, which appeared in 1800.

AWAKE, my soul in joyful lays,
And sing thy great Redeemer's praise;
He justly claims a song from me;
His loving-kindness, O how free![1]

---

[1] Originally: "*is so* free," and so throughout. See ROGERS, p. 400.

He saw me ruined in the fall,
Yet loved me notwithstanding all;
He saved me from my lost estate;
His loving-kindness, O how great!

When I was Satan's easy prey,
And deep in debt and bondage lay,
He paid His life for my discharge;
His loving-kindness, O how large!

Through mighty hosts of cruel foes,
Where earth and hell my way oppose,
He safely leads my soul along;
His loving-kindness, O how strong!

When earthly friends forsake me quite,
And I have neither skill nor might,
He's sure my helper to appear;
His loving-kindness, O how near!

Often I feel my sinful heart
Prone from my Jesus to depart;
But though I have Him oft forgot,
His loving-kindness changes not!

When I shall pass death's gloomy vale,
And life and mortal powers must fail,
Oh! may my last expiring breath
His loving-kindness sing in death.

Then shall I mount and soar away
To the bright world of endless day;
And sing with rapture and surprise
His loving-kindness in the skies.

There with their golden harps I'll join,
And with their anthems mingle mine,
And loudly sound on every chord
The loving-kindness of my Lord.

HOSANNA TO THE LIVING LORD!

Bishop Reginald Heber, of Calcutta. 1827. For Advent Sunday. The text from his "Poetical Works." Lond. 1854, p. 42.

HOSANNA to the living Lord!
Hosanna to the Incarnate Word!
To Christ, Creator, Saviour, King,
Let earth, let heaven, Hosanna sing!
   Hosanna, Lord! Hosanna in the highest!

Hosanna, Lord! Thine angels cry;
Hosanna, Lord! Thy saints reply;
Above, beneath us, and around,
The dead and living swell the sound:
   Hosanna, Lord! Hosanna in the highest!

Oh, Saviour! with protecting care,
Return to this Thy house of prayer;
Assembled in Thy sacred name,
Where we Thy parting promise claim:
   Hosanna, Lord! Hosanna in the highest!

But, chiefest, in our cleansed breast,
Eternal, bid Thy Spirit rest;
And make our secret soul to be
A temple pure, and worthy Thee:
   Hosanna, Lord! Hosanna in the highest!

So, in the last and dreadful day,
When earth and heaven shall melt away,
Thy flock, redeemed from sinful stain,
Shall swell the sound of praise again:
   Hosanna, Lord! Hosanna in the highest!

THOU WHOM WE SEEK.

(Du, den wir suchen auf so finstern Wegen.)

"To the Invisible" ("An den Unsichtbaren"). A sonnet, by LUDWIG UHLAND, one of the purest, most patriotic, and most popular poets of Germany; the head of the "Swabian School;" b. 1787, at Tübingen, where he lived in happy independence and modest retirement till his death, in 1862. Of his poems, which appeared first in 1815, a new edition has been published, since 1833, almost every year. This sonnet, as also his "Shepherd's Sunday Hymn," and his "Lost Church," reveal a genuine and deep religious feeling; although it was not so fully developed in him as in his bosom friends and Swabian fellow-poets, Gustav Schwab and Justinus Kerner. Faithfully translated by Mrs. ELIZABETH L. SMITH, New York, 1868. Contributed. Another translation, by SAMUEL J. PIKE, commences:

"Thou whom we seek in paths where shadows reign."

THOU whom we seek in darkness, still unseen,
    And cannot with our searching thoughts embrace,
Once Thou didst leave the cloud which hides Thy face,
Before Thy people walking forth serene.

What sweet delight to gaze upon Thy mien,
    And listen to Thy words of truth and grace!
    Oh, blessed they who at Thy board found place!
Oh, blessed he who on Thy breast did lean!

Therefore not strange the longing, when the host
    Of countless pilgrims o'er the seas did press,
And armies fought upon the farthest coast,

Only to pray at Thy sepulchral bed,
    Only in pious fervency to kiss
The holy soil on which Thy feet did tread!

TO HIM, WHO FOR OUR SINS.

ARTHUR TOZER RUSSELL. 1851. From R. PALMER'S "Book of Praise," No. LXVII.

O Him, who for our sins was slain,
    To Him, for all His dying pain,
            Sing we Hallelujah!

To Him, the Lamb our sacrifice,
Who gave His soul our ransom-price,
        Sing we Hallelujah!

To Him, who died that we might die
To sin, and live with him on high,
        Sing we Hallelujah!
To Him, who rose that we might rise
And reign with Him beyond the skies,
        Sing we Hallelujah!

To Him, who now for us doth plead,
And helpeth us in all our need,
        Sing we Hallelujah!
To Him, who doth prepare on high
Our home in immortality,
        Sing we Hallelujah!

To Him be glory evermore;
Ye heavenly hosts, your Lord adore;
        Sing we Hallelujah!
To Father, Son, and Holy Ghost,
One God most great, our joy and boast,
        Sing we Hallelujah!

THOU THAT ART THE FATHER'S WORD.

HENRY ALFORD, D.D., Dean of Canterbury; b. at London, Oct. 7, 1810. Written 1832. From his "Year of Praise," Lond. 1867, No. 32.

THOU that art the Father's Word,
Thou that art the Lamb of God,
Thou that art the Virgin's Son,
Thou that savest souls undone,
    Sacred sacrifice for sin,
    Fount of piety within:
        Hail, Lord Jesus!

Thou to whom Thine angels raise,
Quiring songs of sweetest praise,

Thou that art the flower and fruit,
Virgin born from Jesse's root,
   Shedding holy peace abroad,
   Perfect man and perfect God:
     Hail, Lord Jesus!

Thou that art the door of heaven,
Living bread in mercy given,
Brightness of the Father's face,
Everlasting Prince of Peace,
   Precious pearl beyond all price,
   Brightest star in all the skies:
     Hail, Lord Jesus!

King and Spouse of holy hearts,
Fount of love that ne'er departs,
Sweetest life, and brightest day,
Truest truth, and surest way,
   That leads onward to the blest
   Sabbath of eternal rest:
     Hail, Lord Jesus!

PRAISE TO JESUS!

WILLIAM BALL; bred to the bar; residing near Rydal, Westmoreland; a member of the Society of Friends; author of "Hymns and Lyrics," published, 1864, for private circulation. From ROGERS's "Lyra Brit." p. 645.

PRAISE to Jesus! Praise to God
   For the love He sheds abroad,
   Lightening o'er a world of sin,
Glowing in the heart within.

For the pristine promise made
E'en in Eden's darkened shade,
For the light of sacrifice,
Till the Morning Star should rise.

For the harp of prophecy,
Singing of redemption nigh;
For the Branch of Jesse's stem;
For the birth at Bethlehem.

PRAISE TO JESUS.

For the sacred standard spread;
For the life our Pattern led;
For His precept pure and true;
For His doctrine, like the dew.

For His love's inviting call,
All embracing, seeking all;
For the grace and truth He brought.
For the ransom He hath wrought.

For the crown of thorns He wore;
For the painful cross He bore;
For the dying word He said,
Sealed with blood of sprinkling shed.

For the radiant rising dawn,
For the sting of death withdrawn;
For the victory gained so well
O'er the grave, and over hell.

For His glorious reign on high,
When He rose from Bethany;
For the heavenly peace He leaves;
For the Comforter He gives.

For His parting promise dear
Of His presence, alway near;
For the blest assurance made
Of His intercessory aid.

For the pledge that we shall rise,
In His likeness, to the skies;
For the merciful decree
That our Friend our Judge shall be.

All redeeming bounty gives;
All that humble faith receives;
All that rising doubt restrains;
All that drooping hope sustains,—

Saviour! these to Thee we owe,
From Thy dying love they flow;
And we praise, for grace so free,
Thee, Jehovah-Jesus, Thee!

THOU KING ANOINTED.

(Rex Christe, Factor omnium.)

A HYMN to Christ the King, by the Rev. JAMES INGLIS, New York, 1868. Contributed. Suggested by a Latin hymn of GREGORY THE GREAT (590-604) : " In passione Domini " (al. " In cœna Domini "), DANIEL, I. p. 180.

THOU King anointed, at whose word
    A world from nothing answ'ring came,
The world, redeemed, shall own Thee Lord,
    And yield its honours to Thy name.
To Thee, low-bending down Thine ear,
    The suppliant never pleads in vain,—
Our lowly homage swift to hear,
    Though angels swell the rival strain.

Eternal life flows from Thy wound;
    Grace, in Thy very weakness strong,
Dissolves the tyrant's chains, which bound
    Our souls, to ruin dragged along,
Each star is but another gem
    To garnish the Creator's crown;
Yet Thou, the Babe of Bethlehem,
    The humblest wilt a brother own!

Thy hand the secret influence wove
    That links in one things great and small;
Thy hands were fettered to remove
    The tangled net of Satan's thrall.
Nailed to the cross, Thy piteous cry
    Scarce pierced the shout of hellish rage;
Thy whisper shakes the earth and sky;
    Thy glance sheds darkness on the age.

Almighty Victor! from the height
    Of Thy paternal glory bend;
From dangers of the thick'ning night,
    Thy people, best of kings, defend.
The darkness of the night dispel;
    Reveal the splendours of Thy throne;
O'erthrow the reign of Death and Hell,
    And take the kingdoms for Thine own.

AS ON A VAST ETERNAL SHORE.

By Mrs. Dr. G. L. Prentiss, of New York. 1869. Contributed.

AS on a vast eternal shore,
    The waves unceasing roll.
So He, whom all the worlds adore,
    Blesses thy soul, O child of earth—
    Blesses thy human soul.

Then roll thou back, in tidal waves,
    Thanksgivings to His name;
Sing Christ, sing Christ, who loves and saves,
    Who built thy mortal frame, my soul—
    Who built thy mortal frame.

Day follows day, night follows night;
    And ever on their wings
Christ sends thee joy and peace and light;
    Each hour a blessing brings, my heart—
    Each hour a blessing brings.

Then let each day become a song,
    And every night a hymn;
Each hour the song the hymn prolong,
    Till tears thine eyes bedim, thrice blest!
    Sweet tears thine eyes bedim.

Count up thy mercies, child of clay;
    Recount them o'er and o'er;
Yet canst thou tell, in life's short day,
    The sands upon the shore, O child?
    The sands upon the shore?

Nay then, but thou in heaven shalt sing,
    Sing songs to Christ for aye,
Exultant shall thy praises ring
    Through an eternal day, glad heart—
    Through an eternal day!

GLORY BE TO GOD THE FATHER!

HORATIUS BONAR, D.D. "Hymns of Faith and Hope," Third Series, 1868.

GLORY be to God the Father!
　　Glory be to God the Son!
　Glory be to God the Spirit!
Great Jehovah, Three in One!
　　Glory, glory,
While eternal ages run!

Glory be to Him who loved us,
　Washed us from each spot and stain!
Glory be to Him who bought us,
　Made us kings with Him to reign!
　　Glory, glory
To the Lamb that once was slain!

Glory to the King of angels!
　Glory to the Church's King!
Glory to the King of nations!
　Heaven and earth your praises bring,—
　　Glory, glory
To the King of glory bring!

Glory, blessing, praise eternal!
　Thus the choir of angels sings;
Honour, riches, power, dominion!
　Thus its praise creation brings;
　　Glory, glory,
Glory to the King of kings!

CHRIST THE THEME OF SONG IN ALL AGES.

By Anson D. F. Randolph. Written for this Collection, as a finale, New York, September, 1863.

OH, endless theme of never-ceasing song
    And music, wakened by supremest love!
    How hath it broke from feeble lips and strong,
        The power divine, and matchless grace to prove:
Christ Son of God, and Christ the Son of Man;
    Christ on the Cross, and Christ in kingly Reign.
So through the ages, since the song began,
    With swelling hosts, the saints repeat the strain.

On hills and plains the Israelite only knew,
    On classic soil, on drifting desert sand,
Where'er the Roman eagles swiftly flew,
    Or roamed abroad the fierce ungoverned band;
'Mong Jew and Gentile, as in wandering horde,
    Barbarian, Scythian, all, the bond, or free,—
There were who watched and waited for the Lord,
    And some who did His mighty wonders see.

How from the warm and ever-ruddy East,
    Far to the rugged North and golden West,
The knowledge of this wondrous Christ increased,
    With life and hope the dying nations blessed:
Thence saints, exultant, onward bore His sign
    From land to land, and compassed every shore;
One Lord, one faith, one aim, one end divine,
    Their theme and song, their life for evermore!

Since holy women bowed their heads and wept,
    Where from the grave the angel rolled the stone,—
That grave where He, the Son of God, had slept
    As Son of Man, in darkness and alone,—

What countless names the world's applause have won!
    What notes of praise have men to these inscribed!
How soon were they forgotten, one by one,
    And earth's poor honours to the dead denied!

Not mightiest kings the earth has ever seen,
    Nor time, nor powers men honoured or abhorred,
Could crush the memory of the Nazarene,
    Or shut the saints from presence of their Lord:
In kingly courts, in prisons foul and damp,
    In scenes tumultuous, as in homes of peace,
There, with His own, God's Angel would encamp,
    There rise the songs that nevermore shall cease!

Thus through the years of ages long ago,
    Thus in the changes of these latter days:
ONE ONLY LORD, OUR LORD, ABOVE, BELOW,
    AND HE THE OBJECT OF OUR ENDLESS PRAISE:
This the same key-note of unnumbered lyres,
    This, too, th' unending song of sweet accord.
O world! ye have no theme that thus inspires:
    Ye still reject and crucify the Lord.

In furnace-fires, on mountains drear and cold;
    In peasant hut, as in the palace-hall,
The story of His life for ever told.
    And His dear love the burning theme of all:
From lips too weak aught human to express,
    From noble hearts that held the world at bay,
What songs have risen, and what strains confess
    The blessed ONE whom I would praise to-day!

CHRIST SON OF GOD, AND CHRIST THE SON OF MAN;
    CHRIST ON THE CROSS, AND CHRIST IN KINGLY REIGN!
So sang the saints when first the song began,
    So shall it rise a never-ending strain.
Come, Thou, and touch my lips, that I may sing;
    Come, fill my heart with love to overflow:
My Lord, my Life, I would some tribute bring,
    And tell the world how much to Thee I owe!

THE END.

GENERAL ALPHABETICAL LIST OF HYMNS.

	PAGE
ABIDE with me! fast falls the eventide . . .	419
A Child is born in Bethlehem .	38
A great and mighty wonder .	31
A hymn of glory let us sing .	239
A pilgrim through this lonely world	116
A sinful man am I	374
A star shines forth in heaven .	85
Again the Lord of life and light	218
Ah! Jesus let me hear Thy voice	450
All hail the power of Jesus' name	253
All hail, thou night	37
All my heart this night rejoices	45
All praise to Thee, eternal Lord	42
All ye Gentile lands awake .	89
Alone with Thee, alone with Thee!	416
Amid life's wild commotion .	425
Amid the darkness when the storm	383
Angels, from the realms of glory	57
Angels, roll the rock away . .	229
Are there no wounds for me .	175
Art thou weary, art thou languid	354
As on a vast eternal shore . .	565
Ask ye what great thing I know	165
Asleep in Jesus! blessed sleep.	521
As with gladness men of old .	95
At the cross her station keeping	136
Awake, and sing the song . .	554
Awake glad soul, awake! awake!	230
Awake, my soul, in joyful lays	557
Awake, sweet harp of Judah, wake	362

	PAGE
BEHOLD, the Bridegroom cometh	10
Behold the day the Lord hath made	195
Behold the glories of the Lamb	271
Behold, where, in a mortal form	107
Beneath the shadow of the Cross	341
Bethlehem, of noblest cities .	86
Blest morning, whose young .	210
Body of Jesus, O sweet food .	474
Bound upon the accursed tree	163
Bride of the Lamb, awake! awake!	310
Brief life is here our portion .	512
Brightest and best of the sons .	92
By Christ redeemed, in Christ restored	476

	PAGE
CAROL, brothers, carol . . .	62
Cease, ye tearful mourners . .	506
Chief of sinners, though I be .	454
Christ is arisen	222
Christ, the Life of all the living	146
Christ the Lord is risen again	203
Christ the Lord is risen to-day	212
Christ, Thou the champion. .	267
Christ, whose first appearance lighted	93
Cling to the Crucified	166
Come hither, ye faithful . . .	37
Come, let us join our cheerful songs	551
Come, Jesus! come!	8
Come, Lord, and tarry not . .	308
Come, my Way, my Truth, my Life	102
Come, to Calvary's holy mountain	160

GENERAL ALPHABETICAL

	Page
Come, weary souls, with sin distressed	394
Come, ye faithful, raise the strain	191
Come, ye lofty! come, ye lowly!	63
Come, ye saints, look here and wonder	217
Compared with Christ, in all beside	492
Conquering Prince and Lord of glory	250
Courage, my sorely tempted heart	356
Day of judgment! Day of wonders	303
Day of wrath! O Day of mourning	293
Day of wrath! that Day foretold	290
Dear Saviour! we are Thine. See *My Saviour! I am*.	
Dearest of all the names above	329
Deck thyself, my soul, with gladness	470
Draw nigh, draw nigh, Emmanuel	13
Earth has nothing sweet or fair	103
Ere yet the dawn has filled the skies	206
Eternal God of earth and air	421
Ever is my peril near	438
Ever would I fain be reading	109
Exalt, exalt, the heavenly gates	240
Fairest Lord Jesus	325
Fierce was the wild billow	353
Fling out the Banner! let it float	100
For thee, O dear, dear Country	513
For ever with the Lord	523
Forth flames the standard of our King	130
From every stormy wind that blows	364
From lands that see the sun arise	35
From where the rising sun goes forth	32
Glorious Head, Thou livest now	212
Glory be to God the Father	566
Go and dig my grave to-day	536
God comes;—and who shall stand	285
Good news from heaven	43
Guide me, O thou great Jehovah	521

	Page
Hail, Day of days! in peals of praise	185
Hail, infant martyrs	80
Hail the day that sees Him rise	251
Hail! Thou Head!	130
Hail, Thou once despised Jesus	555
Hallelujah! Hallelujah	194
Hallelujah! I believe	428
Hark! how all the welkin rings	51
Hark, my soul! it is the Lord	333
Hark! the glad sound	52
Hark! the voice of love and mercy	157
Hark! what mean those holy voices	56
Heart of Christ my King!	322
Height of heaven, why art Thou lying	40
Heavenward still our pathway tends	249
Here would I feed	464
He comes, no royal vesture wearing	25
He who on earth as man was known	274
He is gone; beyond the skies	261
Him on yonder cross I love	151
Hope of our hearts, O Lord! appear	309
Hosanna! raise the pealing hymn	277
Hosanna to the living Lord	559
Hosanna to the Prince of light	248
How lovely shines the Morning Star	441
How sweet the name of Jesus sounds	334
How wondrous are the works of God	331
I bore with thee long weary days	345
I give my heart to Thee	482
I greet Thee	549
I heard the voice of Jesus say	374
I know in whom I put my trust	426
I lay my sins on Jesus	167
I leave Thee not: Thou art my Jesus	444
I need Thee, precious Jesus	384
I once was a stranger	430
I place an offering at Thy shrine	487
I say to all men, far and near	215
I've found a joy in sorrow	410
I was a wandering sheep	336
I would not live alway	525
If only I have Thee	399
If the dark and awful tomb	190

LIST OF HYMNS.

	Page
Immortal Love, for ever full	117
In Bethlehem, the Lord of glory	69
In memory of the Saviour's love	473
In the bonds of Death He lay	204
In the cross of Christ I glory	158
In the hours of pain and sorrow	380
In the silent midnight watches	342
In Thy glorious Resurrection	232
In Thy service will I ever	452
It came upon the midnight clear	67
It is not death to die	532
Jerusalem the golden	515
Jesu, lover of my soul	359
Jesu, my Lord, my God, my All	499
Jesu, name all names above	317
Jesu, the very thought of Thee	318
Jesu, to Thy table led	475
Jesus Christ is risen to-day	198
Jesus! gentle Sufferer say	170
Jesus' holy Cross and dying	132
Jesus, how much Thy name unfolds	337
Jesus, how sweet Thy memory is	321
Jesus, I live to Thee	459
Jesus, I love Thee,—not because	483
Jesus, I love Thee evermore	484
Jesus, I love Thy charming name	491
Jesus, I my cross have taken	110
Jesus, immutably the same	446
Jesus is God! the solid earth	278
Jesus, lead us with Thy power	448
Jesus lives, and so shall I	214
Jesus, Lord of life eternal	241
Jesus, my chief pleasure	389
Jesus, my Lord! my life, my all	398
Jesus, my Lord, Thy nearness	394
Jesus, my Lord, 'tis sweet to rest	413
Jesus, my Redeemer, lives	207
Jesus' name shall ever be	341
Jesus, pro me perforatus	361
Jesus shall reign where'er the sun	270
Jesus, still lead on	105
Jesus, the rays divine	418
Jesus, these eyes have never seen	500
Jesus, Thou Joy of loving hearts	481
Jesus, Thy blood and righteousness	153
Jesus, Thy boundless love to me	486
Jesus, Thy Church, with longing eyes	305
Jesus! when my soul is parting	535
Joy and gladness! joy and gladness	65
Joy to the world, the Lord is come	50
Just as I am,—without one plea	369
Just as thou art, without one trace	370
King of kings, and wilt Thou deign	280
Lamb, the once crucified	256
Late, late, so late!	307
Let me be with Thee where Thou art	522
Let not your heart be faint	411
Let the earth now praise the Lord	16
Let Zion's sons and daughters say	199
Lift up your heads, ye mighty gates	15
Life's mystery—deep, restless	434
Listen to the wondrous story	346
Lo! God, our God, has come	68
Lo! God to heaven ascendeth	246
Lo! He comes! Let all adore Him	21
Lo! He comes with clouds descending	301
Lo, the Day!—the Day of Life	296
Lo, the feast is spread to-day	477
Lo, the storms of life are breaking	375
Long did I toil	402
Long hast thou wept	372
Lord, how shall I be meeting	17
Lord, it belongs not to my care	519
Lord Jesus Christ, in Thee alone	355
Lord, let my heart still turn to Thee	456
Lord, Thou art mine, and I am Thine	443
Love divine, all loves excelling	330
"Lovest thou Me?"	498
Mary! put thy grief away	200
Messiah, at Thy glad approach	20
More than all, one thing my heart	497
Morning breaks upon the tomb	218
Most holy Jesus, fount of light	101
My dear Redeemer and my Lord	104
My faith looks up to Thee	427
My home in heaven	505
My Jesus, if the seraphim	268
My Saviour! I am Thine	446
My Saviour, 'mid life's varied scene	378
My sins, my sins, my Saviour	169

GENERAL ALPHABETICAL

	Page
No more, ah, no more	508
No, no, it is not dying	531
Not all the blood of beasts	149
Now I have found a friend	405
Now I have found the ground wherein	357
Now let our cheerful eyes survey	273
Now let us join	556
Now thy gentle Lamb, O Sion	197
O ABIDE, abide in Jesus	495
O blessed Lord	460
O blessed Sun, whose splendour	403
O Bread of Life from heaven	469
O Christ, our true and only light	88
O Christ, the Lord of heaven, to Thee	281
O Christ, who hast prepared a place	243
O for a closer walk with God	396
O for a thousand tongues to sing	552
O Friend of souls! how blest the time	391
O God, unseen, yet ever near	474
O happy house	453
O Head so full of bruises	173
O Heaven! Sweet Heaven!	539
O holy Saviour, Friend unseen	429
O Jesu, who art gone before	244
O Jesu! King most wonderful	320
O Jesu! Thou the beauty art	320
O Jesus! sweet the tears I shed	172
O Jesus! when I think of Thee	229
O Lamb of God, who, bleeding	465
O Lord! I love Thee from my heart	485
O Love divine, how sweet Thou art	490
O Love too boundless to be shewn	150
O Love, who formedst me to wear	325
O Paradise! O Paradise!	530
O risen Lord! O conquering King!	208
O sacred Head! now wounded	142
O sacred Head, surrounded	145
O sweet home-echo!	533
O Thou Redeemer of our race	9
O Thou! who by a star didst guide	94
O wondrous mother!	81
O world! behold upon the tree	140
O'er the distant mountains	27
O'erwhelmed in depths of woe	135
Of the Father's love begotten	34
Oh, endless theme	567
Oh for a heart to praise my God	106
O for the peace which floweth	541

	Page
O for the robes of whiteness	540
Oh, gift of gifts	422
Oh how could I forget Him	494
Oh, how wondrous is the story	53
Oh, Jesus Christ, grow Thou in me	108
Oh! long and darksome was the night	1
Oh, Paradise must fairer be	529
On earth awhile, 'mid sufferings tried	241
On Jordan's bank, the Baptist's cry	12
On Thee, O Jesus! strongly leaning	455
Once He came in blessing	14
One there is, above all others	335
One thing's needful: then, Lord Jesus	327
Oppressed with noon-day scorching	166
Our Lord is risen from the dead	253
Our lot is fallen in pleasant places	339
PLUNGED in a gulf of dark despair	19
Ponder thou the cross all holy	134
Praise to Jesus! Praise to God	562
REGION of life and light	516
Rejoice! the Lord is King	272
Rejoice, all ye believers	299
Resting from His work to-day	181
Rest of the weary, Joy of the sad	412
Rest of the weary! Thou	180
Rest, weary Son of God	182
Rest, weary soul!	409
Ride on, ride on in majesty	163
Rock of ages, cleft for me	360, 361
SAVIOUR! when, in dust, to Thee	365
See a poor sinner, dearest Lord	424
See, the Conqueror mounts in triumph	259
See the ransomed millions stand	277
Shepherd of tender youth	547
Since Christ is gone to heaven	245
Since o'er thy footstool here below	526
Sing aloud, children	233
Sing, and the mystery declare	468
Sing, my tongue, the mystery telling	465
Sing, my tongue, the Saviour's battle	125

LIST OF HYMNS.

	Page
Sing, O Heavens! O Earth, rejoice!	262
Sleep, Holy Babe	77
Soft cloud, that, while the breeze	255
Sons of men, behold from far	91
Soon and for ever	542
Souls of men, why will ye scatter	344
Star of morn and even	538
Still on Thy loving heart let me repose	338
Still, still with Thee	458
Still thy sorrow, Magdalena	201
Strong Son of God	433
Suffering Saviour, Lamb of God	471
Sun of my soul, Thou Saviour dear	448
Sun, shine forth in all thy splendour	220
Surely Christ thy griefs has borne	155
Sweet the moments, rich in blessing	154
Sweet was the hour, O Lord! to Thee	415
Tell me not of earthly love	406
That Day of wrath!	295
That great Day of wrath and terror	287
That Holy One	500
That mystic word of Thine	457
The atoning work is done	276
The chariot! the chariot!	306
The children of the world	420
The Church has waited long	26
The Church of God lifts up her voice	189
The Day is near	286
The foe behind, the deep before	223
The God whom earth and sea and sky	75
The grave is empty now	216
The happy Christmas comes	61
The Head that once was crowned	275
The Heavenly Jerusalem	511
The Life above, the Life on high	517
The Lord of all things	488
The Lord of life is risen	224
The Lord will come	304
The morning purples all the sky	193
The Royal Banners forward go	128
The Saviour! O, what endless charms	332
The sepulchre is holding	179
The shadow of the rock	352

	Page
The Supper of the Lamb to share	186
The Throne of His Glory	306
The time draws near	66
The tomb is empty	227
The way is long and dreary	379
The wise men to Thy cradle-throne	96
The wondering sages trace from far	91
The world can neither give nor take	393
Thee we adore, eternal Lord	548
There comes a galley laden	41
There is a blessed home	537
There is a fountain filled with blood	156
There is an everlasting home	376
There is no love like the love of Jesus	343
There was no angel 'midst the throng	347
They gave to Thee myrrh	89
Thine Handmaid, Saviour! can it be	115
This holy morn, so fair and bright	192
This is the month	48
Thou art the Way; to Thee alone	111
Thou fairest Child Divine	49
Thou hidden Source of calm repose	392
Thou Holiest Love, whom most I love	147
Thou King anointed, at whose word	564
Thou Lord of all, on earth hast dwelt	114
Thou shalt rise! my dust	520
Thou stand'st between the earth	78
Thou that art the Father's word	561
Thou who didst hang upon a barren tree	171
Thou whom we seek in darkness	560
Through the love of God our Saviour	407
Thou knowest, Lord	408
Thus far the Lord	382
To-day above the sky He soared	242
To day in Bethlehem, hear I	36
To-day our Lord went up on high	244
To Him, who for our sins was slain	560
To Him who loved the souls of men	546
Tossed with rough winds	377
Trembling before Thine awful throne	400

ALPHABETICAL LIST OF HYMNS.

	Page		Page
Trustingly, trustingly, Jesus, to Thee	121	When Jordan hushed his waters still	55
'Tis come, the time so oft foretold	60	When our heads are bowed with woe	367
'Tis the Day of Resurrection	190	When o'er Judea's vales and hills	112
'Twas on that dark, that doleful night	472	When sins and fears prevailing rise	423
		When this passing world is done	492
WAKE, awake, for night is flying	298	When through the torn sail	363
Wake, the startling watch-cry pealeth	297	When time seems short	437
Watcher, who watchest	381	When winds are raging	416
Watchman! tell us of the night	22	When, within His mother's arms	76
We are the Lord's	496	When, wounded sore, the stricken soul	174
We come not with a costly store	96	Wherefore weep we over Jesus	161
We keep the festival	187	Where high the heavenly temple stands	273
We shall see Him in our nature	543	Where is mercy and compassion	371
We sing the praise of Him who died	159	While faith is with me, I am blest	431
We sing to Thee, Immanuel	44	While to Bethlehem we are going	47
We speak of the realms of the blessed	523	Why should I fear the darkest hour	397
We walk by faith	432	Why should these eyes be tearful	234
We were not with the faithful few	434	With tearful eyes I look around	368
We welcome thee, dear Easter-day	225	With terror Thou dost strike me now	510
Welcome, Thou Victor in the strife	210	Without Thy presence	387
What laws, my blessed Saviour	138	Wonder of wonders! on the cross	173
What shall we be?	527	Wouldst thou learn the depth of sin	168
What star is this, with beams so bright	87		
What sudden blaze of song	58	YES: I will always love	489
When across the heart	414	Ye, servants of God	553
When gathering clouds around I view	366	Yes! my Redeemer lives	435
When I survey the wondrous cross	149	Yes! our Shepherd leads	401
When in the hour of lonely woe	451	Yes,—the Easter bells	184
When Jesus came to earth of old	23	ZION, at thy shining gates	24

LATIN HYMNS.

	PAGE
A SOLIS ortùs cardine ad usque	35
A solis ortûs cardine et usque	32
Ad cœnam Agni providi	186
Ad regias Agni dapes	187
Adeste fideles	37
Alleluia, Alleluia!	194
Altitudo, quid hic jaces	40
Apparebit repentina	287
Arte mirâ, miro consilio	336
Aurora cœlum purpurat	192, 193
Cœlos ascendit hodie	242
Corde natus ex Parentis	34
Cor meum Tibi dedo	482
Dies illa, dies vitæ	296
Dies iræ, dies illa	290
Fœno jacere pertulit	68
Grates nunc omnes reddamus	42
Gravi me terrore pulsas	510
Hic breve vivitur	512
Hora novissima	511
Hymnum canamus gloriæ	239
In terris adhuc positam	241
Jam mœsta quiesce querela	506, 508
Jesu, decus angelicum	320
Jesu dulcis memoria	318
Jesu, plena caritate	167
Jesu, Rex admirabilis	320
Jesus, dulcedo cordium	481
Jesus, pro me perforatus	361
Jordanis oras prævia	12
Judex mundi quum sedebit	283
Lauda, Sion, Salvatorem	545
Mitis Agnus, Leo fortis	197
Nobis Olympo redditus	243
O bona patria	513

	PAGE
O Christe, qui noster poli	244
O Deus, ego amo Te, Nam prior	484
O Deus, ego amo Te, Nec amo	480, 483
O Domine Deus	351
O esca viatorum	469
O filii et filiæ	199
O Jesu, mi dulcissime	83
O nox vel medio splendidior die	37
O quam sanctus panis iste	464
O sola magnarum urbium	56
Pange, lingua, gloriosi corporis	464, 465, 468
Pange, lingua, gloriosi prœlium	125
Parvum quando cerno Deum	76
Pone luctum, Magdalena	200, 201
Puer natus in Bethlehem	38
Quæ stella sole pulchrior	87
Quem terra, pontus, sidera	75
Qui penetravit inferas	237
Recordare sanctæ crucis	132, 134
Rex Christe, Factor omnium	564
Sævo dolorum turbine	135
Salve, Caput cruentatum	130
Salve, Dies dierum gloria	195
Salve, festa dies	185
Salvete, flores martyrum	80
Stabat Mater Dolorosa	136
Stabat Mater Speciosa	73
Stupenda lex mysterii	183
Summi regis cor, aveto	322
Surrexit Christus hodie	198
Tandem fluctus, tandem luctus	7
Tecum volo vulnerari	166
Te Deum laudamus	677
Urbs Syon aurea	515
Veni, Redemptor gentium	9
Veni, veni, Emmanuel	13
Vexilla Regis prodeunt	128

GREEK HYMNS.

	Page		Page
Ἀναστάσεως ἡμέρα	190	Ἰησοῦ γλυκύτατε	317
Ἄσωμεν πάντες λαοί	191	Ἰησοῦς ὁ Ζωοδότης	241
Δόξα ἐν ὑψίστοις Θεῷ	36	Κόπον τε καὶ κάματον	354
Εἰ καὶ ἐν τάφῳ	190	Μέγα καὶ παράδοξον θαῦμα	31
Ἐπάρατε πυλάς	240	Μούνη μοι πάτρη περιλείπετο	505
Ἐφέστηκεν ἡ ἡμέρα	286	Ὁ Κύριος ἔρχεται	285
Ζοφερᾶς τρικυμίας	353	Στόμιον πώλων ἀδαῶν	547

GERMAN HYMNS.

Ach mein Herr Jesu, Dein Nabesein	394	Gott fähret auf gen Himmel	246
Allein auf Christi Himmelfahrt	245	Gott sei Dank durch alle Welt	16
Allein zu Dir, Herr Jesu Christ	355	Gottes Sohn ist kommen	14
Auf diesen Tag bedenken wir	244		
Auferstehn, ja auferstehn	520	Heil! Jesus Christus ist erstanden	184
Aus irdischem Getümmel	425	Heiligster Jesu, Heil'gungsquelle	101
		Herz, du hast viel geweinet	372
Bei dir, Jesu, will ich bleiben	552	Herzlich lieb hab ich Dich, o Herr	485
Bleibt bei Dem, der euretwillen	495	Herzliebster Jesu, was hast Du	138
Brich durch, mein angefocht'nes Herz	356	Himmelan geht unsre Bahn	249
Christ lag in Todesbanden	204	Ich glaube, Hallelujah	428
Christe, Du Beistand Deiner	267	Ich habe nun den Grund gefunden	357
Christi Blut und Gerechtigkeit	153	Ich lass Dich nicht	444
Christus ist erstanden	203	Ich sag es jedem, dass Er lebt	215
Das Paradies muss schöner sein	529	Ich weiss, an wen ich glaube	426
Das Grab ist leer	216	Ich weiss, dass mein Erlöser lebet	435
Dein König kommt in niedern Hüllen	25	Im Abend blinkt der Morgenstern	91
Der am Kreuz ist meine Liebe	151	Immer muss ich wieder lesen	109
Der Du in der Nacht des Todes	93		
Der Herr ist auferstanden	224	Ja fürwahr! uns führt	401
Du, den wir suchen	560	Jesu, geh voran	105
Du schönstes Gottes-Kind	49	Jesu, meine Freude	389
		Jesu, meines Lebens Leben	146
Ein lieblich Loos ist uns gefallen	339	Jesus lebt, mit Ihm auch ich	214
Eines wünsch ich mir	497	Jesus, meine Zuversicht	207
Eins ist noth: ach Herr, diess Eine	327	Keine Schönheit hat die Welt	103
Er ist in Bethlehem geboren	69		
Ermuntert euch, ihr Frommen	299	Lamm, das gelitten und Löwe	256
Es kommt ein Schiff geladen	41	Liebe, die Du mich zum Bilde	325
Fröhlich soll mein Herze springen	45	Macht hoch die Thür'	15
Früh morgens, da die Sonn' aufgeht	206	Mein Jesu, dem die Seraphinen	268
Geht nun hin und grabt mein Grab	536	O auferstand'ner Siegesfürst	208
		O Du Liebe meiner Liebe	147

LIST OF GERMAN HYMNS.

	Page
O Haupt voll Blut und Wunden	142, 145
O Jesu Christ, mein schönstes Licht	486
O Jesu Christe, wahres Licht	88
O Jesu, meine Sonne	403
O Jesus Christus, wachs in mir	108
O Lamm Gottes unschuldig	465
O selig Haus, wo man Dich	453
O Welt, sieh hier dein Leben	140
Saget mir von keinem Lieben	406
Schmücke dich, o liebe Seele	470
Schönster Herr Jesu	325
Siegesfürst und Ehrenkönig	250
So ruhest Du, O meine Ruh'	180
Still an Deinem liebevollen Herzen	338
Vom Himmel hoch da komm ich her	43
Wachet auf! ruft uns die Stimme	297
Wandle leuchtender und schöner	220
Weint nicht über Jesu Schmerzen	161
Wenn ich Ihn nur habe	399
Werde Licht, du Volk der Heiden	89
Wie könnt ich Sein vergessen	494
Wie schön leuchtet der Morgenstern	441
Wie soll ich Dich empfangen	17
Wie wird uns sein	527
Wie wohl ist mir, o Freund der Seelen	391
Willkommen, lieber Ostertag	225
Willkomm, verklärter Gottessohn	212
Willkommen, Held im Streite	210
Wir sind des Herrn	496
Wir singen Dir, Immanuel	44
Wir werden bei dem Herrn sein	533
Wo ist göttliches Erbarmen	371

Hymns from the Syriac, p. 85; from the Spanish, pp. 516, 517; from the French, pp. 487, 488, 489, 531, 532, 549; from the Dutch, p. 101; from the Danish, p. 61.

A Pastor's Sketches 1 & 2
by Dr. Ichabod Spencer

"*A Pastor's Sketches* is a sobering and challenging reminder that the Holy Spirit is the true agent of conversion. This book is urgently needed today when so much of our evangelism is patterned after current marketing methods. It has deeply convicted me to always seek to be in tune with the Holy Spirit as I minister to others." **Jerry Bridges**

"Dr. Spencer's *Sketches*, reprinted after a lapse of many years, are a veritable treasury of pastoral wisdom. They will amply repay careful reading by pastors and serious Christians in our day." **Maurice Roberts**

"The Spencer extracts are superb and will be of great benefit when printed. This is very sobering but enlightening material. It is quite contrary to much of today's practice and all pastors need to read it." **Peter Jeffery**

"Spencer is a master at flushing sinners out of hiding and directing them to Jesus Christ for salvation through Spirit-worked, simple faith. The responses he makes to inquirers is, in the main, biblical, doctrinal, practical, and experiential. His perceptive counsel certainly has produced much fruit. *A Pastor's Sketches* is a compelling read for pastors and Christian workers; its pages contain the nuts and bolts of biblical evangelism." **Joel R. Beeke**

"The republication of Spencer's sketches gives a rare opportunity for contemporary pastors, who have few if any models of pastors who understand the 'work of evangelism.' These sketches show a doctrinal depth and an experiential savvy perfectly meshed in one who had the cure of souls as his passion." **Tom Nettles**

"Ichabod Spencer was gifted by God with a passion for the pastoral care of souls. Any pastor desiring to shepherd the sheep, or to see God's elect drawn to Christ, will find page after page of wise and sage counsel in this work. It is practical, pious, personal, and precious." **James White**

List Price for each volume **$12.95**
Purchase both from SGCB for **$22.00**

Solid Ground Christian Books
Call us toll free at **1-877-666-9469**
E-mail us at **sgcb@charter.net**
Visit us on the web at **solid-ground-books.com**

SGCB Classic Reprints

In addition to *Christ in Song* which you hold in your hand, Solid Ground has been privileged to uncover dozens of "buried treasures" from the past. Some of them include:

The Poor Man's New Testament Commentary by Robert Hawker, which has been unavailable for more than one hundred years. Spurgeon said of this commentary set, *"There is always such a savor of the Lord Jesus Christ in Dr. Hawker that you cannot read him without profit."*

The Sunday School Teacher's Guide by John A. James, which was written near the time Sunday Schools were first founded by Robert Raikes. This should be read by every Christian teacher.

The Devotional Life of the Sunday School Teacher by J.R. Miller, is an absolute gem of a book. Hundreds of copies sold in the first few weeks it was available again. No one who cares about the souls of others should fail to read this Christ-centered volume.

The Church Member's Guide by John Angell James was once the most popular volume in the US and the UK for instruction on the duties of church members. Wisdom is found on every page, and nothing but good can accompany the use of this volume in our day, when far too few take their membership vows seriously.

A Pastor's Sketches: 1 & 2 by Ichabod Spencer, which has drawn the praise of great Christian's all over the world. In these volumes we view true evangelism in the trenches as a 19th century pastor from Brooklyn, NY presses the claims of Christ on those who are dead in their trespasses and sins. Life-changing volumes!

The Pastor's Daughter by Louisa Payson Hopkins is the true story of the faithful, patient and loving ministry of Rev. Edward Payson to his oldest daughter. This is parental evangelism at its best, as a godly, legendary pastor leads his daughter to conversion over a ten year period of time. Every parent must read this book!

The Young Lady's Guide by Harvey Newcomb is a veritable manual of life and godliness for young ladies who care about their souls and eternity. The perfect birthday or graduation gift!

Call us Toll Free at **1-877-666-9469**
E-mail us at **sgcb@charter.net**
Visit our website at **http://solid-ground-books.com**

www.ingramcontent.com/pod-product-compliance
Lightning Source LLC
Chambersburg PA
CBHW021713300426
44114CB00009B/124